AFRICAN HISTORICAL DICTIONARIES
Edited by Jon Woronoff

HISTORICAL DICTIONARY OF ALGERIA
Second Edition

by
Phillip Chiviges Naylor
and
Alf Andrew Heggoy

African Historical Dictionaries, No. 66

The Scarecrow Press, Inc.
Lanham, Md., & London

The following maps are the property of the United States Government:

Extracted from Department of Army Pamphlet 550-44, **Algeria: A Country Study** *© 1985, United States Government as represented by the Secretary of the Army. Reprinted with permission.*

British Library Cataloguing-in-Publication data available

Library-of-Congress Cataloging-in-Publication Data

Naylor, Phillip Chiviges.
    The historical dictionary of Algeria / by Phillip Chiviges Naylor and Alf Andrew Heggoy. — 2nd ed.
       p.   cm. — (African historical dictionaries ; no. 66)
    Heggoy's name appears first on the 1st ed.
    ''Substantially expanded and updated by Professor Phillip Naylor''— Editor's foreword.
    Includes bibliographical references (p. 370-374).
    ISBN 0-8108-2748-4 (alk. paper)
    1. Algeria—History—Dictionaries.   I. Heggoy, Alf Andrew.
II. Title.   III. Series.
DT283.7.N39   1994
965'.003—dc20   93-26302

To David E. Gardinier

CONTENTS

v

LIST OF MAPS

PREFACE TO THE SECOND EDITION

The late Professor Alf Andrew Heggoy's commitment to the historical study of Algeria, as demonstrated by his books, articles, and teaching, paved the way for a new generation of scholars. In addition, his help in organizing the French Colonial Historical Society promoted collegial professional development and new opportunities for publication. Beyond his academic accomplishments, Alf's integrity, warmth, courage, and humanity will be missed.

I have adopted Professor Heggoy's transliteration method of Arabic names (rather than subscribe to the Library of Congress Cataloging Service, "Bulletin 49," Washington D.C., 1958). Heggoy's practical rationale remains persuasive: "The spelling of many Arabic names was fixed in our Latin alphabet by French colonial officials who were not necessarily linguists. In general, publications of the independent Algerian government have continued to use the spellings." This means that diacritical marks are not always transliterated (e.g., Abd al-Qadir for 'Abd al-Qadir). Names and terms are listed as they usually appear in English or French literature on Algeria. I have furnished other often used spellings with entries (e.g., Abd el-Kader [French transliteration]).

As in the first edition, the words Ben, Ibn, Abou, Abu, Bou, Bu, etc., are alphabetized as part of the name. Thus Ben Yahia is listed under "B" rather than "Y" and Abu Yazid is under "A" and not "Y." Prefixes such as al- or el- have been alphabetically ignored. Cross-references (q.v.) are provided. There is an extensive glossary and a list of acronyms and abbreviations. Several new appendices and tables have been added as well as an essay format to the updated bibliography. In addition, I wish to thank the

ix

Department of the Army for permission to use maps from *Algeria: A Country Study* (DA Pam 550–44).

Also, the entry "Abd al-Qadir" is adapted from my article "Abd el-Kader," published in *The International Encyclopedia* (pp. 62–66) by Academic International Press (1992) and used by permission.

The student or scholar of Algerian history often experiences difficulties acquiring information. Even when information is found, it can be biased, inaccurate, and contradictory, which poses heuristic problems. In this book, entries are often less complete than others in spite of valuable publications since the appearance of the first edition. The objective of the second edition is to update, to revise, and, to borrow a Benjedidist term, to "enrich" the first.

I share Professor Heggoy's feeling that "to have included too many French public figures might well have drowned the Algerians, might have tended to make this a historical dictionary of French colonial Algeria rather than a historical dictionary of Algeria." Algeria's history is a multifaceted heritage; the French experience remains influential among others.

This book is dedicated to Professor David Gardinier, my dissertation director, who introduced me to his close friend, Alf Heggoy. Alex Naylor, Peter deRosa, Lewis Livesay, Ronald Johnson, Helen Hanigan, Satoko Thomas, Sylvia Pressman, Peter Ford, John Entelis, Robert Mortimer, Mildred Mortimer, Gretchen Walsh, Mette Shayne, Dan Britz, and the Computer Centers of Merrimack College and Marquette University provided particular assistance. This work also benefited from my associateships at the African Studies Center (Boston University) and the Center for Middle Eastern Studies (Harvard University). Most of all, my wife, Kitty, and our two children, Alexander and Athena, contributed in many ways toward making this project personally worthwhile.

Phillip C. Naylor
Shorewood, Wisconsin

EDITOR'S FOREWORD—ALGERIA

Algeria is one of Africa's more important countries. It is larger than most in sheer size, stretching along the Mediterranean and reaching deep into the Sahara. It is rich in natural resources. And it has a large and active population. Given its location in Africa, it is bound to play a crucial role among the Maghrib countries and, just across from Europe, in relations with the European Community. Yet, just what it does will depend crucially on which path it takes over the coming years.

This leaves Algeria, despite its significance and potential, a bit of a question mark. Its earlier history is less well known than that of more prestigious dynasties elsewhere in northern Africa. Even the events of the long and terrible war of liberation are sometimes controversial.

As for the post-colonial period, it has been so tumultuous that most outsiders cannot follow the twists and turns, from one regime to the next, from one ideology to the next. To expect them to imagine future scenarios would be yet more unrealistic.

This makes it essential to develop our knowledge further, to know more of Algeria's past and present and use it to picture the future. This second edition of *The Historical Dictionary of Algeria,* like its predecessor, does much to provide such knowledge. It delves into the past, reaching all the way back, then deals more intensively with French colonization and takes an even more detailed look as it works its way to the present day. In so doing, it reviews a multitude of events, institutions, economic, social, and cultural aspects, and especially persons. Finally, in an excellent bibliography, it indicates where additional information can be found.

The first edition was written by Professor Alf Heggoy, who was born and educated partially in Algeria. A specialist on French and North African affairs, he wrote *Insurgency and Counter-Insurgency in Algeria* and *The French Conquest of Algiers, 1830.* This work was substantially expanded and updated by Professor Phillip Naylor. His doctoral dissertation was on conflict and cooperation with France during the 1960s and 1970s. Since then, along with various articles and papers, he has coedited a book entitled *Algeria: State and Society.*

Jon Woronoff
Series Editor

ACRONYMS AND ABBREVIATIONS

Please note that many of these acronyms and abbreviations also have separate entries.

ACD. Alliance Centriste et Démocrate; Organization uniting parties sharing social democratic values (e.g., FNR, PNSD, PSD, PSL)

AEDHF. Association pour l'Egalité des Droits entre les Hommes et les Femmes

AEMAN. Association des Etudiants Musulmans d'Afrique du Nord; colonial Muslim student organization

AEMNA. Association des Etudiants Musulmans Nord-Africains; Muslim student organization founded in Paris

AENA. Association des Etudiants Nord-Africains; North African student group.

AGTA. Association Générale des Travailleurs Algériens; labor union created in 1962 to represent Algerian workers in France; affiliated with UGTA

ALN. Armée de Libération Nationale, 1954–1962; revolutionary army during War of Independence; renamed ANP

AML. Amis du Manifeste et de la Liberté; party formed by Ferhat Abbas active in 1944–1945; brief nationalist solidarity during this time

AMU. Arab Maghrib (Maghreb) Union; also *Union du Maghreb Arabe* (UMA)

ANP. Armée Nationale et Populaire; post-independence army

APC. Assemblée Populaire Communale

APN. Assemblée Populaire Nationale

APS. Algérie Presse Service

BAD. Banque Algérienne de Développement

BADR. Banque Agricole et du Développement

BCA. Banque Centrale d'Algérie

BEA. Banque Extérieure d'Algérie

BNA. Banque Nationale d'Algérie

BNASS. Bureau National d'Animation du Secteur Socialiste; bureaucracy produced to manage self-management enterprises immediately after independence

BP. Bureau Politique; organization established by Ahmed Ben Bella and Houari Boumedienne in opposition to the GPRA; also known as the "Tlemcen Group"; refers also to a subsequent organization within the FLN party apparatus

CAPER. Caisse d'Accession à la Propriété et l'Exploitation Rurale; established in 1956 during the War of Independence to stimulate European land redistribution to the *fellahin*; done by purchasing, even by expropriating (a form of "nationalization") land, and by the transfer of public lands; Algerians accepting land risked retribution by the ALN

CCAA. Conseil Communal d'Animation d'Autogestion; council represented by army, government, and presidents of management committees

CCE. Comité de Coordination et d'Exécution; first executive body of the FLN created at Soummam Congress; five members initially, then expanded to nine

CCN. Conseil Consultatif National; established in April 1992 to assist the HCS

CCRA. Centres Coopératifs de la Réforme Agraire; organization charged with marketing produce of self-management farms

CEDA. Caisse d'Equipment pour le Développpment de l'Algérie; the financial organization associated with the Constantine Plan

CGT. Confédération Générale du Travail; communist-dominated French labor union

CNAN. Compagnie Nationale Algérienne de Navigation; national shipping corporation

CNDR. Comité National pour la Défense de la Révolution; a short-lived opposition party to Ben Bella's regime; prominent role played by FFS and PRS members

CNRA. Comite National de la Révolution Algérienne; legislative body of the FLN

CNS. Corps National de Sécurité; security force established after independence

CRUA. Comité Révolutionnaire pour d'unite et l'Action; a group of nine to 30 men (depending on interpretation) who planned and initiated the War of Independence; replaced by the FLN

DA. Dinars algériens

ENA. Etoile Nord-Africaine; nationalist movement organized in 1926 and eventually dominated by Messali Hadj

ESDNC. Entreprise Socialiste pour le Développement National de la Construction

FAF. Front de l'Algérie Française; an extremist *pied-noir* group that predated the OAS

FAS. Fonds d'Action Sociale; established in December 1958 by French Government to promote the social welfare of the emigrant worker community in France

FEMA. Fédération des Elus Musulmans d'Algérie; assimilationist organization founded by Dr. Mohammed Saleh Bendjelloul

FFFLN. Fédération de France du Front de Libération Nationale; branch of FLN founded during War of Independence to organize Algerian workers in France and to combat the influence of Messali Hadj's MNA; replaced by AGTA

FFS. Front des Forces Socialistes; party established in 1963 by Hocine Aït Ahmed to promote Berber interests; now a legalized opposition party

FIS. Front Islamique du Salut (Islamic Salvation Front); most powerful Islamic party in Algeria; lost legal status in March 1992

FLN. Front de Libération Nationale; organization that led Algeria to independence; the single legal party since independence until 1989 constitutional reforms; now discredited and factionalized

FNR. Front National de Renouvellement; party legalized during 1989 liberalization (see ACD)

GPRA. Gouvernment Provisoire de la République Algérienne;
provisional government established by FLN on September
19, 1958; opposed by the Political Bureau (''Tlemcen
Group'') during the immediate postcolonial period

HCS. High Council of State; Higher Council of State; High State
Council; Supreme State Council (first called High Council of
Security [High Security Council]) replaced the presidency of
Chadli Benjedid in January 1992

HSC. High State Council (HSC); see HCS

JFLN. Jeunesse du Front de Libération Nationale; FLN youth
organization founded in 1963

LADDH. Ligue Algérienne de Défense des Droits de l'Homme;
human rights group led by Abdennour Ali Yahia

LADH. Ligue Algérienne des Droits de l'Homme; leading human
rights group led until December 1989 by Miloud Brahimi

LNG. Liquefied Natural Gas

LPG. Liquefied Petroleum Gas

MAJD. Mouvement Algérien pour la Justice et le Développement; party headed by Kasdi Merbah

MCB. Mouvement pour la Culture Berbère; Berber party that
competes with FFS and RCD

MDA. Mouvement pour la Démocratie en Algérie; Ahmed Ben
Bella's opposition party founded in 1984

MDRA. Mouvement Démocratique de la Révolution Algérienne;
opposition group established in late 1960s by Belkacem
Krim; became a liberal opposition party supporting a market
economy

MIA. Mouvement Islamique Armé; Islamist organization in
conflict with HCS's security forces; Abdelkader Chebouti
regarded as its leader

MMBtu. Million British Thermal Units

MNA. Mouvement National Algérien; party created by Messali
Hadj in 1954 to counter the FLN

MNI. Mouvement de Nahda Islamique (Movement of the Revival
of Islam); an Islamic opposition party

MTLD. Mouvement pour le Triomphe des Libertés Démocratiques; Messali Hadj's party, which replaced the PPA after World War II

OAS. Organisation de l'Armée Secrète; European terrorist organization mobilized in 1961 to combat imminent independence of Algeria

OAU. Organization of African Unity

OCRA. Organisation Clandestine de la Révolution Algérienne; opposition party organized in April 1966 by Hocine Aït Ahmed and Mohamed Lebjaoui

OCRS. Organisation Commune des Régions Sahariennes; proposed energy condominium in French-controlled Saharan region

OFAMO. Office Algérien de la Main-d'Oeuvre; organization established by the French government in 1956 concerning emigrant worker community

ONACO. Office National de Commercialisation; inaugurated in December 1962 to control agricultural marketing

ONAMO. Office National de la Main-d'Oeuvre; an emigration agency of the Algerian government set up in 1963

ONRA. Office National de la Réforme Agraire; organization established in October 1962 to monitor and to supervise agricultural committees during self-management (*autogestion*) period

OPEC. Organization of Petroleum Exporting Countries

ORP. Organisation de la Résistance Populaire; clandestine opposition party proclaimed in August 1965 that called for the liberation of Ahmed Ben Bella and others after Houari Boumedienne's coup in June 1965

ORT. Organisation Révolutionnaire des Travailleurs; Trotskyite party created in 1973

OS. Organisation Spéciale; clandestine paramilitary group formed by impatient young nationalists in MTLD; operated from 1947–1950; suffered severe crackdown by French police; many OS members eventually prepared and participated in War of Independence

OST. Organisation Socialiste des Travailleurs; Trotskyite opposition party

PAGS. Parti d'Avant Garde Socialiste; opposition party that is ideological heir to PCA and ORP; organized in 1966; legalized after constitutional reforms of 1989

PAHC. Parti Algérien de l'Homme Capital; liberal opposition party

PCA. Parti Communiste Algérien; autonomous of French parent organization in 1936; outlawed in 1962; PAGS now its heir

PCF. Parti Communiste Français; French Communist Party that helped establish ENA; ambivalent support for PCA and the FLN during the War of Independence

PDR. Parti Démocratique Progressif

PNA. Parti National Algérien; liberal opposition party (see ACD)

PNSD. Parti National pour la Solidarité et le Développement; liberal opposition party

POLISARIO. Frente Popular para la Liberación de Saghia el Hamra y Río de Oro; Sahrawi liberation organization formed in 1973 aiming to attain an independent Western Sahara; first against Spain then Mauritania (ended hostilities in 1979) and Morocco; supported by Algeria

PPA. Parti du Peuple Algérien; founded in 1937 by Messali Hadj; replaced the ENA; brief reappearance in 1962 until outlawed; unsuccessful attempt of legalization after 1989 constitutional reforms

PRA. Parti du Renouveau Algérien; a liberal party headed by Noureddine Boukhrouh that advocates "modernist" Islam

PRP. Parti Republicain Progressif

PRS. Parti de la Révolution Socialiste; clandestine opposition party founded immediately after independence by Mohamed Boudiaf; Mohammed Khider also became a supporter

PSD. Parti Social Démocrate; legalized social democratic opposition party (see ACD)

PSL. Parti Social Libéral; liberal opposition party (see ACD)

PST. Parti Socialiste des Travailleurs; leftist party; received legalized status

PUAID. Parti de l'Union Arabo-Islamique Démocratique; Pan-

Arabic movement headed by Belhadj (Ben Hadj) Khelil Harfi

RADP. République Algérienne Démocratique et Populaire; official name of Algeria

RAI. Rassemblement Arabique-Islamique; party for increased Arabization.

RCD. Rassemblement pour la Culture et la Démocratie; Berber secular party that competes with FFS and MCB; Saïd Saadi is its secretary-general

RFMA. Rassemblement Franco-Musulman Algérien; a party founded in 1938 by Dr. Mohammed Saleh Bendjelloul demanding equality of Algerians with Europeans

RND. Le Rassemblement National pour la Démocratie; opposition group of Ali Mahsas

RTA. Radiodiffusion Télévision Algérienne

SAP. Société Agricole de Prévoyance; replaced SIP in 1952 to aid *fellahin*

SAR. Secteur d'Amélioration Rurale; established in 1946 to provide aid in first sector to *fellahin*; subordinated to SAP; continued after independence

SAS. Sections Administratives Spécialisées; initiated by Governor-General Jacques Soustelle to ameliorate social conditions in the countryside; a counterinsurgency strategem; mission reminiscent of *bureaux arabes*

SIP. Société Indigène de Prévoyance; established in 1893 to assist *fellahin*; replaced by SAP

SMA. Scouts Musulmans Algériens; Algerian boy scout organizaton associated with Association of Algerian *Ulama*; integrated into JFLN

SNS. Société Nationale de Sidérugie; national steel company

SONACOME. Société Nationale de Constructions Mécaniques; national mechanical company

SONAREM. Société Nationale de Recherches et d'Exploitations Minières

SONATRACH. Société Nationale de Transport et de Commercialisation des Hydrocarbures; national oil and gas company founded in December 1963

SONELEC. Société Nationale de Fabrication et de Montage du Matériel Eléctrique et Electronique; national electrical company

SONELGAZ. Société Nationale de l'Electricité et du Gaz; national electricity and gas company

SONITEX. Société Nationale des Industries Textiles; national textile company

UDMA. Union Démocratique du Manifeste Algérien; liberal movement organized in 1946 by Ferhat Abbas; sought Algerian autonomy within French system

UDRS. Union pour la Défense de la Révolution Socialiste; opposition party founded in 1963 by Mohamed Boudiaf; Mohand ou el-Hadj, Belkacem Krim, and others

UFD. Union des Forces Démocratiques; opposition party where Ahmed Mahsas has played a leading role

UGEMA. Union Générale des Etudiants Musulmans Algériens; FLN's student organization during War of National Liberation

UGTA. Union Générale des Travailleurs Algériens; FLN affiliated labor union created in 1956 to mobilize Algerian working classes for the national liberation movement

UMA. See AMU

UNEA. Union Nationale des Etudiants Algériens

UNFA. Union Nationale des Femmes Algériennes

UNFD. Union des Forces Démocratiques; political party as a result of 1989 liberalization

UNJA. Union Nationale de la Jeunesse Algérien

UNLD. Union Nationale pour la Liberté et la Démocratie; opposition group led by Ben Youssef Ben Khedda

UNPA. Union Nationale des Paysans Algériens

UPA. Union Populaire Algérienne; a party formed in 1938 by Ferhat Abbas calling for full citizenship for all Algerian Muslims

USTA. Union Syndicale des Travailleurs Algériens; founded in 1956 by the MNA to confront with FLN (i.e., FFFLN) over the allegiance of the emigrant worker community

GLOSSARY

A collection of terms that may be encountered in historical studies of Algeria.
Please note that some of these terms also have separate entries.

Abid	Refers to Almoravid ascetics; also servants or slaves
Adjutant	French sergeant major
Agha	Captain-general of Turkish forces; commander in chief; tribal chief under Abd al-Qadir
Aghalik	Jurisdiction of an agha under Turks
Alfa	Esparto grass used in paper manufacturing
Amir	Prince; commander
Amir al-Mu'minin	Commander of the Faithful
Amir al-Muslimin	Commander of Muslims; Almoravid title
Ancien combattant	Ex-serviceman, veteran
Arrondissement	French administrative subdivision of departments
Arsch	*Arsh*; Inalienable property that may be inherited; tribal land; property based on labor invested in the land;

	difficult to delineate; collective or communal land
Asabiyya	Tribal "group feeling"; "solidarity"; idea developed by Ibn Khaldun
Aspirant	French officer candidate
Atji-bashi	Head of horses; supervised *Dey*'s household
Autogestion	Self-management system of farms and industrial plants immediately after independence
Azel	Public domain during the Turkish period
Baccalaureate	Secondary-school leaving—university entrance examination
Bachaga	Algerian "governors"; highest rank in the *caidat* system of "native" administration in the French system
Baladiyat	Commune; a subdivision of a *daira*
Baldis	*Baladis*; native citizens of Algiers (pre-Ottoman)
Baraka	Spiritual quality of blessedness; grace; special power, usually from divine source, that may radiate to others; marabouts are supposed to possess *baraka*
Barbary	This geographic term stems from Berber; the Barbary states extended from Libya to Morocco
Barbouze	Undercover French government agents employed against the OAS

during the Algerian War of Independence

Bay'ah — Oath of allegiance to a new ruler

Beni-Oui-Oui — "Sons of/people of yes [speakers]"; derogatory term used to describe Algerian administrators or political persons who collaborated with France

Beur — Derived from the word *arabe* spelled backward and street jargon; a member of the emigrant community's "second generation" in France

Bey — Turkish title of the Dey of Algiers's three principal vassals, the governors of Oran, Constantine, and Titteri.

Beylerbey — Commander of commanders; title of Regency leader in 16th century; governor-general

Bicot — Abusive French term used to refer to Algerians

Bidonville — Shantytown

Bled — *Balad*; countryside

Bleu — French double agent; (*bleuite*, the state of being affected by a double agent)

Bordj — Fort

Burnous — Loose woolen cloak woven into one piece

Cachabia — Heavy, usually woolen winter garment worn by Algerian men

Cadi	See Qadi
Caid	See *Qa'id*
Caidat	French system of "native" administration
Cantonnement	The policy of confining Muslims to certain areas
Captain Pasha	Commanding officer of the Ottoman fleet; post often given to the *Beylerbeys* of Algiers
Casbah	Kasba(h)/Qasba(h); citadel; famous Berber, then Turkish section of Algiers; in general, native quarters of colonial cities
Chechia	Woolen caps worn by many traditional Algerian men
Cheikh	See *Shaykh*
Chekliines	Jews from the Balearics who arrived in Algiers in the late twelfth century
Chott	See *Shatt*
Chouhada	Martyr in the revolutionary war
Code de l'Indigénat	Colonial law code allowing arbitrary, summary justice
Çoff	*Saff*; *soff*; political party (informal), federation; method of establishing tribal divisions
Colon	European settler; especially agrarian settler
Colonat	The term for the settler agricultural "lobby" that influenced political and economic colonial policy

Comité de gestion	Management committee associated with *autogestion*
Commune de plein exercise	Communes of colonial Algeria with large European proportion of inhabitants that were given same administration as metropolitan communes
Commune mixte	Communes in which European minority were. governed by European administrators who controlled Algerians through *caids*
Da'i	Shi'i propagandists and agitators; "callers" or "summoners" to Shi'ism
Da'ira	Daïra; daira (from Arabic dar/ *diyar*); circle (of authority); district; a subdivision of a *wilaya*; an administrative region usually named after a major city
Dar al-Sultan	Residence of the Beylerbeys and Deys of Algiers
Dawair	*Duwwar*; a group of families attached to a chief
Department	*Département*; largest administrative subdivision
Dey	The head of the Regency since the eighteenth century; governor of Algiers
Dinar	Algerian unit of currency
Disparus	The "disappeared"; during the chaos of Algerian decolonization, many Europeans disappeared mysteriously; occasional reports of their

	being interned or sighted have affected French-Algerian relations
Divan	Council of State during Regency; usually consisted of high Turkish functionaries who assisted the *Dey*; could also select *Dey*
Djebel	*Jabal*; mountain
Djemaa	See Jama'a
Djoundi	ALN soldier
Douar	Village; group of tents; administrative unit
Duwwar	Clan
Erg	Sand dune area (in Sahara)
Evolué	Educated Algerian who had been influenced by the French; especially wanted to realize the ideal of assimilation
Exarch	Byzantine administrator (governor)
Exode	Exodus; repatriation/expatriation of European settlers in 1962
Failek	ALN battalion
Faoudj	ALN section
Fatma	Maid; Algerian domestic servant
Fatwa	Islamic legal opinion
Fellagh	Outlaw; Algerian guerrilla fighter
Fellah	Peasant; small farmer (pl. *fellahin*)

Fida'iyin	Combattants of the faith; urban terrorists
Figuier	Fig tree; also French abusive term for Algerians
Fiqh	Term for Islamic jurisprudence
Firman	Offical decree by Turkish Dey
Formation	Training of cadres
Fraction	Part of a tribe or of a village
Fuqaha'	Doctors of canon law, especially Malikite (Maliki) (s. faqih)
Garde-champêtre	Rural policeman
Goum	Dialectical form of *qawm* or *kawm*; armed horsemen in service of Regency; advance guard among *makhzen* tribes enforcing Turkish rule; auxiliaries
Gourbi	Shack; small house of poor peasant
Groupe	Squad
Habous	*Habus*; pious donation of land for a foundation devoted to religious, charitable, or cultural purpose; religious endowments; also known as *waqf*
Hadith	Qur'anic commentary; tradition relating to the life and actions of the Prophet Muhammad
Hadj	*Hajj*; the pilgrimage to Mecca; one who has performed this act of faith
Haik	Sheetlike garment, in white or black, worn by Algerian women when they go out in public

Harki	Algerian soldier serving France
Hidjab	Muslim long robe worn by women
Hitiste	Arabic-French amalgam; "one who holds up walls"; refers to the masses of contemporary jobless young men
Hubs	See *Habous*
Ifriqiya	The general region of Tunisia and far eastern Algeria
Ikhwan	Brethren; as members of Sufi order
Imam	Sunni prayer leader; religious and political leader of Shi'a
Istemeyiz	Janissary warcry
Jabal	See *Djebel*
Jama'a	Village assembly; assembly of elders; Berber institution
Janissaries	Elite Turkish infantry
Jaysh	Army
Jihad	Holy war (see *Moudjahid*)
Jizyah	Capitation tax levied by Islamic state upon non-Muslims
Kasma	Party council of the FLN at the commune level
Katiba	ALN company
Képis bleus	Blue caps; term used to refer to SAS officers and men

Khalifa	Deputy; district governors of Abd al-Qadir
Khamis	Muslim long robe worn by men
Khammes	*Khammas*; sharecropper; tenant farmers who get one-fifth of the harvest for their labor and tools
Kharaj	Land tax
Khaznadar	Dey's personal treasurer
Khaznaji	Officer in charge of the Regency state treasury
Khujas	Regency secretaries
Khujat al-kheyl	*Khujat al Khil*; master of cavalry; responsible for logistics; receiver of tribute during Regency
Kiboussiines	Jews from Spain who arrived in Algiers in late thirteenth century and especially after 1492
Kouloughlis	*Kulughlis*; children of Turks and local women
Ksour	Fortified village; fort
Litham	Face scarf; muffler; made famous by Almoravids
Lycée	Secondary school leading to baccalaureate and to universities
Madrasa	*Médersa*; higher Islamic educational institution
Maghrib	"Place where sun sets"; Northwest Africa; the country of Morocco

Mahallas	Turkish expeditionary units; often sent out to collect taxes
Mahdi	"Guided one"; a redeemer in Shi'i theology
Makhzan	*Makhzen*; tax-exempt tribes allied with Turkish rulers; *ahl al-makhzan* paid taxes
Mansulagha	Honorary agha
Maquis	Dense underbrush; term used by the French to describe nationalist sanctuaries; maquisards were guerrillas; *maquis rouge* referred to PCA guerrillas during the War of Independence
Marabout	*Marabut*; a saintly or venerated Muslim leader; often charismatic; a descendant or leader of a sufi (mystic) order
Mechta	Village, area
Melk	*Milk/Mulk/Malk*; freehold form of private property that is implicitly inalienable; difficult to delineate
Métropole	Metropolitan (colonial) power; France
Militant	Active member of the FLN
Mintaka	A region, a subdivision of a *wilaya*
Moudjahid	*Mujahid*; combattant, ALN soldier; guerrilla. The word is derived from the Arabic verb *jahada* meaning to struggle. It can mean a fighter in a holy war. In Islam it is especially

	the struggle within oneself to be a good Muslim
Mousseblin	Militiaman; ALN guerrilla
Mufti	Islamic jurisconsultant; interpreter of the law
Munas	Turkish garrisons
Muqaddem	*Moqaddam*; leader of a religious brotherhood; a regional leader
Oda	Barrack rooms
Ojaq	*Odjak*; military corps of janissaries; the *ojaq* often influenced the selection of the Regency's *Deys*
Orta	Military unit (company-sized)
Oued	*Wadi*; river or dry riverbed
Paras	French paratroopers; name popularized during Algerian War of Independence
Pasha	Turkish officer or official of high rank; governor of an Ottoman province; title of *Dey* of Algiers
Pashalik	A region under the control of a pasha
Pied-noir	"Black foot"; refers to European settlers in Algeria
Préfet	Prefect; administrator of a department
Qa'id	*Caid*; a leader; high official in the military or civil government; Algerian administrator during French colonial period

Quartier	Sector
Rai	*Raï*; *ray*; personal opinion or judgment; popular form of contemporary Algerian (and Maghribi) music reminiscent of American folk and rap styles
Raïs	*Reïs/Ra'is*; leader or chief; corsair captain; president
Ratissage	Raking over; a "pacification" operation
Ratonnade	"Rat hunt"; European extremists looking for "Arabs" to kill during the War of Independence
Razzia	*Ghazya*; foray; raid; coup; campaign
Refoulement	Forcible removal of native population after active resistance especially during earlier stages of French colonization
Regroupement	Regrouping Muslims into encampments during the War of Independence in order to isolate the ALN
Ribat	Fortified stronghold, retreat, or monastery; a place to prepare a group for a jihad
Rum	Arabic term for Roman; used in general for Christians
R'ya	*Raya*; tribes at least partially subdued by the Turks and *makhzan* tribes
Saff	See *Çoff*

Sayyid	Descendant of Abd al-Mumin; honorific term
Section	Platoon
Sergent-chef	Lowest-ranked sergeant
Shari'a	Islamic law based on Muhammad's revelation
Sharif	A descendant of Muhammad through his daughter Fatima
Shatt	*Chott*; salt marsh; also *chott*
Shawshs	Bailiffs
Shaykh	*Shaikh*; *cheikh*; spiritual leader; elder; arbiter; religious teacher; descendant of important Almohad family
Shi'a	Muslim sects recognizing Ali as true successor of Muhammad and his descendants (imams)
Sidi	Sayyid; honorific title before a name, usually marabouts
Sirocco	Hot wind from the Sahara
Soff	See *Çoff*
Souk	Covered market (traditional)
Sous-préfet	Administrator of an *arrondissement*
Spahis	Cavalry in Turkish forces
Sufi	Muslim mystic
Sunni	Muslims who follow the customs (*sunna*) of the Prophet

Ta'ifa	*Taifa*; *taïfa*; corsair captains; a group or organization of ship captains
Taqlid	Strict adherence to religious tradition and law
Tariqa	Way, path; a ritual practiced by Muslim brotherhoods
Ulama	Learned persons, religious leaders well versed in Qur'anic studies
Ultras	Defiant European settlers who resisted any accommodation
Umma	The community of Muslims
Wadi	See *oued*
Wali	Chief administrator at the district level (Turkish); governor of a *wilaya*
Watan	Administrative unit within *beylik*
Wekil al-kharj	*Wakil al-kharj*; *Vakil khariji*; Regency ministry of the marine also charged with foreign affairs
Wilaya	Administrative provinces; war zones during the War of Independence (I: Aurès region; II: Little Kabylia and eastern Algeria: III: Great Kabylia; IV: Algiers, Mitidja, Ouarsenais, central Algeria; V: Oran and western Algeria; VI: southern zone (northern Sahara)
Yoldash	Private Janissaries
Zawiya	*Zawia; Zawaya* (pl.); buildings for religious study; monasteries; hostelries

CHRONOLOGY

6000 B.C.–A.D. 100
Pictorial history at Tassili N'Ajjer illustrating Saharan prehistoric cultures; frescoes include hunters, herders, and warriors

1200 B.C.–202 B.C.
Phoenicians enter western Mediterranean (possibly Minoans along Algerian littoral c. 2000 B.C.); founding of Carthage (traditional date 814 B.C.); expansion of Carthaginian influence along North African coastline (800–220 B.C.); Berber kingdoms in hinterland

c. 240–148 B.C.
Dynamic reign of King Masinissa, King of Numidia; collaborates with Rome v. Carthage in Second Punic War; builds an impressive kingdom; capital Cirta (Qirta/Constantine)

112–105 B.C.
Jugurtha, King of the Numidians, wars against the Romans

46 B.C.
Numidia, a protectorate, becomes a province of Rome after Caesar defeats followers of the late Pompey and their ally, King Juba, at the Battle of Thapsus. Roman territory is trebled to include several provinces; Africa Nova; most of the old Numidian Kingdom. Mauretania annexed to Empire in A.D. 40

43 B.C.–A.D. 430
Romanization and Christianization of the Maghrib. Berbers restive; Christian martyrs and schismatics; Saint Augustine, Bishop of Hippo (396–430)

429–533
The Vandals arrive; persecution of Roman Catholics

533–34
Belisarius routs the Vandals; reestablishment of a central (Eastern) Roman administration; resistance of petty Berber states

7th century
First Arab invasion of Maghrib (647); 'Uqba (Okba) ben Nafi and the first "soldiers of Allah" traverse the Maghrib, before his death in combat near Biskra. Opposition to Arabs and Islam by victorious Berber leaders (Kusayla [683]; al-Kahina [695])

8th–9th centuries
Islamicization and Arabization progresses. Three influential states: Ibadi (Rustamids) at Tahert (Tiaret) in the center; the Aghlabids in the East; the Idrisids at Tlemcen

10th century
Fatimids dominate North Africa; Ibadi amirate to the M'zab; founding of Algiers by the Zirids.

11th century
Founding of Qal'a by Hammadids; Banu Hilal and Banu Sulaym migration; Hammadids to Bejaïa; Almoravids invade

12th century
The Almohads unify the Maghrib

13th century–16th centuries
Tlemcen in its glory under the Abd al-Wadids; apogee of the Arab-Andalusian culture

16th century
Spanish enclaves on the coast; the brothers Barbarossa (Aruj and Khayr al-Din) establish a Turkish presence; Algiers becomes

maritime power; part of Ottoman Empire; disaster of Charles V before Algiers (1541); Turkish penetration of the interior

17th–18th centuries
Continuation of struggles between Ottoman Turks and Europeans; Algiers continues its cosmopolitan development; Regency acting autonomously

19th century
French expedition v. Algiers (1830); resistance of Abd al-Qadir (surrenders 1847); major revolts in 1857, 1864, and 1871; continuing French colonization and land expropriation; colonists secure internal control of the colony

20th century

GROWTH OF ALGERIAN NATIONALISM

Young Algerian movement; Clemenceau/Jonnart legislation (1919); Emir Khaled's agitation; establishment of the ENA (1926); establishment of Association of Algerian Muslim *Ulama* (1931); Blum-Viollette legislation fails (1936–1938); establishment of PPA (1937); Manifesto of the Algerian People (1943); de Gaulle's ordinance (1944); establishment of AML (1944–45); Sétif rioting (1945); establishment of MTLD and UDMA in 1946; Algerian Statute (1947); organization and operation of OS (1947–1950); dissension in MTLD between Messalists and Centralists (1953–1954); meeting of the CRUA (1954)

WAR OF LIBERATION (1954–1962)

Proclamation of November 1, 1954; Soustelle as governor-general (1955–56); Soummam Conference (August 1956); FLN leaders hijacked (October 1956); Battle of Algiers (1956–1957);

fall of Fourth Republic; de Gaulle to power (May 1958); inauguration of GPRA (September 1958); "Peace of the Brave" initiative and Constantine Plan (October 1958); Challe Plan and French military success (1959); de Gaulle offers self-determination (September 1959); Algiers insurrection (January 1960); Melun discussions (June 1960); demonstrations of settlers and by Muslim masses (December 1960); OAS formed (1961); referendum on de Gaulle's policies (January 1961); French generals' putsch (April 1961); opening of Evian negotiations (May 1961); second GPRA (August 1961); negotiations reopen at Les Rousses (February 1962); Evian Accords (March 1962); FLN-OAS accord (June 1962); Tripoli Program (June 1962); referendum on Algerian self-determination (July 1, 1962); proclamation of Algerian independence (July 3); intraelite conflict (summer 1962)

BEN BELLA ADMINISTRATION (1962–1965)

Ben Bella premier (1962)/president (1963); expropriation of European property (1962–1963); border war with Morocco (October-November 1963); Kabylia revolts (Fall 1963); SONATRACH inaugurated (December 1963); Charter of Algiers (1964)

BOUMEDIENNE ADMINISTRATION (1965–1978)

Col. Boumedienne overthrows Ben Bella (June 19, 1965); Algiers Accord signed with France (July 1965); nationalization of mines (1966); state planning initiated (1967); nationalization of French hydrocarbon concessions (1971); Agrarian Revolution (1971); Cultural Revolution (1971); Algeria demonstrates leadership in special session at U.N. (1974); President Giscard d'Estaing of France visits (1975); Algeria supports POLISARIO after Morocco and Mauritania invade ex-Spanish Sahara (1975); new

Constitution and National Charter (1976); Boumedienne dies of rare blood disease (1978)

BENJEDID ADMINISTRATION (1979–1992)

Benjedid becomes president (1979); gradual political decentralization and economic liberalization; five-year plan initiated (1980); Maghrib unity accords with Tunisia and Mauritania (1983); Benjedid first president to have state visit to France (1985); "enriched" National Charter (1986); rioting throughout Algeria (1988); constitutional reform (1988–1989); democratization of political system begins (1989); Arab Maghrib Union formed (1989); FIS wins local elections (1990); national elections postponed after violence; FIS leaders arrested (June 1991); FIS publications banned (August 1991); FIS wins first round of rescheduled national elections (December 1991); Benjedid deposed in civilian-military coup (January 1992)

HIGH COUNCIL OF STATE (1992–)

High Security Council then High Council of State (HCS) established (January 1992); national elections canceled (January); FIS loses its legal status (March); continued unrest and violence throughout Algeria; assassination of HCS President Mohamed Boudiaf (June 1992); FIS leaders sentenced (July); continuing violence and government crackdowns; erosion of political and civil rights; economy deteriorating; austerity policies emphasized by HCS and Prime Minister Belaïd Abdesselam; Algeria on brink of national implosion; escalating violence results in estimated 4,000 deaths by end of 1993; High Council of State selects General Liamine Zéroual as president (January 1994)

INTRODUCTION

For being Africa's second largest nation, Algeria has remained historically one of the least studied countries on the continent. It is a land of striking geographic, topographic, and ethnic diversity matched by an impressive history.

THE NATURAL SETTING

The Democratic and Popular Republic of Algeria encompasses an area of 2,381,741 square kilometers (919,595 square miles). Its landmass is slightly larger than the entire area of the United States east of the Mississippi and more than four times larger than France. Most of the country is desert. Its only natural border is the Mediterranean Sea to the north. Algeria shares frontiers, clockwise from east to west, with Tunisia (q.v.), Libya, Niger, Mali, Mauritania, Western Sahara (q.v.), and Morocco (q.v.).

Approximately 95 percent of the nearly 25 million Algerians live within a 160 kilometer (100 mile) belt bordering on the Mediterranean Sea, or roughly within 10 to 12 percent of the total area, lying north of the arid Sahara. This portion of the country has a subtropical climate. South from its 1,104 kilometer (686 mile) shoreline, the country has an extremely varied terrain. Even the narrow northern coastal plain is often broken up by mountains, some of which slope directly into the sea, as does the especially striking Chenoua massif near the ancient Roman town of Tipasa, west of Algiers (q.v.). Northern Algeria is dominated by two mountain ranges that run east-west from Tunisia to Morocco. Northernmost is the irregular Tell Atlas Mountain group, which reaches heights more than 2,300 meters (7,500 feet) including the

TUNISIA

MEDITERRANEAN SEA

MOROCCO

SAHARA

Chott Melrhir

Constantine High Plains

Aurès Massif

Constantine

Lesser Kabylia

Bejaïa

Greater Kabylia

Djurdjura Mountains

Algiers

Setif

Hodna Mts.

Chott El Hodna

Bou-Saâda

Hills of the Zab

Biskra

Dahra Mts.

Middle Plain

Ouarsenis Mts.

Oued Chelif

Oran

Sebkha of Oran

ATLAS

Oued Djedi

Oued Touil

TELLIAN PLATEAUS

Chott Ech Chergui

HIGH

SAHARAN

ATLAS

Djebel Amour

Ksour Mts.

Oran

Landforms of Northern Algeria

Hodna range and the Djudjura massif. It is flanked by a high plateau of dry, undulating stretches, which give way to the Saharan plateau and then the Saharan Atlas reaching 2,100 meters (7,000 feet), which are a continuation of the Moroccan High Atlas range. Both mountain ranges descend toward the East and ultimately settle into the coastal plains of Tunisia.

The morphology of the Sahara includes sand, pebbles, and bare rocks. In the southern Sahara, the rocky plateau of Tassili N'Ajjer rises 1,700 meters (5,500 feet). The far south is distinguished by Algeria's highest elevations including the Assekrem Plateau at 2,728 meters (8,950 feet), and the isolated and awesome peaks of the Ahaggar (Hoggar) range, which feature Mount Ilamane at 2,739 meters (8,986 feet) and Mount Tahat at 2,918 meters (9,573 feet), the tallest mountain in Algeria.

The coastal regions average 762 millimeters (30 inches) of rainfall annually. Another area just to the south, but extending up to the coast west of Algiers, receives between 610 and 813 millimeters (24 to 32 inches). A third region, bordering those already mentioned but also encompassing most of the coastline between Algiers and Oran, receives only 406 to 610 millimeters (16 to 24 inches). From Oran to the Moroccan border, more arid conditions prevail. Similar to the high plateaus further south, this region averages from 203 to 406 millimeters (8 to 16 inches) annually, making it unsuitable for agriculture but for pastoralism. The Saharan Atlas averaging a mere 102 to 203 millimeters (4 to 8 inches) qualifies closely as desert. The vast Sahara receives virtually no precipitation.

The agricultural north (q.v. Agriculture) features market garden and industrial produce. Cereals (e.g., wheat, barley) are grown throughout the north in the coastal and inland plains (e.g., Constantine, Oran areas) and plateaus. Production varies with the unpredictable precipitation. Plateau grass (e.g., esparto) nourishes herds of livestock (e.g., sheep, goats, camels).

The most important industry is hydrocarbons (q.v. Hydrocarbons), given the country's significant reserves of oil and especially natural gas (seventh largest in the world). Algeria also

Northern Algeria-Rainfall Pattern

Under 4 inches
4 – 8
8 – 16
16 – 24
24 – 32
Over 32 inches

ORAN
ALGIERS
TIZI-OUZOU
BISKRA

possesses one of the most impressive hydrocarbon infrastructures in the world (trunk lines and refineries [particularly natural gas liquefaction]). The principal solid mineral deposits are iron ore, coal, phosphates, lead, and zinc. Uranium has been found in the Ahaggar range.

Among Algeria's wildlife are the jackal, Barbary ape, gazelle, jerboa, boar, antelope, fennec fox, and ibex. The mountainous north is forested with pine, juniper, cedar, olive, and cork oak. Acacia, dwarf palm, and jujube trees are in the more arid zones. Date palm groves are renowned in Saharan oases.

Algeria faces major environmental challenges such as the relentless encroachment of the Sahara northward (q.v. *Barrage vert*) and the country's burgeoning population (more than 3 percent annual growth). At this juncture, as Algeria struggles for political and economic stability, the generally recognized need for careful planning and management of natural resources assumes a greater urgency.

A HISTORICAL SURVEY

PREHISTORY TO THE ARAB CONQUEST

Algeria had a vigorous Neolithic culture in the predesiccated Sahara as depicted at Tassili N'Ajjer (q.v.) in one of the greatest displays of prehistoric art in the world. Illustrations date from 6000 B.C. to 1500 B.C. For as long as its recorded history, there have been inhabitants in North Africa whom outsiders named Berbers (q.v.), and who call themselves, *Imazighen*, which roughly translated means "noblemen" or "free men." They probably migrated from west Asia and northeast and southeast Africa and eventually melded throughout northwest Africa. The Berbers remained independent of foreign control though they were influenced (e.g., linguistically) by the establishment of Carthage (q.v.) in the ninth century B.C. and its subsequent expansion along the North African littoral, including eastern Algeria.

Berber leaders began to assert themselves during the Second Punic War (218–202 B.C.) between Carthage (q.v.) and Rome (q.v.). The Massyli (q.v.) monarch Masinissa (q.v.) allied with Rome and was recognized as King of Numidia (q.v.) ruling from his capital, Cirta (Qirta; q.v. Constantine). Masinissa expanded Numidia, and eventually this impressive kingdom stretched 700 miles along the North African coast from Carthaginian territory (Tunisia) in the east to the River Muluccha (Moulouya) (Morocco) in the west. After the final destruction of Carthage in 146 B.C., the alliance between Rome and Numidia was no longer as expedient or as strategic. Jugurtha (q.v.), a grandson of Masinissa, pursued his own independent ambitions and confronted Rome in the Jugurthine War (112–105 B.C.), which was detailed by the Roman official and historian Sallust (q.v.). Jugurtha's resistance made him a hero of modern Algeria. Juba II (q.v.) (25 B.C.–A.D. 23) was the last Massyli monarch and a close Roman client.

Rome colonized Algeria, whose coastal plains became a leading granary of the Empire. Remarkable cities were built such as at Timgad (q.v.) deep in the hinterland. Roman legions reached the Sahara and quelled occasional uprisings. It is easy to imagine the comfort of life in Roman Africa among the ruins of coastal Tipassa. Many Berbers were Romanized and later converted to Christianity, among them the great Church Father, St. Augustine (q.v.), who was born in eastern Algeria and became the Bishop of Hippo (Annaba [q.v.]). North Africa was also the site of often violent conflicts among Christian sects (e.g., the Donatists [q.v.], Arians, Catholics/Orthodox).

The invasion of the Vandals (q.v.) in the fifth century ended Roman rule but had little effect upon the Berber population in the interior. The Vandals were defeated in the sixth century by the Byzantines (q.v.), who also maintained a coastal and ephemeral presence.

The next wave of invaders did make a difference.

FROM THE ARAB CONQUEST TO THE TURKISH REGENCY

In the mid- to late seventh century, Muslim Arabs undertook their conquest of Northwest Africa, which would hereafter be known as the "Maghrib," or the land of the setting sun (the west). The Berbers offered stiff and inspirational resistance, especially in the Aurès region under Kusayla (q.v.) and the redoubtable al-Kahina (q.v.). Nevertheless, the Arabs finally subdued the northern region and infused it with their culture. The name "Algeria" is derived from the Arabic word for the "islets" located off the shoreline of what would be the modern capital of Algiers (q.v.). The Berbers converted to Islam, but they maintained their own language and withstood "Arabization."

Though Algeria was neither a unified state nor a "nation," it was highly influenced by its local dynasties and those of its neighboring regions. The Khariji(te) (q.v. Kharijism) Rustumid (q.v.) dynasty secured itself in Tahert in the late eighth century and eventually stretched from Tlemcen to Tripoli. This was the first Muslim state in the Maghrib. The establishment in the ninth century of the Aghlabid dynasty (q.v.) in neighboring Ifriqiya (Tunisia) brought much of eastern Algeria under its control. After the defeat and displacement of the Aghlabids in the tenth century, the Isma'ili Fatimids (q.v.) controlled Ifriqiya, northern Algeria, and much of Morocco. When the Fatimids embarked for Egypt in the tenth century, the western provinces were left to the local Berber Zirid dynasty (q.v.). The Zirids were rivaled by the Berber Hammadid (q.v.) dynasty at Qal'a and then at Bejaïa (q.v.). The onslaught of the Banu Hilal (q.v.) and the Banu Sulaym severely pressured both the Zirids and Hammadids in the eleventh century. Later in that century, the Almoravids (q.v.) swept into western and central Algeria. They were deposed in the twelfth century by the Almohads (q.v.) under Abd al-Mu'min (q.v.), who united the Maghrib from the Atlantic to Ifriqiya.

After the breakup of the Almohad empire in the middle of the thirteenth century, Algeria featured the Abd al-Wadid (q.v.)

(Ziyanid) state with its capital at Tlemcen (q.v.). The size of this state varied in proportion to the power asserted by the rival Hafsids of Tunis and the Marinids of Fez. This was the beginning of a collateral geopolitical trilateralism that one views today with the neighboring countries of Tunisia and Morocco. During this time, cities along the coast such as Algiers often asserted their independence.

Throughout these ''medieval'' centuries, Algeria continued to be a rich agricultural area despite recurrent conquests. (The degree of devastation to the Algerian economy caused by the Banu Hilal and Banu Sulaym invasions remains debatable.) Furthermore, the integration of northern Algeria with the Umayyad (q.v.) and Abbasid (q.v.) Caliphates stimulated the development of expansive international commerce and flourishing cities. Algeria had an established maritime economy long before the arrival of the Ottomans.

Culturally, cities such as Constantine, Tlemcen, Annaba (Bône), Bejaïa (Bougie), and Algiers were distinguished centers of learning besides commerce. Ibn Khaldun (q.v.) lived in several Algerian cities before settling in Tunis. Under the Almoravids, Maliki (q.v. Malikism) Islam was entrenched in Algeria. Furthermore, as a consequence of Almoravid and Almohad invasions, Algeria was influenced by the great Ibero-Islamic civilization. Correspondingly, the arrival of displaced Andalusian Muslims and Jews (q.v.), a consequence of the Christian reconquest (*reconquista*), enriched Algeria's cultural heritage and contribution (q.v. Literature in Arabic).

THE TURKISH REGENCY

In the early sixteenth century, Spanish military and crusading incursions along the Northwest African coast created enclaves including Algiers and Oran (q.v.). The militant Spanish were matched, however, by the ambitious and adventurous ''Barbarossa'' brothers (Aruj [q.v.], Khayr al-Din [q.v.], Ishaq, and

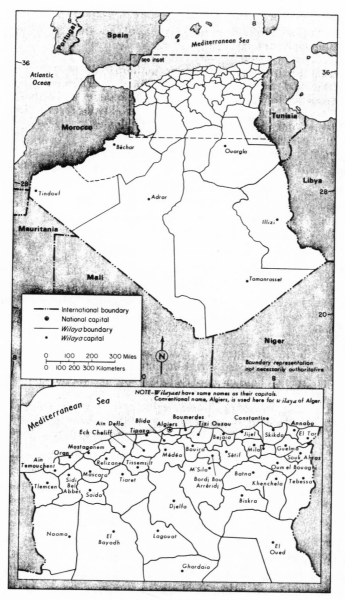

Algeria 1985

Elias). These Turkified Greek privateers raided and occupied regions along the Algerian littoral and in the northern hinterland. The inauguration of the Algerian Regency (q.v.), while theoretically under the rule of the Ottoman Empire, was in practice an autonomous state; the Turks were known as "Algerians." Indeed, the renowned historian, Tawfiq al-Madani (q.v.), referred to the Regency as an "Algerian Ottoman Republic." Under *Beylerbeys*, *Pashas*, *Aghas*, and *Deys* supported by subordinate *Beys* in Mascara (later moved to Oran), Constantine, and Titteri, the Turks governed northern Algeria from the early 1500s until the French conquests of Algiers in 1830 and later Constantine in 1837. Led by such dauntless leaders as Hassan Pasha (q.v.) and Eulj Ali (q.v.), Algeria became a formidable state that earned the respect and fear of Europe.

The economy of the Regency was based not only on its infamous piracy, which was concurrently practiced by Europeans, but also upon Algeria's agricultural and manufacturing production. Protected by its formidable fortifications, Algiers became one of the greatest cosmopolitan centers of the Mediterranean, distinguished, too, by impressive mosques and public works.

THE FRENCH COLONIAL ESTABLISHMENT

France's internal affairs generated incidental imperialist ambitions toward Algeria. In order to divert his subjects' restlessness concerning his unpopular domestic policies, King Charles X (q.v.) exploited a number of commercial and political contentions with the Regency. The chief issue was the Bourbon government's refusal to honor a debt dating back to the Revolutionary period owed to an Algerian exporting firm. This nagging issue contributed to an inopportune event for the Regency in 1827 when Dey Husayn (q.v.) slapped the French consul (Pierre Deval) with a fly whisk. The King ordered a blockade of Algiers and then, three years later, an invasion. Under the command of General Louis de Bourmont (q.v.), French troops used contingency plans drawn up years before for

Napoleon and landed on June 14, 1830, west of Algiers at Sidi Fredj (Ferruch). After defeating Turkish and allied Berber forces, Algiers capitulated to the invaders on July 5. Ironically, after this success Charles X was deposed several weeks later.

Louis-Philippe (q.v.) inherited this conquest and dispatched a "Special Commission" to help him assess the situation. The Commission, which was enlarged in 1833 and renamed the "African Commission," acknowledged that there had been injustices committed against the native population. Nevertheless, it also listed appealing nationalist rationales for maintaining a French presence, such as the availability of new markets and strategic military sites, the enduring civilizing mission, and the promotion of France's international prestige. Louis-Philippe was particularly sensitive to the Commission's report that the conquest was popular in France. This was the decisive argument that convinced him to endorse colonization.

Though the French dismantled the Ottoman Regency, it was clear that the concept of an Algerian state or an embryonic Algerian "nationalism" existed at the time. For example, when the French attacked Algiers, peripheral tribes from areas that routinely refused to pay taxes to central authorities sent soldiers to defend the city. As France debated what to do with this conquest, an Algerian began to fill the power vacuum.

In western Algeria the Amir Abd al-Qadir (q.v.) organized a successor Islamic state, which posed a very serious threat to French colonial plans. This amirate eventually controlled about two-thirds of Algeria's inhabited land area of Algeria and a like proportion of its Arab and Berber inhabitants who consensually did not want "infidels" intruding on Muslim territory. Abd al-Qadir demonstrated impressive statecraft as he attempted, though unsuccessfully, to gain diplomatic recognition from England and Spain. Although he also encountered difficulty in obtaining modern weapons, he and his followers stoutly resisted the French. By the Treaty of Tafna (May 1837) (q.v.), his theocratic state was recognized by the French. War resumed soon afterward as the Amir's territorial ambitions competed with those

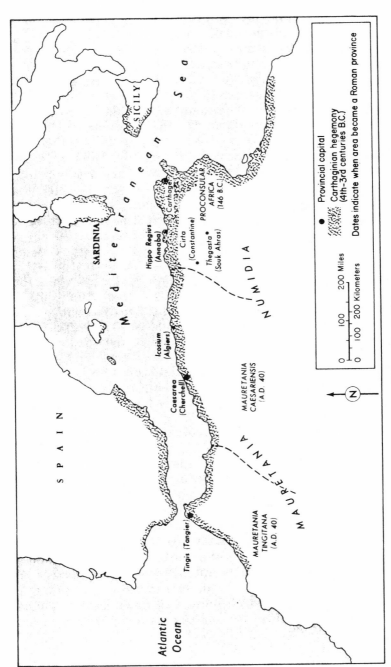

Roman North Africa

of the French. Faced with the determined Marshal Thomas-Robert Bugeaud (q.v.) commanding overwhelming forces, the Amir found himself hard-pressed. The French Army effectively adapted to the campaign by using Muslim raiding tactics, but also resorted to atrocities that terrorized and demoralized the native population. The Amir was forced to surrender in 1847. The enduring resistance of Abd al-Qadir and his followers can be understood only by appreciating the incipient nationalistic sentiments of the Algerians. To view them as merely religious and xenophobic resisters is to embrace a deeply rooted fallacy that has long been the standard of Eurocentric colonial historiography. It is essential to recall that a "national" sentiment rooted in Abd al-Qadir's endeavors remained throughout the colonial period.

Algeria's heroic resistance to French penetration did not end with the capture, imprisonment, and exile of Abd al-Qadir. The French were compelled to fight on until 1859 in order to subdue other intractable foes. Among the most troublesome were the Awlad Sidi Shaykh (q.v.) revolt in western Algeria in 1864 and the Kabyle Revolt of 1871–1872 (q.v.).

Concurrently, there was an administrative conflict between the Army and the settlers. The colonists resented the military government, or the "rule of the sabre." Though northern Algeria became an integral part of France when it was divided into three departments in 1848, the military continued its administration except during the short-lived Ministry of Algeria and Colonies (1858–1860). Napoleon III's (q.v.) directives (e.g., the Senatus-Consultes of 1863 and 1865 [q.v.]) sought to lessen the negative consequences of colonialism. The Franco-Prussian War interrupted another initiative (June 1870) that would have further eroded the French settlers' power by permitting greater political participation of Muslims, Jews (who had just benefited from the Crémieux Decree [q.v.]), and the European foreign population.

After the humiliating French defeat in Europe, the difficult suppression of the Kabyle Revolt of 1871–1872, and the establishment of the Third Republic, civilian (settler) rule was finally secured and safeguarded in Paris by Eugène Etienne (q.v.)

and his *parti colonial*. Nevertheless, an investigative Senate study (1892) reappraised the Algerian situation and leveled serious charges against the civilian administration. Governor-General Jules Cambon's efforts to implement reforms to improve native conditions incited intense colonial opposition. Threatened politically by Paris and compounded by domestic economic problems and rising anti-Semitism, Algeria experienced a European insurrection in 1898, which even suggested an independent settler state. Paris backed down and reaffirmed Algeria's civil personality by permitting an autonomous budget controlled in Algiers by a *Délégations financières* (q.v.) and a reorganized *Conseil supérieur de l'Algérie* (q.v.). This was confirmed by law in December 1900.

Though officially assimilated within the French administrative system, colonial Algeria featured many anomalies. Unlike the metropolitan departments, Algeria had a governor-general, clearly a colonial office, as the chief administrator rather than a prefect. The *Délégations financières* allowed for a large degree of administrative and fiscal autonomy when compared with other French departments. Only Europeans could vote, although France had established universal manhood suffrage in 1871. Native Algerian males were not allowed to vote until 1919. Even then, only 421,000 of them gained access to the ballot box. After World War II, Algerians were permitted to vote in a second electoral college (the first being reserved for Europeans, a small number of naturalized Frenchmen of Algerian origin, and Jews). Universal suffrage was instituted during the War of Independence.

The colonial period was a disaster for the disinherited colonized. From 1830 to 1940 almost 3.5 million hectares (8.64 million acres) were taken over by the colonialists. The severity of this economic deprivation had profound social effects. Approximately 3 million people lived in Algeria at the time of the French invasion (1830). By 1871, years of warfare, disease, and famine reduced the native population by about one-third. The gradual introduction of modern sanitation, hygiene, and medicine, however, increased the colonized's population at an extraordinary rate. In 1921, there were about 5 million Muslims; by 1956, their numbers inflated to approximately 8.5 million. This caused a Malthusian nightmare of vast underemployment and unemployment forcing Algerians to seek work in France (q.v. Emigrant Labor). Furthermore, the colonized were also deprived of educational opportunities (q.v. Education). Muslims fortunate enough to go to school received a French education that impressed another culture upon their own repressed one compounding an identity dilemma. By 1954, more than 90 percent of the colonized were illiterate and only one out of ten Muslim children attended school.

Approximately 10,000 Europeans (about 5,000 French) in 1834, excluding military forces, waited for Louis-Philippe's decision concerning the colonial future of Algeria. By 1845, there were 100,000 Europeans in Algeria, which almost matched the number of soldiers in pursuit of the elusive Abd al-Qadir. The population reached 250,000 settlers (130,000 French) in 1870. The settlers eventually were known as *colons* and *pieds-noirs* (q.v.). When Algeria became financially autonomous in 1900, their numbers had swelled to more than 600,000. From 1922 to 1954, the population grew from 800,000 to just over 1 million. The Europeans exercised civil and political rights and received greater economic and educational opportunities. For example, modern agricultural machinery was made more accessible to them which underscored the first sector's modern/traditional dichotomy between settlers and natives. Though the image of the settlers was often associated with the wealth and influence of the relatively few *grands colons*, most Europeans lived modestly and at levels just slightly better than the colonized Muslims.

Adversely affecting both the colonized and the colonialists, the metropolitan power characteristically prevented economic competition by impeding innovation and diversification. This resulted in a deeply dependent or "extroverted" Algerian economy. Before the War of Independence, France provided about 80 percent of Algeria's imports (another 10 percent from the French Union). France also imported about 75 percent of Algeria's

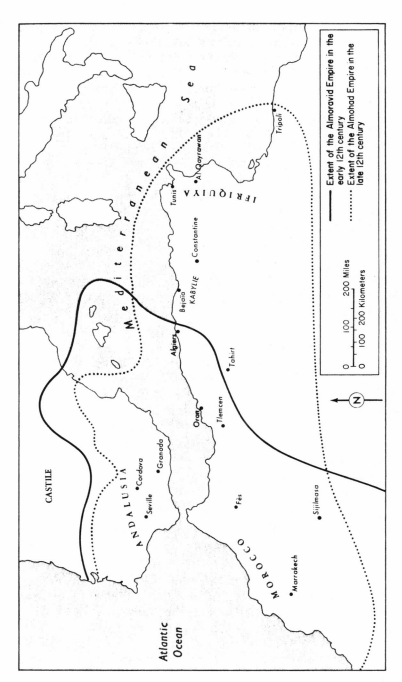

The Maghrib in the Middle Ages

CASTILE

ANDALUSIA
•Seville •Cordova •Granada

Atlantic
Ocean

Mediterranean Sea

•Oran •Tlemcen
Algiers•
Bejaia•
KABYLIE
•Constantine
Tunis•
IFRIQUIYA
•Al-Qayrawan
•Tripoli

•Tahirt

MOROCCO
•Fès
•Sijilmasa
•Marrakech

| Extent of the Almoravid Empire in the early 12th century |
| Extent of the Almohad Empire in the late 12th century |

0   100   200 Miles
0   100   200 Kilometers

N

exports with another 10 percent going to the French Union. Viticulture acted as colonial Algeria's chief economic pursuit after phylloxera infestations ravaged French vineyards in the late 1870s. In order to maximize profits, cereal fields were replaced with vineyards in a land where hunger haunted millions. In 1880, there were 40,000 hectares devoted to viticulture, but this increased tenfold by 1940. During the War of Independence, significant petroleum and huge natural gas deposits (q.v. Hydrocarbons) were discovered, which elevated Algeria's strategic importance and economic promise.

The multiple social and economic dislocations caused by colonialism would be bequested to independent Algeria. Collectively, these conditions exacerbated the frustrating political exclusion of the Algerian people and provoked a desperate and violent liberation struggle.

THE DEVELOPMENT OF ALGERIAN NATIONALISM

Algerian nationalism began before World War I, though the first "nationalists" were hardly revolutionaries. They were educated in French schools and had "assimilated" French culture. A number of these *évolués* argued with Cartesian logic that the realization of authentic assimilation meant the conscription of all Algerians, the availability of educational opportunities, the eradication of the *Code de l'Indigénat* (q.v.), the initiation of fiscal equality, and the extension of citizenship. These "Young Algerians" (q.v.) were very moderate politically; however, they amplified the paradoxes inherent in the colonial relationship.

World War I had pivotal significance for the colonized. Besides supplying soldiers, France imported nearly 120,000 Algerians to replace French workers sent to the front. The Algerians joined the thousands who had already emigrated before the war in search of work and subsistence. It was the extraordinary commitment and service of the colonized (25,000 dead; 22,000 European settlers also perished) on the fronts and in the factories during World

War I that so impressed Premier Georges Clemenceau that he proposed legislation (q.v. Clemenceau Reforms; Jonnart Law) to provide Muslims more opportunities to participate in government and to acquire full French citizenship. Determined colonialist opposition, however, effectively minimized reform.

The failure to enact fully this legislation galvanized Algerian nationalism. The Amir Khalid (Emir Khaled [q.v.]), a grandson of the renowned Abd al-Qadir and a veteran promoted to the highest rank attainable by an Algerian Muslim (captain), articulated ideas that went beyond those of the Young Algerians. Khalid proposed the end of European immigration to Algeria, abolition of the *communes mixtes* (q.v.), compulsory education in French and Arabic, equal political representation in colonial assemblies, and especially French citizenship without the loss of Muslim status. These demands compelled colonial authorities to deport Khalid in 1923.

Khalid's efforts, however, influenced others. Ferhat Abbas (q.v.) was at first an earnest assimilationist embracing French ideals. Nevertheless, continuing colonial oppression and especially insensitivity to the legitimate aspirations of *évolués* symbolized by the rejection of the Blum-Viollette legislation (q.v.) of 1936 turned Abbas and other moderates toward more radical courses. Messali Hadj (q.v.) presented another nationalist alternative. Messali, like Abbas, headed many organizations, but his objective never wavered from national independence and social revolution. Shaykh Abd al-Hamid ibn Badis (q.v. Ben Badis) was a cultural nationalist who believed that French assimilation was impossible. In 1931 he formed the Association of Algerian Reformist *Ulama* (q.v.), a group of religious scholars who criticized superstitious practices, upheld orthodox Islamic traditions, and promoted the learning of Arabic. His efforts to preserve and protect an Algerian cultural identity also led to a political one. Colonialism's inherent divisive and distorted social structures produced the elite's heterogeneity and consequently its disunity, which jeopardized Algeria's potential for national regeneration and recuperation.

In February 1943, Abbas proclaimed the Manifesto of the Algerian People (q.v.), which called for an autonomous Algeria. It was spurned by colonial authorities. Charles de Gaulle's (q.v.) subsequent Ordinance of March 1944 (q.v.), which finally granted citizenship to tens of thousands of Algerians without losing their Muslim status, was a response to nationalist restlessness, but it failed to impress the increasingly impatient elite. Indeed, the nationalists found themselves united as never before. Taking advantage of this situation, Abbas organized the *Association des Amis de la Manifeste* (AML) (q.v.). At its first Congress in March 1945, Messali was recognized as its leader. The colonialists attempted to crack nationalist solidarity by deporting Messali. This decision, which disclosed official insensibility to the incendiary political climate, ignited violence at Sétif (q.v.) and Guelma in May 1945. Demonstrations in these cities celebrating the end of World War II in Europe included the display of nationalist placards, which provoked severe rioting leading to terrible police and military reprisals. The uprising fractured the fragile unity of the nationalists and convinced many Algerians that the only recourse against colonialism was violence.

The enactment and misapplication of the Statute of 1947 (q.v.) compounded by Abbas's and Messali's policies of activism and abstention alienated the brooding younger nationalists. In 1947 they mobilized a paramilitary movement called the *Organisation Spéciale* (OS) (q.v.), which still associated itself with Messali's recently formed *Mouvement pour le Triomphe des Libertés Démocratiques* (MTLD) (q.v.). Colonialist police eventually broke up the OS, but its members (e.g., Ahmed Ben Bella [q.v.], Rabah Bitat [q.v.], Hocine Aït Ahmed [q.v.], Mohammed Khider [q.v.], Mourad Didouche [q.v.], Mohamed Boudiaf [q.v.], Larbi Ben M'hidi [q.v.], Belkacem Krim [q.v.], and Mostepha Ben Boulaïd [q.v.], collectively known as the "historic leaders/ chiefs" [q.v.]), became the nucleus of the future *Comité Révolutionnaire pour l'Unité et l'Action* (CRUA) (q.v.) in 1953 and then the *Front de Libération Nationale* (FLN) (q.v.) the following year. The young elite prepared for national revolution.

THE WAR OF INDEPENDENCE/NATIONAL LIBERATION

The Algerian War of Independence ranks as one of the great Third World struggles of decolonization. Independence was achieved because of three reasons: (1) the relentless pursuit of fundamental FLN objectives as listed by the Proclamation of November 1, 1954 (q.v.), as reinforced by the resolutions of the nationalists' Soummam Conference (q.v.) and other declarations; (2) the ability of the FLN to pose a security threat to French authority and to attract international attention; and (3) the FLN's ability to remain politically viable in spite of its endemic dissension and fratricidal tendencies.

After the initial coordinated operations of October 31– November 1, 1954, the repeated attacks of the *Armée de Libération* (ALN) (q.v.) convinced French authorities that the rebellion was serious. Premier Pierre Mendès-France pressed for a military solution while addressing social and economic needs. In general, this would be the policy pursued by the governments of the Fourth Republic and subsequently that of Charles de Gaulle's Fifth Republic. Mendès-France and his interior minister, François Mitterrand (q.v.), recognized the gravity of the situation and the anachronistic Algerian colonial condition, but they did not have the political strength to implement a decolonization process or to persuade credible Algerian nationalist interlocutors to initiate dialogue and possibly negotiation. Before his government fell (February 1955), Mendès-France appointed Jacques Soustelle (q.v.) as governor-general.

Soustelle introduced the idea of "integration" (q.v.), which called for a complete political and economic amalgamation of Algeria with France. Carried to its logical conclusion, this ultimate assimilation implied the democratization of Algeria. Soustelle energetically promoted social service highlighted by the creation of the *Sections Administratives Spécialisées* (SAS). While the settlers considered the ominous ramifications of integration, military operations intensified.

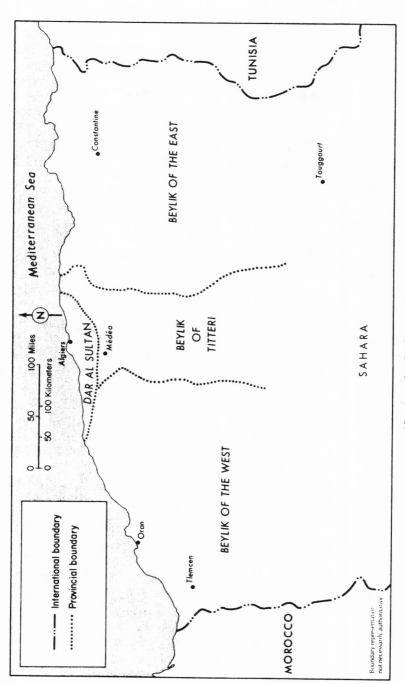

Algeria under the Ottoman Regency

The war suddenly reached a dramatic and terrible height of violence in the FLN-planned brutal massacres in the Constantinois (region of Philippeville [Skikda]) in August 1955 and in the indiscriminate massive French retribution based on "collective responsibility." The vengeful French response to the atrocities, however, alienated the moderate Muslims, as 61 Muslim second college deputies of the Algerian Assembly, symbolized by the signing of a "Declaration of the Sixty-One" (q.v.), denounced French policy (September 25, 1955). The fall of the Edgar Faure government also brought down Soustelle's administration. Guy Mollet became the premier carrying a reputation sympathetic to Algerian nationalist aspirations. Soon after coming to power he visited Algiers in February 1956 and was ignominiously pelted by tomatoes hurled by anxious supporters of French Algeria. Though secret diplomatic contacts were later made with the FLN, Mollet's government adhered to the policy aiming to quell the revolt while investing development monies.

Concurrently the ALN suffered greatly at the expense of the French army, which had learned the lessons of "revolutionary warfare" (*guerre révolutionnaire*) from its grievous humiliation by the Vietminh in Indochina. As the war progressed, the French refined a sophisticated use of counterinsurgency tactics. The Algerians rarely fielded battalion-sized units. Nevertheless, the ALN secured a section of Kabylia undetected by the French, which allowed the FLN to hold the significant Soummam Conference.

Dominated by the fiery Ramdane Abane (q.v.), the conference reiterated FLN objectives, and its "platform" fashioned a preliminary framework for the development of the future state. It created a 34-member *Comité National de la Révolution Algérienne* (CNRA) (q.v.) and a five-member *Comité de Coordination et d'Exécution* (CCE) (q.v.) to manage policies between deliberations of the larger body. The growing internal versus external elite rivalry intensified since Kabyles played a prominent role at Soummam, which upset Ben Bella and other FLN Arabs operating in foreign capitals, who heard about the Conference after it had taken place. Furthermore, the construction of the Morice Line (q.v.) along the Tunisian border effectively prevented exterior ALN sappers from reaching their isolated and often demoralized fighting comrades in the interior. This impeded military support and embittered relations between ALN "external" and "internal" forces.

The Algerian War of Independence featured not only the FLN's intraelite contention but also interelite conflict. A month after the FLN's November Proclamation, Messali Hadj mobilized his *Mouvement Nationaliste Algérien* (MNA) (q.v.). Failed efforts to unite the two organizations had hostile and tragic consequences. As French forces laid back, ALN and MNA units conducted ferocious attacks on each other. The degree of fratricidal violence was symbolized by the ALN massacre of MNA sympathizers at Mélouza (q.v.) in May 1957. Even after the MNA was no longer viable, Messali refused to recognize the FLN's legitimacy or its claim to be the sole voice of the Algerian nationalist movement.

The most controversial strategic decision reached at Soummam was to initiate an urban guerrilla campaign. Targeting Algiers, the ALN used tactics of assassinations and bombings (often conducted by attractive young Algerian women passing as Europeans), which gripped the city in terror. General Jacques Massu's paratroopers (*paras*) were called in from the field (*bled*) to terminate the assaults. The ALN organization was defeated, but the political consequence was costly because the French had resorted to torture in order to obtain information. This amplified the war internationally, which had already attracted worldwide attention given United Nations deliberations and especially the October 1956 air hijacking of the "historic leaders" Ben Bella, Khider, Boudiaf, Aït Ahmed, and Bitat.

The French military, aiming to expunge its humiliation in Indochina, prided itself on its Algerian successes. It feared, however, that the civilian government would negate its achievement. This led to distrust and disobedience of the government's command and control as exemplified by the unauthorized air assault into Tunisia (q.v. Sakiet Sidi Youssef). In May 1958, the

Army and insurrectionary settlers seized the offices of the governor-general. The Fourth Republic's authority suddenly vanished as a hastily organized "Committee of Public Safety" in Algiers demanded that General de Gaulle be given office. The military and the settlers' conclusion that de Gaulle was the only one who could preserve French Algeria was their decisive miscalculation.

After coming to power, de Gaulle's immediate policy toward Algeria was a continuation of Fourth Republic initiatives. Though de Gaulle's discourse has been termed "Delphic," he had indicated several years earlier before returning to power that he supported a new French-Algerian relationship. He perceived that French financial, technical, and cultural (educational) assistance could secure a reformulated "association," which would protect strategic French interests and preserve an influential long-term presence. Financial allocations in all sectors rose rapidly (q.v. Constantine Plan). More children attended Algerian schools from 1958 to 1962 than between 1830 and 1958. Attention was also given to the emigrant worker community in France. It was a symbiotic relationship rather than a politically integrationist one that de Gaulle wanted to achieve—and in many ways he succeeded.

As political momentum grew in Paris, the FLN responded with its formation in September 1958 of a "Provisional Government of the Algerian Republic" (GPRA) (q.v.) presided by Ferhat Abbas. It rebuffed de Gaulle's suggestion of a "Peace of the Brave" (q.v.) in October 1958 and criticized his projected "special place" for Algeria within the French Community. de Gaulle's internal political reforms (e.g., more Algerian departments) failed to sway the nationalists or, more important, the native masses. In September 1959, de Gaulle concluded that self-determination would be his government's new policy. This provoked a settler uprising in Algiers in January 1960, which de Gaulle ended with difficulty through persuasion.

At this time French armed forces, under the able command of General Maurice Challe (q.v.), conducted very effective airmobile operations, which crippled the ALN, in desperate need at that time of logistical support. In June 1960, de Gaulle invited the FLN to preliminary discussions. A week later, Ali Boumendjel (q.v.) and Mohammed Ben Yahia (q.v.) met with French officials in Melun (q.v. Melun Conference) outside of Paris. While talks held there were not substantial, they were cordial. In November, de Gaulle spoke of an ''Algerian Algeria.'' This further alienated the settler establishment and angered politicized professional soldiers. When campaigning in Algeria in support of the referendum of January 1961, which confirmed French support for self-determination, de Gaulle observed that Muslims rather than settlers welcomed him. Concurrently, grisly violence in Algiers (December 1960) between the Muslim and settler communities convinced de Gaulle that decolonization must end soon.

In April 1961, de Gaulle reaffirmed publicly that his policy was decolonization. Later that month four generals, Challe, Raoul Salan (q.v.), Edmond Jouhaud, and André Zeller, led a revolt in Algiers, banking on the collaboration of other professional units. de Gaulle's indomitable presence and stature again predominated. Challe and Zeller surrendered while Salan and Jouhaud joined the *Organisation de l'Armée Secrète* (OAS) (q.v.).

THE EVIAN ACCORDS (Q.V.) AND THE TRANSITION TO INDEPENDENCE

Earnest negotiations began in Evian, France, on May 20 between the Algerian delegation, led by Belkacem Krim and its French counterpart led by Louis Joxe (q.v.). On June 13, talks broke down, particularly over Algerian sovereignty of the Sahara, which the French claimed was not really part of Algeria, and the political status of the European community in the future independent state. An attempt to revitalize discussions in July failed. Meanwhile terrorism in Algeria and France increased. Anarchy and savagery heightened the alienation between both communities in Algeria and France.

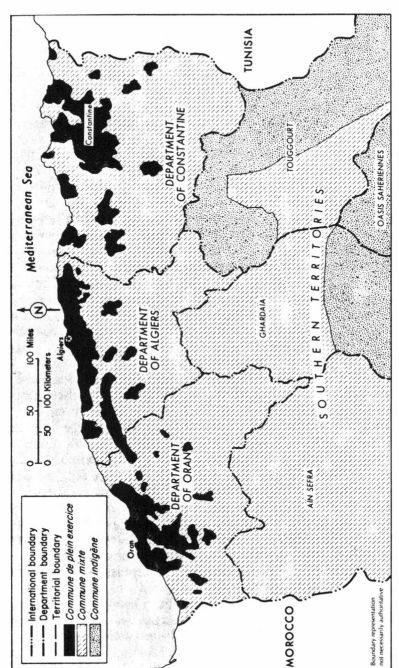

French Algeria

Both sides returned to negotiations held secretly at Les Rousses in the Jura Mountains in February 1962 where an agreement was reached. Final negotiations at Evian began on March 7 and at last a cease-fire was proclaimed at noon on March 19. The Evian Accords provided for Algerian political independence while preserving a French presence through "cooperation" (q.v.). On the other hand, France retained control of the Saharan fields and its military bases while continuing its social and economic aid. There would be no double citizenship for the settlers. After three years, they would have to choose between being French or Algerian.

The conclusion of the Evian Accords did not mean the end of the conflict. Abderrahmane Farès (q.v.), the head of the transitional Provisional Executive administration, tried unsuccessfully to reconcile the settler and native communities. Even with arrests of its leaders, the OAS's violence intensified into a nihilistic "scorched earth" campaign further ravaging the war-torn country. The resultant chaos provoked the flight of hundreds of thousands of settlers to France, leaving their land and property behind. The OAS finally resigned itself to the pressing realities and signed an agreement in June with the FLN that mirrored the guarantees to the settlers as stipulated by the increasingly anachronistic Evian Accords.

The Accords were not only vitiated by the settlers' sudden and massive repatriation, but also by the FLN's Tripoli Program (q.v.). This document challenged the neocolonial impositions of the Accords and proclaimed the elite's exercise of a "socialist option." Under these rapidly changing circumstances, a referendum was held on July 1 by which 91 percent of the Algerian voters selected independence. de Gaulle proclaimed Algeria independent on July 3. Algeria officially declared its national liberation on July 5, 1962, 132 years after the French seizure of Algiers.

Official Algerian estimates claimed that 1.5 million colonized perished in the struggle. These numbers have caused considerable historiographical controversies. Xavier Yacono disputed these numbers, given the numbers who participated in the referendum of July 1 and the census of 1966. Belkacem Krim contended that 300,000 met their deaths. Alistair Horne and David C. Gordon have calculated that wartime deprivations such as population displacement added casualties that could bring the figure nearer to 1 million. Despite the quantitative controversy, all would agree that the country was in a condition of multiple dislocation.

Politically, it took several more months to achieve peace. The fragile unity maintained by the FLN/ALN during the War of Independence fractured as various political and military national elites began to compete for power. The GPRA, under President Ben Youssef Ben Khedda (q.v.), who had replaced Ferhat Abbas in August 1961, wished to continue its authority. It was immediately challenged by other GPRA members who had been held in French prisons (e.g., Ben Bella, Khider, Boudiaf, Aït Ahmed, Bitat) and Abbas. With a few exceptions, the internal military liked neither the "external" ALN based in Morocco and Tunisia nor the politicians of the GPRA.

Ben Khedda arrived in Algiers first. ALN chief Houari Boumedienne (q.v.), however, refused to obey orders from the GPRA's president and came to terms with Ben Bella. The two crossed into Algeria and set up headquarters in Tlemcen on July 11, 1962. Ben Bella, Khider, and Aït Ahmed then created a "Political Bureau" (also known as the Tlemcen Group) to oppose the GPRA. As the external ALN troops moved toward Algiers, they had to fight several pitched battles with internal units. It was a tragic culmination that tainted the nationalists' heroic revolutionary legacy. The FLN never recovered from this fratricide or tolerated the same degree of pluralism until forced to by the consequence of the October 1988 riots (q.v.). The new nation drifted toward authoritarianism and soon military dictatorship. Full-blown civil war was avoided because of the intervention of mass demonstrations organized by the *Union Générale des Travailleurs Algériens* (UGTA).

After considerable political maneuvering, an Algerian Assembly with constituent powers was elected; it met on September 25, 1962, and chose Ferhat Abbas as its president. The next day, Ben

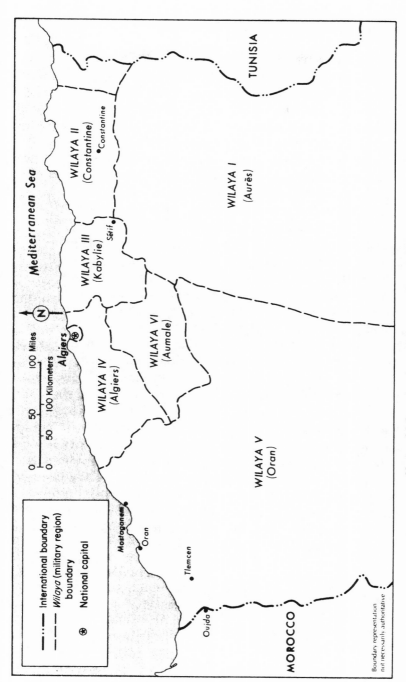

National Liberation Army Military Regions, 1954–62

Bella was elected prime minister. He immediately organized a cabinet staffed by his partisans, by associates of Boumedienne, and by a few "historic leaders." The new government faced grievous economic problems.

The extroverted, "disarticulated" colonial economy needed a total reorientation. The FLN's "socialist option" inferred state planning and projected in the long term the introversion of an integrated national economy. With the untapped potential of Saharan hydrocarbons, the outlook appeared promising. In the short term, however, the flight of colonial cadres and capital severely dislocated the economy because few of the colonized were trained to manage strategic sectors. Furthermore, the ineluctable postcolonial ties to France (perpetuated, too, by the policy of cooperation) qualified Algeria's revolutionary image besides independence.

Socially, the dislocation was dreadful. The massive repatriation, or "expatriation," of the European community, including skilled professionals such as teachers and doctors, was not anticipated by either French or Algerian authorities. Furthermore, native society, already destructured by colonialism, was devastated by the war, producing a demographic disaster. Besides the enormous casualties, more than 2 million colonized had been displaced and "regrouped." The turmoil and terror in the countryside (*bled*) forced the colonized to flee to the cities, resulting in overcrowding exacerbating inadequate services.

Above all, independence left Algeria existentially disoriented. Algeria had to free itself from foreign political, economic, social, and cultural structures (i.e., mentalities) in order to experience an authentic liberation. The definition of an inclusive national identity taking into account Algeria's historic cultural pluralism remains a persistent and problematic project.

ALGERIA UNDER AHMED BEN BELLA, 1962–1965

Once in power, Ahmed Ben Bella moved to consolidate his position. His government outlawed opposition parties (e.g., the

PCA [q.v. Algerian Communist Party], the regenerated PPA [q.v.], which had been the MNA, and the recently formed PRS [q.v.]). Henceforth, the FLN would be the only legal party. Ben Bella then maneuvered to gain FLN control over the UGTA, which he managed to do by packing the Union's Congress early in 1963. He pushed a constitution (q.v.) through the Algerian Assembly, which created a presidential republic with a one-party (the FLN) system. This constitution was adopted by a national referendum followed by elections. In September 1963, Ben Bella was elected to a five-year term as president.

There was both symbolic and serious resistance to Ben Bella's increasing authoritarianism. A disappointed Ferhat Abbas resigned as president of the National Assembly in protest of Ben Bella's amassed personal power. Mohammed Khider criticized the growing influence of the military, and he, too, resigned from his post of secretary-general of the FLN and chose exile. Beginning in October-November 1963, Ben Bella had to fight off an armed rebellion based in Kabylia led by Aït Ahmed and Mohand Ou El Hadj (q.v.). A military insurrection commenced in the southeast in 1964 commanded by Colonel Mohamed Chaabani (q.v.). Although both Aït Ahmed and Chaabani were captured (the latter was executed), Ben Bella remained politically insecure during his years in power.

Nevertheless, Ben Bella provided, as Robert Merle (q.v. Bibliography) contended, "purpose and direction" to Algerian independence. He asserted Algerian sovereignty and gained considerable popular support by nationalizing vacated European lands and properties (March and October 1963 Decrees) and by adopting the "self-management" (*autogestion* [q.v.]) system, which he proclaimed to be Algeria's unique contribution to socialism. His foreign policy effectively presented Algeria as a Third World leader championing national liberation movements and struggles against colonialism and neocolonialism. Algeria's most important international relationship was with France. Ben Bella and his successor, Houari Boumedienne, delicately balanced conflict with cooperation. Critical of the neocolonial

presence of French military bases and of hydrocarbon concessions, Ben Bella also realized that Algeria was dependent upon
France in every way, especially with regard to technical and
educational services. Bilateral relations were particularly strained
over the nationalization of settler property, French atomic testing,
and the inaugural construction of a third oil trunk line by the
national enterprise SONATRACH (q.v. Hydrocarbons)

Though relations with its Maghribi neighbors had been
"fraternal" during the war, they cooled immediately after
independence. President Bourguiba of Tunisia had hoped to
adjust Algerian borders in order to share hydrocarbon wealth.
Furthermore, Bourguiba accused Algeria of harboring plotters
conspiring against his government. Relations declined also with
Morocco. The FLN had agreed to negotiate the contentious
colonial frontiers after the war, but Ben Bella now claimed that
they were unalterable. This led to the outbreak of the brief Border
War of October-November 1963 (q.v.).

By mid-1964, after Ben Bella had eliminated practically all the
"Historic Leaders" from public life, he began to move against the
supporters of Boumedienne, his erstwhile ally. First he ordered all
prefects to report directly to the presidency; Ahmed Medeghri
(q.v.), the minister of the interior and one of Boumedienne's
staunchest supporters, resigned in protest (July 1964). Next, Ben
Bella attempted to dismiss Abdelaziz Bouteflika (q.v.), the
minister of foreign affairs. Boumedienne retaliated by launching
a bloodless coup d'état, dubbed the "historical rectification" of
June 17, 1965, which deposed Ben Bella.

ALGERIA UNDER HOUARI BOUMEDIENNE

A new body called the Council of the Revolution (q.v.)
assumed political authority; Boumedienne emerged as president
of the Council, prime minister, and minister of defense. He moved
quickly to create a new government (July 10, 1965), which
included several men who had served under Ben Bella (most

notably Medeghri and Bouteflika). Soldiers dominated the Council, which frequently met with the Cabinet. The new ministers were generally civilian technocrats as well as military men. Another change was the creation of a five-man Secretariat for the FLN. This new institution was charged with the task of revitalizing the party besides expediting relations between the FLN and the government. Boumedienne also dismissed a number of European advisers, men of Communist, Trotskyist, and Maoist convictions, who had surrounded Ben Bella. He felt that these consultants had no roots in Algeria; they neither understood nor valued Algeria's Arabic and Islamic culture. ''Algeria,'' Boumedienne declared in a June 30, 1965, speech, ''wants to be Algeria, and that is all.''

By far, Boumedienne's most important initiatives during his presidency concerned economic planning and state building. His government implemented a Three-Year (Pre-Plan) and two Four-Year Plans (q.v. State Plans) (1967–1977) that concentrated on capital-intensive export industry (i.e., hydrocarbons) in order to accumulate revenues for reinvestment. This was strategically important because Algeria, although allowing foreign investment (though under stringent codes), expected to finance its own development.

Besides accelerating Algeria's ''industrial revolution,'' Boumedienne inaugurated an ''Agrarian Revolution'' (q.v.) and a ''Cultural Revolution'' (q.v.) in 1971. These ambitious enterprises correlated with the government's carefully cultivated revolutionary image. During his rule, Boumedienne encouraged the growth of the UGTA and organized the UNPA (peasants) and the UNJA (youth). These official efforts to mobilize the masses were a mixed success.

Foreign policy continued to be an expression and extension of internal policy. Mirroring Ben Bella's policy, but not his flamboyance, Boumedienne also projected Algeria as a Third World leader and reaffirmed the need for a North-South dialogue. It was Boumedienne's Algeria that championed the ''Group of 77'' less-developed countries in their quest to publicize the economic plight of the developing world. Algeria also sponsored the special session of the United Nations in 1974, which proposed a new economic order between the have and have-not countries.

The relationship with France inevitably transformed. Algeria welcomed the Algiers Accords, an innovative hydrocarbons and industrial development agreement (q.v. Hydrocarbons). Boumedienne continued, however, the systematic policy of postcolonial decolonization by eventually removing French military and hydrocarbon presences. The last French base (at Bou Sfer) was handed over in December 1970. Then in February 1971, after an arduous negotiation, French hydrocarbon concessions were nationalized, which was called a victory in "the battle for oil." This temporarily ended the privileged French-Algerian relationship. Furthermore, Algeria prohibited further emigration to France in September 1973, given the hostility directed against that community.

When President Giscard d'Estaing visited Algiers in April 1975, Boumedienne expressed his wish to "turn the page." Anticipation of better relations, if not renewed privileged relations were dashed by France's reluctance to redress the trade imbalance and especially by Paris's support of the Tripartite or Madrid Accords (q.v.) of November 1975, which partitioned the bordering Spanish Sahara between Morocco and Mauritania. Algeria responded by providing havens for refugees and the POLISARIO (q.v.), the Sahrawi people's liberation organization. French aerial intervention against the POLISARIO (1977–1978) especially angered Algeria.

Boumedienne's command of the military and his paternalistic attitude toward the growth of an Algerian technocracy allowed him to amass immense political authority and to build a state. His power was threatened only during the early years of his regime. In 1965–1966 and 1968, sporadic student protests occurred. In December 1967, Boumedienne destroyed an attempted military coup led by Tahar Zbiri (q.v.), and in April 1968 he survived an assassination attempt. There was also the formation of opposition parties (e.g., ORP, OCRA, PRS, MDRA). The mysterious deaths of exiled Mohammed Khider (1967) and Belkacem Krim (1970) eliminated influential rivals. Former President Ben Bella remained in house arrest despite international protest. Uncharacteristically, Boumedienne allowed considerable public debate concerning the drafting of the National Charter (q.v.). The Charter and Constitution proclaimed in 1976 were the capstones of Boumedienne's political institutionalization.

On December 27, 1978, Boumedienne died from a rare blood disease. Rabah Bitat, the president of the National Assembly, became interim president of the Republic. An FLN Party Congress then selected a compromise candidate, Chadli Benjedid (q.v.), as secretary-general of the FLN and sole candidate for the presidency of Algeria; he was elected on February 7, 1979. The smooth transition of power bore witness to the effectiveness of the timely institutional changes engineered by Boumedienne.

ALGERIA UNDER CHADLI BENJEDID, 1979–1992

Unlike Presidents Ben Bella and Boumedienne, Chadli Benjedid was more pragmatic than ideological. At first, President Benjedid appeared committed to his predecessor's socialist state-building model; however, he soon proposed more balanced economic development.

Benjedid's First 5-Year Plan (1980–1984) devoted significant attention to agriculture and infrastructure while braking the accelerated capital-intensive heavy industrialization of Boumedienne's planners. The second sector was not neglected because projects from earlier plans continued to be addressed. Nevertheless, since domestic agricultural production accounted for only about 30 percent of the country's alimentary needs, the first sector needed immediate development. Benjedid's government also symbolically reversed the Agrarian Revolution of the 1970s by resolving to return 450,000 hectares to private hands. Algeria's burgeoning population growth necessitated greater allocations to the tertiary sector, especially toward housing construction.

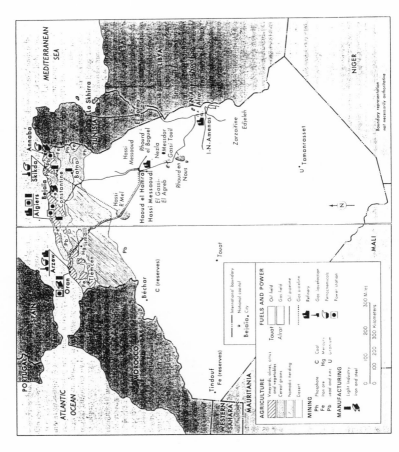

Economic Activity, 1985

AGRICULTURE

- Vineyards, olives, citrus and vegetables
- Cereal grains
- Nomadic herding
- Desert

MINING

- Ph   Phosphate
- Fe   Iron ore
- Pb   Lead and zinc
- C   Coal
- Hg   Mercury
- U   Uranium

MANUFACTURING

- Light industry
- Iron and steel

FUELS AND POWER

- Touat Oil field
- Alrar Gas field
- Oil pipeline
- Gas pipeline
- Refinery
- Gas liquefaction
- Petrochemicals
- Power station

- International boundary
- National capital
- ★ Bejaïa ● City

0   100   200   300 Miles
0   100   200   300 Kilometers

Boundary representation not necessarily authoritative

MEDITERRANEAN SEA

PORTUGAL
SPAIN
ATLANTIC OCEAN
MOROCCO
WESTERN SAHARA
MAURITANIA
MALI
NIGER
LIBYA
TUNISIA

Annaba
Skikda
Bejaïa
Algiers
Constantine
Batna
Oran
Arzew
Tlemcen
Béchar
Tindouf
Hassi R'Mel
Haoud el Hamra
Hassi Messaoud
El Gassi-El Agreb
Rhourd en Nous
Rhourd el Baguel
Nezla
Gassi Touil
Messdar
Hassi Messaoud
El Borma
I.N.Amenas
Zarzatine
Edjeleh
Alrar
I.N.Amenas Nord
In Amenas
Touat
U'Tamanrasset

Fe (reserves)
C (reserves)
Pb
Fe

Deteriorating economic conditions qualified the Second Five-Year Plan (1985–1989), which featured an objective of horizontally integrating sectors. Financing the investment and introversion of the economy continued to be hydrocarbon export revenues. Consequently, as long as its oil prices remained high and export market demand stayed relatively inelastic, index-based revenues (with regard to natural gas) could sustain ambitious development plans. The government also attempted to attract greater foreign investment especially in hydrocarbons (e.g., liberal 1986 legislation).

Benjedid inaugurated the decentralization of the government's statist economic and political structures. Powerful state companies such as SONATRACH were "restructured" into smaller operations. In addition, this socialist country quietly and later openly encouraged private enterprise. The establishment of new *wilayat* (states) (from 34 to 48) also permitted greater local participation and control.

Algeria's changing domestic policy was reflected in its foreign relations. Benjedid attempted to temper Algeria's past radicalism while maintaining its avant-garde Third World reputation. Taking advantage of its extraordinary range of diplomatic associations, Algeria offered itself as a mediating Third World "parley" (rather than "proxy") state to disputing nations (e.g., United States–Iran, Iraq–Iran, and France–Lebanon [i.e., its political factions]). In addition, its global activism was redirected toward regional Maghribi and western Mediterranean affairs.

Benjedid attempted to resolve differences with neighboring states by pursuing Maghrib unity (q.v.), an elusive economic and political objective. This resulted in 1983 with amity accords with Tunisia and Mauritania (which signed an accord in 1979 with the POLISARIO terminating its involvement in Western Sahara's partition). Sharp differences over the Western Sahara prevented a similar reconciliation with Morocco. Benjedid and King Hassan II met in 1983 and 1987, which marginally improved relations but still contributed toward the restoration of relations in June 1988. Algeria's aspiration to solve the Western Saharan War within the framework of a Greater Maghrib was underscored when Morocco and POLISARIO consented to a U.N.-promoted peace proposal in August 1988. Though a final settlement of the Saharan War was not reached (a self-determination referendum projected before the end of 1991 never took place), the overall promising regional initiatives and achievements contributed to the creation in February 1989 of the ''Arab Maghrib Union'' (q.v.) dedicated to regional cooperation and integration.

Benjedid also pursued a more positive relationship with France. This was highlighted by President François Mitterrand's (q.v.) visit to Algiers in 1981, which resulted in a memorable Liquefied Natural Gas (LNG) Accord in February 1982 (q.v. Hydrocarbons) and a period of heightened cooperation (termed at that time as ''co-development''). Relations declined in the mid-1980s, but France revived its economic and political support after the 1988 riots (q.v.) (financial and LNG accords [January 1989]; Mitterrand visit [March 1989]).

Though Benjedid's administration received general public support, there were threats to its stability. First, there were the ousted ''superindustrialist'' planners (e.g., Belaïd Abdesselam [q.v.]) from the Boumedienne era, who questioned the reoriented state planning. Benjedid responded by streamlining the governing Political Bureau and staffing it with loyalists, while offering ideological opponents other positions. Second, the disconcerting emergence of Islamic populism challenged the government's secularism. Benjedid signaled his sensibility by releasing imprisoned Islamist leaders in May 1984. Furthermore, the Family Law of 1984 (q.v.) reinforced traditional Islamic law, while disappointing women's groups (q.v. Women). Third, Berber unrest over cultural identity questions incited disturbances in 1980, 1982, and 1986. Fourth, the rising expectations of Algeria's youth, the rapidly maturing national generation, were frustrated by a lack of social and economic opportunities. Educational opportunity was a primary postcolonial objective, but highly trained Algerians found it impossible to find employment. By the late 1980s, these political and social problems were compounded by depressed hydrocarbon prices and economic shortages. Public distress and discontent provoked the fierce and widespread October 1988 riots (q.v.), causing heavy casualties, which discredited the FLN's political legitimacy and historic legacy.

Benjedid quickly initiated reforms. A referendum in November 1988 reduced presidential power by giving the prime minister more responsibility. (Benjedid was reelected president in December.) The Constitution of February 1989 (q.v.) was acclaimed by referendum and projected a multiparty state, thereby terminating the FLN's monopoly of power. Legislation enacted in July 1989 permitted the legalization of opposition parties. Political liberalization generated a variety of political parties, newspapers, organizations, etc., (q.v. Appendices), which collectively illustrated the vitality and diversity of Algerian historical, besides political, culture. In September, the Islamic Salvation Front (FIS) (q.v.), the chief Islamist party, received its legal status as an oppostion party. Hocine Aït Ahmed, the enduring opposition leader, repatriated in December after 23 years of exile. Ben Bella returned the following year.

In June 1990, the first free elections in Algeria's history gave the FIS stunning victories in local races (q.v. Elections of June 1990). Observers considered the Islamist success a consequence of protest voting against the political establishment. Parliamentary elections were slated for the following June. Electoral law changes enacted in April by the FLN-dominated *Assemblée Nationale Populaire* (ANP) particularly infuriated the FIS and led to protests in May and June, which culminated with the arrests of its leaders Abassi Madani (q.v.) and Ali Ben Hadj (q.v.) (q.v. Elections of June 1991). Elections were rescheduled for December, when the first round resulted in another astonishing FIS triumph (q.v. Elections of December 1991).

THE HIGH COUNCIL OF STATE (JANUARY 1992–)

The spectre of an Islamist party in power alarmed civilian and military elites. The realization that Benjedid remained committed to the democratic process and the completion of the second electoral round compelled a powerful group to confront the president. On January 11, 1992, President Benjedid was forced to resign by a "High Council of Security." It was renamed on January 14, as the "High Council of State" (HCS) (q.v.) and officially took over power presided over by the former historic chief, Mohamed Boudiaf. The elections were cancelled and the HCS declared a yearlong national state of emergency. The Islamist rejection of the HCS forced massive arrests and the subsequent establishment of controversial internment camps. This produced domestic outrage and international disapproval. Student unrest also necessitated police intervention on national campuses. Most distressing, Islamist protest turned violent (especially after the FIS lost its legal status) as the *Mouvement Islamique Armé* (MIA) (q.v.) targeted police officers and soldiers. By the end of 1992, it was estimated that between 200 and 400 members of security forces had been killed.

President Boudiaf, a fiercely independent man, hoped to earn the confidence of the country while strengthening his political position. In April, a consultative body (*Conseil consultatif national* [CCN] [q.v.]) convened to assist or at least accommodate the HCS. In June, the President appealed for a "national patriotic rally" (*Rassemblement National Patriotique*), a thinly disguised attempt to mobilize a unity party. Boudiaf attacked corruption highlighted by the indictment in May of General Mostefa Benloucif (Belloucif) (q.v.), the former Chief of the General Staff. Boudiaf's increasingly assertive leadership ended on June 29, when he was assassinated while delivering a speech in Annaba. The subsequent inconclusive investigation of his death cast suspicions on not only the Islamist opposition, but also Boudiaf's own government.

Ali Kafi (q.v.), a member of the HCS, became president; along with Prime Minister Belaïd Abdesselam he now faces enormous problems. The anarchic political situation has worsened as symbolized by the gruesome bombing at the Algiers airport in August 1992 (9 reported deaths and many wounded). The government's efforts to end the violence has threatened the recently gained civil and constitutional rights. (In October President Kafi signed a law that would permit sentences without recourse to appeal from five years to the death penalty for acts of terror.) In addition, the economy is collapsing under a $26 billion foreign debt burden (consuming about three-quarters of external receipts) compounded by an inflation rate of 30 percent. Unemployment is modestly estimated at 25 percent. In August 1993, Reda Malek (q.v.) replaced Abdesselam as prime minister. During that same month the increasing violence claimed the life of ex-prime minister Kasdi Merbah (q.v.) and members of his family. The HCS appointed in January 1994 Liamine Zéroual (q.v.) as Algeria's sixth president. He appears determined to initiate a dialogue with the Islamists in order to stem the escalating internecine conflict that has taken approximately 4,000 lives (April 1994). Though politics and economics usually receive the most attention, there is also the enduring and intensifying cultural issue, which has taken on heightened significance during this protracted crisis: the national inability to recognize and reconcile its historical and social legacies. Algeria is poised before an epochal transformation, which will lead toward national deliverance or disintegration.

THE DICTIONARY

ABA, NOUREDDINE (b. 1921). Poet. Noureddine Aba was born in Sétif (q.v.), but he spent a large part of his life in France. During World War II, he served in the Italian and French campaigns. After the war he was a journalist and became an activist for the Palestinian cause. He returned to Algeria in 1977. Among his published poetic works are: *L'Aube de l'amour* (1941); *La Toussaint des énigmes* (1963); *Montjoie Palestine! ou l'an dernier à Jérusalem* (1970); *Le Chant perdu au pays retrouvé* (1978); and *Gazelle après minuit: Chants d'amour et de guerre de la Révolution algérienne* (1979); and *C'était hier Sabra et Chatila* (1983). He won the *Prix de l'Afrique méditerranéenne* for *Le Chant perdu* and *Gazelle après minuit*. He has also written children's stories (*La Gazelle égarée* [*The Stray Gazelle*] [1979] in Arabic; *Les Quatres ânes et l'écureuil*). Several of his plays have been broadcast by the ORTF (*Office de la Radio et Télévision Française*): *Le Gain d'une défaite, Ziryab l'enchanteur, La Vérité à portant*. According to Jean Déjeux (q.v. Bibliography), Noureddine Aba's contributions resemble those of Mohammed Dib's (q.v.) works because they explore the universal qualities of human beings beyond pretense and politics.

ABANE (ABBANE), RAMDANE (1920–1957). FLN (q.v.) leader during the War of Independence. A Kabyle (q.v.) born in Azouza, Abane served as a noncommissioned officer in the French Army during World War II and as a functionary in the colonial administration. He was attracted, however, to the PPA (q.v.) and soon left his job to devote himself full time to the nationalist organization. He quickly rose to the position of party leader in the Sétif region. Abane was arrested in the wake of the French discovery of the OS (q.v.), although he was apparently not an active member of that secret paramilitary organization. Released in January 1955, he joined the FLN (q.v.) (after being contacted by Amar Ouamrane [q.v.]). He was apparently instrumental in getting members of the UDMA (q.v.), the PCA, and the Association of Reformist *Ulama* (q.v.) to join the liberation organization.

Abane is best known for his role at the Soummam Congress (q.v.), which, under his fiery leadership, adopted a platform and administrative organization of which members of the external delegation of the FLN (particularly Ahmed Ben Bella [q.v] and Mohamed Boudiaf [q.v.]) disapproved. Though Soummam had presented a framework for collegial or collective political leadership, Abane was the unofficial leader. He was a member of the CNRA (q.v.) and of the CCE (q.v.) from 1956 until his assassination in December 1957. Abane's role at the Soummam Congress and his refusal to abandon his thesis that the internal leadership of the ALN (q.v.)-FLN should dominate the external delegation and that the civilian FLN should control the military made him very unpopular in several nationalist quarters. With his political power and position endangered, Ramdane castigated the "colonels" (ALN commanders; there were no "generals" in order to promote a sense of equality among commanders) and their "*wilayism.*" Abane's acerbity was directed particularly at the powerful Wilaya V commander, Abdelhafid Boussouf (q.v.). Abane's rancor also alienated sympathetic ALN commanders. His murder by the military in December 1957 eliminated the tempestuous Kabyle, but it also removed a dynamic ideologist who could have possibly presented a social and economic program for the revolution. His death signaled that the military had become the decisive force in Algerian politics. Recent historiography has reassessed Abane's contribution to the Revolution and rehabilitated his reputation as a vigorous nationalist.

ABBAS, FERHAT (1899–1985). Nationalist; president of the GPRA (q.v.), National Assembly. Abbas was born in Taher into a family prominently associated with French rule. His father, a *caid* at Chahna near Constantine (q.v.), was a recipient of the silver braid and a rosette of the Legion of Honor. In 1909, Abbas entered the lycée at Philippeville (Skikda). After three years in the French army's medical service, he enrolled in the pharmacy school at the University of Algiers (opened a pharmacy in Sétif [q.v.] in 1931).

Abbas's political career evolved from an assimilationist to a revolutionary. In his first book, *Le Jeune Algérien: De la colonie vers la province* (1931), he criticized the failure of French colonialism to fulfill its assimilationist ideals. Abbas and Dr. Mohammed Saleh Bendjelloul (q.v.) led the *Fédération des Elus indigènes* (founded in 1927), which promoted the moderate reforms called for earlier by the Young Algerians (q.v.). He also held the posts of municipal councilor for Sétif (1935) and general councilor for Constantine (1934). He became a member of the *Délégations financières* (q.v.) in 1936.

Abbas enthusiastically embraced the Blum-Viollette Bill (q.v.), which would have granted full French citizenship to 20,000 to 30,000 assimilated Algerians. The failure of the Blum-Viollette Bill split the moderates as Dr. Bendjelloul founded the *Rassemblement Franco-Musulman Algérien* while Abbas organized the *Union Populaire Algérien* (UPA), a party that called for full citizenship for all Muslims and that asserted that Algeria had a separate identity from that of France. This latter position had profound personal and political significance for Abbas because it represented a redefinition of his contention in a famous 1936 article in the *Fédération*'s newspaper, *Entente*, where he wrote that he was unable to find an Algerian nation and thereby linked Algeria's future to France.

Abbas volunteered for service at the beginning of World War II, but he was alienated by the French defeat, Vichy administration, and then by Free French General Giraud's insensibility toward reform while he concurrently exhorted Muslims to enlist (though not on an equal basis) and to sacrifice their lives. Abbas reacted by promulgating the "Manifesto of the Algerian People" (*Le Manifeste du Peuple algérien* [q.v.]) in February 1943 followed by a more explicit supplement (influenced by Messalists) called the *Projet de réformes faisant suite au Manifeste* in May. These documents proposed an autonomous Algerian state associated with France.

Though Charles de Gaulle's Ordinance of March 7, 1944 (q.v.) surpassed the Blum-Viollette Bill's provisions, assimilation no longer coincided with the aspirations of the moderate nationalist elite. Concurrently, Abbas organized the *Association des Amis du Manifeste et de la Liberté* (AML) (q.v.), which briefly unified the Association of Reformist *Ulama* (q.v.) and Messali Hadj's PPA (q.v.). Messali was recognized as the leader of AML. The elite demanded the establishment of an Algerian republic federated to France. Under PPA pressure, the AML took an even more radical position, calling for an Algerian government with a reduced French attachment.

Messalist agitation (exacerbated by the decision to deport Messali in April 1945, compounded by economic frustrations) contributed to the bloody uprisings at Sétif and Guelma in May and the consequent fierce colonialist retributions. Abbas was confined to house arrest. After his release, he founded the *Union Démocratique du Manifeste Algérien* (UDMA) (q.v.) in 1946, which sought an autonomous Algerian state within the French Union. Abbas also served in the Second French Constituent Assembly and as a member of the Muslim College of the Algerian Assembly (1947–1955).

During the first 18 months of the War of Independence, Abbas attempted to act as an intermediary between the *Front de Libération Nationale* (FLN) (q.v.) and the French, though the UDMA itself was targeted by the ALN (q.v.). Finally in April 1956, Abbas along with other moderates declared for the FLN and joined the liberation organization.

Recognizing Abbas's international prestige, the FLN appointed Abbas on September 19, 1958, as the president of the *Gouvernement Provisoire de la République Algérienne* (GPRA) (q.v.). Though Abbas's chief preoccupation was Algerian independence, he also pursued activities that related to the country's independent future. For example, he participated in January 1961 at a continental conference that convened to plan and propose an African Charter. Abbas also signed an agreement with King Hassan II of Morocco in July 1961 to resolve enduring border disputes after Algeria received its independence. In August he was involuntarily replaced, however, by the more radical Ben Youssef Ben Khedda (q.v.), which signaled a crucial shift toward a more uncompromising FLN leadership.

In fall 1962, Abbas returned to political prominence as president of the National Constituent Assembly. Abbas envisioned a pluralistic parliamentary government; however, his liberal democratic viewpoint appeared anachronistic to the revolutionary Nasserist younger elite (e.g., Premier Ahmed Ben Bella [q.v.]). Abbas resigned in August 1963 after a constitution was constructed that disregarded the Constitutent Assembly's deliberations. Furthermore, Abbas condemned Ben Bella's authoritarian accretion of power. Abbas was subsequently removed from the FLN, which represented a repudiation of a historic legacy that had aimed at liberal reform and close ties with France. He was arrested in 1964.

Released after Houari Boumedienne (q.v.) overthrew Ben Bella's government in June 1965, Abbas declined to serve the military government. Indeed, in March 1976 he collaborated with Ben Khedda, Hocine Lahouel (q.v.), and Mohamed Kheireddine (q.v.) and signed the "New Appeal to the Algerian People," (q.v.) a manifesto critical of Boumedienne's government. Abbas was placed under house arrest, and his pharmacy was expropriated. President Benjedid (q.v.) later released Abbas and returned his property.

Ferhat Abbas's nationalist contribution was publicly recognized in the "enhanced" National Charter of 1986 (q.v.), which was published soon after his death. Abbas would have encouraged Algeria's recent steps toward political democracy since the October 1988 riots (q.v.). He would have opposed, however, the Islamist objectives embraced by the *Front de Salut Islamique* (FIS) (q.v.).

Besides *Le Jeune Algérien* (1931), Abbas authored several other books. *Guerre et Révolution d'Algérie: La Nuit coloniale* (1962) and *Autopsie d'une guerre* (1980) reflect on the struggle for independence. In *L'Indépendance confisquée, 1962–1978* (1984), Abbas disclosed his disillusionment with independent Algeria, but he also dedicated the work to the emerging new generation. In some ways, his appeal for the youth to restore the true meaning of the Revolution has been heard since the October 1988 riots (q.v.).

ABBASID DYNASTY. The successor to the Umayyad dynasty, it lasted from 750 to 1258. The dynasty was founded by Abbas, a descendant of the Prophet Muhammad's uncle. The Abbasid coalition, which overwhelmed the Umayyads in 750, was composed of Shi'i (q.v.), *mawali* (or non-Arab Muslims), and other dissidents.The capital was moved from Damascus to Baghdad. The Abbasids failed to keep the political integrity of the *Umma* (Muslim community, i.e., the Arab Empire) as independent amirates and dynasties arose such as the Aghlabids (q.v.), Fatimids (q.v.), and Idrisids in the Maghrib.

ABD AL-MUMIN (Abd al-Mu'min ibn Ali) (1094?–1163). The first and greatest caliph of the Almohad (q.v.) dynasty. Abd al-Mumin was born in Tagra in southern Morocco to a son of a potter of the Kumiya tribe of the Zenata Berbers (q.v.). He distinguished himself in Islamic studies in his village, which led him to Tlemcen (q.v.) and then to Bejaïa (Bougie) (q.v.).

He met Ibn Tumart (q.v.), the leader and eventually the *Mahdi* (guided one) of the Almohad movement. Ibn Tumart was deeply impressed with Abd al-Mumin and chose him to be his *khalifa* (deputy). After Ibn Tumart's death (c. 1130), Abd al-Mumin became the Caliph of Ibn Tumart and was known to his followers as the *Amir al-Muminin* (Prince/ Commander of the Faithful).

Abd al-Mumin organized an Almohad army that operated at first in the Atlas and eventually the Rif. His strength increased to the point where he confronted the Almoravid ruler, Tashfin ibn Ali, near Tlemcen in 1145 and defeated him and pushed the Almoravid (q.v.) forces into the coastal plain near Oran. After Tashfin's accidental death (horse fall), his son was invested as the Almoravid sovereign in Marrakesh. Abd al-Mumin took Fez and finally Marrakesh in 1146, which ended the Almoravid line. Morocco was secured by 1148.

After an Almohad intervention in Spain that produced a protectorate in southwestern Andalusia, Abd al-Mumin campaigned again in the central Maghrib and took Bejaïa in 1151 and, in the process, destroyed the Hammadid (q.v.) kingdom. In 1152, the Almohads destroyed the Banu Hilal (Arab Hilalians) (q.v.) at Sétif (q.v.). In 1159–1160, Tunis, Sousse, and the Norman-controlled Mahdiya were taken. With the fall of Ifriqiya (eastern Maghrib), the entire Maghrib was under the unified control of a Maghribi state. Ironically, Abd al-Mumin forcibly moved nomadic Arab tribes into the western Maghrib where they would eventually destabilize the region.

Abd al-Mumin was most concerned with the establishment of a political and military state. He commissioned a survey of his empire for administrative purposes and introduced fixed tax rates for tribes besides the *kharaj*. Non-Almohad Muslims could have their property expropriated, which could then become *habus* (*habous*). Charles-André Julien (q.v.) noted that a kind of "federative and aristocratic republic" envisioned by Ibn Tumart had become instead a monarchy. Abd al-Mumin did maintain the consultative Council of Fifty and the complementary assemblies established by the *Mahdi*, but they became an administrative facade as royal authority dominated the system. This was also illustrated by the distinguishing between the *sayyid* (descendants of Abd al-Mumin) and the *shaykhs* (*shaikhs*) (descendants of great Almohad families).

As other Maghribi leaders, Abd al-Mumin built impressive landmarks and particularly the city Ribat al-Fath (Rabat) in 1150. Before his death in 1163, the Caliph appeared prepared for a major campaign in Spain.

Abd al-Mumin's empire was powerful and impressive. The memory of a united northwest Africa remained a historical inspiration for the recent steps toward Maghrib Unity (q.v.).

ABD AL-QADIR AL-DJILANI (Abd al-Qadir al-Jilali) (d. 1166). Islamic brotherhood founder. Abd al-Qadir al-Djilani was the founder and patron saint of the Qadiriyya, an Islamic brotherhood with many Algerian followers, particularly in western Algeria. Two of the most famous Algerian Qadiri *shaykhs* were Muhyi al-Din ibn Mustafa and his son, the Amir Abd al-Qadir (q.v.). After the defeat of the Amir, Qadiri *shaykhs* resigned themselves to French rule.

Like other brotherhoods, affiliates received the *tariqa* to enhance their spirituality. Though Abd al-Qadir al-Djilani was a principal of a Hanbali law *madrasa* and *ribat*, his ideas had wide application and interpretation. "Djilalism" is one form practiced in North Africa, which has pre-Islamic influences. The Qadiriyya particularly appealed to Muslim intellectuals.

ABD AL-QADIR (Abd el-Kader) BEN MUHYI AL-DIN AL-HASANI (May 26, 1807–1883). Amir of Mascara; resistant of French military and colonial expansion. Abd al-Qadir founded and administered a veritable Arab-Berber theocracy in western Algeria during the 1830s and 1840s. He was born near Mascara to the Hashim tribe, which was headed by Abd al-Qadir's father, the *shaykh* Muhyi al-Din ibn Mustafa (1757–1833), who also was the *muqaddam,* or head, of the regional *Qadiriyya* (q.v.) order. Both the *Qadiriyya* and its rival the *Tijaniyya* (q.v.) were operating actively against the Turks. In 1826–1828 Abd al-Qadir and his father performed the *hajj* (pilgrimage) to Mecca, which also offered opportunities to study in Damascus, Baghdad, and at al-Azhar in Cairo. When the French began expanding westward along the Algerian littoral after seizing Algiers in 1830, the Hashim and other tribes (with support from Morocco's Sultanate) resisted the infidel invader.

Muhyi al-Din initially led attacks against the French and their native allies in 1832 in the *Oranais* (region by Oran), but he knew he was too old to campaign effectively. Abd al-Qadir's religious reputation and redoubtable character made him not only a logical successor, but also enabled him to unite Arabs and Berbers in a jihad against the French. French expansion accelerated the disintegration of the isolated and decentralized Turkish administration, which expedited Abd al-Qadir's political consolidation of western Algeria. As he monitored French debate over the future of their conquest, Abd al-Qadir established himself at Mascara in the former residence of the Turkish beys.

When the French Government decided to pursue a policy of "limited occupation" restricted to the littoral, it had to negotiate with Abd al-Qadir, which was tantamount to recognizing his sovereignty. In a treaty with General Louis-Alexis Desmichels (q.v.) in February 1834, Abd al-Qadir permitted French occupation of western coastal cities (e.g., Oran [q.v.], Arzew, and Mostaganem). By the Arabic text, the Amir could appoint consuls to the French enclaves. Desmichels considered Abd al-Qadir an ally and supplied him with arms, which facilitated the Amir's victory over Mustafa ibn Ismail's forces in July 1834 and other rivals in the following months.

Hostilities resumed between the French and Abd al-Qadir for several reasons. The French felt threatened by the Amir's territorial ambitions vis-à-vis Titteri (Tittari). They were also irritated by Abd al-Qadir's independent commercial activities, which shrewdly bypassed French middlemen and merchants in Oran. Finally, Governor Jean-Baptiste Drouet d'Erlon decided to undermine the Desmichels agreement. General Camille-Alphonse Trézel replaced Desmichels and organized tribal opposition to Abd al-Qadir. This resulted in a humiliating defeat for the French and their Muslim allies at Macta (q.v.) in June 1835. Marshal Bertrand Clauzel (q.v.) retaliated by capturing Mascara, but the Amir had withdrawn from it.

Exploiting surprise, speed, mobility, and familiarity with the terrain, Abd al-Qadir continually harassed the French. Though General Thomas-Robert Bugeaud (q.v.) defeated the Amir at Sikkak in July 1836, the general French position remained adverse. Stout resistance to the French in eastern Algeria led by Ahmad (Ahmed) Bey (q.v.) centered at the fortress city of Constantine (q.v.) permitted Abd al-Qadir to obtain very favorable terms in May 1837 by the Treaty of Tafna (q.v.), which was negotiated with General Bugeaud.

The treaty redefined the Amir's territorial boundaries (thereby reaffirming his sovereignty) and reasserted France's policy of limited occupation. It permitted Abd al-Qadir's theocratic state to encompass about two-thirds of (northern) Algeria while France preserved its coastal enclaves. Nevertheless, the agreement was not realistic given its expedient negotiation and the conflicting ambitions of both sides.

During this time Abd al-Qadir fashioned a viable theocracy. Its administration was hierarchical, but it respected tribal traditions. The Amir headed the state assisted by *khalifas*, who governed large districts while local rule was left to *aghas*. Tribes were supervised by the Amir's representatives, who assured loyalty and who managed military and economic activities. The Amirate monopolized trade, collected taxes, and struck coins. He also promoted education. By dispatching one of his *khalifas* to Paris (q.v. Miloud Ben Arrash), Abd al-Qadir cultivated an image of an able and energetic sovereign leader who exercised modern statecraft.

The Amir consolidated his hold over the territory stipulated by the Treaty of Tafna. In Titteri, he attacked Ayn Madi, the center of the rival *Tijaniyya* brotherhood (its leaders had their own political ambitions and would eventually ally themselves with the French). The Amir never marshaled more than 10,000 regular troops. His command usually included mustered regional auxiliaries. As Abd al-Qadir secured his dominion, his influence spread to eastern Algeria.

The difficult conquest of Constantine in October 1837 extended the French occupation of the hinterland. There is some controversy over the Amir's lack of assistance to Ahmad Bey. Abd al-Qadir had opposed the Turks and dismissed Ahmad Bey's political ambitions (i.e., a new Ottoman-Algerian regency). Nevertheless, the Bey of Constantine posed less of a threat than the expansion of French power in eastern Algeria.

With eastern Algeria temporarily "pacified," Governor-General Sylvain-Charles Valée attempted to persuade Abd al-Qadir to revise the Treaty of Tafna. Despite arguments on both sides concerning the Treaty's semantics and border delineations, it was clear that the French had abandoned their policy of limited occupation and that Abd al-Qadir was prepared to resist their expansion and promote his own. When the French moved into disputed territory to secure communications with Constantine in November 1839, war broke out. Abd al-Qadir countered the French provocation by raiding the Mitijda region near Algiers. Valée was replaced with General (soon to be Marshal) Bugeaud, who also served as governor-general from February 1841 to September 1847.

Bugeaud's objective was total conquest, which meant the end of the Amir's sovereignty. The campaign against Abd al-Qadir was ruthless and relentless. (It also influenced the development of an exceptionally severe colonial establishment in Algeria.) The French Army modified the tribal tactic of *ghazya* (*razzia* [French transliteration]), or raids, in order to destroy all means of native livelihood. This resulted in large-scale, systematic destruction of villages, crops, livestock, and vegetation (especially forests). The devastated Muslim population became demoralized by this brutal offensive, which included atrocities such as the burning alive of surrendering Muslims trapped in caves. Abd al-Qadir faced an army many times the size of his own (about 108,000 French soldiers campaigning by 1847) and suffered the steady reduction of his dominion.

In November 1843 the Amir withdrew to Morocco where he sought and received traditional neighborly support from the Sultanate. The French victory over the Moroccans at (Wadi) Isly in August 1844, however, led to the Treaty of Tangier (September 1844), which also called for the Sultanate's cooperation against Abd al-Qadir. A timely rebellion in the Dahra championed by a young *marabout* named Bu Maza (Muhammad bn Abdallah) (q.v.) enabled the irrepressible Amir to return to Algeria where he had some heartening, if minor, victories. Nevertheless, his vulnerable situation compelled his return to Morocco. He settled in the Rif where he appealed for and received tribal support.

Abd al-Qadir's resentment of the Moroccan government's compliance with the French coupled with Sultan Abd al-Rahman's suspicions of the Amir's political designs bred more war. After scoring some successes, the Amir was decisively defeated by the Moroccans. He retreated to Algeria but soon confronted a French army under General Louis-Léon de Lamoricière (La Morcière). Given his untenable position, the Amir surrendered in December 1847 to the Duc d'Aumale, a son of King Louis-Philippe who was the new Governor-General.

Public pressure prevented Abd al-Qadir's exile to Acre or Alexandria, which had been assured by d'Aumale. Instead, the Amir was incarcerated in France until Napoleon III permitted his permanent exile in 1852. After living in Bursa (Brusa), Turkey (until 1855), he settled in Damascus.

While in exile, the Amir wrote about politics and displayed a keen interest in science. In 1860 Abd al-Qadir saved 12,000 Christians and many others during rioting. Napoleon III (q.v.) was impressed by his virtuous nature and noble stature and accorded him the "Grand Cordon de la Légion d'Honneur." The Amir was brought to Paris and honored in 1865. He died in Damascus in 1883 as a respected foe of France.

The influence of Abd al-Qadir continued to pervade Algeria after his deportation and death. Emir Khaled (Amir Khalid) (q.v.), his grandson, was a prominent leader of the incipient nationalist movement. During the War of Independence (1954–1962), the memory of Abd al-Qadir's resistance inspired the *Armée de la Libération Nationale* (ALN) (q.v.). After independence was attained in 1962, a monument dedicated to the Amir replaced one to Bugeaud in downtown Algiers. In 1968, his remains were returned to rest in Algeria. In many respects, Abd al-Qadir incarnated the national ideals of modern Algeria.

ABD AL-WADID DYNASTY (ABDALWADIDES; BANU(I) ABD AL-WAD; BANU ZAIYAN; ZIYANIDS; ZAYYA-NIDS) (1235–1545) (see individual entries for significant monarchs). Established by Yaghmorasan ibn Ziyan (q.v.) as the Almohad (q.v.) empire disintegrated, this Zenata Berber (q.v.) dynasty produced 27 rulers who governed the central Maghrib from their capital, Tlemcen (q.v.), a renowned cultural center. Geopolitically, the kingdom was situated between the Hafsids of *Ifriqiya* and the Marinids (Merinids) of Morocco (Fez). In addition, the dynasty often faced the hostility of rival Zenata tribes. The size of the Abd al-Wadid kingdom was determined by its own power and the ambitions and strength of its neighbors. Unlike other Maghribi kingdoms/states, the history of the dynasty has been well documented (q.v. Ibn Khaldun).

ABDELGHANI, MOHAMED BEN AHMED (BENHAMED MOHAMMED) (b. 1927). Officer; prime minister. Abdelghani was born in Marnia. Attracted to Messali Hadj's (q.v.) movement, he joined the paramilitary OS (q.v.). During the War of Independence, he was involved in trying to move troops across Algeria's barricaded borders. He became an ''external'' in the FLN's intraelite rivalry. He was promoted to the rank of captain in the ALN (q.v.) and kept his commission after independence when it became the ANP (q.v.). Abdelghani assumed command of the First Military Region (Blida) in 1962, the Fourth Military Region (Ouargla) in 1965, and the Second Region (Oran) in 1967.

As a Boumedienne loyalist (q.v.), he became a member of the Revolutionary Council (q.v.) in 1965. Boumedienne valued Abdelghani's talents and charged him with considerable responsibilities. He organized the symbolic deployment of Algerian troops to support Arab allies as a consequence of the October War (1973) and after the death of Ahmed Medeghri (q.v.) in late 1974, he became minister of the interior in 1975.

In a collegial and politically significant move (to enlist the Boumedienne faction), President Chadli Benjedid (q.v.) selected Abdelghani to be his first government's prime minister in March 1979 who still maintained the interior portfolio (until 1980). Abdelghani remained prime minister until January 1984 when he was replaced by Abdelhamid Brahimi (q.v.). Abdelghani then became a minister of state to the presidency.

ABDELKADER, HADJ ALI (1883–1957). Political organizer in France. A Kabyle (q.v.), Hadj Ali Abdelkader was a naturalized Frenchman and a member of the French Communist Party. He was a founder of the *Etoile Nord-Africaine* (ENA) (q.v.), which was activated in March 1926. According to historian Charles-Robert Ageron (q.v. Bibliography), Abdelkader's precise role in the founding of this organization is not entirely clear given police, communist, and Messalist interpretations. He directed it until June 1926. The ENA was taken over by Messali Hadj (q.v.), but Abdelkader still played an important role in its direction until 1928. Given his communist affiliation, Abdelkader envisioned the ENA as an international emigrant worker organization. Eventually, it became more of an Algerian nationalist organization. Invited by Messali to join the regenerated ENA, Abdelkader preferred serving the *Ligue de défense des intérêts musulmans* and eventually subscribed to the policies of Ferhat Abbas's (q.v.) UDMA (q.v.).

ABDESSELAM (ABDESSLAM, ABDESSALAM), BELAID (b. 1928). Technocrat ("Father of Algerian Industry"); prime minister. Abdesselam was born in Aïn El Kebira to a landed property Kabyle (q.v.) family. Messalist (q.v. Messali Hadj) oriented, he was a medical student at the University of Grenoble and, according to Benjamin Stora (q.v. Bibliography), the "veritable founder" of the *Union Générale des Etudiants Musulmans Algériens* (UGEMA) in 1953. During the War of Independence he politicized Algerian students in France and was an instructor in the FLN (q.v.) school at Oujda (Morocco). Abdesselam also served under the GPRA (q.v.) ministries of Social Affairs and Culture. He was an adviser in Ben Youssef Ben Khedda's (q.v.) cabinet in 1961 and headed the Bureau of Economic Affairs of the FLN in 1962. Under President Ahmed Ben Bella (q.v.), Abdesselam became director of the Algerian Office of Hydrocarbons in 1964. Furthermore, he organized and supervised the state hydrocarbon enterprise SONATRACH (q.v.) in 1963–1964.

In 1965 Abdesselam became Minister of Industry and Energy and was given the responsibility of organizing a coherent and comprehensive development policy that would be characterized by "industrializing industries." This meant using Algeria's hydrocarbon wealth as an economic multiplier, or as he stated: "It is necessary to plant petroleum in order to harvest industry." Given the emphasis placed on state planning and the second sector by President Houari Boumedienne (q.v.), Abdesselam exercised enormous influence and power. His efforts were highlighted by the "pre-plan" or "three-year plan" and two four-year plans (1970–1977) (q.v. State Plans). In 1970–1971, as Algeria negotiated (by Foreign Minister Abdelaziz Bouteflika [q.v.]) with France concerning the latter's hydrocarbon concessions in the Sahara, Abdessalam gained a global reputation symbolizing Algeria's determination to control its own economic destiny. He earned the title of "father of Algerian industry."

From 1977 to 1979 he served as Minister of Light Industry, but was removed from office and eventually accused of "errors and negligence." There were other implications involved here. Abdessalam represented the Boumedienne (d. 1978) clique. Furthermore, the failure of the promising Algerian-American El Paso gas contract (q.v. Hydrocarbons) was associated with the former Minister of Industry and Energy. In December 1981 he was suspended from the Central Committee of the FLN and in 1983 he was charged with corruption. Nevertheless, Abdessalam returned to politics in November 1989 with his election to the enlarged Central Committee of the FLN. He resigned in July 1991 protesting the FLN's leadership and direction. Abdesselam was also very critical of President Chadli Benjedid's (q.v.) drift from state socialism to economic liberalism, especially with regard to hydrocarbons.

In July 1992, he was selected by the High Council of State (HCS) (q.v.) as prime minister, replacing his longtime colleague Sid Ahmed Ghozali (q.v.). Abdesselam has vigorously confronted Islamist opposition (at a cost of civil and constitutional liberties) in an attempt to restore order. He has methodically dismantled the FIS presence (e.g., FIS charities, business associations, etc.). Nevertheless, violence has continued. In October 1992 a ''sabotage and terrorism'' law was passed and in December a curfew was imposed. By the end of the tumultuous year, approximately 300 security forces members had been killed. In addition, he has signaled his preference for state rather than private enterprises to pull Algeria out of its economic morass, which could complicate relations with the International Monetary Fund (IMF) and a number of financial as well as commercial partners.

ABDUH, MUHAMMAD (1849–1905). Egyptian scholar, jurist, and reformer; ''Father of Islamic Modernism.'' Muhammad Abduh believed that Islam was compatible to the modern world. He was heavily influenced by Jamal al-Din al-Afghani (q.v.). Like al-Afghani, Abduh perceived how the modern world had been deeply changed by European power and technology. He advocated modernization in Islamic law, administration, and education (with emphasis on the sciences) but not at the expense of fundamental Muslim beliefs, values, and cultures. He criticized both popular un-Islamic notions as well as the idea of *taqlid* (imitation), which stifled Muslim jurisprudence and scholasticism. This movement was called the *Salafiyya* (q.v.), which referred to the culture of Muslim ancestors of Muhammad's generation/Medinan Caliphate/the Umayyad and early Abbasid empires (according to various Salafi intellectuals). This movement aimed to restore and reinvigorate Islam.

In the Algerian context, Abduh's program led his followers to reprove *marabout* brotherhoods for being dangerous local misinterpretations of Islam, and also the Young Algerians (q.v.) for not understanding that they need not become Frenchmen to be cultured men. Abduh visited Algiers in September 1903 and gave a series of talks. His writings had preceded him and he had a following among Algerian elites who were well-read in Arabic. Among his disciples were Abd al-Halim Ibn Smaya, a professor at the *Madrasa* in Algiers, Muhammad al-Sa'id al-Zawawi, a Kabyle, who published a short book in 1904 that clearly argued Abduh's precepts about maraboutic brotherhoods and *zawiyas* (meditation centers), and Ibn al-Mansur al Sanhagi, who founded an Arabic language reformist Muslim weekly, *Du-l-Faqar*, which was entirely devoted to the spread of Abduh's ideas.

Eventually, Abd al-Hamid ibn Badis (*Shaykh* Ben Badis) (q.v.) and the Association of Reformist *Ulama* (q.v.) embraced Abduh's ideas and work and created institutions that could convince his countrymen that they could choose to be Algerians, Arabs, and Muslims; they need not be assimilated into French culture.

ABU HAMMU MUSA I (r. 1308–1318). Abd al-Wadid (q.v.) ruler. Abu Hammu repaired the previous devastation that had been wrought on Tlemcen (q.v.) during the siege by the Marinids (1299–1307). His reign was distinguished by restoring prosperity and regenerating Abd al-Wadid political power. He extended the dynasty's authority over the Tudjin and the Maghrawa tribes of the Chélifian plain. He was assassinated as a result of a palace plot that involved his son Abu Tashfin I (q.v.).

ABU HAMMU MUSA II (1323/1324–1389). Abd al-Wadid (q.v.) ruler. Abu Hammu Musa II was born in Spain where his family had been exiled by Abu Tashfin I (q.v.). After the defeat of the Abd al-Wadids by the Marinids at the plain of Angad (1352), he fled to Tunis with his uncle, Abu Thabit. With the support of the governor of Tunis and some *Ifriqiyan* chiefs, Abu Hammu Musa marched on Tlemcen (q.v.), where he arrived at the time of the death of the Marinid prince. He entered the capital and was proclaimed ruler in 1359. Though forced to surrender Tlemcen three times to the Marinids (indicative of the transitory power struggles during this period among rival kingdoms), he returned in 1372. During his reign he also suppressed several revolts by his subjects. He wrote a treatise on political ethics in 1379, built a new school at Tlemcen, and installed there the renowned teacher Sherif Abu Abd Allah.

ABU TASHFIN I (1293–1337; r. 1318–1337). Abd al-Wadid (q.v.) ruler. He seized power following the assassination of his father, Abu Hammu Musa I (q.v.). Abu Tashfin began his reign by exiling all pretenders to the throne. His reign was greatly influenced by his Christian Catalonian adviser, Hilal. During the reign, he built the *Madrasa Tashfiniya*. Its construction demonstrated the strong cultural orientation of the Abd al-Wadids. He aided Hafsid dissidents, hoping to exploit weakness in *Ifriqiya* for his own expansion. Nevertheless, Hafsid and Marinid collaboration led to a campaign in 1335 by the Marinids. For three years the Marinids besieged Tlemcen, where Abu Tashfin died defending his capital.

ABU TASHFIN II (1351–1393). Abd al-Wadid (q.v.) ruler (1389–1393). Abu Tashfin II was raised in Fez during the exile of his grandfather and his father, Abu Hammu II. After Abu Hammu II returned to the throne at Tlemcen, Abu Tashfin treacherously plotted against his father. With the support of the Marinid army, Abu Hammu II was defeated and killed in 1389. Abu Tashfin II took over, but as an actual vassal of the Marinids.

ABU YAZID (Makhlad ibn Kaydad) (880–885?–947). Ibadi (q.v. Ibadism) opponent of Fatimids (q.v.). Abu Yazid received a Kharijite (q.v. Kharijism) education and taught at Tahart. The Fatimids imprisoned him in Qayrawan in 937, but his followers freed him. Abu Yazid was admired for his humility (called "the man on the ass" for his usual mode of transportation) and austerity. He was lame and frail but remarkably articulate and energetic for his advanced age. He organized his rebellion in the Aurès (q.v.) against the Fatimids in 943. It was fabulously successful as Qayrawan fell in 944 and Mahdiyya was besieged. Sanhaja raids, however, weakened Abu Yazid's army. The Fatimid Caliph Isma'il (al-Mansur [q.v.]) defeated Abu Yazid's forces at Susa and before Qayrawan. Abu Yazid was forced to flee and died shortly after being captured.

ABU ZAIYAN (ZIYAN, ZAYAN). Name of several Abd al-Wadid rulers. Abu Zaiyan I (r. 1304–1308) was proclaimed ruler during the siege of Tlemcen by the Marinid Abu Yakub (1299–1307). After Abu Yakub's assassination, Abu Zaiyan I negotiated with one of his successors, Abu Thabit, to raise the siege of Tlemcen and its surrounding territories (including the fortified camp of Mansura). Abu Zaiyan campaigned against eastern tribes who had supported the Marinids. Before he was able to complete the rebuilding of Tlemcen, he became ill and died. Abu Zaiyan II ruled in 1360 as a Marinid client and was driven out by Abu Hammu Musa II (q.v.). Abu Zaiyan II tried to take Tlemcen several times but failed. Abu Zaiyan III was installed in Tlemcen by the Marinids of Fez in 1393. Like other Abd al-Wadid rulers he supported letters and arts. He was driven from the throne by his brother and then assassinated in 1398. By the time Abu Zaiyan IV became ruler (1540), Algeria was being competed for between the Spanish and the Turks. The Spanish supported his brother. In 1543, the Spanish succeeded in taking Tlemcen after avenging an earlier loss and placed his brother on the throne. The populace overthrew him and Abu Zaiyan IV was restored. His actual service as a Turkish vassal ended the independent Abd al-Wadid state. He ruled until 1550.

ACHOUR, MOULOUD (b. 1944). Novelist. Achour's style has been compared to that of Mouloud Feraoun's (q.v.). His writings have especially described the difference in values between rural and urban Algeria. His works include *Le Survivant et autres nouvelles* (1971) and *Héliotropes* (1973).

AL-AFGHANI, JAMAL AL-DIN (1838–1897). An activist born in Iran who popularized the Muslim modernist movement. Al-Afghani urged a strict adherence to fundamental Islamic beliefs, but found no contradiction in studying modern science and technology. He observed how the Islamic World had been colonized by countries with greater technological abilities. His position was reformist and also anti-colonial. Al-Afghani's greatest contribution is publicizing these ideas and influencing other Muslim intellectuals such as Muhammad Abduh (q.v.). He criticized *taqlid* (absolute imitation of tradition) and called for the reopening of *ijtihad* (interpretation of Islamic law). His ideas interpreted through Abduh would influence Algerian *ulama* (Muslim scholars) such as the *Shaykh* Abd al-Hamid Ben Badis (q.v.).

AGHLABID DYNASTY (800–909). Founded by Ibrahim ibn al-Aghlab, an Abbasid governor in *Ifriqiya*, he became an Amir in 800. Aghlabid power centered in Tunisia (Qayra- wan) and eventually spread westward reaching Annaba but bordering Lesser Kabylia (q.v.) and the Aurès (q.v.). The Aghlabids also conquered Sicily and campaigned in Italy, forcing the Pope to flee Rome. In 876, a new capital was established at Raqqada. The Aghlabids' colorful courtlife promoted cultural activities. The Fatimids (q.v.) ended the dynasty in 909.

AGRARIAN REVOLUTION. An agricultural initiative in the 1970s. The Charter of the Agrarian Revolution was proclaimed in November 1971 and aimed at extending socialism in the first sector through a series of phases. The Agrarian Revolution was highlighted by projecting the construction of 1,000 "socialist villages" and the reclamation and redistribution of land. It complemented the revolutionary discourse of the Houari Boumedienne (q.v.) presidency (e.g., Industrial and Cultural Revolutions [q.v.]). Nevertheless, the private sector was maintained, though absentee landlordship was addressed and for the most part eliminated. Unlike the *autogestion* (q.v.) phenomenon in 1962, the Agrarian Revolution was a systematic plan for the *fellahin* (farmers) (though participating farmers in both operations complained of bureaucratic interference). The government nationalized 1.5 million hectares and reallocated another 1.3 million (though many landowners privately "reallocated" among family members). In general, resistance by the dominant private landowners effectively reduced the reforming impetus. Furthermore, the socialist sector's production and profits remained unimpressive. President Benjedid's (q.v.) liberalization policies in the agricultural sector, including returning nationalized land to the private sector, were in part a response to the failure of the Agrarian Revolution.

AGRICULTURE. Algeria's coastal plain is very fertile and since antiquity was viewed as a food-producing area. The Romans called the area a "granary." In spite of recurrent conquests, even that of the destructive Banu Hilal (q.v.), the area remained productive. Indeed, one of the causes of the French invasion of 1830 was over a grain debt owed to an Algerian exporting firm.

French colonialism changed the first sector dramatically. Given the need to complement or integrate the colonial economy with that of the metropolitan power, the land was used for viticulture rather than traditional grain production.

Algerian wines were stronger than domestic French production and were attractive particularly to strengthen metropolitan volumes.

The result of this change was disastrous for the colonized since their lands were expropriated by settlers and the subsequent wine production was incompatible with their Islamic culture, which prohibited its consumption. The colonized often suffered from food shortages and occasionally famine. During the War of Independence, agrarian reform was a plank of the Soummam Conference's (q.v.) platform. The Evian Accords (q.v.) also recognized the need for change in the sector.

After independence was attained this sector was initially favored, given the *autogestion* (q.v.) phenomenon. The creation of spontaneous self-management committees was heralded as a unique Algerian type of socialism. The March and October 1963 Decrees nationalized former settler properties. The sector was subordinated to the second sector during the Boumedienne planning era until the Agrarian Revolution (q.v.) of the 1970s, which attempted to institute a socialist system for the sector. In spite of these efforts, the sector's production remained unsatisfactory. Under Benjedid (q.v.), agrarian socialism was replaced by initiatives promoting private enterprise in the sector. The government declared its intent to return 450,000 hectares to the private sector. This was a symbolic repudiation of the Agrarian Revolution. The five-year plans (q.v. State Plans) devoted more attention to the first sector. In 1982 an Agricultural and Rural Development Bank was inaugurated, and by the end of the decade, the grand socialist edifice was being reorganized (*exploitations agricoles collectives*) or being replaced (*exploitations agricoles individuelles*).

Algeria's agricultural production features (as it has for centuries) cereals such as wheat and barley, citrus fruits, olives, dates (one of the world's largest exporters), market vegetables (carrots, artichokes, tomatoes, potatoes), industrial produce (sugar beets, tobacco, cotton, tomatoes), dry legumes (chickpeas, lentils, broad beans), and grapes. Viticulture areas have been decreased significantly as well as production (1.5 hls in 1988 from 3.8 million hls in 1978). Citrus fruit production reached 277,000 tons in 1987, which was almost matched by Saharan dates (224,000). Olive oil volumes average 150,000 hls annually. The Chélif River features rice production.

In general, this sector has been plagued less by nature than by mismanagement (e.g., bureaucratization) and by failure to modernize it efficiently. It has been estimated that about one-third of Algeria's revenues are devoted to food importation. In the early 1980s, approximately two-thirds of its cereals and three-quarters of its eggs were imported. There has been encouraging improvements (e.g., self-sufficiency in egg production). Nevertheless, Algeria still must import about one-half of its alimentary needs.

AHMAD BEY (AHMAD IBN MUHAMMAD) (1785?–1850). *Bey* of Constantine Province (1826–1837). His father was an Ottoman and his mother was from the prominent Ben Ghana tribe; Ahmad was a *kouloughlu*. He performed the *Hajj* and spent time in Egypt where he observed the modernizing initiatives of Muhammad Ali. Returning to Constantine, he served as *khalifa* (deputy) of the Bey from 1817 to 1818. Ahmad, now the *Bey* of Constantine, took part in the defense of Algiers (q.v.) in 1830. After the *Dey*'s defeat, Ahmad viewed himself as the logical successor of the Regency (q.v.) and kept in communication with the Porte (Constantinople). During this time, he reformed the *Beylik*'s government, permitting greater participation by Arabs. He successfully withstood French efforts to occupy Constantine in 1836. Ahmad's hopes of assistance from Abd al-Qadir (q.v.) were frustrated by the Amir's reluctance to assist Turks. The following year he was overpowered by the French and fled to the south from which he conducted periodic raids on the

French. He surrendered in 1848 and died in Algiers two years later. His resistance to the French was championed by Algerian nationalists and revolutionaries.

AISSAT, IDIR (1919–1959). Nationalist; union organizer. Idir Aïssat's political career began at first in the PPA (q.v.), then in the MTLD (q.v.), and in the CGT. He was the founder of the UGTA (q.v.) and, by February 1956, its secretary-general. Arrested by French authorities in May 1956, he was apparently tortured and moved from prison to prison until he died in July 1959. French authorities announced that he had committed suicide, but no investigation into the exact cause of his death was ever permitted.

AIT AHMED, HOCINE (b. 1926). Kabyle (q.v.) leader; "historic chief" (q.v.). Hocine Aït Ahmed was born to a well-to-do Kabyle family, his father having served the French colonial regime as a *caid*. Nevertheless, Aït Ahmed joined the PPA (q.v.) when he was still in secondary school and later was a member of the MTLD (q.v.). In 1947, he helped create and became the first director of a secret paramilitary organization, the OS (q.v.). In 1950, he was replaced at the head of the OS by Ahmed Ben Bella (q.v.), ostensibly because Aït Ahmed had proved himself to be too much of a Berberist (q.v.). He left Algeria in 1951 after French courts had condemned him in *absentia* for various crimes against the state. He took refuge in Cairo, traveling widely as a spokesman for the MTLD.

A "historic chief" of the revolution as one of the first partisans of armed insurrection against the French colonial regime, he continued to travel widely to defend FLN (q.v.) positions as a member of the party's external delegation (e.g., his attendance at the Bandung Conference of 1955). The Soummam Congress of August 20, 1956, elected him to the CNRA. Captured by the French authorities in the skyjacking of October 22, 1956, he spent the rest of the war in prison.

After independence, Aït Ahmed opposed the Ben Bella group, which, with the backing of the general staff of the ALN, seized power in Algiers. He refused membership in the Political Bureau of the FLN, but was elected a deputy in the first National Assembly of independent Algeria. In 1962 he helped draw up the Tripoli Program (q.v.) (1962) and the *autogestion* (q.v.) decrees. Still critical of Ben Bella, he organized the *Front des Forces Socialistes* (FFS) and instigated an insurgency in October and November 1963 from bases in Kabylia (q.v.). Captured by the government after his military ally Colonel Mohand Ou el Hadj (q.v.) made peace with Ben Bella (q.v. Border War with Morocco), Aït Ahmed was condemned to death. He made his peace with Ben Bella shortly before the latter was overthown by Boumedienne in June 1965. Kept in detainment by the Boumedienne regime, Aït Ahmed escaped from El Harrach in 1966 and began a life in exile in France and Switzerland.

He reconciled with the recently released Ben Bella, and in December 1984 jointly called for elections for constitutional reforms (specifically, a constituent assembly) and for political rights in Algeria. After the October 1988 riots (q.v.), Aït Hocine returned from exile on December 15, 1989. The FFS was also legalized as an opposition party. In 1990, Aït Ahmed's restoration as a legitimate political leader was symbolized by a meeting with President Chadli Benjedid (q.v.). Aït Ahmed's boycott of the elections of June 1990 (q.v.) was seen by many analysts as a political blunder because it enhanced the Islamist FIS (q.v.) success.

Aït Ahmed and the Kabyles were particularly upset with the December 1990 legislation (q.v. Arabization) concerning the use of Arabic because it threatened Berber culture. In addition, many of the Kabyles are Francophone. He campaigned actively during the 1991–1992 parliamentary elections, though the FFS like other parties was overwhelmed by the first round success of the FIS (q.v. Elections of December

1991). Aït Ahmed supported the democratic process in spite of his reservations concerning the possibility of an Islamist government. He led a huge rally in January 1992 in support of democracy, which was an implicit appeal to vote in the second round against the FIS. He criticized the suspension and cancellation of elections after the High Council of State (q.v.) deposed President Benjedid. Despite the gradual loss of civil and constitutional rights in contemporary Algeria, the FFS has kept its legal status. Aït Ahmed can still be regarded to be in opposition and continues to be a chief guardian of Kabyle rights. An excellent theoretician, Aït Ahmed authored *La Guerre et l'après-guerre* (1964) and *Mémoires d'un Combattant* (1983).

AIT AL-HOCINE, MOHAND. He was named to the FLN's (q.v.) Central Committee in April 1964 and presided over the *Amicale* in Paris (q.v. Emigrant Labor). After the Houari Boumedienne (q.v.) seizure of power, Aït al-Hocine along with Mohammed Lebjaoui (q.v.) founded the anti-Boumedienne *Organisation Clandestine de la Révolution Algérienne* (OCRA) (q.v.).

AL-ALAWI, ABU AL-ABBAS AHMAD B. MUSTAFA (1869–1934). Sufi. Al-Alawi was a cobbler who became a follower of Muhammad al-Buzidi, who made him a *muqaddam* in 1894. He succeeded al-Buzidi as *shaykh* in 1909 and declared the independence of his *zawiya* from the mother *zawiya* in Morocco (1914) based on his practice of the *khalwa* (spiritual retreat). Because of his preeminent position in sufism, he became literary target of reformist *Salafiyya* (q.v.) groups. He began printing a weekly newspaper in Algiers to defend his conservative views, *Al-Balagh al-Djazai'iri*. He opposed wearing of Western dress and other tendencies toward westernization, which brought him into disharmony with French authorities. He also published many works in Arabic on Sufism.

ALGERIAN COMMUNIST PARTY (*Parti Communiste Algérien*) (PCA). The PCA was organized after World War I. (There is some historiographical contention concerning when it was officially organized [c. 1920; according to others, certainly by 1933; recognized by Comintern in 1935; First Congress in Algiers in July 1936). Its history before the revolution often disclosed a lack of political sensibility concerning the aspirations of the colonized. Undoubtedly this was because of its *pied-noir* (q.v.) majority in the PCA's overall membership (approximately 12,000 to 15,000, including Albert Camus [q.v.]). For example, it supported both the Blum-Viollette law (q.v.) and the repression at Sétif (q.v.) in 1945.

Nevertheless, many Muslims were attracted to the PCA (e.g., Ahmed Akkache, Ben Ali Boukourt, Amar Ouzegane [q.v.], Sadek Hadjerès [q.v], Bachir Hadj Ali [q.v], and Larbi Bouhali [q.v.]). During Vichy (q.v.) rule, PCA member Kaddour Belkaim was arrested and died in prison as a political martyr.). When the War of Independence began, the PCA found itself torn. In general, its Muslim membership wanted to join the nationalists unlike most of the Europeans. The PCA's ambiguity was mirrored by the French Communist Party's (PCF) evasive and equivocal positions. In July 1955 the PCA's Central Committee voted to join the revolution but kept its independent internal administration. PCA members distinguished themselves during the war. Henri Maillot secured arms for the nationalists and was killed while serving the *maquis rouge*. Henri Alleg (q.v. Bibliography), the editor of *Alger Républicain*, was arrested and tortured. His book entitled *The Question* publicized the inhumanity of the war before the world. While the PCA's collaboration with the FLN was often heroic, there were accusations that the communists were discriminated against during operations and even purposely placed in more dangerous situations.

The PCA refused to take sides during the postwar struggle between the GPRA (q.v.) and the Political Bureau (q.v.). In 1962 its newspaper, *al-Hurriya*, however, and the PCA itself, were suppressed. In 1964 *Alger Républicain* was taken over by the FLN. Communists still played an important role initially in the Ben Bella government in publications such as *Révolution africaine*. The *Parti de l'Avant-Garde Socialiste* (PAGS) (q.v.) has carried on the legacy of the PCA.

ALGERIAN MUSLIM CONGRESS. A short-lived organization aspiring to unify nationalists. The Congress was inspired by Dr. Mohammed Saleh Bendjelloul (q.v.) as a means to mobilize Muslim support for the Blum-Viollette legislation (q.v.). For a brief period it united the most significant Algerian leaders and nationalists (i.e., Ferhat Abbas [q.v.]; Messali Hadj [q.v.]; and *Shaykh* Abd al-Hamid Ben Badis [q.v.]) and the Algerian Communist Party. It convened on June 7, 1936. The Congress produced a Charter (*Charte revendicative du peuple algérien musulman*) that called for full equality, assimilation, and complete integration with France. The *Ulama* advocated the use of Arabic besides French as an official rather than ''foreign'' language. Messali refused to support this document.

The Charter was presented in Paris to the Blum government. A second Congress gathered on July 11, 1937 (without Messali) and threatened the resignation of Muslim elected officials if the Blum-Viollette legislation failed. By the end of the year, 3,000 resigned temporarily. The legislation was ultimately rejected in 1938.

The failure of the Blum-Viollette Bill ended the Congress and resulted in a split among the moderates as Abbas, in particular, questioned if assimilation and integration were actually possible. It reaffirmed to other members of the elite that independence was the only recourse. Muslim unity would not be attained again until the organization of AML (q.v.).

ALGERIAN SAHARA. Vast region south of the Saharan Atlas with an area of more than 804,000 square miles. The most significant physical characteristic is the lack of rainfall, generally less than four inches per year; usually the relative humidity is in the range of 4 to 5 percent. Topographically the area consists mostly of plains and plateaus with scattered mountains including the surreal Hoggar (Ahaggar) range. The surface consists of sand dunes (ergs), plains of stones (regs), tables of denuded rocks (hammadas), and basins. Due to the scarcity of arable land, there is severe overpopulation in the oases. Land-use patterns vary greatly from nomadic grazing to intensive irrigation farming. The most extensive developments in this region (eastern Algeria) have been a result of the growth of the petroleum and natural gas industries, which have been sources of economic development in the region (q.v. Introduction; Hydrocarbons). Its inhabitants include the Tuareg (q.v.) and the Haratin (q.v.).

ALGIERS. Capital of Algeria. The site was named Ikosin (Ikosim) by the Phoenicians and then Icosium by the Romans. The name has legendary significance as the settlement of "twenty" (*eikosi* in Greek) companions of Hercules. Icosium was a rather insignificant site as Cherchell, or Caesarea, was Rome's administrative center. Icosium became a Latin colony during the reign of the Emperor Vespasian (69–79) and was taken over in 371–372 by Firmus, a Berber prince. Eventually the city returned to Roman rule and became the seat of a Bishopric. A series of conquests (Vandal, Byzantine, and Arab) left the city destroyed and deserted until the middle of the tenth century.

The generally recognized founder of a regenerated Algiers was Bulukkin (q.v.), a Zirid (q.v.) *amir*, who named it *al-Jaza'ir* (islands) for its islets in the harbor. The city was controlled by a variety of rulers who swept in and out of the central Maghrib's littoral between the eleventh and sixteenth centuries, such as the Hammadids (q.v.), the Almoravids (q.v.), Almohads (q.v.), the Hafsids, Abd al-Wadids (q.v.), the Marinids, the Spanish, and the Turks.

Between conquests, Algiers was a city-state under the leadership of native citizenry (*Baldis*). The scholarly and saintly Sidi Abd al-Rahman al Tha'alibi (q.v.) distinguished the town during the fifteenth century. The arrival of the Spanish in the early sixteenth century followed the influx of fugitive Moors and Jews from Spain. Pedro Navarro (q.v.) took possession of the islet Peñon (q.v.) in the harbor in 1511. Aruj (q.v.), the corsair leader, removed the Spanish supporters from the city and laid the foundation for the Regency (q.v.). His brother Khayr al-Din (Khair) (q.v.) destroyed Peñon in 1529. In 1541 Charles V (q.v.) attacked Algiers, but he was repelled by the besieged and by the weather.

Besides building highly effective maritime fortifications and landward fortresses, the Turkish rulers (*Beylerbeys, Pashas, Aghas,* and *Deys*) built a striking city. The Turks, who called themselves "Algerians" (q.v. Regency), were highly influenced by Asia Minor architecture, which resulted in the commissioning of impressive mosques and monuments. Construction of the Casbah (q.v.) began in earnest in the sixteenth century. Eventually the *Dey*'s palace was situated there. Algiers numbered about 60,000 inhabitants in 1580. The population rose to 100,000 in the seventeenth century and "accommodated" also about 30,000 captives. Epidemics, famines, and the general decline of piracy reduced the population of this once bustling cosmopolitan entrepôt to about 30,000 at the time of the French conquest.

While piracy is usually associated with the Regency, Algerines had engaged in it before the Turkish establishment. The city withstood many bombardments (e.g., the English [1622, 1655, 1672, 1816], the Danes [1770], the French [1661, 1665, 1682, and 1683], and the Spanish [1783; after an unsuccessful land attack in 1775]. Using a plan developed by Napoleon's staff, the French finally seized Algiers in 1830.

Algiers received an excellent infrastructure as a result of colonialism. This included the striking facade along the port and many new buildings. In 1954 the city's population was nearly 600,000 with about one-half of its citizens being European. During the War of Independence, it was the site of dramatic events. The "Battle of Algiers" (q.v.) was an intense urban guerrilla warfare campaign launched by the ALN in 1956–1957 that amplified the war internationally. The successful colonialist insurrection of 1958 occurred there, which toppled the Fourth Republic. In January 1960, Europeans barricaded themselves in Algiers to protest de Gaulle's policies. Decolonization led to the April 1961 "putsch" by four French generals who rebelled from Algiers. During the last days of French Algeria, Algiers suffered from terrorism on all sides. About 300,000 Europeans fled Algiers leaving their properties.

There are more than 2 million people now living in Algiers (1,483,000 in 1987 census), though all statistics are inaccurate given the increasing congestion caused by urban migration. Because state plans (q.v.) allocated most funding toward the second sector, services received scant relative attention until the 1980s. A metro may be operating by the end of the century. Algiers is, however, in a state of chronic crisis. The water quality is poor and its flow is often intermittent. This caused public protest in the Casbah and private complaint elsewhere. In 1985, a building collapsed there and provoked rioting over the lack of attention to urban affairs. A small earthquake west of Algiers in 1989 caused another Casbah building to crumble and provoked more protests. (The Casbah's 1,700 buildings, most of which are hundreds of years old, hold about 70,000 people). In general, there is an immediate need for thousands of housing units. Even in this state of disrepair, Algiers remains a resplendent city still deserving the colonial title of "Alger la blanche" (Algiers the White).

As Algeria's capital, it was the epicenter of the October 1988 riots (q.v.) and the violent protests associated with the elections of June 1991 (q.v.). Algiers has become the site of escalating violence between the forces of order and Islamist sympathizers, especially since the cancellation of national elections by the High Council of State (HCS) after it deposed President Benjedid (q.v.) and derailed the democratic process in January 1992. In December 1992 a curfew was imposed in the city and surrounding areas. The security measures and tactics have evoked haunting memories of the "Battle of Algiers."

ALGIERS ACCORD (July 29, 1965) (q.v. Hydrocarbons).

ALGIERS AGREEMENT (August 5, 1979). An agreement between the POLISARIO (q.v.), supported by Algeria, and Mauritania that ended Mauritania's direct involvement in the Western Saharan war. (Mauritania had participated with Morocco [q.v.] in the Madrid Accords [q.v.], which partitioned the ex-Spanish Sahara between both countries.) The agreement stated notably that "the Islamic Republic of Mauritania solemnly declares that it does not have and will not have territorial or any other claims over Western Sahara" and that "the Islamic Republic of Mauritania decides to withdraw from the unjust war in Western Sahara." This amounted to the renunciation by Mauritania of its claim to Tiris el-Gharbia (southern of the ex-Spanish Sahara).

ALGIERS CHARTER (q.v. Charter of Algiers).

ALLIED INVASION OF ALGERIA (November 8, 1942— "Operation Torch" of World War II). Based upon the faulty assumption that the Vichy (q.v.) French in North Africa would not resist, a force of 107,000 American and British troops, commanded by General Dwight D. Eisenhower, invaded Oran in western Algeria and Algiers. A third allied force invaded Morocco. Algiers capitulated first that evening when French General Alphonse Juin surrendered to a joint U.S.-British force of 32,000 commanded by General Charles Ryder. Troops moved on to occupy Bejaïa (Bougie) on November 11, and Annaba (Bône) the following day before crossing into Tunisia on November 15. French forces at Oran, however, resisted for two days, before surrendering to General Lloyd Fredendall's 31,000-man force.

ALMOHAD EMPIRE (ALMOHADS; ALMOHADES; AL-MUWAHHIDUN). Powerful Zenata Berber (q.v.) state (1147–1269). The founder of the Almohad movement and the Islamic doctrine that motivated them was Muhammad ibn Tumart (q.v.), who took the title of *Mahdi*. Ibn Tumart emphasized the basic belief in the unity of God. The dynasty was founded by Abd al-Mumin (q.v.), who conquered Morocco (q.v.) in 1147 from the Almoravids (q.v.) and took the title of Caliph. Abd al-Mumin extended Almohad power as far as *Ifriqiya,* thus unifying the Maghrib. He also carved out a protectorate in Spain. Under Yaqub al-Mansur (r. 1184–1199), the Almohad empire enjoyed its highest point. Al-Mansur's brilliant court also featured the presence of Ibn Rushd, the brilliant Andalusian scholastic and jurist.

In 1236, the Almohad state broke up as the Hafsids took over control in *Ifriqiya* and the Bani Abd al-Wad (q.v. Abd al-Wadids) established themselves in Tlemcen. In 1248, the Bani Marin (Marinids) secured their power in Fez. Almohads also lost territory in Spain to the Nasrid princes of Granada. The legacy of the Almohad unification of Northwest Africa provided an inspiring legacy for modern initiatives of Maghrib Unity (q.v.).

ALMORAVID STATE (ALMORAVIDS; AL-MURABITUN). Sanhaja (q.v.) Berber (q.v.) state of the eleventh and twelfth centuries. This state was organized by a powerful Sanhaja tribe known as the Lemtouna located in the Adrar in Mauritania. The origin of the Almoravid movement began when Yahya ibn Ibrahim al-Gadali led a group from the tribe in the hajj (pilgrimage to Mecca). During their return they stopped at Qayrawan (Tunisia) and met a famous Moroccan Maliki (q.v.) scholar named Abu Imran al-Fasi. The Lemtouna requested a name of a scholar who could instruct the Qur'an to the Sanhaja. Eventually, they were introduced to Abd Allah ibn Yasin, who decided to return with the pilgrims. The Lemtouna soon became strict adherents to Malikism.

Ibn Yasin organized a military *ribat* (monastic fortress), which trained and disciplined the initiates. (*Murabitun* means men of the *ribat*). The Almoravids attacked south ending the fabulous Soninke Kingdom of Ghana with the capture of Awdaghost (Awdaghust, Aoudaghost). Turning north, Sijilmasa was laid siege to and taken in 1055–1056. Ibn Yasin acted as spiritual chief while a Lemtouna, Yahya ibn Umar, commanded the military forces. In 1056 Yahya's brother, Abu Bakr ibn Umar, succeeded his brother and continued the conquests.

The Almoravids expanded under one of Umar's commanders, Yusuf ibn Tashfin (q.v.), who built Marrakesh (c. 1060) and extended Almoravid power. Fez was taken in 1069, and Algiers was reached in 1082 after taking Tlemcen, Oran, and Ténès. The Almoravids also established themselves in Spain after a great victory against Alphonso VI in 1086. After Abu Bakr's death, Ibn Tashfin became the head of the movement.

The Almoravid was at its zenith during Ibn Tashfin's reign (d. 1106). As a consequence of the Almoravids' success in Spain, the Maghrib received a cultural infusion from Andalusia. Malikism (q.v.) also secured itself in northwest Africa. To many Muslims, Malikism's legalism lacked spiritual satisfaction, which contributed to the appeal of the

Almohad (q.v.) movement. Furthermore, Spanish Christian assaults constantly pressured the Almoravids. Almohad power finally overwhelmed the Almoravids as Marrakesh was taken in 1147.

AMIROUCHE (Aït Hamouda) (1926–1959). Kabyle (q.v.) ALN (q.v.) *wilaya* commander. Before the War of Independence, he was influenced by the Ulama movement (q.v. Association of Reformist Ulama) and the MTLD (q.v.). He was arrested in 1950 during the OS (q.v.) repression. He was released in 1952 and lived in Paris politicizing the emigrant community (q.v. Emigrant Labor).

It was during the War of Independence where this young Kabyle earned his infamous reputation. Aït Hamouda, whose nom de guerre was "Amirouche," organized his own guerrilla group in eastern Kabylia (q.v.). Eventually he commanded *Wilaya* III with approximately 800 troops.

Amirouche controlled his sector through sheer terror and brutality. He assaulted any Algerian nationalist competition to his position such as Bellounis (q.v.)/ MNA. (q.v.) (e.g., the Battle of Guenzet in 1955). It was Amirouche who guaranteed security for the Soummam Conference (q.v.) in August 1956.

French intelligence manipulated his violent nature by infiltrating the FLN and by falsely implicating effective nationalist cadres. This incited Amirouche's fierce character as he conducted purges that eliminated many innocent people. Eventually a French airmobile operation cornered and killed Amirouche during a firefight in March 1959.

AMIS DU MANIFESTE ET DE LA LIBERTE (AML). A political organization formed by Ferhat Abbas (q.v.) in March 1944. Abbas aimed to make this an umbrella nationalist party. Besides his own liberal nationalist faction, the Association of Reformist Ulama (q.v.) and the more radical PPA (q.v.) supported this initiative. The AML membership was estimated at 350,000. In a gesture of elite unity, Abbas proclaimed his nationalist rival, Messali Hadj (q.v.), as the leader of the movement.

The AML criticized de Gaulle's wartime reforms (e.g., Ordinance of March 7, 1944 [q.v.]) because they did not provide Algerians with enough freedom. The AML was dissolved in 1945 as part of the French reaction to the Sétif Riots (q.v.). Even before dissolution, this organization had not managed to coordinate and control the various factions that supposedly supported it. Indeed, the Messalists instilled an insurrectionary influence before Sétif. The AML did enjoy a wider support than any other party before the FLN.

AMROUCHE, JEAN (El Mouhoub) (1906–1962). Francophone poet and essayist. Jean Amrouche may represent better than anyone else the plight of North Africans caught between two civilizations, that of their African ancestors and that of the colonizing French. Amrouche's parents were Kabyles (q.v.) who had converted to Christianity. The quality of Jean Amrouche's literary production clearly demonstrates how well he assimilated French culture. Throughout his life, he tried to describe Algeria and its soul to the rest of the world.

Amrouche also lived and taught in Tunis (Albert Memmi was one of his students). He was a friend of Charles de Gaulle (q.v.) and acted as an intermediary between Ferhat Abbas (q.v.) and the General. Though he was not a member of the FLN (q.v.), he was very critical of French repression.

Among his most renowned publications were *Cendres* in 1934 and *Etoile secrète* in 1937. In 1939 he published a translation of Kabyle songs, which appeared as *Chants berbères de Kabylie*. In 1943 he published the brilliant essay that he entitled *L'Eternel Jugurtha,* which may well be the best attempt to explain the Algerian soul. Henri Kréa (q.v.) stated that Amrouche was the "intellectual reincarnation of Jugurtha." Amrouche highly influenced the "generation of 1954" (q.v.), i.e., Algerian authors who wrote about the independence struggle. Amrouche's life was epitomized by his statement: "France is the spirit of my soul[;] Algeria is the soul of my spirit."

ANAS, MALIK IBN (d. 795). Founder of Maliki school. This Meccan imam was hostile to rational interpretation (e.g., Mu'tazilism and *'aql* [reason]) as a fundamental source of religious knowledge. Instead, the consensus of the Medinan community was upheld in contrast to general consensus, private opinion, and analogy. Malikism (q.v.) was entrenched in North Africa as a result of the Almoravids (q.v.). Its legalism, however, contributed to the rise of the Almohads (q.v.) and more emotional forms of Islam associated with *marabouts*.

ANNABA (Bône). A major port city in eastern Algeria. Originally a Phoenician settlement known as Hippona, it was successively occupied by the Carthaginians, the Numidians, and the Romans, who renamed it Hippo Regius. Augustine (q.v.) served there as Christian bishop from 395 to 430. Taken by the Vandals in 430, it was recaptured by the Byzantines. The Arabs occupied toward the end of the seventh century. As a pirate port, it was attacked by the Pisans and Genoese in 1034. King Roger II of Sicily captured it in 1153 and established the Hammadids (q.v.) there. The Almohads (q.v.) took the city in 1160. The Hafsids annexed it to their realm during the thirteenth century. At its request, the city was taken over by Khayr al-Din (q.v.), who established a Turkish garrison that remained there until 1830. Bône became an important center of settler colonialism especially under Mayor Joseph Bertagna. It was bombarded by the German Navy in August 1914. Its population in 1983 was 348,322.

Annaba is also an industrial site. It is the location of the huge El-Hadjar steel plant. It also exports iron and phosphates.

ARAB MAGHRIB (MAGHREB) UNION (q.v. MAGHRIB UNITY) (AMU). This longtime dream of Maghribi peoples was established in a multilateral accord in February 1989 calling for cooperation and collaboration concerning defense, economic, cultural, and international affairs among Algeria, Libya, Mauritania, Morocco, and Tunisia. The AMU has a Consultative Council composed of 50 members (10 per country) and a Presidential Council composed of the heads of state.

ARABIZATION. This was the objective of the Cultural Revolution (q.v.) and remains a vitally important project of contemporary Algeria as seen in the Arabization Law of December 1990. By a 1938 law, the colonial administration viewed Arabic as a foreign language. In 1961 this law was abrogated as Arabic became mandatory in "first degree" schools. Since independence, Arabization was seen as the means to purge Algerians of their colonial past in order to rediscover an authentic national identity. While not an Arabist (i.e., Arabic speaker/writer), President Ahmed Ben Bella (q.v.) linked the Arabization of the state to the success of socialism. Arabization of primary classes began during his presidency.

Houari Boumedienne (q.v.), an Arabist, called for an accelerated Arabization, especially when the Cultural Revolution was inaugurated. The policy was very controversial. Actions such as the changing of street signs to Arabic names created confusion (done in the late 1970s). Mostapha Lacheraf (q.v.) as minister of education questioned Arabization, given its practical use and the texts available for its study. He even reinstituted bilingualism. The use of French in technical and scientific training also created cultural as well as historical contradictions.

The ideas of an Arab nation imposing its language disaffected the Berbers (q.v.), resulting in chronic unrest and even violent protest in the 1980s. (Many of the Berbers are also Francophone.) President Chadli Benjedid (q.v.) continued this policy as all primary-school classes and most secondary-school classes became Arabized. This was symbolized by the highly charged appropriation of Algiers's Lycée Descartes in 1988. Furthermore, the Arabization Law of December 1990 projected the complete Arabization of official activities during 1992 and for higher education by 1997. The rise of the Islamist and Arabist FIS (q.v.) added another dimension to the language controversy.

The practical problems of Arabization also relate to the difference between the written language and the spoken language; Algerian Arabic is a dialect. Algerians fear that they will ironically suffer a "bilingual illiteracy," a linguistic limbo, by not being able to express themselves adequately in Arabic or French. This could also impede technological transfers. Indeed, English has been used at the *Institut National d'Electricité et d'Electronique* at Boumerdes.

ARMEE DE LA LIBERATION NATIONALE (ALN). The National Liberation Army. This was the name of the revolutionary force that fought the French during the War of Independence (1954–1962) (q.v. Introduction). While the ALN rarely fielded battalion-sized units, its guerrilla rural and urban campaigns tied down hundreds of thousands of French troops. ALN units were often at the edge of physical and mental exhaustion given their inability to receive logistical support. Nevertheless, in spite of their weakness, they still posed threats.

The "internal" ALN fought within Algeria, while the "external" ALN trained in bordering countries and occasionally attempted to infiltrate French frontier barriers such as the Morice Line. In order to maintain a sense of collegiality, the highest rank was colonel. Rivalries between ALN factions contributed to the intraelite strife after the Evian Accords (q.v.). Today the Army is called the *Armée Nationale Populaire* (ANP).

ARMEE NATIONALE POPULAIRE (ANP). The ALN (q.v.) was changed to the ANP after independence was achieved. The ANP was initially led by Houari Boumedienne (q.v.) who used it effectively to overthrow his political rival, Ahmed Ben Bella (q.v.) in June 1965. Therefore, the ANP's role has been political besides military. Under President Chadli Benjedid (q.v.), himself a former colonel, ANP officers received for the first time the rank of general. In 1990, the Army included 120,000 soldiers in three armored, five mechanized, and 12 motorized brigades; 31 infantry, four paratroop, five artillery, five air defense, and four engineer battalions; and 12 companies of desert troops.

ARSLAN, CHEKIB (SHAKIB) (1869–1946). A Druze amir and a pan-Arabist. Messali Hadj (q.v.) met Arslan in Geneva in 1936. Arslan apparently convinced Messali Hadj to emphasize Islam and Arabism in the *Etoile Nord Africaine* (ENA) (q.v.) and to move away from the communist ideology that had led to the founding of that organization.

ARUJ (ARUDJ, AROUJ, URUJ), IBN YAKUM ABU YUSUF (BARBAROSSA I) (1473?-1518). Turkish corsair captain and a founder of the Regency (q.v.). Though his early life has been obscured by legend, Aruj was probably born in Mitylene (Lesbos). Brought up as a pirate in the Greek archipelago, he was captured and forced to serve a term on the galleys of the Knights of Saint John. Afterward he returned to his piracy along the coast of Spain. By 1510, he had acquired an armed force of more than a thousand men and about a dozen ships. The Hafsid sultan of Tunis allied himself with Aruj and offered him the governorship of the island of Djerba, which became his headquarters. Aruj's personal territorial ambitions led him to establish alliances with local rulers, especially in eastern Algeria and in Kabylia. In 1514 he was in control of Djidjelli (Jijel).

At the request of the *shaykh* of Algiers (q.v.), Salim al-Tumi, Aruj undertook an attack to free the city from the Spanish, who controlled the port by its fortress on the islet of Peñon (q.v.). Though Peñon remained in Spanish hands, Aruj took over the city. When unrest began to spread against the Turkish force, Aruj had the *Shaykh* strangled in his bath and himself proclaimed sultan by his forces. A Spanish expedition to recapture Algiers failed in 1516.

At the request of townspeople from Tlemcen (q.v.), Aruj left Algiers in 1517 to seize that town from the control of the Abd al-Wadid (q.v.), Abu Hammu III, a Spanish ally. He placed his brother, Khayr al-Din (q.v.), in his stead at Algiers and proceeded to Tlemcen. Instead of restoring the pretender Abd al-Wadid (q.v.), Abu Zaiyan, Aruj took control of Tlemcen. A Spanish force from Oran besieged the town for six months in 1518. Aruj attempted to flee to the sea but was pursued by Spanish cavalry. He was slain at the ford of the Salado River.

Aruj demonstrated that an effectively commanded, small, determined force could take advantage of native rivalries in the Maghrib. His conquests of Mitidja, the Chélif Valley, Titteri, the Dahra, Ouarsenais, and Tlemcen inspired Khayr al-Din to pursue successfully Aruj's territorial ambitions and secure Turkish power in Algeria.

ASABIYYA. Arabic word popularized by Ibn Khaldun (q.v.) in his renowned work the *Muqqadima,* which might be translated as "group feeling"/"clannishness"/"esprit de corps"/"natural solidarity." Ibn Khaldun thought that *asabiyya* acted as a chief historical agent concerning the rise and fall of North African dynasties.

EL-ASNAM (q.v. Ech-Chlef).

ASSEMBLEE ALGERIENNE (ALGERIAN ASSEMBLY). Legislative institution formed by the Statute of Algeria (q.v.) of

1947. This body was composed of 120 delegates, half of whom were Algerians. The Algerian Assembly was created to give Algeria more autonomy. The French were still very much in control, however, as the governor-general could exercise the veto. Another way to control Algerians was through electoral manipulation. The 1948 elections, for example, were notoriously manipulated. As a result, many Algerians became alienated from the political process and turned toward more radical alternatives.

ASSEMBLEE POPULAIRE NATIONALE (APN). The APN was a product of the Constitution of 1976. Its first election was on February 25, 1977. The 261 deputies were members of the FLN. The first free national legislative elections featuring Algeria's new political parties were to take place in June 1991 (q.v. Elections of June 1991) until violent protests in Algiers forced their postponement. The rescheduled elections in December resulted in the astonishing success of the Islamist FIS party after the first round of elections (q.v. Elections of December 1991). The fearful uncertainty of an Islamist government led to the deposal of President Chadli Benjedid (q.v.) and the cancellation of the elections by the High Council of State (HCS) (q.v.). The Counseil Consultatif National (CCN) (q.v.) today represents a "legislative" branch in the new government though it has no legislative power.

ASSIMILATION POLICY. A French colonial policy. In the Algerian context, assimilation aimed in theory to make Frenchmen of Muslim subjects. This objective was to be reached through contact and education. In fact, the policy foundered especially because of the Algerians' fervent allegiance to Islam. While the policy was in effect, Algerians who acquired the accoutrements of French civilization, including language, dress, education, and, if not religion, at least the willingness to abandon a personal status based in part on Islamic law, could petition for French citizenship. In fact, the process was so complicated that relatively few Algerians ever became French citizens. More Algerians might have been assimilated if the procedures had not involved giving up a personal status defined in Islamic law and if the policy had not been applied by colonial officials who were often against the policy and thus made the workings of the law next to impossible.

The problem of acquiring French citizenship in Algeria was highlighted by the colonial establishment's resistance to the Blum-Viollette legislation (q.v.), which would have granted citizenship to tens of thousands of Algerians. By the time of the March 1944 Ordinance (q.v.) that realized the Blum-Viollette's objectives, the idea of assimilation had lost its appeal to the increasingly nationalist elite.

ASSOCIATION GENERAL DES TRAVAILLEURS ALGERI-ENS (AGTA) (General Association of Algerian Workers). A union founded in 1962 to help protect the interests of some 800,000 Algerian workers who had emigrated to France in their search for work. The AGTA was affiliated with the *Union Générale des Travailleurs Algériens* (UGTA) (q.v.).

ASSOCIATION OF ALGERIAN REFORMIST ULAMA (*Association des oulémas réformistes algériens*). A reformist Islamic organization that also opposed French colonialism. Founded in 1931 by Abd al-Hamid Ben Badis (q.v.), it was most active in the Constantine region, but it quickly spread throughout Algeria. Other important members included Bachir al-Ibrahimi (q.v.), Tawfiq al-Madani (q.v.), and Tayyib al-Uqbi (q.v.). The Association was ostensibly not a political party but a religious group. Nevertheless, its cultural and educational program fostered the growth of an Algerian national spirit.

By 1936, this *Ulama* organization had 130 schools in Constantine department alone. In *Ulama* schools, pupils learned in Arabic. There was no French content and, indeed, many of the *Ulama* did not know French. In their schools and in the Algerian boy scout movement, which they also directed, the *Ulama* taught young Algerians in a spirit best exemplified by their slogan: "Islam is my religion; Arabic is my language; Algeria is my fatherland."

In the mid-1930s, the *Ulama* joined the FEMA, the ENA (q.v.), and the PCA (q.v. Algerian Communist Party) in the Algerian Muslim Congress (q.v.), an attempt to unify all Algerian opposition to the colonial regime. After the beginning of the War of Independence, like the moderate UDMA (q.v.), it initially reserved its support for the FLN (q.v.). The association called for a general organization including all nationalist groups. Nevertheless, it, too, became alienated by French repression and the lack of conciliatory initiatives. Sensitive to the increasing attachment by the Muslim youth to the War of Independence, the association aligned itself with the FLN.

After independence, the *Ulama* continued to have some influence in independent Algeria since the socialist governmental system did define itself as an Islamic government. The Ministry of Religious Foundations (*habous*), for example, generally was held by members of the *Ulama* group. The Cultural Revolution (q.v.), which featured accelerated Arabization, related directly to the enduring influence of the *Ulama* movement. Nevertheless, the close association of the "establishment *ulama*" with the FLN was discredited given the "Events" of October 1988 (q.v.), the subsequent instability, and especially the emergence of the Islamist FIS.

ASSOCIATION OF ALGERIAN SUNNITE ULAMA. Anti-Reformist organization formed in Algiers on September 15, 1932, in opposition to the Association of Reformist Algerian *Ulama* (q.v.). In opposition to the journal *al-Shihab*, they established an Arabic newspaper named *Al-Ihlas* (Sincerity) in December 1932.

ASSOCIATION POLICY. A French colonial policy. When the assimilation (q.v.) policy proved unworkable, French officials applied the theory of association. Algerians (and other colonial subjects), it was thought, would be brought into the modern social and economic world by association with the superior civilization of France. In practice, this meant a more indirect rather than direct administration of the colonized. "Association" was another means to perpetuate the colonial establishment in spite of idealistic platitudes. Assimilation was practiced more in urban areas and association in the countryside (*bled*). In the deep Sahara, the French ruled through the military.

ATERIAN. A prehistoric civilization, named for a major archaeological site, Bir el-Ater, located 100 kilometers south of Tebessa. Arriving in the area at the time of the last ice age, it is believed that the Aterian culture extended from the Nile to the Atlantic down to the edges of the Sahara.

AUDISIO, GABRIEL (1900–1977). Writer. Audisio was born in Marseilles and occasionally visited Algeria. He was awarded the *Prix littéraire* in 1925 for *Trois hommes et un minaret*. Audisio was struck by the natural beauty of the country (its sun and sea), which eventually through his works became known as the "Mediterranean sensibility" (*sensibilité méditerranéene*). This can be seen in *Jeunesse de la Méditerranée* (1935) and *Le Sel de la mer* (1936). He saw Algeria as a mélange of Mediterranean cultures unlike the more nationalist *Algérianiste* interpretation by Louis Bertrand (q.v.). Audisio especially influenced the writings of Albert Camus (q.v.).

AUGUSTINE (AURELIUS AUGUSTINUS) (354–430). A famous Christian "Father" and Bishop of Hippo Regius (modern Annaba [q.v.]) (396–430). Augustine was born in Tagaste (Souk-Ahras) in eastern Numidia and educated in

Madauros and Carthage. He went to Rome in 383. Though he was a Manichaean who was also influenced by Neoplatonism, Bishop (St.) Ambrose of Milan had a profound impression upon this young man in restless spiritual search. This led to Augustine's baptism by Ambrose on Easter in 387, and, after a short stay in Rome, he returned to Tagaste the following year. There he founded a monastery where he remained until 391 when he became a priest at Hippo.

Augustine succeeded Valerius as Bishop of Hippo and continued to reside there until his death during the siege of the city by the Vandals (q.v.). He devoted much of his energies as bishop toward healing the Donatist (q.v.) schism within the Christian Church. Unlike the Donatists, Augustine believed in cooperation with Rome. Augustine also championed Catholicism against Manichaeanism and Pelagianism. His most famous works are the *Confessions* and *The City of God. Confessions* is an autobiography that chronicles his worldly interests and spiritual development; *The City of God* presents a philosophy of history. Augustine perceived history as paradoxical, but providential and teleological leading to the Parousia (Second Coming of Christ). Augustine encouraged education, which produced the Augustinian Order of priests. He is venerated in the Catholic Church as a saint, as is his mother, St. Monica.

AURES MOUNTAINS. Great massif of Southeastern Algeria and the Saharan Atlas. It contains Jabal (Djebel) (Mount) Chélia, which rises 2,326 meters (7,638 feet). The Aurès is populated by the Chaouia (q.v.), a Berber (q.v.) people. Located in the northern part of the massif, the Chaouia are sedentary and combine agriculture with seminomadic herding. Because of its remoteness and ruggedness, the Aurès sustained effective resistance against the Romans, the Arabs, the Turks, and the French in 1850, 1859, 1916, and during the War of Independence (1954–1962).

AUTOGESTION (SELF-MANAGEMENT). A socialist initiative during the immediate period after independence. Anguished over their future and terrorized by the OAS and the FLN, hundreds of thousands of European settlers fled Algeria in 1962. The "vacationing" settler factories and farms were seized by Algerians, who began to manage these enterprises themselves. Ahmed Ben Bella (q.v.) touted the spontaneous mobilization of *autogestion* ("self-management") committees as a unique example of an Algerian brand of socialism. In a series of decrees (October, November 1962; March, October 1963), the Algerian government institutionalized and bureaucratized the self-management system that according to observers vitiated socialist initiative and enterprise.

It was argued that the 5,000 farms that were nationalized compensated for the 8,000 villages destroyed during the War of Independence. This expropriation of French property strained bilateral relations and effectively nullified in the short-term the agricultural cooperation as implied in the Evian Accords (q.v.). Algerian agricultural reform continued in the early 1970s with the Agrarian Revolution (q.v.).

AWLAD SIDI SHAYKH (OULED SIDI CHEIKH). Confederation of tribes in western Algeria. This tribal group derived from a Muslim "saint," Sidi Shaykh, a descendant from Abu Bakr, the first caliph, and the Prophet Muhammad's best friend and father-in-law. In their history, the Awlad Sidi Shaykh were often influenced by the Moroccan Sultanate. During the French occupation, they first cooperated with Governor-General Thomas-Robert Bugeaud (q.v.) against the Amir Abd al-Qadir (q.v.). In the early 1850s, the Awlad under Mohammed ben Abdallah fought the French while others under Si Hamza cooperated with colonial forces. The French, however, faced a serious rebellion by the Awlad in 1864–1865 when incompetent officers of the *Bureaux Arabes* insulted tribal leadership traditions. During the major

Kabyle (q.v.) revolt in 1870, the Awlad Sidi Shaykh remained restive as reminded by occasional raids until 1883 and were passive afterward.

AZEGGAGH, AHMED (1942–). Journalist, poet, and playwright. Azeggagh was born in Bejaïa, but he lived in France until returning to Algeria after 1962. He eventually settled again in France. His collection of poetry entitled *Chacun son métier* (1968) illustrated a disillusionment with independence. Among his other literary works are the novel *L'Héritage* (1966), another poetic work, *Les Récits du silence* (1974), and a play *République des ombres* (1976). Azeggagh devoted the poetry of *Blanc c'est blanc* (1987) to the emigrant labor (q.v.) problem.

AZZEDINE (Rabah Zerari). ALN (q.v.) leader. Azzedine was a welder who joined the guerrillas in 1955. After being arrested in July 1956, he escaped. He became an ALN commander in 1958. Captured and imprisoned by the French in November 1958, he tricked his captors by claiming that he advocated de Gaulle's (q.v.) "Peace of the Brave." He rejoined his comrades in Tunis in March 1959 and served as a member of the CNRA from 1959 to 1962, and the General Staff from 1960 to 1962. He headed the "autonomous zone" of Algiers from January to July 1962. Ben Bella (q.v.) considered him a political enemy and imprisoned him in 1964. He is the author of *On nous appelait fellaghas* (1976) and *Et Alger ne brûla pas* (1980).

BANU HILAL. Along with the Banu Sulaym, this Arab tribe had taken part in the Qarmatian revolt against the Abbasids (q.v.). Though they were Shi'a, their unruly behavior discredited them in the eyes of the Fatimids (q.v.), who forcibly dispatched them westward against the rebellious Zirids (q.v.) where they devastated the eastern and central Maghrib during the middle of the eleventh century. Qayrawan was pillaged in *Ifriqiya* and the Zirids fortified themselves for the onslaught in Mahdiya. The Hammadids (q.v.) were pressured to move from Qal'a to Bejaïa (q.v.).

The cultural significance of the arrival of the Banu Hilal was reminiscent of the arrival of the Germans in the Roman Empire and the Turks in the Abbasid Empire. It changed the civilization of North Africa from a Berber to a more Arab one, especially linguistically. Though the invasion occurred before the great Almoravid (q.v.) and Almohad (q.v.) Berber dynasties, the Banu Hilal cultural legacy became entrenched in North African society. Economically, the damage was consequential, destroying agricultural regions that had been very productive for centuries. Jamil Abun-Nasr points out (q.v. Bibliography), however, that the extent of the devastation may have been exaggerated given historiographical prejudices against nomads. The arrival of the Banu Hilal represents one of the greatest events in Maghribi history.

BARBAROSSA (q.v. Aruj; Khayr al-Din). A group of brothers born to an ex-Janissary and daughter of a Greek Orthodox priest, who established the Algerian Regency (q.v.).

BARBARY WARS. The American name given to a series of conflicts fought from 1800 to 1805 and, especially concerning Algeria, in 1815 between the United States and the states of the Maghrib. In 1812 the Dey of Algiers sought increased tribute for the passage of American commerce through the Mediterranean. Upon the conclusion of the American War of 1812 (1812 to 1815), American Commodores Bainbridge and Stephen Decatur (q.v.) led a naval force against the Algerian fleet, capturing its flagship (q.v. Hamidou *raïs*). Decatur then moved into the harbor of Algiers, threatening to bombard the port. In June 1815, the Dey signed a treaty that stipulated the elimination of tribute from the United States, the return of confiscated American property, the release of Christian hostages, and the payment of an indemnity for a captured brig.

BARRAGE VERT ("Green Barricade"). Environmental initiative. In the mid-1970s, the Houari Boumedienne (q.v.) government embarked on an ambitious environmental project. The plan was to construct a belt of hardy, drought resistant vegetation (e.g., Aleppo Pines) traversing the country from Morocco to Tunisia (1,500 kms; ranging in width from 5 to 20 kms) to stop the relentless advance of the Sahara northward. It was designed, too, as a complement to the Agrarian Revolution (q.v.). Critical observers believed that the monies allocated could have been directed toward restoring eroded soils. This initiative has not been completely fulfilled.

BATTLE OF ALGIERS (q.v.) (1956–1957). A terrorism campaign authorized by the CCE (q.v.) of the FLN (q.v.). Yacef Saadi (q.v.) was the chief FLN figure in Algiers (after Rabah Bitat's [q.v.] arrest). Saadi organized an urban guerrilla working from the Casbah (q.v.) with approximately 1,400 operatives in which women played a strategic tactical role (q.v. Introduction; Zohra Drif; Djamila Bouhired; Women]). Particularly dauntless operatives included Hassiba Ben Bouali, Djamila Bouazza, Samia Lakhdari, and Ali Amara known as Ali la Pointe, who assassinated Mayor Amédée Froger of Boufarik, the president of the Federation of Mayors of Algeria, in December 1956. The French responded to the random assaults and the bombings (e.g., popular European settings such as the Milk-Bar, the

Cafétéria, and the Coq-Hardi) by sending in elite paratroops ("les paras"). Furthermore, severe suppressive methods (including torture) were initiated. Eventually these measures dismantled the revolutionary apparatus. The CCE had withdrawn (leaving Algeria), though Larbi M'hidi (q.v.) stayed and was captured. Saadi and Zohra Drif were seized in September 1957. Several weeks later, Ali la Pointe, Hassiba Ben Bouali, and Saadi's twelve-year-old nephew were surrounded in the Casbah. A charge designed to knock down a partition apparently detonated explosives killing all three and 17 neighbors. While this campaign was a grievous military loss to the ALN, it publicized the FLN's quest for independence before the world. France also was targeted with international criticism. This is also the name of an impressive film by Gillo Pontecorvo (1965) (q.v. Cinema).

BEDJAOUI, MOHAMMED (b. 1929). Jurist; minister; ambassador. Bedjaoui was born in Sidi-bel-Abbès and attended the University of Grenoble and the *Institut d'Etudes Politiques* (Grenoble). He served as a legal counselor to the GPRA during the War of Liberation. After the war he was briefly the president of the *Société National des Chemins de Fer* (National Railways) and dean of the *Faculté de Droit d'Alger* (1964). He also served as Minister of Justice (1964–1970) before beginning a diplomatic career. In 1969 he became Ambassador to France and in 1979 he was Algeria's United Nations delegate. He also argued in the International Court of Justice (ICJ) on behalf of the POLISARIO (1974–1975). In 1982, Bedjaoui became a justice of the ICJ. Among his publications are *La Révolution algérienne et le droit* (1961); *Non-alignement et droit international* (1977); and *Pour un nouvel ordre économique international* (1979).

BEJAIA (Béjaïa/Bougie). Bejaïa was colonized by the Romans. It gained particular prestige when it became the cosmopolitan capital of the Hammadids (q.v.) during the eleventh century. During Hammadid rule, it may have had 100,000 inhabitants. In 1136, it was besieged by Genoa. In 1151–1152, the Almohads (q.v.) took over the city and ended the Hammadid dynasty. The Almoravid adventurer Ali ibn Ghaniya took over Bejaïa in 1184. The next conquest (c. 1230) was achieved by the Hafsids of Tunisia. Bejaïa asserted its independence in 1284 prior to falling before the rival Hafsids again during the following century.

Like other cities along the North African littoral, Bejaïa pursued piracy. This led to an assault in 1509 by Pedro Navarro (q.v.), who left a Spanish garrison there. The Spanish kept the town until 1555 when the Turks took it over. The city declined, losing its splendor and prosperity. After the French captured Algiers, the Turkish garrison was forced out by the citizens of the town and by neighboring Kabyles, who had often harassed the Turks. Though repulsed once, a French invasion under General Camille-Alphonse Trézel that had been outfitted in Toulon took the city in 1833. Bejaïa is an important hydrocarbons export center as a pipeline terminal for Saharan oil. Its population was recorded at 124,122 (1983).

BEKKHOUCHA, MOHAMMED (1904–1970). Poet. Though this talented poet signed his poetry with one K, he used two Ks formally to honor his uncle. He was a teacher and poet who was forced to leave Algeria during the War of Independence. He composed in Arabic and French. His *Poèmes libres* (1946) are particularly significant given the Sétif (q.v.) riots in 1945.

BELHADJ, MOKRANE (q.v. Ou el-Hadj Mohand).

BELHOUCHET, ABDELLAH (b. 1923). ALN/APN officer. Born near Sedrata, Belhouchet had attained the rank of sergeant in the French Army before he joined the ALN. He fought in eastern Algeria (*Wilaya* I and II) before crossing over into Tunisia. He was implicated in a 1958 coup against the GPRA, arrested by Tunisian authorities at the request of the ALN, and imprisoned until the fall of 1960. After his release, he joined an underground group organized along the Mali border by Abdelaziz Bouteflika (q.v.); Belhouchet eventually became commander of this region.

Belhouchet supported the Tlemcen (q.v.) group (Ahmed Ben Bella [q.v.]-Houari Boumedienne [q.v] faction) in the summer of 1962 and was appointed to direct the commando section of the Military Academy at Cherchell. He fought in the ANP during the Border War of 1963 (q.v.), then was appointed commander of the Fifth Military Region (Constantine). He was a member of the Council of the Revolution (q.v.) in 1965. Belhouchet commanded the First Military Region (Algiers) from 1967 to 1979.

A close ally of Presidents Houari Boumedienne and especially Chadli Benjedid (q.v.), Belhouchet became deputy minister for defense in 1980 and also a member of the Political Bureau. He also served as inspector general of the Armed Forces. These positions placed him in a powerful position in the military. In 1984 he was promoted to general. In 1986, General Belhouchet replaced General Mostafa Benloucif (q.v.) as Army chief of staff. After the October riots, Belhouchet lost his position as deputy minister for defense. He still acted as Benjedid's military adviser. Belhouchet retired in August 1989 as a major general.

BELKACEM, CHERIF (b. 1933). Minister. Belkacem was active in the UGEMA in Morocco and then joined *Wilaya* V. By the end of the War of Liberation, he was a close associate of Colonel Houari Boumedienne (q.v.) and in command of the General Staff Command Post-West. He became a member of the National Assembly and played an important role in presenting and passing the Constitution (1963) (q.v.). Though he became minister of education and orientation in

1963 and minister of education the following year, he criticized Ben Bella within the FLN's Central Committee, which demonstrated his continuing attachment to Boumedienne. After the coup of June 1965 (q.v.), Belkacem was charged with reorganizing (and revitalizing) the FLN as "coordinator" of the Executive Secretariat. He held that position until December 1967. The Ottaways (q.v. Bibliography) considered him a "moderate" within the Boumedienne "clan." Belkacem reemerged politically in 1991 with other former Boumedienne supporters in opposition to President Chadli Benjedid.

BELLOUCIF, MOSTEFA (q.v. BENLOUCIF, MOSTEFA).

BELLOUNIS (BEN LOUNIS), MOHAMED (1912–1958). Algerian nationalist who opposed the FLN. Bellounis was a strong supporter of Messali Hadj (q.v.) and served in the PPA (q.v.) and the MTLD (q.v.) and, most significantly, in the MNA (q.v.). The MNA was organized in December 1954 in opposition to the FLN's (q.v.) assertion that it was the sole nationalist voice of the Algerian people. Bellounis was charged by Messali to muster guerrillas within Algeria. The MNA targeted, however, the ALN (q.v.) rather than French forces. In the summer of 1955, under the command of Colonel Amirouche (q.v.), the ALN attacked Bellounis and his 500 MNA fighters at Guenzet in Kabylia (q.v.). Bellounis and a small number of his men survived the assault and escaped to the Mélouza (q.v.) region (north of the Sahara) where there was still considerable Messalist support. The ALN massacre of suspected Messalists at Mélouza (May 1957) forced Bellounis to turn to the French for logistical support. The French were very willing to collaborate (termed "Operation Ollivier"). By August 1957 Bellounis commanded 1,500–3,000 soldiers, who received their own uniforms and flag. Bellounis proclaimed this new force as the *Armée Nationale du Peuple* (or *Populaire*) *Algérien*

(ANPA) and promoted himself to the rank of two-star general. Messali never gave this self-styled organization his official approval. Bellounis had initial success against the ALN, but his increasing megalomania and counterproductive harsh treatment of local civilians besides his own soldiers forced the French to end their association. He was tracked down and killed in July 1958. Bellounis was the only serious rival nationalist military threat mounted against the ALN.

BEN ALLA (BENALLA), HADJ (b. 1923). Nationalist. Ben Alla was a member of the PPA (q.v.) in Oran. After the Allied invasion of North Africa (1942) (q.v.), he served in the Italian, French, and German campaigns. He was a member of the paramilitary OS (q.v.) and imprisoned. He became an officer in the ALN (q.v.) during the War of Independence and was a companion of Larbi Ben M'Hidi (q.v.). Ben Alla was arrested in November 1956 and released in 1962.

He was a member of Ahmed Ben Bella's (q.v.) Political Bureau (q.v.) and of the FLN's (q.v.) Central Committee after independence. In 1963 he was his party's director in charge of national organizations. He also served as president of the National Assembly. Ben Alla was considered to be very close politically to Ben Bella; therefore, he was arrested, too, when Houari Boumedienne (q.v.) took over the government in June 1965. Ben Alla was released from prison in 1968. He was kept under surveillance until completely freed in 1978.

BENAOUDA, AMAR BEN MOSTEFA. Nationalist. Benaouda was from Annaba (q.v.) and was attracted to Messali Hadj's (q.v.) PPA (q.v.) and later the paramilitary OS (q.v.). He was arrested by French colonial authorities in 1950, but escaped from prison in 1951. As an outlaw, he moved about Algeria, but particularly in Kabylia (q.v.) until the outbreak of the War of Independence in November 1954. He favored armed revolution and, at the Soummam Congress of August 1956 (q.v.), he was named a member of the CNRA (q.v.). One of his first duties with the CNRA was to go from Algeria to Tunis to argue the supremacy of the interior delegation of the FLN (q.v.). Later he served as a member of the Algerian negotiating team for talks with France. After independence Benaouda pursued a diplomatic career, including service as a military attaché (Cairo, Paris, and Tunis) and as an ambassador (Libya).

BEN ARRASH, MILOUD (fl. 1830s). Prior to 1830 he served as an *agha* in the service of Hasan Bey of Oran. Under Abd al-Qadir (q.v.), he served as a *khalifa* and as the Amir's representative to France. Ben Arrash's mission (1838) symbolized Abd al-Qadir's sovereignty as recognized by the Treaty of Tafna (1837) (q.v.).

BEN BADIS, ABDEL HAMID (Abdelhamid; Abd al-Hamid bn Badis) (1889–1940). Founder of the Association of Reformist *Ulama* (religious scholars) (q.v.) and indirectly a cultural nationalist. Born in Constantine (q.v.) into a traditional Muslim family (though his father was a member of the *Conseil supérieur*), he was educated in his native city, in Tunis (Zituna University), and in other Muslim centers in the Middle East. He was influenced by the *Salafiyya* movement (q.v.) and the ideas of Muhammad Abduh (q.v.). Ben Badis founded two journals after he returned to Algeria, *al-Muntaqid* and *al-Shihab*. In 1931, he helped create the Algerian Association of Reformist Ulama which was to have a great deal of influence in shaping Algeria's Arabic Renaissance (*Nahda*). His motto, which became that of the Algerian Muslim Boy Scouts' Movement was ''Islam is my religion, Arabic my language, Algeria my fatherland.''

Though he was not a nationalist, Ben Badis asserted an Algerian identity. He believed that assimilation was impossible and that Algerians had to assert their Islamic identity. He refuted Ferhat Abbas (q.v.) and the liberal elite by asserting: "This Algerian nation is not France, cannot be France, and does not wish to be France." The *Ulama* did participate, however, in the Algerian Muslim Congress (q.v.).

Shaykh Ben Badis's emphasis on cultural values appealed to nationalists. Though the contributions of Abbas and Messali Hadj (q.v.) were usually ignored or castigated by the FLN (before the National Charter of 1986 [q.v.]), Ben Badis's legacy was respected and has heightened given the current Islamic revival in Algerian political and social affairs.

BEN BELLA, AHMED (b. 1916) (q.v. Introduction). First premier and president of independent Algeria. Ahmed Ben Bella was also the best-known member of the small group of men ("historic leaders" [q.v.]) who as members of the CRUA (q.v.) planned and launched the Algerian War of Independence.

Ben Bella was born into a relatively comfortable farming family in Marnia and was the youngest child in a family of five boys and several girls. His father apparently insisted on the proper observance of Islam and native customs. Nevertheless, Ben Bella was not well versed in Arabic, but he did manage to finish French primary school by the time he was thirteen years old. He was drafted into the 14th regiment of Algerian Sharpshooters before the outbreak of World War II and served with distinction in the Italian campaign, earning a Military Cross for valor. Returning to Algeria in 1945, he witnessed the terrible repression of the Sétif (q.v.) uprising and quickly joined the illegal PPA (q.v.). He was later a member of the OS (q.v.), participated in an attack on the main post office in Oran (April 4, 1949), and was captured by the French police. He was imprisoned from 1950 until his escape in 1952.

Ben Bella fled to Cairo where he joined Mohamed Khider (q.v.), Mohamed Boudiaf (q.v.), and Hocine Aït Ahmed (q.v.) in the planning for the revolution, thereby earning membership among the "historic leaders." After the War of Independence began in November 1954, Ben Bella headed the "external" faction of the FLN, which soon rivaled the "internal" faction for control of the revolution. His chief objective was to direct the collection of funds and materiel for the ALN (q.v.). Ben Bella was not invited to the Soummam Conference (q.v.) (August 1956), which asserted the primacy of the "internals." In October 1956 he and other "historic chiefs" (Aït Ahmed, Boudiaf, and Khider) were skyjacked by the French while en route from Morocco to Tunisia. He was held prisoner in France until 1962.

After the war, Ben Bella teamed with the powerful external military commander Houari Boumedienne (q.v.) and formed the Political Bureau (Tlemcen group) (q.v.) in opposition to the GPRA (q.v.). After a brief and tragic intraelite conflict, Ben Bella emerged with the support of Boumedienne as the most powerful political figure in Algeria. He became Algeria's first prime minister (1962–1963), then was elected president of the Algerian Republic (1963–1965). While in power, Ben Bella helped restore order in Algeria, steered his country toward a socialist economy, pushed for agrarian reforms (e.g., the self-management [*autogestion*] [q.v.] system), and spent considerable sums on education. In foreign policy, he supported wars of national liberation.

Ben Bella faced many problems and threats to his authority. In 1963–1964, Kabyle (q.v.) unrest resulted in a serious rebellion instigated by his former colleague, Aït Ahmed. Algeria also engaged in a brief border war (q.v.) with Morocco in October-November 1963. In 1964 Col. Mohammed Chaabani (q.v.) led an unsuccessful military revolt against Ben Bella. Ben Bella perceived the political ambitions of Vice President Boumedienne and attempted to remove his supporters from his cabinet (e.g., Ahmed Kaid [q.v.], Chérif Belkacem [q.v.], Ahmed Medeghri [q.v.] and Abdelaziz Bouteflika [q.v.]). On June 19, 1965, Boumedienne (q.v.) deposed him (q.v. Coup of June 19, 1965). While Ben Bella was reproached for his rule, his controversial recovery of land and property was a stunning achievement; and policies challenging the French military and hydrocarbon presences (e.g., the inauguration of SONATRACH [q.v.]) represented significant initiatives which aimed at securing full Algerian sovereignty.

Ben Bella's fate after his arrest during the coup of 1965 was not known, which mobilized a variety of pro-Ben Bella and anti-Boumedienne organizations. He was freed from house arrest in July 1979 by President Chadli Benjedid (q.v.). All restrictions were lifted in October 1980 and Ben Bella left for France.

In May 1984 Ben Bella formed an opposition party called the *Mouvement pour la Démocratie en Algérie* (MDA) that called for a democratic and multiparty Algerian government. He even espoused Islamist positions. After reconciling with fellow political exile, Aït Ahmed, both men demanded in December 1985 a constituent assembly ensuring political rights in Algeria. In 1990 Ben Bella was allowed to return to Algeria and for a brief political moment, observers thought that the former president could reconcile secular and Islamist groups. In 1991 he declared himself a candidate for the Presidency. After the deposal of Benjedid in January 1992 by the High Council of State, soon headed by another former colleague, Boudiaf, Ben Bella still remained on the political periphery though he is regarded as an important historic symbol.

BEN BOULAID, MOSTEFA (1917–1956). "Historic leader" (q.v.) and ALN (q.v.) commander. Ben Boulaïd was born into a family of impoverished peasants. He served with distinction in the Italian campaign (like Ahmed Ben Bella [q.v.]) in World War II. Ben Boulaïd became a miller and eventually was able to buy a bus line that served the Arris-Batna region. His political activity led him, however, into difficulties with the French authorities, and he lost his business license in 1951. By then, he had already been an active nationalist politically aligned with Messali Hadj (q.v.). Ben Boulaïd ran for the Algerian Assembly in 1948, won a majority of votes, but was denied his seat by the colonial authorities. He was a founding member of the CRUA (q.v.), thereby regarded as a "historic chief."

When the War of Independence began, he commanded the Aurès region (*Wilaya* I). His men conducted the first operation of the revolution at Biskra on October 31, and continued in the Aurès the following morning, resulting in the deaths of a *caïd* and Guy Monnerot, who along with his wounded wife were dedicated French teachers. Through intermediaries, Salah Maïza and Hamoud El-Hachemi, who were members of the Central Committee of the MTLD (q.v.), he tried to convince Messali Hadj to join in the armed rebellion. This effort failed. Meanwhile, he sold much of what he owned to help finance the revolution in the Aurès, a *wilaya* he kept together only with great difficulty. The French authorities managed to arrest him in February 1955, but he escaped on November 4, of the same year. He died on March 27, 1956, while trying to operate a field radio that had been booby-trapped by the French army's special services.

BENCHENEB, MOHAMMED (1869–1929). Writer; translator. Bencheneb translated numerous Arabic texts into French (chronicles, philosophical, poetic, and philological books) and authored books of his own (e.g., *Traité de prosodie arabe* [1906] and *Proverbes arabes d'Algérie et du Maghreb* [3 vols. 1905–1907]). Among the Arabic authors he translated or published critical editions about their works were Ibn Maryam, al-Ghobrini, al-Zadjadji, and Aboul Arab al-Khochani (q.v. Literature in Arabic).

BENCHENEB, SAADEDDINE (1907–1968). Writer. Son of Mohammed Bencheneb (q.v.), he, too, published a great deal about Arabic literature. Some of his books were in Arabic, but most were in French. His best-known works are *La Poésie arabe moderne* (1945) and *Contes d'Alger* (1946). He was awarded the Algerian Grand Literary Prize for these two books.

BENCHRIF, AHMED (b. 1927). Officer; minister. A native of Djelfa, Benchrif had been promoted to the rank of second lieutenant in the French Army before he deserted to join the ALN (q.v.) in July 1957. He was appointed director of a nationalist military school located in southern Tunisia. He went underground in 1959 and became commander of *Wilaya* IV with the rank of major in 1960. Benchrif was also a member of the CNRA. He was condemned to death after his capture in October 1960. The sentence was not carried out and he was released from French prison after the signing of the Evian Accords (q.v.). He was promoted to colonel in the ALN (q.v.) and was put in charge of the Algerian gendarmerie. He was a key actor in Houari Boumedienne's (q.v.) coup of June 1965 (q.v.) and became a member of the Council of the Revolution (q.v.). He also had considerable influence in the ANP (q.v.). In 1977 he became minister of hydraulics and environment and a member of the Political Bureau (q.v.) in 1979. In 1980 he was removed from Political Bureau and in 1981 from the Central Committee.

BENDJELLOUL, DR. MOHAMMED SALEH (b. 1896). Moderate nationalist. Bendjelloul continued the work of the Young Algerians (q.v.) and aimed to realize personally and publicly the French ideal of assimilation (q.v.). He founded the *Fédération des Elus Musulmans d'Algérie* (FEMA) during the time of the pending Blum-Viollette legislation (q.v.). Bendjelloul was at the height of his influence during this period as he called for an Algerian Muslim Congress (q.v.) to coordinate colonized support for the legislation. After the parliamentary repudiation of the legislation, the moderates split (q.v. Ferhat Abbas), and Bendjelloul organized in 1938 the *Rassemblement Franco-Musulman Algérien* (RFMA).

Bendjelloul continued to work within the system. He eventually became a deputy to the French National Assembly. When the War of Independence broke out, he reminded the French of the past opportunities to satisfy native political aspirations, which were squandered. Ironically, Bendjelloul contributed, too, to the revolutionary effort. He was deeply disturbed by the FLN-instigated massacres and the French retribution (''collective responsibility'') (q.v. Jacques Soustelle) at Philippeville (Skikda). He once again organized a meeting that produced the ''Declaration of Sixty-One'' (26 September 1955) (q.v.), underscoring how French policies alienated the Algerian moderates. It was tantamount to a statement of support for the FLN (q.v.).

BENHADDOU, BOUHADJAR (Si Othmane) (b. 1927). ALN (q.v.) officer. Born near Oran, Benhaddou was a farmhand before the 1954 War of Independence. He was a member of the OS (q.v.) and was arrested for terrorist activities in 1950; he was released in 1953. Benhaddou joined the ALN in 1954 and eventually became commander of *Wilaya* V. During the intraelite conflict in the summer of 1962, he supported the Political Bureau (q.v.) of Ahmed Ben Bella (q.v.) and Houari Boumedienne (q.v.). Benhaddou became Ben Bella's cabinet chief and was promoted to the FLN's Central Committee in April 1964. After the coup of June 1965, he served on the Council of the Revolution (q.v.).

BENHADJ (BELHADJ), ALI (b. 1956). Militant imam (of the al-Sunna mosque, Bab el-Oued, Algiers). Benhadj was born in Tunis, though his family was from the Béchar region. He was a supporter of Mustapha Bouili (q.v.) and was imprisoned from 1982 to 1985. Benhadj devoutly embraced the idea to realize an Islamic state in Algeria linked to an Arab nation (*umma*). Benhadj became Abassi Madani's (q.v.)

cofounder and deputy leader of the *Front Islamique du Salut* (FIS). (Within the FIS, he is regarded as the chief *salafiste*, or internationalist Islamist.) His fiery sermons attracted many of the alienated and disillusioned youth. He alarmed Westerners with his anti-democratic rhetoric and has been significantly influenced by the Iranian Revolution. Above all, he has been an ardent critic of the FLN (q.v.). He was arrested along with Madani on June 30, 1991 after violent protests by FIS led to the calling of a state of siege and postponement of the first free national legislative elections (q.v. Elections of June 1991). Along with Madani, he was given a 12-year sentence in July 1992, which observers regarded as a moderate punishment signaling a reconciling approach by the Algerian government (i.e., the High Council of State [HCS] [q.v.]) with recalcitrant Islamist factions.

BENHAMOUDA, BOUALEM (b. 1933). FLN (q.v.) minister. Benhamouda, who holds a doctorate in law, played a very important role within the FLN, including being the president of the party's Fourth Congress (February 1979). He also served as minister of the *Mujahidin* (1965–1970); minister of justice (1970–1977); minister of public works (1977–1979); minister of the interior (1980–1982); and minister of finances (1982–1986). He also served as director of the *Institut d'Etudes Stratégiques Globales* (INESG) until 1990. By that time, Benhamouda became critical of President Chadli Benjedid's (q.v.) liberalization policies and became identified with the opposition associated with other ex-Boumedienne (q.v.) officials.

BENHEDOUGA, ABDELHAMID (b. 1929) (q.v. Literature in Arabic). Writer and poet. Benhedouga was born in Mansoura near Sétif and is one of Algeria's leading authors and poets, who always writes in Arabic though he knows French well. In 1958, he published an essay entitled *Algeria Between Yesterday and Today,* and, at about the same time, he joined the ALN-FLN underground as a propagandist. Beginning with the War of Independence, Benhedouga began to earn a reputation through his short stories. He is best known, however, for his novel *The Wind from the South,* which was published in 1971. This book has been translated internationally. It is a story that examines generational conflicts and the role of women in Algerian rural life. Among his other works are *Empty Souls, The End of Winter* (1975), *Morning Has Risen* (1980), and *Jaziya and the Dervishes* (1980). He has also been a frequent commentator on radio and television.

BEN IBRAHIM, SLIMANE (Baâmer) (1870–1953). Writer, collaborator, and companion of Etienne Dinet (q.v.). Ben Ibrahim was Dinet's friend, mentor, and guide regarding Maghribi life and Islam. They worked together for 45 years. Among the works of Ben Ibrahim and Dinet are *Rabia el Kouloub ou le printemps des coeurs* (1902); *Mirages. Scènes de la vie arabe* (1906); *Tableaux de la vie arabe* (1908); *Khadra, la danseuse des Ouled Naïl* (1910); and *L'Orient vu de l'Occident* (1921).

BENJEDID (BENDJEDID), CHADLI (b. 1929). Third president of Algeria. Born in Bouteldja in the Annaba (q.v.) region, he was the son of a small landholder. He received some schooling at Annaba.

Joining the ALN (q.v.), he was regional commander in 1956 and an assistant commander in 1957. He was wounded in 1957 and promoted to captain in 1958. In 1960, Chief of Staff Houari Boumedienne (q.v.) appointed Benjedid to the Operational Command of the nationalists' Northern Military Zone.

After the war, Benjedid, now a major, commanded the 5th military (Constantine) region and monitored the withdrawal of French troops. He was transferred to the 2nd Military (Oran) Region in June 1964 and pursued a similar mission in that part of Algeria, including the withdrawal from the naval base of Mers-el-Kébir in 1968.

Not surprisingly, Benjedid supported Boumedienne's coup of June 1965 and became a member of the Council of the Revolution (q.v.). In 1969, on the fourth anniversary of the takeover, he was promoted to colonel, the highest rank in the ANP (until Benjedid created [permitted] the rank of General during his presidency). He accompanied Boumedienne to Morocco in 1969, a trip resulting in a treaty of cooperation and even Benjedid's decoration by King Hassan II.

Benjedid's command in Oran became much more strategic given the War in Western Sahara (q.v.). On the whole, however, he was a professional and loyal army officer who played only minor political roles until President Boumedienne's health worsened in 1978.

As the eight members of the Council of the Revolution assumed more responsibility, Benjedid was given more power concerning military defense and security. After President Boumedienne's death in December 1978, Benjedid emerged as a compromise candidate among political factions in the FLN. After becoming Secretary-General of the FLN on 25 January 1979, he was elected President on 7 February. He also held the Defense portfolio.

Benjedid was not as ideological as his predecessors and was generally regarded as a pragmatist. He reoriented direction of state-planning from the heavy capitalization of the second sector to a more balanced development thereby giving more attention to the relatively neglected first sector. He also dismantled enormous state companies and created smaller enterprises. His foreign policy emphasized regional affairs; especially the idea of a Greater Maghrib (q.v.). This meant reconciliation with Morocco which had broken relations over the War in Western Sahara and especially Algeria's support of the POLISARIO (q.v.). In February 1989 an Arab Maghrib Union (AMU) (q.v.) was established which aimed to integrate the policies of Morocco, Mauritania, Algeria, Tunisia, and Libya.

Benjedid was reelected in 1985. In January 1986, an "enriched" "National Charter" (q.v.) was published, reaffirming Algeria's Arab and socialist identity. Nevertheless, that image had been already attacked by Berber (q.v.) groups (e.g., protests in 1980) which feared a cultural imposition of Arabism. Algeria's pursuit of socialism was regarded as a foreign ideology by politicized and inimical Islamists. Chronic under- and unemployment alienated a more educated youth. Furthermore, oil prices collapsed in the mid 1980s (q.v. Hydrocarbons), which had a severe effect upon the economy. These variables led to popular uprisings in October 1988 (q.v.), resulting in the proclamation of a state of siege and hundreds of casualties. The FLN was forced to give up its monopoly of political power as the Constitution was revised (February 1989) (q.v.), permitting political pluralism and guaranteeing civil rights. In addition, the prime minister received more governing authority.

Benjedid's survival of this crisis was a testament to his popularity in Algeria, although he was tainted by the violence. He was reelected president in 1989 (third term). Nevertheless, the surprising success of the Islamist FIS in the June 1990 local elections (q.v. Elections of June 1990) weakened his position. In June 1991 (q.v. Elections of June 1991), he had to declare a state of siege again after violent protests by the FIS over the electoral process during national elections. On June 26, 1991, Benjedid resigned as head of the FLN. Remaining president, he faced deepening political, economic, and social problems.

The first round of the rescheduled parliamentary elections were held in December 1991 (q.v. Elections of December 1991). The FIS again earned a remarkable success. The second round was sure to place it in power. Benjedid prepared to continue the democratic process and to share power with the the Islamists. On January 11, 1992, a group of civilian and military leaders, apprehensive of the prospect of an FIS-dominated government, engineered a coup and deposed Benjedid, replacing him with the High Council of State (HCS) (q.v.). He was placed in house arrest. Given the indictment against General Mostefa Benloucif (q.v.) for corruption, there have been reports that Chadli Benjedid may also be charged with abusing the privileges of his presidency.

BENKACI, ABDELKADER (1936–1986). Ambassador. Benkaci had a distinguished career of public service. He studied in Cairo where he joined the FLN (q.v.) during the Revolution. He served within the Ministry of Information of the GPRA (q.v.). He was a member of the Algerian mission to the U.N. before heading the Arab world section of the Foreign Ministry. He became the Ambassador to Damascus. He was the deputy secretary-general of the Ministry of Foreign Affairs before he was tabbed to head the Department of Foreign Affairs and Cooperation of the Presidency. Benkaci played an important role in upgrading relations with Egypt. He died of injuries after being hit by an automobile in Paris.

BEN KERIOU, ABDALLAH (q.v. Oral Tradition).

BEN KHEDDA, BEN YOUSSEF (b. 1922). Second president of the GPRA (q.v.). Ben Khedda's father was a Muslim magistrate. After receiving a scholarship, Ben Khedda attended the lycée at Blida and eventually became a pharmacist. He joined the PPA (q.v.) during World War II. He was secretary-general of the MTLD (q.v.) in 1954 when that party split into two groups, the Messalists (q.v. Messali Hadj) and the Centralists (Ben Khedda was on the Central Committee). He was arrested in November 1954 after protesting French repressive policies. After his release he joined the FLN (q.v.). Along with Ramdane Abane (q.v.) and Saad Dahlab (q.v.), he drafted the Soummam Platform (q.v.). In 1957 he and Belkacem Krim (q.v.) reached Tunis after an adventurous trek. He served as minister for social affairs in the first GPRA and as a member of the CNRA (q.v.) and CCE (q.v.). In December 1958 he led the FLN's first delegation to China. Though he resigned from the GPRA in 1960, he continued to serve the FLN in various diplomatic delegations and to write in *El-Moudjahid* (q.v.).

Though Ben Khedda had not taken sides in the elite struggle, he did believe in civilian control. He was chosen in August 1961 to replace Ferhat Abbas (q.v.) as president of the GPRA. Ben Khedda, with a reputation as a Marxist theorist, was regarded as a hard-liner with regard to negotiations with the French. This made him politically palatable to Colonel Houari Boumedienne (q.v.) and the General Staff of the ALN.

After the completion of the Evian Accords (q.v.), Ben Khedda and the GPRA were confronted by the Political Bureau led by elite rivals Ahmed Ben Bella (q.v.) and Boumedienne. This political struggle resulted in the defeat of the GPRA.

Ben Khedda retired to private life until 1976 when he, Ferhat Abbas, and several others published a manifesto (q.v. "New Appeal to the Algerian People") criticizing the policies of the Boumedienne options. This led to his house arrest (released by President Benjedid [q.v.]). He organized the opposition group called the *Union Nationale pour la Liberté et la Démocratie* (UNLD). After the constitutional reforms of 1989, Ben Khedda mobilized a political party called *Oumma*. The name means nation, but also means Islamic community. He has attempted to coordinate opposition Islamist parties.

BEN KHEIR, MOHAMMED (q.v. Oral Tradition).

BENLOUCIF, MOSTEFA. ANP officer. As a military man close to President Chadli Benjedid (q.v.), Benloucif was selected secretary-general of the Ministry of Defense in 1980. He was chosen as an alternate member of the Political Bureau (q.v.) of the FLN (q.v.) in January 1984, was promoted to Major General in October, and became the ANP's chief of staff in November. Though he retired in 1987, he was indicted for corruption in 1992 and sentenced to a 15-year imprisonment in 1993. The indictment signaled the High Council of State's (HCS) (q.v.) determination to present an image of a government resolved to reform and disassociate itself with the former governing establishment.

BEN M'HIDI, LARBI (1923–1957). "Historic leader" (q.v.); revolutionary leader. Ben M'Hidi was born in Ain M'Lila in Constantinois (region of Constantine) into a family of relatively well-to-do farmers. He was attracted to Messali Hadj's (q.v.) nationalist appeal and was in the PPA (q.v.) and in the OS (q.v.). He was a founding member of the CRUA (q.v.), thereby gaining the reputation as a founder ("historic leader") of the FLN (q.v.). Ben M'Hidi was the first commander of the Oran *wilaya* (V).

At the Soummam Congress he was elected to the Committee for Coordination and Execution (CCE). (He gave command of Oran province to Abdelhafid Bossouf [q.v.].) Ben M'Hidi supported the theses advanced by Ramdane Abane (q.v.) and Belkacem Krim (q.v.) that the "interior" elite should lead the revolution. During the Battle of Algiers (q.v.), Ben M'Hidi directed the ALN (q.v.) until his capture. Though he was supposed to be treated well, he died mysteriously in prison. Interpretations vary about his death, which was officially reported as a suicide. He was probably tortured during his incarceration.

BENNABI, MALEK (1905–1973). Writer. Bennabi received both an Arabic and French education and wrote in both languages. Besides being a celebrated author, he was also an electrical engineer. Before the revolution he contributed to *La République Algérienne* (1950) and *Jeune Musulman*

(1952–1953). After the war he wrote for *Révolution afri-caine* (1964–1968). His political leanings were liberal (toward the UDMA [q.v.]), but he also identified strongly with the *Ulama*. Bennabi understood the need for Algerians to reexamine themselves. His writings complement the existential theme to modern Algerian history. Among his works are: *Le Phénomène coranique. Essai d'une théorie sur le Coran* (1947); *Lebbeik, pèlerinage de pauvres* (1948); *Discours sur la condition de la renaissance Algérienne. Le Problème d'une civilisation* (1949); *Vocation de l'Islam* (1954); *The Ideological Struggle in a Colonized Country* (in Arabic; 1957); *SOS Algeria* (Arabic; 1957); *Le Sens de l'étape* (1970); *The Muslim Role in the Last Third of the Twentieth Century* (Arabic; 1973).

BENNOUR, MOUHOUD. Writer. Bennour wrote *Les Enfants des jours sombres,* which chronicled the War of Independence as viewed by a family. It received a national literary award commemorating the revolution.

BEN OTHMAN, MOHAMED (r. 1766–1791). *Dey.* Ben Othman reasserted the Regency's (q.v.) power by imposing tribute upon maritime activities (among the payers were Great Britain, the United States, and the Kingdom of Two Sicilies) and by successful military campaigns in the interior. He also repulsed the Spanish invasion (q.v. O'Reilly). He was politically and militarily the last dynamic *Dey.*

BEN RAHAL, M'HAMED (MOHAMED) (1855–1928). Alge-rian colonial administrator; reformer and writer. Ben Rahal was the son of an *agha* and eventually succeeded his father as *caïd* of Nédroma. Ben Rahal studied at the *Collège impérial.* Though he was a member of the colonial establishment, Ben Rahal tried to change the system for the benefit of the indigenous population. He provided testimony in 1891 for the investigating Senate Committee that was critical of the colonial government. Ben Rahal became attracted to sufism and became an initiate to the Darqawa (q.v.) brotherhood. He was identified as a leading member of the *Vieux Turbans* (q.v.). Not surprisingly, he did not embrace the "Young Algerians." Nevertheless, he eventually supported the Emir Khaled's (q.v.) proposals. In 1922 Ben Rahal called for the abrogation of the arbitrary *Code de l'Indigénat* (q.v.). Ben Rahal also served on the *Conseil général* of Nédroma, but he failed to be elected to the *Délégations financières* (q.v.).

Besides his political activities, he published in the *Bulletins de Géographie d'Oran* and is credited (by Jean Déjeux [q.v. Bibliography]) as having published the first Algerian short story written in French. He was also an associate member of the Académie des Sciences coloniales.

BEN SAHLA, MOHAMMED (q.v. Oral Tradition).

BEN SAID, FARHAT (d. 1840). An Arab *shaykh* from the South (eastern Sahara). Saïd opposed the eastern *beylik* (Constantine) and rebelled against its authority (1820–22). Though he settled his differences with the Turks, he was dismissed by Ahmad Bey in 1830 and renewed hostilities against the *beylik* which lasted until he joined the Amir Abd al-Qadir (q.v.). He accepted the title of *khalifa* of Ziban and the eastern Sahara for the Amir.

BENSALEM, ABDERRAHMANE (b. 1923). Soldier. Born in the region along the Tunisian border, Bensalem was a decorated officer in the French army (fought in Italy during World War II and Indochina) who deserted to the ALN (q.v.) in 1956. He was a supporter of Houari Boumedienne (q.v.) against the GPRA (q.v.). After the War he became a member of the General Staff of the ANP (1964) and served on the Central Committee of the FLN.

BEN THAMI (BENTAMI), BELKACEM (DJILALI). Reformer. A resident of Algiers and an ophthalmologist by profession, Ben Thami was a "Young Algerian" (q.v.) who led a delegation to Paris in 1912. In meetings with Raymond Poincaré and other French political leaders, he requested an increase in rights for Algerians. His group suggested that Algerian soldiers should be able to choose naturalization without being forced to renounce their personal rights as defined by Islamic law. Other demands included a call for an end of the *Code de l'indigénat* (q.v.) and for significant representation for Algerians at every level of government, including some elected representatives in Paris itself, either in the Chamber of Deputies or in some special body. These demands of the "Young Algerians" created quite a debate in the French press, and influenced the shape and content of the Clemenceau (q.v.) and Jonnart (q.v.) reforms, though this legislation generally disappointed "Young Algerian" aspirations.

BEN TOBBAL, LAKHDAR (b. 1925). FLN leader; wartime minister. Ben Tobbal was active in the PPA (q.v.) and the OS (q.v.) and condemned to death in 1950. He went underground and later joined the FLN (q.v.). Ben Tobbal was Youssef Zighout's (q.v.) adjutant in *Wilaya* II (North-Constantinois). He supported the plan to attack the European community in the Philippeville region (August 1955) in order to demonstrate to Algeria, France, and the world that the FLN aimed to achieve by any means its objective of destroying colonialism (q.v. Introduction). He was a representative at the Soummam Congress (q.v.) and was elected to the CNRA (q.v.). He served the GPRA (q.v.) and from 1958 to 1961 as minister of the interior and then as a minister of state in the Ben Youssef Ben Khedda (q.v.) government. He was on the negotiating team that resulted in the Evian Accords (q.v.). After independence Ben Tobbal became active in Algeria's economic development and became president and director general of Algeria's national steel enterprise.

BEN YAHIA (Benyahia), MOHAMMED SEDIK (1932–1982). Minister. Ben Yahia was born in Djidjelli in Kabylia (q.v.). His mother spoke only Arabic, but she encouraged her son to get as much modern (i.e., French) education as possible. He eventually earned a *licence* (equivalent to an M.A.) in Law in 1953. Collaborating with Ahmed Taleb Ibrahimi (q.v.), Belaïd Abdesselam (q.v.), and Lamine Khène, he helped organize the *Union Générale des Etudiants Musulmans Algériens* (UGEMA), a pro-FLN student union.

Between 1954 and 1956, he defended victims of repression in Algiers. He left for Cairo shortly before French authorities were to arrest him. Ben Yahia was a member of the CNRA (q.v.) in 1956 and represented this group in Djakarta. He served under Ahmed Francis (q.v.), the finance minister of the GPRA (q.v.), then as the director of the cabinet under President Ferhat Abbas (q.v.). Diplomatically, he was present at the Melun (q.v.) discussions and the Evian (q.v.) negotiations. Ben Yahia also served on Ben Youssef Ben Khedda's (q.v.) staff during the third GPRA. He co-wrote the Tripoli Program (June 1962) (q.v.).

Ben Yahia was named his country's ambassador to Moscow in 1963 and then was assigned to London in 1965. President Houari Boumedienne (q.v.) tabbed Ben Yahia as minister of information in 1966. He later headed the Ministries of Higher Education and Scientific Research and Finance (1977–1979). He replaced Abdelaziz Bouteflika (q.v.) as foreign minister in January 1979. In September and October 1980 he concluded important agreements with France concerning emigrant labor and social security. In February 1982 he completed a significant liquefied natural gas accord (LNG) with France (q.v. Hydrocarbons). This led to a remarkable period of privileged relations with the ex-*métropole* known as "codevelopment." Ben Yahia died in an air crash in May while trying to negotiate a settlement to the Iran-Iraq War.

BERBERIST CRISIS (1949–1950). This MTLD (q.v.) crisis was a consequence of Messali Hadj's (q.v.) emphasis on Arabism, which alienated Berber (q.v.) members. In addition, the Berbers (q.v.) resented the growing "personality cult" surrounding the great nationalist. The Berberist crisis did not provoke a mass desertion of the Berbers, but it did contribute to Arab-Berber tensions. In addition, Hocine Aït Ahmed (q.v.) was replaced as the leader of the OS (q.v.), a Messalist associated organization.

BERBERS. Although the Berbers (q.v. Kabyles) describe themselves as *Imazighen* (sing. *Amazigh*), meaning the noble or free born, it was the Latin name "Berber" that has been used to refer to them. The word is derived from the Latin *barbari*, for peoples who spoke neither Latin nor Greek. The early Greek writers used "Libyan" as a generic name to refer to the indigenous population of the Maghrib. By the third century B.C., the Greeks had come to use the term "Libyan" to refer specifically to the non-Phoenicians living within the Carthaginian state, while speaking of other Berbers as the Numidians, the "Nomads," a name that reflected the fact that most of them were pastoralists. The Arabs also adopted this name and derived from it an adjective *barbariyya*, which means primitive and foreign. The Berbers are historically renowned for their love of independence. In times of crisis, they often formed confederations.

Their ethnic origins remain a mystery, though the prehistoric indigenous population was probably infused with migrations from northeast and southeast Africa and probably from the sub-Sahara and Western Europe. Berbers divided over kinship, not language. Linguistically, dialects (possibly derived from a Hamitic past) are difficult as a consequence of a lack of a universal alphabet and no common literature (though there is a strong oral tradition [q.v.]). Furthermore, over the centuries there have been ethno-cultural symbioses with the conquerors (e.g., Carthaginian, Roman, Arab, and French). Major Berber areas are in Kabylia, the Aurès (q.v.), the M'zab (q.v.), and the southern Sahara.

King Masinissa (q.v.) of the Massylis (q.v.) established the first renowned Berber state, Numidia (q.v.). After his death, Numidia became associated as a Roman client. After Jugurtha's (q.v.) failure to assert Massyli independence, Numidia became a Roman protectorate until it was incorporated into the Empire's provincial system.

Though Roman rule and colonists brought a great degree of prosperity and stability to the region, the Berbers were often forced into the hinterland. They mounted numerous rebellions, even including those who had assimilated Roman culture such as Tacfarinas (A.D. 17 to 29). The arrival of Christianity produced more dissension and dispute given the popularity of Donatism (q.v.). One Berber who especially distinguished himself during this religious controversy was the Bishop of Hippo (Annaba [q.v.]), Augustine (q.v.). Concurrently, revolts led by Firmus (372–375) and Gildon (398) further weakened Roman control, which expedited their displacement by the Vandals (q.v.).

The Vandals never controlled the area as successfully as the Romans had, as many Berber regions asserted their independence. Nevertheless, the Vandals recognized the fighting abilities of the Berbers and recruited them. The Byzantines (q.v.) also admired the military prowess of the Berbers, but like the Vandals, they found it impossible to extend their administration over all Berber territory.

The Berbers under Kusayla (q.v.) and al-Kahina (q.v.) mounted formidable resistance against the Arabs' expansion in North Africa. The Arabs, like their predecessors, realized it would be more strategic to enlist Berbers in their armies rather than to encounter them as enemies on the battlefield.

As Berbers converted to Islam, they also provided the military means to conquer the Maghrib and Andalusia (Spain). As with the experience with Christianity, the Berbers pursued their independence and heterodoxy, subscribing to different Islamic doctrines (Kharijism [q.v.], Ibadism [q.v.], Shi'ism [q.v.]). This led to political movements and states (e.g., Khariji/Ibadi resistance to the Fatimids [q.v.]; the Shi'i Kutama [q.v.]; and the Ibadi Rustumid [q.v.] dynasty).

Berbers developed dynamic dynasties such as the Zirids (q.v.) and Hammadids (q.v.). The most famous Maghribi Berber dynasties were the Almoravids (q.v.) and the Almohads (q.v.), who distinguished themselves by their military and cultural achievements. They were able to unite Maghribi Berbers, if for relatively short periods. After the decline of the Almohads, smaller Berber dynasties established themselves, such as the Abd al-Wadids (q.v.) in Tlemcen.

The Turks, like other conquerors, had trouble controlling the Berber population. Berbers living in the Aurès (q.v. Chaoui) asserted their independence from Turkish rule as well as sections of Kabylia. With difficulty the French managed to subdue these regions during the 1850s, though revolt, especially in 1871 (q.v. Revolt of 1871), and brigandage remained constant concerns. Among the Saharan Berbers (Tuareg [q.v.]), the French governed eventually (late nineteenth to early twentieth century) through the military.

During the War of Independence, Berbers played leading roles (e.g., Belkacem Krim [q.v.]; Ramdane Abane [q.v.]; Ben Youssef Ben Khedda [q.v.]; Hocine Aït Ahmed [q.v.]; Mohammed Ben Yahia [q.v.]; Col. Amirouche [q.v.]). Kabylia and the Aurès were especially insurrectionary. Traditional Berber-Arab rivalries (q.v. Berberist Crisis) threatened the liberation movement and contributed to the brief but violent power struggle after independence.

Berbers have remained extremely sensitive to threats to their culture. The Cultural Revolution's (q.v.) emphasis on

Arabization (q.v.) has been particularly resisted as disclosed by riots in 1980. There have been other incidents. In October 1985 demonstrators and police confronted each other in Tizi Ouzou as Kabyles demanded the release of Berber activists, including the singer Lounis Aït Menguellet. The Berbers were also restive during the October 1988 riots (q.v.). Berbers have been particularly vocal as a result of the December 1990 Arabization law.

Since the constitutional reforms of 1989, there have been several active Berber opposition parties; among them are the *Rassemblement pour la Culture et la Démocratisation* (RCD); *Mouvement Culturel Berbère* (MCB); and particularly Aït Ahmed's *Front des Forces Socialistes* (FFS). These Berber parties share many objectives, but in April 1990 the RCD and the MCB had a violent confrontation.

Berbers have played significant official roles in independent Algeria (e.g., Belaïd Abdesselem [q.v.]; Ben Yahia; Kasdi Merbah [q.v.]; Nordine Aït Laoussine [q.v. Hydrocarbons]). The Berbers make up approximately 20 percent of the present population of Algeria (17 percent in 1987).

BERTRAND, LOUIS (1866–1941). Writer. Bertrand was very influential as a stylist of the *Mouvement algérianiste,* which viewed French colonization as inheriting the legacy of Roman Africa. He taught at the *Lycée* of Algiers after arriving in Algeria in 1891. Among his most famous works are *Le Sang des races* (1899), *Pépète le bien-aimé* (1901), *La Cina* (1901), and *Les Villes d'or* (1921).

BESSAIH, BOUALEM (b. 1930). Diplomat and minister. Bessaih served in the ALN during the War of Liberation and was a member of the CNRA. After independence he was ambassador with service in Belgium, Luxemburg, the Netherlands, Egypt, and Kuwait (1963–1971). He was a representative to the Arab League from 1971 to 1974. He returned to Kuwait as ambassador in 1979 and then became secretary-general of the Ministry of Foreign Affairs in 1980. Bessaih attained the rank of minister, being appointed to hold the portfolios of Information and Culture (1981), Postal and Telecommunications (1984), and Foreign Affairs (1988). Bessaih is respected as a negotiator and has been sent to Beirut in order to help resolve Shi'i-Palestinian differences.

BEURS (q.v. Emigrant Labor).

BISKRA. An oasis and city in the northern Sahara. The present city is built on the site of the Roman town of Vescera. It was given its current name by the Aghlabids (q.v.), who conquered it in the eleventh century. The city was contested among the Abd al-Wadids (q.v.), the (Tunisian) Hafsids, and the (Moroccan) Marinids. Under the Hafsids, it was essentially an autonomous city, prospering from the caravan trade between the Sahara and the Tell. The Turks ruled the city indirectly through the head of the Beni Oukhaz family. It continued to prosper, though rivalries between the Beni Oukhaz and the Ben Gana families produced instability.

In the nineteenth century the Amir Abd al-Qadir (q.v.) took over the city, forcing the former Bey Ahmad (Ahmed [q.v.]) to flee. The French supported the Ben Gana, and the duc d'Aumale (one of Louis-Philippe's sons) occupied it in 1844. Bu Zian's (q.v.) revolt against the French in the Biskra area in 1849 was also suppressed.

After independence, Biskra was the center of Colonel Mohamed Chaabani's revolt against President Ahmed Ben Bella. The population of the city was estimated to be 108,320 in 1983.

BITAT, RABAH (b. 1926?). "Historic leader" (q.v.); president of the APN. Bitat, like many other young nationalists, was attracted to Messali Hadj's (q.v.) nationalist message. He became active in the PPA (q.v.) before being drafted into the

French Army in 1939. Bitat was appalled by the horrible Sétif (q.v.) repression of 1945. He joined the MTLD (q.v.) in 1948 and then the OS (q.v.). He attracted enough official colonial attention by 1950 to have earned condemnation in *absentia* to five years exile from Algeria. Nevertheless he never left his native land, preferring to go underground to work for national liberation. He was a founder of the CRUA (q.v.) and the FLN (q.v.), thus earning the appellation of "historic leader."

Bitat commanded revolutionary forces within Algeria itself, first in northern Constantine province, then around and in Algiers. He was captured by the French police in 1955 and spent the rest of the war in prison. Bitat was named an honorary member (minister of state) of the GPRA (1958–1962) (q.v.). He became a member (vice president) of the Political Bureau (q.v.) in 1962, but two years later he joined a group in Paris opposed to Ahmed Ben Bella. During Houari Boumedienne's (q.v.) presidency, he served as minister of transportation (1965–1977) and after the implementation of the new Constitution of 1976 (q.v.), he presided over the *Assemblée Populaire Nationale* (APN).

When Boumedienne died in 1978, Bitat served briefly as interim head of state until the election of Chadli Benjedid (q.v.). In 1990 Bitat resigned as president of the APN (replaced by Abdelaziz Belkhadem) in protest over the rapid reforms and the decline of the economy (especially the *Dinar Algérien* [DA]). He became associated with disaffected FLN party members Mohammed Salah Yahiaoui (q.v.), Chérif Messadia (q.v.), Ahmed Taleb Ibrahimi (q.v.), Abdelaziz Bouteflika (q.v.), and Boualem Benhamouda (q.v.).

Bitat's wife is Zohra Drif (q.v.), a heroine of the Battle of Algiers (q.v.).

BITCHNIN, ALI (fl. seventeenth century). Successful *raïs* during the flourishing period of the Regency (q.v.). Bitchnin was an Italian pirate who converted to Islam. His exploits during the

Regency gave him great wealth (two palaces in Algiers) and his own private army. He refused to send an Algerian naval contingent to the Sultan in Istanbul unless he was paid a subsidy in advance. This insubordination prompted the Sultan to send an emissary to Algiers with orders to have Bitchnin executed. The *raïs*'s followers forced the emissary and the *pasha* to seek haven in a mosque. Nevertheless, Bitchnin was forced to flee when the Janissaries asked him to provide their salaries. Eventually, he was pardoned and later possibly poisoned.

BLUM-VIOLLETTE LEGISLATION (BILL, PROPOSAL, LAW). Effort by the Popular Front Government of French Socialist Premier Léon Blum (with the particular assistance of Minister of State [and former Governor-General] Maurice Viollette and historian, Charles-André Julien [q.v.]) to satisfy the aspirations of Algerian moderates. Presented in 1936, the legislation proposed that a certain number of educated Algerian Muslims (10,000 to 20,000) be allowed to become French citizens without surrendering their Muslim personal status in matters such as marriage, divorce, and inheritance. Due to strident European settler opposition, the legislation was never brought to the floor of the Chamber of Deputies. The Senate defeated it in 1938. This led to disillusionment among many Algerian moderates (q.v. Ferhat Abbas; Mohammed Saleh Bendjelloul). Many historians view the failure to pass the Blum-Viollette legislation as a "lost opportunity."

BONE (q.v. Annaba).

BORDER WAR ("War of the Sands"); (q.v. Morocco). Conflict between Algeria and Morocco lasting several weeks (October to November 1963). This war was a consequence of colonialism, decolonization, and the national ambitions of both states. It has been called Africa's first postcolonial conflict, but it was rooted in the border demarcated by competing Moroccan and Algerian colonial bureaucracies.

Before the end of Algeria's War of Independence, Moroccan and Algerian leaders began serious discussions concerning their shared border. On July 6, 1961, Ferhat Abbas (q.v.) concluded an agreement with Rabat that stated that the contested frontier would be addressed immediately after Algeria gained its independence. From the FLN's (q.v.) perspective, this agreement ensured that there would be no separate agreement between Paris and Rabat concerning frontiers. In addition, it underscored Morocco's support for Algeria's colonial territorial integrity. (Concurrently, President Charles de Gaulle [q.v.] had threatened to partition the Sahara [q.v. Introduction]).

When Algeria achieved its formal independence in July 1962, Moroccan *Forces Armées Royales* (FAR) advanced into Algerian territory anticipating the implementation of the July agreement. After Ahmed Ben Bella (q.v.) came to power, King Hassan II kept the pressure on him, though FAR units withdrew across the border (with violence at Tindouf in October 1962). Compounding this issue was the ideological differences between Algeria's republican, revolutionary socialist state and Morocco's monarchy. Hassan's visit to Algiers in March 1963 did not settle the issue. Border incidents occurred during the summer.

When Algiers faced the Kabyle insurrection in October 1963 (q.v. Hocine Aït Ahmed; Kabyles), Hassan poised the FAR on the border. Conflicting reports claimed that on October 1, Moroccan or Algerian troops violated the other's frontier initiating fighting. There were three main areas of fighting: (1) 500 km southwest of (Colomb-)Béchar at Hassi Beida and Tindjoub; (2) the Tindouf region; and (3) in Moroccan territory at Ich-Figuig. Given the national crisis, Kabyles chose national over ethnic interests (q.v. Mohand ou el-Hadj), which effectively reduced the internal danger to Ben Bella's government. Mediation by President Modibo

Keita of Mali and especially Emperor Haile Selassie of Ethiopia produced a summit at Bamako, Mali, on October 30, where Ben Bella and King Hassan agreed to a cease-fire. Fighting finally broke off several days later. According to the Paris daily, *Le Monde*, the ANP lost 60 dead with 250 wounded. In general, this "war of the sands" showed that Morocco had a superior military force than Algeria's. This led to Algeria's buildup of its military, which was achieved primarily with the assistance of the Soviet Union.

The OAU was charged with settling the issue. It managed to circumscribe a demilitarized zone, which was accepted by both sides in February 1964. By this time Ben Bella had repudiated the Abbas agreement and subscribed to the OAU principle of July 1964 respecting colonial borders and territorial integrity.

Relations warmed between Algeria and Morocco in the late 1960s and early 1970s, culminating in the conventions of 1972, which demarcated a border and called for economic collaboration concerning the mineral riches in the contested area. Algeria ratified the agreements but Morocco did not. The border issue reemerged during the decolonization of the Spanish Sahara (q.v. Western Sahara). With the establishment of the AMU (q.v. Maghrib Unity) in February 1989, Morocco finally ratified the 1972 conventions.

BOUALAM, (BACHAGA) BENAISSA SAID (1906–1982). Most reknown *harki* (q.v.) leader. Boualam was born in Souk-Ahras and was an officer in the French Army. He was elected to the French National Assembly in 1958 (deputy from Orléansville/El Asnam/Ech-Chlef[q.v.]). The Bachaga also organized effective anti-ALN units and was a fervent proponent of the mobilization of loyal Algerian units (*harkis*) to be deployed against the ALN.

Boualam managed to escape with several hundred of his *harkis,* which saved these French loyalists from certain persecution and probable death. He settled in Le Mas

Thibert. He campaigned tirelessly for France to recognize the *harkis* and to provide adequate services (especially housing and education) for them. Elevated within the Legion of Honor, he used his personal prestige to remind the ex-metropolitan power how French Muslims continued to be casualties of Algerian decolonization because of discrimination and non-integration. He headed the *Front National des Rapatriés de Confession Musulmane*. He wrote three books concerning the *harkis*: *Mon pays, la France* (1962); *Les Harkis au service de la France* (1963); and *L'Algérie sans la France* (1964). Boualam's family has continued his efforts on behalf of the *harkis*.

BOU BAGHLA (q.v. Bu Baghla).

BOUBNIDER, SALAH (Saout-el-Arab) (b. 1925). Officer. Born in Oued Zenati near Constantine, Boubnider was a member of the PPA-MTLD and favored armed action against French colonialism. He joined the FLN and led a commando group on October 31 to November 1, 1954, the opening night of hostilities. He rose within the ALN to the post of military assistant to the commander of *Wilaya* II in late 1959 and was promoted to the rank of colonel in early 1962. He opposed Ahmed Ben Bella (q.v.) and was arrested in July 1962. He reconciled with Ben Bella soon afterward (August) and part of his power was restored (directing public and administrative affairs of *Wilaya* II). He became a founding member of the opposition PRS and subsequently was arrested and released again.

Returning again to favor (member of FLN's [q.v.] Central Committee), Boubnider worked hard to establish a special relationship between the Syrian Baath party and the FLN. He supported Houari Boumedienne's (q.v.) coup of June 1965 (q.v.) and became a member of the Council of the Revolution (q.v.) He shared with Chérif Belkacem (q.v.) and Mohand Ou El Hadj (q.v.) leadership within the FLN until 1967.

BOUDA, AHMED (b. 1907). Nationalist. Bouda was a member of the ENA (q.v.) and the PPA (q.v.). He was also a delegate in the Algerian Assembly (q.v.) in 1948. He eventually broke with the MTLD (q.v.) and Messali Hadj (q.v.). French authorities arrested him in November 1954, but released him in April 1955. Bouda left Algeria and became the FLN's representative in Libya. He tried to mediate between the GPRA (q.v.) and Ben Bella's Political Bureau (q.v.) during the summer of 1962. After this initiative failed, he gave up politics to become a teacher in Algiers.

BOUDIAF, MOHAMED (1919–92). "Historic leader" (q.v.); first President of the High Council of State (HSC) (q.v.). Boudiaf was born in M'Sila. He was drafted into the French Army in 1943 where he tried to organize nationalist cells among Algerian soldiers. In 1947, he created a branch of the OS (q.v.) in the department of Constantine. Boudiaf escaped French authorities and went underground while being held in contempt of court. In 1953–1954, he was a party organizer for the MTLD (q.v.) in France.

Reacting to the recent split in that organization, Boudiaf played a very significant role in organizing the CRUA (q.v.) in Spring-Summer 1954 earning his membership among the "historic leaders" of the Algerian Revolution. In late October 1954, he was the key liaison officer between the internal and the external members of the CRUA.

Boudiaf served with the "external" FLN during the war and was captured on 22 October 1956 along with Ahmed Ben Bella (q.v.), Hocine Aït Ahmed (q.v.), Mohammed Khider (q.v), and Professor Mostefa Lacheraf (q.v. Arabization) in the infamous skyjacking of a Moroccan Air-Atlas airplane. He spent the rest of the war in prison.

After independence, Boudiaf emerged as an opposition leader to Ben Bella. He refused membership to the Political Bureau (q.v.) and he viewed the electoral process (i.e., selection of candidates) of the National Constituent Assembly as illegitimate. He responded by founding the opposition *Parti de la Révolution Socialiste* (PRS). In June 1963 he was kidnapped in Algiers and condemned to death. He was eventually forced into exile in France and Morocco. He remained in exile and in opposition after Houari Boumedienne's June 1965 military coup. Nevertheless, he kept a critical watch on Algerian political developments. In July 1989, after the October 1988 riots (q.v.), Boudiaf called for a national political organization in opposition to the FLN.

The forced resignation of President Chadli Benjedid by the High Security (then State) Council in January 1992 suddenly brought Boudiaf back into political prominence. He accepted the post of President of the HCS. At first, it was believed that he would serve symbolically, as a needed historic figure to bolster the HSC's legitimacy. Boudiaf, always an individualist, proved, however, that he would be an activist president. He tirelessly called upon the "silent majority" to promote national unity and consensus. He tried, for example, to mobilize a political party, the *Rassemblement National Patriotique* (National Patriotic Rally). Under his presidency the *Conseil Consultatif National* (CCN) (q.v.) was inaugurated in April 1992. It was viewed as an advisory rather than a legislative body. In June 1992, Boudiaf was assassinated in Annaba while delivering a speech. An inquiry investigating this tragedy was inconclusive, generating rumors concerning accountability of this murderous act from Islamists to the HCS government itself.

Boudiaf was one of the few "historic leaders" who published books. In *Où va l'Algérie?* he explains some of his theoretical disagreements with Ben Bella. He also wrote *La Préparation du 1er novembre* (1976) including *La Lettre aux Algériens*.

BOUDJEDRA, RACHID (b. 1941). Novelist. Boudjedra was born in Aïn-Beïda and went to school in Tunis. He joined the ALN at seventeen and was wounded. Boudjedra then served as an FLN representative in Spain. After the war he completed a philosophy degree at the Sorbonne in 1965. He taught at a lycée for women at Blida and then returned to France from 1969 to 1972. He then went to Morocco and taught there until 1975 before returning to Algeria.

In 1977 Boudjedra was an adviser to the Ministry of Information and Culture and, beginning in 1981, a consultant for the national publishing press, the *Société Nationale d'Edition et de Diffusion* (SNED). He also taught at the Institut des Sciences Politiques in Algiers.

Boudjedra's fame rests particularly on his literary talent. Two critically acclaimed novels are *La Répudiation* (1969) and *L'Insolation* (1972). These books include psychologically wracked carnal characters. Boudjedra examined male and female roles in traditional Algerian society. Implicitly, he questioned the effect of the revolution on Algerian society. Among his other works are *Topographie idéale pour une agression caractérisée* (1975); *L'Escargot entêté* (1977); *Les 1001 années de la nostalgie* (1979); and *Le Vainqueur de coupe* (1981). In 1982 Boudjedra declared that he would no longer write in French. He translated his novel written in Arabic, *Ettafakouk* (1982), as *Le Démantèlement* (1982). Boudjedra is among a remarkable group of Algerian writers who share themes, such as the conflict between Algeria's traditional and revolutionary cultures.

BOUDJENANE, AHMED (1929–1968). Officer. Boudjenane was born in Ouled Ali near Tlemcen (q.v.). Boudjenane was an activist in the MTLD (q.v.) who had gone into Moroccan exile as early as 1948. While in Morocco, he studied at the University of al-Quarawiyin (Karaouiyyin) in Fez. He joined the ALN's (q.v.) *Wilaya* V, rising to the rank of captain in command of the *Wilaya*'s zone II. In 1961 he was demoted to lieutenant for refusing to cross border fortifications. In the civil war that took place during the summer of 1962, he sided with the Tlemcen group (Ahmed Ben Bella [q.v.]-Boumedienne [q.v.]). He was appointed head of the Second Military Region and was active in the Oran Federation of the FLN. In the spring of 1964, Boudjenane became director of the Military Academy at Cherchell and was named to the General Staff. He died in an automobile crash in January 1968.

BOUHALI, LARBI (b. 1912). PCA (q.v. Algerian Communist Party) leader. As a leading Algerian communist (Central Committee member), he was incarcerated in 1943. He refused to support the AML (q.v.). From 1947 to 1962 he was secretary-general of the PCA and served in its foreign delegation during the War of Independence.

BOUHIRED, DJAMILA. Revolutionary heroine. Bouhired was one of Saadi Yacef's (q.v.) young women agents during the "Battle of Algiers" (q.v.). At the age of twenty-two, she was wounded, arrested, tortured, and charged with the bombings of the "Milk Bar" and the "Brasserie Coq Hardi." Her trial attracted worldwide attention as she became a symbol of Algeria's struggle for liberation from colonialism. She was finally imprisoned in Rheims, where she remained until the end of the war. Bouhired's prestige played a key role in the defeat of the Family Code of 1981. She has been an advocate for women's rights in Algeria (q.v. Women).

BOUIALI, MUSTAPHA (d. 1987). Militant Islamist. Bouiali was a former ALN (q.v.) fighter who opposed the Chadli Benjedid (q.v.) government. In August 1985, militant Islamists raided a police barracks, implicating Bouiali. On January 3, 1987, Bouiali and six of his supporters were killed by police in a gun battle in Larba, south of Algiers. Bouiali's operations portended the violence that particularly has plagued Algeria since the cancellation of national elections (q.v. Elections of December 1991) by the High Council of State (HCS) (q.v.).

BOUKADOUM, MESSAOUD (b. 1910). Nationalist. The son of a well-to-do landowner and bureaucrat, Boukadoum was sent to France for his higher education. He apparently joined Messali Hadj's (q.v.) ENA (q.v.) in 1934, while still a university student. He later joined the PPA (q.v.) and then the AML (q.v.). Boukadoum was elected in 1946 to the French National Assembly as a MTLD (q.v.) deputy. He assisted in the formation of the OS (q.v.) and tried to convince Tunisian nationalists to pursue an armed revolt against French colonialism.

Boukadoum was the GPRA's (q.v.) ambassador to Belgrade (1960–1962) after serving as Foreign Minister Debaghine's (q.v.) cabinet director (1958–1959). After independence he was a deputy in Algeria's National Constituent Assembly. He refused the position of ambassador to Dakar (Senegal) and took instead a position with SONATRACH (q.v. Hydrocarbons) at Skikda.

BOUKHAROUBA, MOHAMMED (q.v. Houari Boumedienne).

BOULAHROUF, TAYEB (b. 1923). Nationalist. Boulahrouf was born to a very poor family and became politicized at an early age, selling the PPA's (q.v.) newspaper, *El-Ouma*. During World War II he continued to work for the PPA and then with the AML (q.v.). He was one of the organizers and participants of the May 1945 demonstrations that had such tragic consequences (q.v. Sétif). He was jailed several times, especially for his OS (q.v.) activities (organized a hunger strike in prison).

Boulahrouf opposed Messali Hadj's (q.v.) moderate course and collaborated with Mostefa Ben Boulaïd (q.v.) and Didouche Mourad (q.v.) in preparing for the revolution. During the War of Independence, he attempted in vain to obtain PCF (*Parti Communiste Français*; French Communist Party) support for the FLN. Boulahrouf led a clandestine life while being sought by French police and, more dangerously, the "Red Hand," a vengeful colonialist terrorist group. He eluded several of the latter's assaults. In 1961 he was involved in secret communications with French officials (including Georges Pompidou), which led to the formal negotiation at Evian (q.v. Evian Accords).

After independence, he distinguished himself as an ambassador serving in Rome, Belgrade, Lima, Bucharest, Buenos Aires, La Paz, and Lisbon.

BOULMERKA, HASSIBA (b. 1969). Athlete. Boulmerka became the 1991 world 1,500 meter champion with the winning time of 4:02.21. Then during the Barcelona Olympics, the twenty-four-year-old champion easily defeated the field with a time of 3:55.30. In one of the most dramatic moments of the Olympiad, Boulmerka pointed to her green jersey, reaffirming her pride in her country and urging the world audience to recognize it. Her training and fame as a woman athlete has drawn Islamist protest, even to the point of a denunciation (*kafr*). Boulmerka viewed her victory as one for Arab and especially Algerian women. Boulmerka and her track compatriot, Noureddine Morceli (q.v.), have focused more attention on Algeria. Indeed, Morceli's victory as the 1,500 meter winner during the 1991 World Championships, made history. In no other time has a country had both world champions in the same event. Both athletes received the Medal of Merit from President Chadli Benjedid (q.v.).

BOU MAZA (q.v. Bu Maza).

BOUMAZA, BACHIR (b. 1927). Minister. Boumaza was originally from the region north of Sétif. While working in France, he became a member of the MTLD (q.v.) and eventually became secretary to Messali Hadj (q.v.). He joined the FLN (q.v.) and served in France until his arrest in December 1958. Boumaza was tortured as disclosed in the controversial book *La Gangrène* (1959). During the civil war

of the summer of 1962, he sided with Ahmed Ben Bella
(q.v.) and Houari Boumedienne (q.v.) (the Tlemcen group/
Political Bureau [q.v.]). In September of that year, he was
appointed minister for labor and social affairs in Ben Bella's
first government. A year later, in Ben Bella's second
government, Boumaza became minister of national economy
(including finance, commerce, and industry). He was kept in
the third government (December 1964) as minister for
industry and energy.

Though initially supporting Colonel Boumedienne's coup
of June 1965 (q.v.), which was symbolized by Boumaza's
membership on the Council of the Revolution (q.v.) and his
new position as minister of information, he became disillusioned in 1966 and fled the country. He became a member of
the opposition OCRA in 1966. As a result of President
Chadli Benjedid's (q.v.) efforts to reconcile FLN factions, he
was invited back to Algeria. Boumaza returned in 1980 and
became a member of the Central Committee of the FLN in
1989. He publicly supported Saddam Hussein in the Gulf
War of 1991 and has actively been involved in trying to have
the suppression of the Sétif uprising (q.v.) of 1945 recognized internationally as a ''crime against humanity.''

BOUMEDIENNE (BOUMEDIENE), HOUARI (Mohammed
Ben Brahim Boukharouba) (1925–1978). Head of the ALN/
ANP; second President of Algeria. ''Boumedienne'' was
Boukharouba's *nom de guerre* and the name of a renowned
teacher in the Tlemcen region (q.v. Literature in Arabic).
Boumedienne was a fervent nationalist and socialist. Fluent
in both Arabic (he studied at al-Azhar in Egypt) and French,
Boumedienne was forceful, authoritarian, and ambitious.
Above all, he was dedicated toward projecting a sovereign,
liberated Algeria as an exemplar for the Third World.

Boumedienne was from Guelma and joined the FLN (q.v.)
in 1955. He led *Wilaya* V in 1957 and by the end of the War
of Independence, was Chief of Staff of the ALN and in

charge of the (external) Algerian armies in Tunisia and Morocco. At independence, he joined forces with Ahmed Ben Bella (q.v.), led his troops into several pitched battles with freedom fighters who had spent the war years within Algeria (i.e. the intraelite internal-external conflict [q.v. Introduction]), and then gained power for the group of political and military elites who were led by Ben Bella (i.e. Tlemcen Group/Political Bureau [q.v.]). A member of Ben Bella's various governments (Vice President, Minister of Defense), he eventually plotted and executed a bloodless military coup (June 1965) (q.v.).

Weak at first because he lacked popular support (as disclosed by student protests), President Boumedienne instituted a collegial system of government (Council of the Revolution [q.v.]). When the military coup led by Col. Tahar Zbiri (q.v.) against his own leadership failed in December 1967, he seized his chance to assert complete control over Algeria. (Boumedienne also escaped an attempt against his life in 1968.) By 1970 he had secured himself in power.

Attracted by revolutionary socialism and inspired by the theoretical possibility of an economically autarkic nation, Boumedienne insisted on four-year plans and governmental control of all significant industrial and agricultural enterprises (q.v. State Plans). He also sought foreign investments though they were subject to strict regulations. Boumedienne's state-building system developed into an elaborate ''state capitalism'' spearheaded by national enterprises such as the hydrocarbons sector's SONATRACH (q.v.). Pursuing his corresponding objective to eliminate neocolonialism in his country, Boumedienne methodically nationalized banks, mines, and symbolically French hydrocarbon concessions (February 1971) (q.v. Hydrocarbons). He also initiated an Agrarian Revolution (q.v.) in 1971 and a Cultural Revolution (q.v.).

Under Boumedienne, Algeria attained great prestige in 1971 with its bold nationalization of French hydrocarbon concessions and also when it championed the United Nations' special session on the need to redistribute world resources equitably in 1974. Beginning the following year, however, a series of events occurred that distressed Boumedienne personally besides officially.

In April 1975, President Boumedienne hosted the visit of French President Valéry Giscard d'Estaing. For Boumedienne the summit represented a "turned page" in the controversial and highly charged bilateral history. Boumedienne anticipated a much improved relationship with France, but this did not occur. Indeed, Giscard found political and personal compatibility with King Hassan II of Morocco. Hassan's own political ambitions was the second setback for Boumedienne in 1975. The Moroccan king was able to pressure Spain (e.g., "the Green March") to conclude the Tripartite (Madrid) Accords of November 1975, which handed over the Spanish Sahara to Morocco and Mauritania (q.v. Western Sahara). This caught Boumedienne's government by surprise since relations with Morocco had improved significantly since the Border War (q.v. Border War; Morocco). Algeria subsequently provided massive support to the Sahrawi liberation movement (q.v. POLISARIO).

In 1976 Boumedienne institutionalized his regime with a National Charter (q.v.), which defined and outlined the goals and aspirations of the country, and a new constitution (q.v. Constitution of 1976). The Constitution particularly expedited the smooth transition in the presidency after Boumedienne died of a rare blood disease in December 1978.

Boumedienne's efforts to construct a socialist Algeria resulted in dramatic achievements in the second sector. Nevertheless, his successor, Chadli Benjedid (q.v.) contended that economic development should have more sectoral balance. His liberalization and decentralization policies as well as the reforms after the October 1988 riots (q.v.) deconstructed Boumedienne's institutions. The emergence in July 1992 of Belaïd Abdesselam (q.v.) as prime minister, who was formerly Boumedienne's chief industrial technocrat, as well as his subsequent statements harkened back to the earlier state-building era.

Ten years after his death, the Prix national Houari Boumedienne was inaugurated to award research and writing in the "national" (Arabic) language.

BOUMENDJEL, AHMAD (1906–1982). Minister. Boumendjel was born in Ben-Yenni. He was a teacher and then a lawyer who became a nationalist. He joined the ENA (q.v.) and then its successor organization the PPA (q.v.). He was Messali Hadj's (q.v.) lawyer from 1939 to 1940. Boumendjel also served as a Municipal Councilor in 1938.

His politics moderated in the 1940s as he coedited Ferhat Abbas's (q.v.) Manifesto (q.v.) and collaborated with him in the founding of the UDMA (q.v.). He was a councilor of the French Union in 1951. In 1955–1956 Boumendjel decided to join the FLN (q.v.). (Ali Boumendjel was Ahmad's brother, who was also a highly respected lawyer and a valuable member of the FLN. His death during the war [falling out of a window] was very controversial and had a significant effect upon the legal community in France.)

Boumendjel prominently participated at the Melun (q.v.) (June 1960) and Evian (q.v.) (May 1961) negotiations for the GPRA (q.v.); he was also involved in secret communications. After the war he served as minister of reconstruction and public works (1962–1963) and minister of reconstruction (1963–1964). In 1964, he was eased out of office in Ben Bella's attempt to gain uncontested power.

BOU MEZRAG (q.v. Bu Mezrag).

BOUPACHA, DJAMILA. Revolutionary heroine. Boupacha was an urban guerrilla for the ALN. She was arrested in February 1960 for throwing a bomb into a café. Her subsequent torture received great publicity as a result of a book by the renowned existentialist and companion of Jean-Paul Sartre, Simone de Beauvoir. Boupacha became a heroine for French opponents of the war. Besides de Beauvoir, other founders of a "Djamila Boupacha Committee" were Germaine Tillion (the renowned social anthropologist) and François Mauriac. Boupacha married Battle of Algiers [q.v.] ALN leader, Yacef Saadi (q.v.).

BOURBOUNE, MOURAD (b. 1938). Writer. Bourboune was born in Jijel. He studied in Constantine, Tunis, and Paris. After the war, he participated in organizing the *Union des Ecrivains Algériens*. He served as the director of the Cabinet of Bachir Boumaza's (q.v.) Ministry of Work and Social Affairs (Ben Bella's [q.v.] first government). He also directed a Cultural Committee of the FLN. Bourboune left for France after the Houari Boumedienne (q.v.) coup of June 1965 (q.v.). He returned to Algeria several years later only to return again to Paris.

Bourboune wrote *Le Mont des genêts* (1962) describing the transformation of Algeria as a result of the revolution. His most famous work is *Le Muezzin* (1968), whose hero is presented as a religious and revolutionary apostate. His writings question the genuine effect of Algeria's social changes as a result of the revolution.

BOURMONT, LOUIS AUGUSTE VICTOR DE (1773–1846). French officer. Bourmont was at first a loyal royalist officer during the revolution, who served in the Vendée. After its pacification by revolutionary forces, he was imprisoned and held under suspicion for conspiracy. Bourmont escaped to Portugal, but he later offered his services to the French military and served in the logistics section. Upon his return to France, he was detained again in Paris, but he was finally allowed to serve again. He distinguished himself in the Russian, Saxon, and French campaigns during Napoleon's decline and became a division general. Bourmont did not support Napoleon during the Hundred Days and offered his services to Louis XVIII after Waterloo. (He also participated as a witness for the prosecution of Marshal Ney.) Bourmont offered his services once again to the Bourbons and participated in the expedition to Spain in 1823. He became minister of war in 1829.

Using contingency plans commissioned by Napoleon, Bourmont invaded Algeria, landing at Sidi Fredj (Ferruch) west of Algiers on June 14, 1830. He subsequently seized and secured Algiers on July 5. He was promoted to Marshal. Bourmont refused to serve the Orléanists after the Revolution of 1830. In 1832 he was linked to another Vendée revolt on behalf of the Duchess of Berry and exiled. He returned to France in 1840 after a general amnesty.

BOUSSENA, SADEK (b. 1948?). Minister. From 1978 to 1982 Boussena served as director-general of the Ministry of Energy then as the secretary-general of this ministry. He was selected in 1988 as minister of energy and petrochemical industries in the Kasdi Merbah (q.v.) government. In June 1990 Boussena was tabbed to head OPEC.

BOUSSOUF, ABDELHAFID (1926–1982). ALN colonel. Boussouf was born in Mila. He joined the PPA (q.v.) and became a leader in the OS (q.v.). He was among the nationalists (q.v. Committee of Twenty-two) at the June 1954 meeting that prepared the revolutionary outbreak of November 1954. Boussouf began the war as Larbi Ben M'Hidi's (q.v.) assistant, then became colonel in charge of *Wilaya* V (Oran). He was elected to the CNRA (q.v.) (1956) then to the CCE (q.v.) (1957), before becoming minister for general liaison and communications (1958) in the GPRA (q.v.). He opposed Ramdane Abane (q.v.) and was involved in his death. Boussouf supported Ferhat Abbas (q.v.), then Ben Youssef Ben Khedda (q.v.) for the presidency of the GPRA. In 1961 he was in charge of supplies and armaments. He retired from direct political activity at the time of the FLN crisis and conflict during the summer of 1962. William Quandt (q.v. Bibliography) placed Boussouf in the late 1960s in "semiopposition" to the Houari Boumedienne (q.v.) regime. Boussouf was also involved in his shipping business.

BOUTEFLIKA, ABDELAZIZ (b. 1937). Foreign minister. Bouteflika was born in Oujda, Morocco. Bouteflika received his primary education in Oujda before continuing in Tlemcen (q.v.). When the UGEMA called a general strike in 1956, he quit school and joined the nationalist underground in *Wilaya* V (Oran). He quickly became the *Wilaya*'s political officer; then he joined the general staff of the ALN (q.v.) in 1960. Bouteflika's nom de guerre was Si Abdelkader el-Mali. In 1962, he was an intermediary between the general staff led by Houari Boumedienne (q.v.) and Ahmed Ben Bella (q.v.), when the latter was still in prison. He sided with Ben Bella and Boumedienne in the political and civil strife that immediately followed independence. Consequently, he became minister for youth sports and tourism in September 1962, then foreign minister in 1963, a position he held until 1979. He was also a member of the FLN's Political Bureau (q.v.).

Ben Bella's attempt to remove Bouteflika as foreign minister contributed to the coup of June 1965 (q.v.) by which Boumedienne took control of Algeria. Bouteflika distinguished himself in 1970–1971 during negotiations with the French, resulting in the nationalization of their hydrocarbon concessions (q.v. Hydrocarbons) and in 1974 while chairing the United Nations's Special Session on North-South relations. Bouteflika's unswerving loyalty was underscored by his delivery of the eulogy at President Boumedienne's funeral. The foreign minister was considered a prominent candidate to replace Boumedienne and was considered less ideological. After President Chadli Benjedid's (q.v.) election, he held the position of a minister without portfolio and adviser.

In July 1981 he was suspended from the FLN's Political Bureau and in December from the Central Committee. In May 1983 Bouteflika was charged with corruption and embezzlement (60 million dinars=$12,370,000). (Bouteflika began a self-imposed exile in 1982.) He returned in 1987, which was viewed as an FLN (q.v.) effort for intraparty reconciliation. Along with other ex-Boumedienne officials (e.g., Belaïd Abdesselam [q.v.]), Bouteflika began to play a role again with the FLN. As a result of the 1989 third Extraordinary Congress of the FLN, he became a member of the expanded Central Committee. Bouteflika actively campaigned for the FLN in local elections in 1990. The HCS considered him a candidate for the presidency in January 1994.

BRAHIMI, ABDELHAMID (b. 1936). Prime minister. Brahimi was a guerrilla during the War of Independence. As a consequence of the Algiers Accord of 1965 (q.v. Hydrocarbons), he served as the director of the OCI (*Organisme de Coopération Industrielle*). (He is a *Docteur en Sciences économiques.*) He also represented SONATRACH in the United States (1976-January 1979) before his appointment to the Abdelghani cabinet in 1979 as minister of planning and organization of national territory. In January 1984 he became prime minister and served until after the October 1988 riots (q.v.).

BRAHIMI, LAKHDAR (b. 1934). Foreign minister. Brahimi received an excellent education in Algeria (University of Algiers) and France (Paris, Faculté de Droit; Institut des Sciences Politiques). During the War of Independence, he representing the FLN in Southeast Asia. He was appointed Secretary-General of the Ministry of Foreign Affairs (1961–63) and then became Algeria's Ambassador to Egypt, representing his country, too, at the Arab League, then Ambassador to Sudan (1963–70). In 1971, he was selected to be Ambassador to the United Kingdom. Brahimi was an adviser in the administration of President Chadli Benjedid (q.v.). In June 1991, he was tabbed by Prime Minister Sid Ahmed Ghozali (q.v.) as foreign minister. He kept this post until February 1993 (replaced by Redha Malek [q.v.]). This period was a difficult one given Algeria's domestic problems. His chief objective was to gain international confidence, especially after the establishment of the Higher Council of State (HCS) (q.v.) in January 1992.

BU BAGHLA (BOU BAGHLA) ("Mule man") (d. 1854). Rahmaniyya *sharif* of the 1851 uprising in Kabylia against the French. As a consequence of their pursuit of the elusive Bu Baghla, who was killed in battle, the French expanded their authority into Kabylia (q.v.).

BUGEAUD, THOMAS-ROBERT, born BUGEAUD DE LA PICONNERIE (1784–1849). Marshal of France and governor-general of Algeria. Born of a noble family of Périgord, Bugeaud could not be admitted to the school for senior officers at Fontainebleau, but in 1804 he entered the ranks of the grenadiers of the guard, which served as a training ground for junior officers. He joined the Army of the Rhine and participated in the German campaign of 1805. In 1808 he was with the Army of Spain where he distinguished himself at the Battles of Saragossa (1809) and Lerida (1810). In 1811 he was promoted to major and he became a colonel. Following his marriage in 1818, he settled down to the life of a gentleman farmer. He wrote a number of tracts promoting improved agricultural techniques. He was elected as a deputy representing Dordogne (1831). As a result of the July Revolution, he was able to return to the army that same year.

Bugeaud opposed the French occupation of Algeria, but in 1836, he was ordered to confront Abd al-Qadir (q.v.) in order to relieve the Muslim siege of the French camp at the Tafna River. He dealt the Amir a solid defeat at its tributary, the

Sikkak. Bugeaud was later authorized to negotiate a treaty with Abd al-Qadir. The Treaty of Tafna (May 30, 1837) (q.v.) abandoned the major part of Algeria to the Amir in exchange for peace. By the time he was appointed governor-general by the Soult-Guizot government in December 1840, war had resumed with Abd al-Qadir.

As governor-general, he promoted the idea of *Bureaux arabes* (q.v.), a military system of administration. He also projected a "utopian" colonization of Algeria. During his administration of Algeria, he maintained full control over the local French bureaucracy, which drew protests from the European settlers. He also maintained constant pressure on Abd al-Qadir. Bugeaud eventually resigned his post in June 1847, particularly because he could not obtain permission to pursue the Amir into Morocco (as had been done before) and because of inroads on his civil authority as a result of the Ordinance of April 15, 1845. Furthermore, atrocities committed by French troops also discredited the governor-general. The final blow was rejection of his plan of military colonization.

Upon his return to French politics, he was elected president of the Chamber of Deputies in January 1848 and was called to command the defense of the Orléanist regime on February 24. After his offer of services to the Provisional Government was rejected, he returned to farming. He was elected deputy from Charente-Inférieure in 1848 and again in 1849. Bugeaud died shortly after being named commander of the army of the Alps.

A square in colonial Algeria honored the governor-general, who was most responsible for Algeria's colonization. After independence, it was renamed after his Algerian rival, the Amir Abd al-Qadir.

BULUKKIN (BOLOGGUIN; BULUGUIN; BOLOQQUIN) (r. 973–984). Berber *amir* of Fatimids (q.v.). After the Fatimid Caliph al-Mu'izz left for Egypt, Bulukkin was left in charge.

He was the son of Ziri (q.v.) and a member of the Zirid (q.v.) dynasty. He expelled the Zenata (q.v.) from the Central Maghrib, destroyed Tiaret, and took Tlemcen (q.v.). He pushed into Morocco in 980, but his presence there was ephemeral as he withdrew from Fez and allowed the Zenata's return. Bulukkin is credited with the naming and "founding" of Algiers (q.v).

BU MASRAQ (BOU MEZRAG) (d. 1906). A Kabyle (q.v.) leader of the insurrection of 1870–1871. Bu Masraq continued the (Great) Kabyle revolt (q.v.) after the death of his brother, Muqrani (q.v.). He was captured in 1872. His death sentence was commuted to exile, and he was sent to Nouméa instead. He was allowed to return to Algeria in 1905, where he died within a year.

BU MAZA (BOU MAZA) (MUHAMMAD BN ABDALLAH) ("The Goat Man") (fl. 1845). *Marabout* who resisted French. Bu Maza proclaimed himself *Mahdi* and led tribes of the Dahra, the Chélif Valley, and the Ouarsenais against the French "infidels" in 1845, which also gave the harassed Abd al-Qadir (q.v.) a brief respite. Bu Maza was finally forced to surrender in April 1847.

BUREAUX ARABES. Colonial administrative institution. The *Bureaux Arabes* were implemented by governor-general Thomas-Robert Bugeaud (q.v.). The *bureaux* maintained control over Muslim populations in areas not under French civil control. Created in 1841, the *bureaux* initially attracted young Arabic-speaking French officers, who were often paternalistic toward native populations. During the next two decades, *bureaux* officers did not display the same type of sensibility as those who served under Bugeaud. This created problems (e.g., the insurgency of the Awlad Sidi Shaykh [q.v.]). The idea that the French Army had a social mission in Algeria was taken up again during the Algerian War (of

Independence) by *Sections Administratives Spécialisées* (q.v. Soustelle) units. Though civilian control was assured in Algeria after 1871, the *bureaux* type of system remained in the military-administered Sahara.

BU RENAN (BOU RENAN) (fl. 1850s). Leader of a Kabyle (q.v.) revolt. French attempts to assert more control over the Awlad Achour and the Ben Azzedin of eastern Kabylia (q.v.) incited a rebellion led by Bu Renan, who had been a French *qa'id*. He was defeated and exiled in 1860. Bu Renan, along with the rebellion of Bu Baghla (q.v.), underscored the French difficulties in subduing Kabylia.

BU ZIAN (BOU ZIAN) (d. 1849). *Marabout* who resisted the French. Bu Zian led a revolt at the Za'atsha (Zaatcha) oasis (southwest of Biskra) that broke out when the French attempted to increase taxes on palms. After the French were repulsed in July 1849 at Za'atsha, Bu Zian's reputation was amplified, influencing sympathy and support from the Hodna and Aurès regions as well as the Ziban. The French returned in greater force in the fall. This was a particularly heinous episode of suppression. The defenders were massacred (approximately 800 dead) and the bodies of Bu Zian and his son were mutilated. Bu Zian's head was displayed publicly.

BYZANTINES. During Emperor Justinian's reign, the Byzantines under Belisarius conquered the Vandal (q.v.) Kingdom in 533. The Byzantines' territorial control of Algeria never matched that of Rome as they could govern only within regions along the littoral.

　　An exarch ruled the province of Africa. Byzantine administration was marked by high taxation, though there were determined efforts to promote an efficient provincial government. Emperor Heraclius, a former exarch, entertained the idea of moving the imperial government to

Carthage during the Sassanid (Persian) wars. The exarch Gregory and his Berber allies were defeated by the Arabs under Abdallah ibn Saad (Abd Allah ibn Sa'd) in 647. It took the Arabs until 698 to take over Carthage permanently (there was a brief ephemeral Byzantine reconquest of Carthage in 697).

CADI, HADJ CHERIF (b. 1867). Assimilated officer. Cadi was born near Souk Ahras. The familial name *Cadi* means judge, reflecting his family's distinguished centuries-long juridical service for his tribe (*Kebetias*). Cadi was an outstanding student who earned a scholarship. This led him to the Ecole Polytechnique in Paris. He was the first Algerian to be admitted to that prestigious institution. In 1889, he became a second lieutenant in the artillery. He became a French citizen and was promoted eventually to the rank of lieutenant-colonel. During World War I he fought at Verdun and served as a military adviser to Amir Ali, a son of Sharif Husayn (Hussein). (He received the honorific title "Hadj" for his pilgrimage.) He remained a Muslim in religion but a fervent Frenchmen. He published a book entitled *Terre d'Islam* in 1925.

CAMUS, ALBERT (1913–1960). Writer. Camus was born in Mondovi. His writings emoted the "Mediterranean sensibility" of settler culture. Among his most famous novels are *The Stranger* (1942), *The Plague* (1947), and *The Fall* (1957). His essays include *The Myth of Sisyphus* (1942) and *The Rebel* (1951). He also wrote short stories. Camus received the Nobel prize for Literature in 1957.

Besides his literary output, Camus was politically engaged in Algerian and French affairs (even briefly associating himself with the PCA [q.v. Algerian Communist Party; Amar Ouzegane]). Before World War II he excoriated the colonial government concerning the condition of the colonized in Kabylia. During the Liberation of France, he worked for the French Underground and edited *Combat*. Camus's works associated him with the French existentialists. He broke, however, with Jean-Paul Sartre after the publication of *The Rebel*. Camus's criticism of ideology leading to nihilism, which was a theme in this book, would have direct application during the War of Independence. During the war, Camus urged moderation and understanding. (He proposed a federated Algerian association.) Finding few on both sides who subscribed to his values or ideas, he went to France. He died in an automobile accident.

CANTONNEMENT. Policy favored by the *bureaux arabes* in the 1850s. It removed the seminomadic tribes from large areas of their former holdings and confined them to Arab-Berber reservations. The objective of this policy was to open Algerian lands to Europeanization. The policy was reversed by Napoleon III (q.v.), who attempted to halt the transfer of Muslim property to Europeans (q.v *Sénatus-consultes*). Unknowingly the Emperor's reforms merely replaced the communal lands with private ownership.

The term also applies to the rounding up of native populations by the French Army during the War of Independence in order to isolate ALN guerrillas.

CAPSIANS. An ancient people who occupied the area of Algeria as early as 6,000 B.C. They were Berbers (q.v.) who had adopted neolithic culture.

CARTHAGE. Located near Tunis, Carthage was Phoenicia's most renowned colony. It was established in the late ninth century B.C. The Phoenician Princess Elissa, or Dido, has been credited as the founder of the colony. The settlement eventually often conflicted with regional Greek colonies, but by the third century, the Carthaginians dominated the western Mediterranean. Carthaginian power spread to eastern Algeria (Numidia). Many of its mercenaries were native North Africans. Both the Mauretanians (q.v.) and the Massyli (q.v.) (q.v. Masinissa) were influenced by Carthaginian culture and agronomy.

Though maintaining its independence as a result of the disastrous Second Punic War, the city was destroyed in the Third Punic War (149–146 B.C.). Though rebuilt, the city never acquired its past political power and influence.

CASBAH (Kasbah or Qasba). The citadel or fortified seat of Turkish authority in the Regency (q.v.) of Algiers. It was also the site of the FLN redoubt during the famous "Battle of Algiers" (q.v.) in 1956–1957. The Casbah was built during the Regency (q.v.) and is renowned for its famous labyrinthine streets and alleys. Today it is seriously overcrowded. Its crumbling infrastructure needs vast attention and has resulted in protests in 1985 and 1989 (q.v. Algiers). It is estimated that there are 70,000 people living in its 1,700 buildings. Algerian authorities have viewed this old part of Algiers as a possible tourist attraction and have lobbied for international assistance (e.g., the United Nations's UNESCO in 1988). It is one of the most famous urban communities in the world.

CHAABANI, MOHAMED (d. 1964). ALN/ANP officer. Colonel Chaabani was a *wilaya* commander during the revolution. After independence he commanded the Fourth Military Region (Sahara). President Ahmed Ben Bella (q.v.) selected Chaabani to serve on the General Staff of the ANP to counterpoise Colonel Houari Boumedienne's (q.v.) power and ambition. Chaabani was also named to the Political Bureau and Central Committee of the FLN in 1964. This maneuver ultimately failed and Ben Bella found himself threatened. At the April 1964 Algiers Congress of the FLN, Chaabani spoke about the need to emphasize Islam's role in Algerian society. This was an implicit criticism of Ben Bella's government. In May Chaabani lost his command of the Fourth Military Region and was removed from the Political Bureau in June. The disaffected Colonel organized and led a revolt from Biskra (q.v.) against Ben Bella, who still faced Hocine Aït Ahmed's (q.v.) Kabyle (q.v.) insurgency. Chaabani was captured in July and executed for treason in September 1964.

CHAAMBA. A nomadic group of the Sahara. The Chaambas, in addition to the nomadic Berber Tuaregs (q.v.) and the sedentary Berber Ibadi (q.v.), are an important Arab group inhabiting the Sahara. The Chaambas are found particularly near Ouargla, Gharadaïa, and El Goléa. The Chaambas, like the Tuareg, are distinguished by their remarkable sense of orientation and direction in the desert. During the colonial period, many served the French as guides and soldiers.

CHALLE, MAURICE (1905–1979). French officer. General Challe was appointed commander-in-chief of French forces in Algeria in 1958 by Charles de Gaulle (q.v.). He effectively deployed airmobile tactics (''Challe Plan'') against the weary ALN (q.v.). Challe was reassigned to NATO in 1960 and then resigned in 1961. The Algerian experience had a profound effect upon this talented officer. With de Gaulle pursuing an inexorable decolonizing policy, Challe became increasingly concerned about Algerians who had been loyal to France (q.v. *Harkis*). He joined with Generals Raoul Salan, Edmond Jouhaud, and André Zeller in Algiers (q.v.) for an insurrection in April 1961. It failed to mobilize military and metropolitan support for the preservation of French Algeria and soon collapsed. Challe was arrested and eventually amnestied in 1968. Challe wrote *Notre révolte* (1968).

CHANDERLI, ABDELKADER (b. 1915). FLN (q.v) representative in the United States during the War of Independence. Chanderli was a veteran of World War II, having campaigned in 1940 and then joining the Free French. He was a journalist before the War of Independence and then worked for the United Nations's UNESCO program. Along with M'hamed Yazid (q.v.), Chanderli effectively promoted the FLN in the United Nations and in the United States. Chanderli influenced John F. Kennedy to speak before the Senate in 1957 on behalf of Algeria. He represented Algeria at the U.N. from 1962 to 1964 and then became director of the General Centre for Industrial Studies and Technology (Algiers).

CHAOUIA. Berber inhabitants of the Aurès (q.v.) mountains. The Chaouïa have maintained a strong ethnicity, given their situation in these remote, inaccessible, and even unapproachable mountains. They speak their own dialect. The Chaouïa are primarily pastoral in the south and sedentary in the north. Like their Kabyle (q.v.) "cousins," the Chaouïa place a great emphasis on family life. They reject polygamy, and women play an influential role within the family and Chaouïa society.

CHARLES V (1500–1558). Habsburg (Hapsburg) emperor (1519–1556). When confronting Ottoman control of the Mediterranean, Charles V targeted Algiers (q.v.). After obtaining French neutrality, Charles ordered Admiral Andrea Doria (q.v.) to attack in 1541. With an armada of more than 500 ships (galleys and transports) carrying approximately 37,500 soldiers and sailors, the assault force landed at the mouth of the Harrach River. The invaders secured the heights over the city. Nevertheless, stormy weather disorganized the attackers, and Turkish and allied Algerian counterattacks successively drove off the Habsburg forces. The Knights of Malta distinguished themselves covering the retreat. Another storm wracked the invasion fleet, destroying 140 ships. As the defeated Habsburgs embarked, the Turkish and Algerian forces celebrated a great victory. The Ottoman Regency's (q.v.) prestige was heightened given this triumph over Europe's most powerful ruler.

CHARLES X (1757–1836) (q.v. Introduction). Last Bourbon King of France (1824–1830). Charles X was embroiled in a commercial dispute with the Regency (q.v.), compounded by the fly whisk affront (when *Dey* Husayn [q.v.] slapped the French consul with a fly whisk). After a three-year blockade of Algiers, Charles ordered the invasion of Algeria in an effort, too, to shift his subjects' attention from his "ultra" conservative polices. Another explanation was his wish to reestablish a Christian presence in North Africa. Algiers was taken on July 5, 1830, but by the end of the month Charles was deposed and replaced by his cousin, Louis-Philippe (q.v.).

CHARTER OF ALGIERS. Promulgated at the April 1964 FLN (q.v.) Congress, it was a policy program that attempted to define the direction of Algeria's future. In general, this document elaborated upon the ideas of the Soummam Conference (q.v.) and the Tripoli Program (q.v.) of June 1962. It reaffirmed that Algeria would follow policies based on scientific socialism (in part through the pursuit of *autogestion* [q.v.]). Arabization would be pursued systematically. Although the Charter was heavily imbued with Marxism discourse (e.g., class struggle), Algeria affirmed its strong attachment to Islamic beliefs. Nevertheless, the Charter blueprinted a statist system under the control of the FLN as the sole ''avant-garde'' party, controlling political, economic, and social affairs.

CHERCHELL (SHARSHAL). Known as Iol by the Carthaginians, it was renamed Caesarea in honor of Augustus by Cleopatra Selene (the daughter of Antony and Cleopatra) and Juba II. Caesarea eventually became the splendid capital of the Roman (q.v. Rome) province of Mauretania. The city suffered severe damage in 373 during Firmus's rebellion (q.v. Berbers). Under the Byzantines, Cherchell regained some of its splendor and significance. It was occupied by the Arabs by about the tenth century. Andalusian refugees also settled in Cherchell. The Marinids seized it in the fourteenth century and Khayr al-Din (q.v.) took it over in 1518. Andrea Doria (q.v.) destroyed part of the Algerian fleet there in 1531, but he could not disembark his troops. The city was also bombarded by Beaufort (1663) and Duquesne (1682). The French occupied it in 1840. The greater Cherchell area (the *daïra*) has a population of about 100,000.

CHEVALLIER, JACQUES (1911–1971). Deputy and especially Mayor of Algiers (1953–1958) (q.v.) during the War of Independence. Chevallier also served as minister for national defense in the Mendès-France government. Chevallier was a liberal who was particularly respected by the Muslim population and opposed by powerful colonialist conservatives. After independence he still served in Algiers's Chamber of Commerce.

ECH-CHLEF (EL-ASNAM/ORLEANSVILLE). City of the interior, about half way between Algiers and Oran and which the French called Orléansville during the colonial period. (It was founded by Marshal Bugeaud [q.v.] in 1843.) El-Asnam was the site of severe earthquakes in 1954, 1980, and 1982. Its population was numbered at 118,996 in 1983.

CINEMA. Algeria cinema has reflected many of the literary themes (q.v. Literature) of heroism, disillusionment, socialism, Islam, rural versus urban values, and so on. Algeria ranks as one of the greatest producers of films within the Arab world. During the War of Liberation, the GPRA produced *L'Attaque des mines de l'Ouenza* (1957) and *L'Algérie en flammes* (1960). Among the most significant directors and productions are: Mohamed Lakhdar Hamina (b. 1934), *Le Vent des Aurès/Assifat al-Aaouras/Wind from the Aurès* (1965–1966), honored at Cannes in 1966 with the "Award for First Feature"; *Décembre* (1972); *Chronique des années de braise/Waqail Sanawat al-Jamr/Chronicle of the Years of Embers* (1975), honored with a Palme d'Or (Grand Prize) at Cannes in 1976; Ahmad Rachedi (b. 1938), *L'Aube des damnés/Dawn of the Damned* (1965); *L'Opium et le Bâton/Al-Afyoun wal-'Asa/The Opium and the Baton* (1970); *Ali au pays des mirages/Ali in the Country of Mirages* (1978); Merzak Allouache (b. 1944), *Omar Gatlato*; *Al-Tahouna/The Mill* (1985); Mustafa Badie (b. 1928), *La Mort de Hassan Tero/The Death of Hassan Tero* (1974);

Mughamarat Zaim/Adventures of a Hero (1978); Moham-med Bouamari (b. 1941), *Le Charbonnier/The Coal-man* (1972); *L'Héritage* (1974); Mohamed Slimane Riad (b. 1932), *La Voie/The Way* (1968); *Le Vent du Sud/Ryah al-Janoub/Wind from the South* (1975); Sid Ali Mazif (b. 1943), *Sueur noire* (1970); *Les Nomades* (1975); *Leïla et les autres/Leïla and the Others* (1977); Tayeb Mefti, *'Urs Moussa/Wedding of Moussa* (1982); Ali Ghalem (b. 1943 and lives in France), *L'Autre France*; *Zawja li Ibni/A Wife for My Son*; and the *Beur* directors Mehdi Charef, *Le Thé au Harem d'Archimède* (1986); *Camomille* (1988); and Rachid Bouchareb (b. 1953), *Baton Rouge*. (Isabelle Adjani, a *Beur*, is one of France's greatest actors.) In October 1987, Rabah Laradji's, *Massinnissa* received first prize at the International Film and Archaeological Society's meeting in Algiers. Assia Djebar (q.v.), the famous novelist, has also distinguished herself directing the film *La Nouba des femmes du Mont Chenoua* (1979) and *Zerda et les chants de l'oubli* (1982).

CLAUZEL, BERTRAND (1772–1845). French officer and ad-ministrator. Clauzel volunteered for service in 1791, and he was a general by 1802. He participated in all the major campaigns and supported Napoleon during the Hundred Days. He was exiled to the United States but was allowed to return. In 1830 he returned to the service and replaced Bourmont (q.v.) as French commander in Algeria. Clauzel was promoted to marshal in 1831 and was appointed governor-general of Algeria in 1835. Clauzel established a "model farm" near Algiers, disclosing his interest in agricultural colonization. He was recalled to France after his defeat before Constantine in 1836.

CLEMENCEAU REFORMS (q.v. Jonnart Law). Georges Cle-menceau was inclined toward reform in Algeria. In 1908 Prime Minister Clemenceau permitted Muslims to elect their members to department general councils. In 1916 the presidents of the Senate and Chamber of Deputies Committees of Foreign Affairs, Georges Clemenceau and Georges Leygues, co-wrote a letter proposing a program of reforms. These proposals included naturalization to French citizenship without loss of Muslim status; extension of Muslim participation in political assemblies (including a presence on the *Conseil supérieur* in Paris; termination of discriminatory Muslim taxes (*impôts arabes*); and Muslim property protection. When Clemenceau became premier in 1917, he aimed to enact this program because he was particularly conscious of the sacrifices of the colonized during World War I and of the impending serious discontent within Algeria. Reappointing Charles Jonnart (q.v.) as governor-general to assist in implementing reforms, Clemenceau initiated the legislative process. In June 1918, the extraordinary Muslim taxes were abolished, and in August Muslims were given authority over communal and village properties through tribal and local assemblies (*jama'a*). The most important initiative was the passage of the Jonnart Law (q.v.) of February 1919. It allowed educated Algerians to obtain French citizenship provided, however, that they would abandon personal status under the Muslim civil law. Few Algerians were willing to make this concession. The Muslim electorate was expanded to about 425,000 voters. Muslims were given one-quarter of the seats in the *Conseils Généraux* (q.v.), and allowed colonized members of *Conseils Municipaux* (q.v.) to vote in mayoral elections. These measures were resisted by the settlers (Eugène Etienne [q.v.]). The reforms did not immediately threaten their entrenched position, but they deepened Muslims' dissatisfaction with the *métropole*'s political sensibility and resolve.

CODE DE L'INDIGENAT. Law code for the colonized Muslims who had not become naturalized Frenchmen. This system was imposed in 1881 and was characterized by arbitrary punishments for a wide variety of offenses. Its application was clearly discriminatory and became the target of the Young Algerians (q.v.) and other Muslim activists. It was somewhat tempered in 1914 and 1919 (q.v. Clemenceau Reforms; Jonnart Law). The Code (or sometimes called the *Indigénat*) remained in effect until Charles de Gaulle's (q.v.) Ordinance of March 7, 1944 (q.v.). Summary justice was again applied during the War of Independence.

COMITE DE COORDINATION ET D'EXECUTION (CCE) (q.v. Appendices). This was the executive body of the FLN (q.v.) created in 1956 at the Soummam Conference (q.v.) to manage the party's affairs between meetings of its legislative body, the CNRA (q.v.). It had five members in 1956 and it was increased to nine the following year. It was the CCE that ordered the urban terrorism which led to the Battle of Algiers (q.v.).

COMITE INTERMINISTERIEL DES AFFAIRES MUSULMA-NES (CIAM). Interministerial Committee on Muslim Affairs, an organization created in 1919 to help coordinate policies toward Muslim subjects. It was generally ignored.

COMITE NATIONAL DE LA REVOLUTION ALGERIENNE (CNRA). This was a body created by the Soummam Conference (q.v.) and meant to serve as a parliament for the revolutionary organization. The FLN's (q.v.) primary authority rested in the CNRA. Between meetings of the CNRA, the CCE (*Comité de Coordination et d'Execution*) (q.v.) exercised supreme authority.

COMITE NATIONAL POUR LA DEFENSE DE LA REVOLU-TION (CNDR). Opposition groups formed in the summer of 1964 by combining the PRS (q.v.) and the FFS (q.v. Hocine Aït Ahmed). Arrests followed the announcement of the organization of the CNDR, including "Liberals" like Ferhat Abbas (q.v.) and Abderrahmane Farès (q.v.) and suspected pro-(Mohammed) Khider (q.v.) sympathizers, including Commander Azzedine (q.v.) (Rabah Zerari), and deputies, presumably protected by parliamentary immunity, Boualem Oussekik, Brahim Mezhoudi, and others. While Ahmed Ben Bella (q.v.) survived the challenge to his authority, which the CNDR represented in the summer of 1964, his position remained unstable.

COMITE REVOLUTIONNAIRE D'UNITE ET D'ACTION (CRUA). Revolutionary group. The CRUA broke from the divisive MTLD (q.v.) struggle between the "Centralists" and "Messalists" in the spring of 1954. Initially aspiring to resolve the fractured Messalist movement, CRUA members soon pursued their own course. Many of the members were former OS (q.v.) operatives. A Committee of Twenty-Two (q.v.) was established under the leadership of Mohamed Boudiaf (q.v.), which eventually selected a leadership team that would be known as the "historic chiefs" (q.v.) who continued to plan for armed revolution. After the coordinated attacks on October 31 to November 1, the CRUA became known as the FLN (q.v.).

COMMITTEE OF TWENTY-TWO (q.v. Appendices). A group of nationalists and operatives who met near Algiers in June or July 1954. Their leaders were the six internal members of the "historic chiefs" (q.v. Historic Leaders) (Mohamed Boudiaf [q.v.], Mostefa Ben Boulaïd [q.v.], Mourad Didouche [q.v.], Belkacem Krim [q.v.], Rabah Bitat [q.v.], and Larbi Ben M'Hidi [q.v.]). Scholars argue about whether the original CRUA (q.v.) or the Committee of Twenty-two organized the revolution. The Committee agreed that an armed revolution should be pursued until the country freed itself from French colonialism.

COMMUNE DE PLEIN EXERCISE. A form of municipal government introduced into Algeria by the French in 1834 and modeled on the French "commune," having an elected mayor and council. In these municipalities, Muslim Algerians were subjected to local justices of the peace.

COMMUNES MIXTES. Municipal government under the French occupation introduced as early as 1868 into those areas that had formerly been under military occupation. These were administered by appointed agents of the governor-general and assisted by commissions. In 1881 the judicial authority formerly held by the justices of the peace were transferred to appointed French officials who held broad discretionary powers (q.v. *Code de l'Indigénat*).

CONGRES MUSULMAN ALGERIEN (q.v. Algerian Muslim Congress).

CONSEIL CONSULTATIF NATIONAL (CCN). A consultative body of 60 members called for by a February 1992 decree by High Council of State (HCS) President Mohamed Boudiaf (q.v.), which was inaugurated in April 1992. The selection process for its membership surveyed candidates in a variety of professions from all over Algeria. Redha Malek (q.v.) became the first president of the CCN. Though it replaced the suspended Assemblée Populaire Nationale (APN), as of this writing, the CCN has no legislative function.

CONSEIL SUPERIEUR DU GOUVERNEMENT. Assembly during the period of French control over Algeria, established by a decree of August 23, 1898. It was composed of high administrative officials and elected and appointed persons. Of the 60 members, 22 were administrators, 31 were elected by the *Délégations financières* (q.v.) or the *Conseils généraux* (q.v.), and seven were appointees of the governor-general. It included only seven Algerian Muslims, four elected by the Muslim section of the *Délégations* and three appointed by the governor-general.

CONSEILS GENERAUX. A parliamentary body at the departmental level of colonial Algeria. After 1855, Algerian representatives were appointed to these *conseils,* but they were always in the minority.

CONSEILS MUNICIPAUX. Municipal councils in colonial Algeria. As early as 1847, Algerians were represented on these councils, although they were always in a minority and they were generally appointed by French authorities. In contrast, the European settlers on the councils were elected and were guaranteed a majority of the seats.

CONSTANTINE. A major city of Algeria located 330 miles east of Algiers (q.v.). Built on a rocky plateau marked on the northeast, northwest, and southeast by deep ravines (cut by the Rhumel [Rummel] River), the city is on a site that serves as a natural bastion.

Roman writers mention the existence of a town named Cirta, evidently of Carthaginian origin. (There is also evidence of prehistoric neolithic culture at Constantine.) At the time of the Punic wars it was the capital of Numidia (q.v.). The town was seized by the Romans (q.v. Rome) during the first century B.C. Emperor Maxentius had Cirta razed in 311 when it supported the usurper Alexander. Constantine rebuilt it in 313, and it was renamed in his honor. Constantine was captured at the time of the Vandal invasion, but it was returned to the Emperor in 442 by Gaiseric (q.v.). After the fall of Rome, Constantine became independent until the Byzantines (q.v.) captured it in 533. It probably fell to Arab conquerors during the seventh century.

The town was loyal to the Almohads (q.v.) until the breakup of the Empire when it recognized the authority of the Hafsid Abu Zakariya. During the fifteenth century the town was under the control of a few strong families. Not until 1534 did the Turks secure firm control of the city. Revolts against Turkish rule occurred in 1567, 1572, and 1642.

During the eighteenth century, it was the object of a major rebuilding program by the Turkish rulers (*beys*). A period of disruption followed, and 17 *beys* ruled during the period from 1792 to 1826. The last bey of Constantine, Ahmad (q.v.) was formally deposed by decree of French General Bertrand Clauzel (q.v.) in 1830; however, the French were unable to enforce it until the siege of 1837. Due to its intransigence, the town remained under French martial law until 1848.

Charles de Gaulle (q.v.) announced in Constantine reform measures for Algeria in December 1943 and in October 1958 (q.v. Constantine Plan). In November 1986 riots broke out in Constantine caused by student protests over campus conditions and examination changes. This resulted in four dead and 186 jailed. Constantine's population was recorded as 448,578 (1983).

CONSTANTINE PLAN. French reform effort announced by Charles de Gaulle on October 3, 1958, in Constantine as a nonmilitary means of gaining Algerian support. It proposed: (1) raising salaries and benefits to metropolitan levels; (2) new housing units to accommodate 1 million persons; (3) jobs for 400,000; (4) the matriculation of two-thirds of school-age Algerian children within five years (100 percent in eight years); (5) the distribution of 250,000 hectares to Muslims; (6) more civil service posts reserved for Muslims; (7) and industrialization (especially in hydrocarbons sector).

The Constantine Plan was significantly influenced by the Maspétiol Report (q.v.), the Frappart Report (q.v.), and the *Perspectives décennales* (q.v.). While its objectives were not all met, there were improvements in infrastructure, soil conservation, hydroelectric production, and industrial and housing construction. The Constantine Plan also acted as an instrument of transition, which enabled France to assume the role of "cooperator" (q.v. Cooperation) for that of colonialist after independence. The Evian Accords (q.v.) stipulated a continuation of Constantine Plan assistance.

CONSTITUTION OF 1963. It was ratified by 96.8 percent of the voters in the September 8, 1963, referendum. The Constitution oriented most power toward the presidency. It reaffirmed the revolutionary commitment to the anti-imperialist struggle and *autogestion* (q.v.). The FLN (q.v.) was declared the only legal party. Arabic was declared to be the official language and Islam, of course, the official religion. The National Assembly was regarded as fundamentally subordinate to the presidency. The Constitution reflected the growing authoritarianism in Algeria and specifically the presidential ambitions of Ahmed Ben Bella (q.v.).

CONSTITUTION OF 1976. This Constitution reaffirmed Algeria as an Islamic and socialist state. The FLN (q.v.) remained the sole legal party. Its Political Bureau and Central Committee were charged with preparing legislation for a new representative body called the *Assemblée Populaire Nationale* (APN) composed of 261 members (elected from slates of candidates selected by the FLN). While the APN had stipulated powers, the real political power remained in the presidency. The president's cabinet was not responsible to the APN. The president could govern by ordinance. He was also the secretary-general of the FLN. While civil and political freedoms were ideally guaranteed by this document, in reality, Algeria remained an authoritarian state with a strong executive that did not have to share power. The Constitution gave President Houari Boumedienne (q.v.) a legitimacy that he did not possess before, given his coup in June 1965 (q.v.).

CONSTITUTION OF (FEBRUARY) 1989. The Constitution was a direct consequence of the October 1988 riots (q.v.). In November 1989, the shaken government of President Chadli Benjedid (q.v.) already had amended the Constitution of 1976 (q.v.), making the cabinet responsible to the *Assemblée Populaire Nationale* (APN). The Constitution of 1989 would be profoundly different from the Constitutions of 1963 and

1976 (q.v.). By the new Constitution, Algeria now defined itself as a "democratic and popular" republic and did not include the word "socialist." Algeria's Islamic character was underscored reflecting the growth of the Islamist movement in the 1980s (q.v. *Front Islamique du Salut*). The FLN was not even mentioned; indeed, a multiparty state was projected. Human and civil rights were included, though the new Constitution did not mention women's rights (unlike the 1976 document). This document was meant to be a vehicle toward reform. In July, legislation established the format for Algeria's new political pluralism. Other legislation created new electoral laws and permitted free expression, which quickly produced a variety of new publications (q.v. Appendices).

COOPERATION (*Coopération*) (q.v. Charles de Gaulle; Constantine Plan; Emigrant Labor, Hydrocarbons; Introduction). The name for postcolonial French aid policies and programs. Cooperation was also stipulated within the Evian Accords (q.v.). The national self-determination referendum (July 1, 1962) called for independence with cooperation. It remains a fundamental principle in French-Algerian relations. Technical (training) and cultural (teaching) cooperation has been especially important to independent Algeria (e.g., Conventions of 1966/1986; establishment of a variety of institutes for training [*formation*]). Cooperation was supplanted briefly (1981–1984) by the concept of "codevelopment" (a more planned or accommodating cooperation) during the Mitterrand (q.v.) presidency. Algeria has also pursued its own cooperation policies with other countries.

COUNCIL OF THE REVOLUTION. An institution created after the Houari Boumedienne (q.v.) coup of June 1965 (q.v.) to replace the National Assembly and the Political Bureau (q.v.) of the FLN (q.v.). The Constitution of 1963 (q.v.) was suspended. This Council was to function as the "supreme authority of the revolution" until the formulation of a new constitution (eventually the Constitution of 1976 [q.v.]). At first it was composed of 26 members but eventually reduced to nine by 1976.

COUP OF JUNE 19, 1965. On June 19, 1965, a group led by Colonel Houari Boumedienne (q.v.) arrested President Ahmed Ben Bella (q.v.) and in a bloodless coup took over power. The stated purpose of this "revolutionary readjustment" was to put an end to Ben Bella's personal rule and to place priority instead on Algeria's need for economic development. Boumedienne's regime projected the disciplined internalization of the revolution and its consolidation through planned programs (q.v. State Plans) and rejected the spontaneity and externalization that had characterized Ben Bella's government.

The coup was particularly provoked by Ben Bella's attempts to bypass the Political Bureau and especially to neutralize the influence of Boumedienne. The new government gave the impression of being one of collegial rule as the executive government was theoretically the new Council of the Revolution (q.v.).

CREMIEUX DECREE (q.v. Jews). A law of October 24, 1870, whereby the French government conferred French citizenship upon approximately 35,000 Algerian Jews. This was opposed by many European settlers. It also reinforced the isolation of the Muslims in Algeria. The Decree was abrogated by the Vichy (q.v.) government and reinstated when Algeria was liberated.

CULTURAL REVOLUTION. A Cultural Revolution was proclaimed in 1971. It demonstrated that Houari Boumedienne's (q.v.) regime believed that the objective of "state-building" was not only tangible but also intangible: mentalities needed liberation. This meant a concerted commitment toward Arabization (q.v.) of Algerian culture and particularly language. Nevertheless, by the end of the decade, Arabization was slowed, and in 1980, Berbers (q.v.) demonstrated against its imposition upon their culture. There were appeals also within the FLN for more sensitivity to Algeria's non-Arab population. In the early 1980s, the idea of a pluralist identity began to be expressed, though Arabism received a powerful boost by the end of the decade with the emergence of Islamist opposition parties (especially the *Front Islamique du Salut* [q.v.]).

Though the revolutionary discourse of the Boumedienne era was dropped during President Benjedid's presidency, the cultural self-exploration of Algeria continued to be promoted. This was seen in the convocation of historical seminars and conferences. The "Memorial to the Martyr" (92 meters/302 feet) towering over Algiers includes a museum dedicated to the history of the nation. The "enriched" National Charter (q.v.) that was published in January 1986 also included a large section entitled "The Historical Foundations of Algerian Society." This section disclosed the "constants" in Algerian history, such as resistance to foreign forces dating back to Masinissa (q.v.) and Jugurtha (q.v.). The repatriation of the "national archives" from France emerged as a contentious bilateral issue underscoring the growing role of history in Algerian cultural affairs.

The Arabization Law of December 1990 projected the complete use of the language in official proceedings and documents and higher education by the end of the century. It received intense criticism from Berbers and from the Francophone population (many of whom are Kabyles [q.v.], and also the emigrant community, i.e., the *Beurs* [q.v. Emigrant Labor]). Indeed, the appropriation of Algiers's Francophone Lycée Descartes in 1988 was a highly charged event underscoring the inherent problems of a policy that has at times disclosed insensitivity toward Algeria's pluralist cultural legacy.

DAHLAB, SAAD (b. 1919?). Nationalist; minister; ambassador; industrialist. Dahlab attended the lycée at Blida and eventually became a member of the PPA (q.v.) and served for a time as Messali Hadj's (q.v.) secretary. Promoted to membership in the Central Committee of the MTLD (q.v.), he opposed Messali. Arrested by the French authorities in November 1954, he was freed in April 1955 and quickly joined the FLN (q.v.). He was elected to the CNRA (q.v.) and to the CCE (q.v.) in August 1956. He lost his seat on the CCE in 1957. Dahlab rose gradually within the GPRA (q.v.), becoming minister for foreign affairs in 1961 under his close colleague, President Ben Youssef Ben Khedda (q.v.). He was one of the chief negotiators at Evian (q.v. Evian Accords) (including secret negotiations with Louis Joxe [q.v.] in January 1962) and the Algerian ambassador to Morocco after independence. He then took on the industrial position of director of Berliet-Algérie.

DANSER, SIMON (fl. early seventeenth century). Sailor born in Flessingue, Holland. He arrived in Marseilles early in the seventeenth century. Having begun a flourishing Mediterranean trade, he moved to Algiers in 1606 and became a corsair captain. In three years he captured more than 40 Christian vessels under the title ''Captain Devil.'' For returning a group of captured Spanish Jesuits to the French King Henry IV, he was acquitted of his crimes against France and was allowed to return to Marseilles in 1609. In gratitude, Danser gave the duc de Guise two brass cannons that actually had been loaned to him by the Turkish Regency (q.v.). When de Guise refused to return the cannons, war broke out between France and Algiers. Marseilles's commerce particularly suffered as a result of this protracted conflict (peace reached in 1628).

DARQAWA (DARKAWAH/DERKAWA). An Islamic Order founded in northern Morocco in the late eighteenth century by the Idrisid *sharif* Sidi Mulay al-Arabi al-Darkawi of Fez, though its doctrine was first promulgated by Ali ibn Abd al-Rahman al-Jamal. The order promoted the practice of frequent prayers in its meeting places. The membership is still concentrated in north and eastern Morocco and western Algeria (especially in the Ouarsenis [mountainous region in western Algeria]). The order has been involved occasionally in the politics of the region. Ibn al-Sharif led a rebellion against the Turks in Oran province from 1803 to 1809. Members of the Order accused Abd al-Qadir (q.v.) of collusion with the French for his treaties (i.e., Desmichels [1834] [q.v.] and Tafna [1837] [q.v.]). In 1864, the Darqawa leadership refrained from encouraging attacks on the French (during the Awlad Sidi Shaykh [q.v.] insurgency). By the end of the nineteenth century, the Order numbered about 14,500 members in Algeria. The Algerian membership resigned themselves to the French, unlike their Moroccan brethren.

DAWAIR. A tribal group of families attached to a chief. Before the French conquest, the term applied especially to four groups attached to the Bey of Oran. Organized as militia, they lived off the land put at their disposal by the Turks, drawing spoils from revolting tribes. The tribe split between Abd al-Qadir (q.v.) and the French during the early 1830s. The assassination in 1843 of their leader, Mustafa ibn Ismail, brought to an end their greatest power.

DEBAGHINE, LAMINE MOHAMMED (b. 1917). Minister. Born in Cherchell (q.v.) and educated as a doctor, Debaghine joined Messali Hadj's (q.v.) PPA (q.v.) in 1939. He opposed the Nazis, but he refused service in the French Army during World War II. During World War II he worked secretly for the PPA (q.v.) and helped draft Ferhat Abbas's (q.v.) "Manifesto of the Algerian People" (q.v.). One month before the Sétif massacre (q.v.) Debaghine proposed an armed insurrection.

Debaghine was a deputy in the French National Assembly form 1946 to 1951, was removed from the MTLD (q.v.) in 1949, and was asked in 1954 to participate in the insurrection as the head of the FLN (q.v.). He sympathized with the idea of armed revolution but refused at that time. Nevertheless, he later joined the FLN and served on the CNRA (1956) (q.v.) and CCE (1957) (q.v.). He received the portfolio for Foreign Affairs in Abbas's first GPRA (q.v.) (1958–1960). He opposed Ferhat Abbas (q.v.), Abdelhafid Boussouf (q.v.), Ahmed Ben Bella (q.v.), and Mohamed Boudiaf (q.v.), thereby alienating himself ideologically and politically from several sides. Debaghine returned to practicing medicine after Algeria achieved independence.

DEBECHE, DJEMILA. Journalist. Born in Sétif, Debeche resided in France where she worked for the ORTF, the official French radio and television organization. She was a thoroughly acculturated Algerian who wrote numerous articles on education and on the social and professional situation faced by Algerian women. Between 1945 and 1947, she edited *L'Action*, a literary and artistic revue directed at women. She also published two novels, *Leila, jeune fille d'Algérie* (1947), and *Aziza* (1955), both of which reflected her interest in women's issues (q.v. Women).

DECATUR, STEPHEN (1779–1820). American naval officer. After his participation in the "quasi-war" with France (1798–1800), Decatur distinguished himself in the Barbary campaigns (Wars) (q.v.). In 1804, he led a small group of "commandos" and destroyed the captured *Philadelphia* at Tripoli. In the War of 1812, he defeated the British frigate *Macedonia* as captain of the *United States*. He was later captured by the British in 1815 when he tried to break the blockade. After his release, Commodore Decatur engaged an Algerian frigate on June 17 near Cape de Gatt and defeated it, killing *raïs* Hamidou (q.v.), one of the last effective

Algerian captains. Decatur then sailed to Algiers and forced the *Dey* to sign a treaty assuring safe passage for American ships.

DECLARATION OF THE SIXTY-ONE. With the escalating violence of the War of Independence as disclosed by the massacres at Philippeville (Skikda) and the terrible retribution by French forces (''collective responsibility''), Dr. Mohammed Saleh Bendjelloul (q.v.) called for a meeting of moderate (non-revolutionary) Muslim elected officials. They convened, passed a resolution, and signed a statement (September 26, 1955) calling for Algerian autonomy, which would allow Algerians to live their own lives. Among the supporters of this declaration were Ferhat Abbas (q.v.) and Ahmed Francis (q.v.), both of whom soon abandoned the search for moderate solutions and joined the FLN (q.v.). The declaration was a blow to the French government and ended the availability of moderate Muslim mediation between colonialists and revolutionaries.

DE FOUCAULD, CHARLES EUGENE (1858–1916). Officer; explorer; priest. This remarkable man has been called by Douglas Porch ''a modern-day Augustine'' (q.v.) (q.v. Bibliography). De Foucauld was a graduate of St. Cyr (1876) and the cavalry school in Saumur (1878). He at first led a dissipated and disorderly life. North Africa intrigued him, however, when he served with the *Chasseurs*. He left the Army and explored Morocco and the Sahara disguised as a servant of a rabbi. This journey resulted in his book *Reconnaisance au Maroc, 1883–84* (1888).

De Foucauld gained an intense appreciation of Islam, asceticism, and spirituality. He went to the Holy Land and entered a Trappist monastery. Though he eventually left the Trappists, he was ordained in 1901. He set up a hermitage at Beni-Abbis and in 1905 moved to his famous retreat at Assekrem in the desolate and awesome Ahaggar (Hoggar)

Mountains near Tamanrasset. This humble ascetic tried to convert the desert tribes by example, as a "universal brother" believing in charity and goodwill. He also learned the Tuareg (q.v.) language, which resulted in a French-Tuareg dictionary. Though he was highly respected by the desert tribes, he was murdered by marauding Tuaregs.

De Foucauld viewed his mission as spiritual, but he also symbolized a French presence in the Sahara. Beatification proceedings were begun in 1927.

DE GAULLE, CHARLES (1890–1970) (q.v. Introduction). French president. As leader of the *Comité Français de la Libération Nationale* during World War II (i.e., Free French), de Gaulle appreciated the support given to his movement by Africans (as viewed at Brazzaville in January-February 1944). Once Algiers was liberated, it became the capital of "Free France." de Gaulle issued his Ordinance of March 1944 (q.v.), which provided citizenship without the loss of Muslim status to approximately 50,000 Muslims and which terminated the *Code de l'Indigénat* (q.v.). Most historians believe that this assimilationist initiative no longer corresponded to the native elite's aspirations. Indeed, it was de Gaulle's provisional government that was in power during the severe repression at Sétif (q.v.) in May 1945.

Leaving the presidency of the provisional government in 1946, de Gaulle kept up his interest in Algerian affairs. He supported the Statute of 1947 (q.v.) but regretted that it was not implemented appropriately. De Gaulle became convinced, especially after the revolution began, that France and Algeria should have a redefined "association." He shared these thoughts privately and worded them publicly in a way that could be interpreted in various ways. When the Fourth Republic fell in May 1958, the Committee of Public Safety in Algiers (led by the military and influential European settlers [q.v. *pieds-noirs*]) called for de Gaulle to assume power.

De Gaulle became the last premier of the Fourth Republic and instituted reforms that established the Fifth Republic. His visit to Algiers in June 1958 featured his famous statement before the excited throng at the Forum: "Je vous ai compris" (I have understood you). To the *pieds-noirs* this indicated that de Gaulle understood that Algeria should remain French. De Gaulle had, however, another interpretation. It was a time to implement an associative relationship. When this failed, de Gaulle saw no other alternative but decolonization. De Gaulle, now as the French president (elected in January 1959 as the first Fifth Republic executive) faced settler unrest (January 1960) and outright military rebellion (April 1961), but he survived these crises as well as an assassination attempt (August 1962).

After Algeria gained its independence as a result of the Evian Accords (q.v.), de Gaulle inaugurated a period of generous "cooperation" (French aid programs) (q.v.). His government viewed Algeria as the "doorway to the Third World." Massive financial, cultural (educational), and technical assistance was given to the struggling new country. The highlight of this period was the conclusion of the Algiers Accord of 1965 (q.v. Hydrocarbons). By the time de Gaulle left office, Algeria was no longer as dependent upon France, and France was no longer dependent upon Algeria. France had gained prestige within the Third World and had significantly improved its relations with the Arab states.

Reda Malek (q.v.), Mahfoud Kaddache (q.v.), Mohamed Bedjaoui (q.v.), and Djamal Eddine Houhou (q.v.) participated at the colloquium commemorating the centenary of de Gaulle's birth (held in Paris, 19–24 November 1990).

DELAVIGNETTE REPORT OF 1955. Study made for the French Economic Council in July 1955. The report revealed the significantly unequal distribution of arable land in Algeria between settlers and Algerian Muslims. Of 15 million acres of arable land, 25,000 Europeans controlled

6,875,000 acres; 15,000 Muslims possessed 1,875,000 acres; and 500,000 Muslim owners held 6,250,000 acres. Additionally, the report demonstrated that the lands held by the settlers were the most fertile. In terms of industrial conditions, the report noted a distinct difference in the minimum hourly industrial wage between Algeria and France. The report asserted that French investments hardly affected the Muslim population.

DELEGATIONS FINANCIERES (Financial Delegations). Colonial institution established by decree of August 23, 1898. It consisted of an assembly under the control and direction of European settlers that performed certain budgetary tasks. It served as a settler-dominated check over the governor-generals. Representing interests rather than individuals, it was composed of three sections: 24 elected by landholding Europeans, 24 elected by Europeans in the cities, and 21 Muslims selected in various ways. Normally the three sections met and voted separately in a final plenary session. Sessions were not public until 1918, and even then, publication of the minutes was under the control of the governor-general. The *Délégations financières* symbolized settler political dominance in Algeria.

DE PAUL, VINCENT (1581–1660). Founder of the Congregation of the Mission (Lazarist/Vincentian Order). De Paul was ordained in 1600. Apocryphal stories of his own Barbary enslavement disclose his interest in North Africa and the physical and spiritual redemption of Christian captives. Consulates were purchased and handed over to the Lazarists (Algiers [1646] and Tunis [1648]). The arrival of the Lazarists and the papal appointment of the clerical consul as bishop and vicar of Barbary irritated Trinitarian, Mercedarian, and Capuchin orders. Nevertheless, the Lazarists also assumed particular risks. When Admiral Duquesne bombarded Algiers in 1683, the *Dey* Mezzo Morto (q.v. Husayn

Pasha) brutally executed the Lazarist Consul of France Père Vacher.

De Paul also served as chaplain general of the French galleys. He was canonized in 1737.

DERDOUR, DJAMEL (b. 1907). Nationalist. Derdour was born in Annaba (q.v.) and was educated as a dentist in Paris. He was a dedicated follower of Messali Hadj (q.v.). He was a leading PPA (q.v.) member of the AML (q.v.) and he contributed to the document «Appel aux Français» ("Appeal to the French") protesting the deportation of Messali and the harsh repression of the May (Sétif [q.v.]) riots of 1945. He was arrested but freed in time to be elected a deputy along with Lamine Mohammed Debaghine (q.v.) and Messaoud Boukadoum (q.v.). He became a leading member of the MTLD (q.v.). Derdour had mixed feelings toward an armed confrontation with the French.

DERRIDA, JACQUES (b. 1930). Leading deconstructionist philosopher. Born to a Jewish (q.v. Jews) family in El Biar, Algiers, Derrida left for Paris where he studied at the *Ecole Normale Supérieure*. From 1960 to 1964 he taught at the Sorbonne and from 1965 to 1984 at the *Ecole Normale*. His "poststructuralist," or "deconstructionist," methodology involves textual criticism and interpretation. He examines particularly the role of linguistics and philosophical presuppositions. These ideas became highly influential in Europe and the United States. Derrida's significant works include: *La Voix et le phénomène*; *L'Ecriture et la différence*; and *De la Grammatologie* in 1967; *Marges de la philosophie* (*Margins of Philosophy*); *Positions*; and *Dissémination* in 1972; *La Vérité en peinture* (1978); and *La Carte postale* (1980).

DESMICHELS, LOUIS-ALEXIS, BARON (1779–1845). French officer. Desmichels campaigned during the Revolutionary and Napoleonic wars and eventually became a member of the Imperial Guard. He commanded the French forces in Oran from 1833 to 1835, negotiating the "Desmichels Treaty" (q.v.) with Abd al-Qadir (q.v.) in 1834. Desmichels was appointed inspector general of cavalry in 1835, was promoted to lieutenant general the following year and reappointed inspector general of cavalry in 1836.

DESMICHELS TREATY OF 1834. An agreement concluded on February 26, 1834 between the commander of the French forces in Oran, General Louis-Alexis Desmichels (q.v.) and the Amir Abd al-Qadir (q.v.). It recognized the Amir's authority in the area of Oran (*Oranais*) (excluding the cities controlled by the French: Arzew, Mostaganem, and Oran). It also provided the Amir with arms to subdue those tribes that rejected his authority over them. Although the treaty was accepted by the French government, it was violated by Governor-General Marshal Bertrand Clauzel. (q.v.) The treaty was superseded in 1837 by the Treaty of Tafna (q.v.).

DEY. European title of the ruler of the Regency (q.v.) of Algiers (q.v.). The Deys of Algiers were generally elected by fellow Janissary officers. There was a succession of some 30 deys between 1671 and 1830. Nominal vassals of the Ottoman empire, deys in fact exercised virtually absolute power in the Regency (q.v.) and acted independently from their suzerains in Constantinople.

DIB, MOHAMMED (b. 1920). Novelist; poet. Dib was born in Tlemcen (q.v.) and is regarded as one of contemporary Algeria's greatest literary figures. His collective work is a chronicle of Algeria's decolonization and its search for a genuine national identity. Three of his novels, *La Grande maison* (1952), *L'Incendie* (1954), and *Le Métier à tisser* (1957), are particularly important because they mirrored what was happening in Algeria just before and during the

War of Independence. In the novels *La Danse du roi* (1968), *Dieu en Barbarie* (1970), and *Le Maitre de chasse* (1973), he provides a critical view of postcolonial identity. Among his other works are the novels: *Qui se souvient de la mer* (1962); *Cours de la rive sauvage* (1964); and *Habel* (1977). Among his poetic works are: *Ombre gardienne* (1961); *Formulaires* (1970); *Omneros* (1975); *Feu beau feu* (1979); and *O vive, Paris* (1987). According to Jean Déjeux (q.v. Bibliography), Dib's most fundamental theme is the need to realize common values and humanity.

After being forced to leave Algeria in 1959, he has lived in France. His international reputation earned him a visiting professorship to UCLA in 1974. Dib is a chief member of a great generation (q.v. Generation of 1954) of Algerian writers (e.g., Kateb Yacine [q.v.], Mouloud Mammeri [q.v.], Mouloud Feraoun [q.v.], and Malek Haddad [q.v.]).

DIDOUCHE, MOURAD (1922–1955). Revolutionary and "historic leader" (chief) (q.v.). Didouche was one of the principal planners of the revolution, earning him membership as one of the "historic leaders." He was the first revolutionary commander in the Constantine region. He was a member of the PPA (q.v.) beginning in 1945, a leader in the OS (q.v.), and an early opponent of Messali Hadj (q.v.) when the latter questioned the timing of an armed insurrection. Sought by the colonial police from 1950 on, he served as Mohamed Boudiaf's (q.v.) associate in France where, before the outbreak of the War of Independence, they organized Algerian workers in support of nationalist causes. He was killed in combat in Algeria while covering the retreat of an armed group that he had personally directed (January 1955). One of the most famous streets of Algiers is named after him (ex-rue Michelet).

DINAR (DA) (q.v. Appendices for dinar-dollar conversions). Introduced in 1963, it is the basic monetary unit of the

Algerian government. At that time it replaced the French franc at par value until the French devaluation of 1969 when it maintained its value. In January 1974, the Algerian government allowed the value of the dinar to ''float.'' In the late 1980s, the dinar's decline symbolized that of the Algerian economy. As part of the effort to liberalize the economy, the dinar was devalued by 22 percent in September 1991.

DINET, ETIENNE (Nasr-Eddine) (1861–1929). Writer. Born in Paris, Dinet emigrated to southern Algeria and wished to become Algerian. He settled in Laghouat, then in Bou Saada. In 1913, he converted to Islam and took the name of Nasr-Eddine. With his Algerian friend and mentor, Slimane Ben Ibrahim (q.v.), he collaborated on a number of works, among which were *Tableaux de la vie arabe* published in 1904 and *Khadra, danseuse des Ouled Naïl* in 1910. Dinet is considered a precursor of Algerian authors who wrote in French (as opposed to French authors who wrote about Algeria).

DJEBAR, ASSIA (Fatima Zohra Imalayen) (b. 1936). Writer; cinematist. Born in Cherchell (q.v.), Djebar interrupted studies at the Ecole normale at Sèvres to participate in the Algerian revolution. She wrote for *El-Moudjahid* and reported on the Algerian refugee situation. She continued her education at Tunis. Djebar taught at the University of Rabat (1959 to 1962) and served at the Faculté d'Alger. From 1965 to 1974 she lived in Paris before returning to Algeria.

Djebar's works particularly concern women. Her novels include: *La Soif* (1957), *Les Impatients* (1958), *Les Enfants du nouveau monde* (1962); *Les Alouettes naïves* (1967); *L'Amour, la fantasia* (1985); and *Ombre sultane* (1987). She also published *Poèmes pour l'Algérie heureuse,* a short story collection entitled *Femmes d'Alger dans leur appartement* (1980). Djebar has also distinguished herself in the theater and particularly in film, directing the award-winning *La Nouba des femmes du Mont Chenoua* (1979); and *La Zerda et les chants de l'oubli* (1982). She is interested in women's issues and their modern identity. She is also one of the few Algerian authors who have had their works translated into English (*A Sister to Scheherazade* [translation of *Ombre sultane*]; *Women of Algiers in Their Apartment*; and *Fantasia: An Algerian Cavalcade*).

DONATISM. Prominent North African Christian sect (regarded as a heresy by the Church). Donatism began in 312 over the election of Caecilian as bishop of Carthage (q.v.). The movement was named for Donatus, primate of Numidia (q.v.), who led opposition to Caecilian's election. In 321 Emperor Constantine granted toleration to the Donatists, but in 347 Emperor Constans exiled the group's leaders to Gaul. In 412 and 414, strict laws denied them ecclesiastical and civil rights. Augustine (q.v.) argued effectively against them and severely weakened the movement. Nevertheless, the arrival of Arian Vandals (q.v.) regenerated the Donatists. They survived in North Africa until the Arab invasions.

Donatists were among the most educated Romanized citizens of Numidia. They claimed that the validity of sacraments required that its ministers be in a state of sinlessness. The Church rejected this idea. This led to theological and often violent disputes between Donatists and Catholics/Orthodox. Since the Donatists opposed the official religion of the Empire, by projection, they also rebelled against its political authority. This made it appealing to the rebellious nature of the population (q.v. Berbers). Donatism was another cause of the decline of Roman power in North Africa.

DORIA, ANDREA (1466–1560). Genoese admiral. Doria owned his own fleet and served Francis I and Charles V. He attacked Cherchell in 1531 in an effort to free Christian slaves, but he sailed off quickly when Khayr al-Din's (q.v.) fleet approached. In general, he earned an excellent reputation as a sailor. He was most concerned about promoting Genoese interests.

DRAGUT (d. 1565). Famous sixteenth-century corsair leader. After gaining a reputation as a corsair captain, Dragut was inspired by the Barbarossa (q.v.) brothers' achievements in western Barbary. He managed to base himself in eastern Barbary (Mahdiya, i.e., in Tunisia), but he was forced out by the Spanish in 1550. Eventually, he pledged himself to the Ottomans and served as governor of Tripoli. Court politics prevented him from becoming Captain *Pasha* of the Ottoman fleet. He died in Malta.

DRAIA, AHMED (1929–1988). Revolutionary; CNS chief. A native of Souk Ahras, Draia joined the ALN (q.v.) early in the War of Independence. He spent two years in Tunisian prisons for his participation in an anti-GPRA (q.v.) conspiracy. By the time independence was achieved, he had been liberated and sent to the area bordering on Mali to help organize nationalist forces there. He joined the *Corps Nationale de Sécurité* (CNS) in 1963, and was named director of the presidency's security force in March 1965. In spite of efforts by Ahmed Ben Bella (q.v.), Draia remained close to Houari Boumedienne (q.v.). After the June 1965 coup, Draia became commander of the CNS (1965–1977). In 1977 he was tabbed as minister of transportation. Draia was also named to the Council of the Revolution (1978) and the Political Bureau of the FLN (q.v.). He was gradually removed from important positions within the FLN (e.g., Central Committee in 1983). After his years of domestic service, Draia entered the foreign ministry and held ambassadorial posts in Switzerland and Portugal.

DRIF, ZOHRA. ALN (q.v.) urban fighter. Drif, who had attended the Lycée Descartes, was famous as one of Yacef Saadi's (q.v.) "girls" who dressed as European women and then planted bombs during the revolutionary terrorism of the Battle of Algiers (1956–1957) (q.v.). She was arrested with Saadi on September 24, 1957 and condemned to 20 years of hard labor. (She was implicated in the bombing attacks of the "Milk-Bar" and the "Coq Hardi" in Algiers.) After the war she married Rabah Bitat (q.v.). Drif also has supported women's rights (q.v. Women).

DUVAL, LEON-ETIENNE (b. 1903). Archbishop of Algiers; cardinal. Cardinal Duval was ordained a priest in Rome in 1926. He became the bishop of Constantine and Hippo in November 1946. In 1954 he was elevated to the archbishop of Algiers.

During the War of Independence, Archbishop Duval called on both sides for justice, peace, and brotherhood. His willingness to help both sides made him suspect to the European settlers who criticized his positions. Archbishop Duval's aim was to perpetuate the Church in North Africa, which he did not equate with the preservation of French colonialism.

After Algeria gained its independence, Duval worked closely with the new government. Negotiations transferred abandoned Church properties to the Algerian state. The famed Ketchoua mosque that had been converted into a Christian church was returned to Islam. Catholic charities and schools also provided valuable assistance during those days of dislocation. In 1965 Archbishop Duval was named a cardinal by Pope Paul VI. During that same year he became an Algerian citizen. It was said that the Algerian (Muslim) government out of its deference for Duval suggested that he be elevated to that prestigious office.

Eventually the government took over Catholic schools, but the Church maintained a moral authority within the Muslim country. He was a founder of the *Ligue Algérienne des Droits de l'Homme* LADH. He has expressed his concern over the tragic violence committed against the emigrant worker community. In 1988 he retired to Notre-Dame d'Afrique (replaced by Mgr. Henri Teissier).

His homilies, speeches, and other statements have been collected in *Paroles de paix* (1955); *Messages de paix* (1962); and *Au nom de la vérité* (1982). His conversations with Marie-Christine Ray are in *Le Cardinal Duval: «Evêque en Algérie»* (1984).

EBERHARDT, ISABELLE (1877–1904). Writer. Eberhardt was a French writer of Russian birth who married an Algerian officer in the Spahis (a native corp), Sliman Ehni, and rode with his unit. She converted to Islam and idealized Arab culture and Muslim mysticism. (She called herself "Si Mahmoud.") She died in a flash flood at Aïn Sefra. Among her works, all published posthumously, are *Notes de route* (1908), *Dans l'ombre chaude de l'Islam* (1921), *Trimardeur* (1922), *Mes Journaliers* (1923), and *Contes et paysages* (1925). Along with Etienne Dinet (q.v.), she is considered a precursor of Algerian authors who wrote in French. In addition, her extraordinary independence has particularly interested researchers concerning feminists.

ECONOMY (q.v. Introduction; Agriculture; Hydrocarbons; State Plans).

EDUCATION. During the medieval period, cities such as Tahert (q.v. Rustamids), Tlemcen (q.v.), Algiers (q.v.), and Bejaïa (q.v.) distinguished themselves as centers of Islamic studies (q.v. Ibadism and Malikism). Great teachers included Sidi Bou Mediene in Tlemcen and Sidi Abd al-Rahman al-Tha'alibi (q.v.) in Algiers. Ibn Khaldun (q.v.) also taught and researched in several Algerian cities. The Turkish Regency (q.v.) promoted Hanafi studies complementing the traditional Maliki and Ibadi, underscoring the diversity of Islamic education in Algeria.

During the colonial period, Europeans received the benefits and opportunities of education. Significant early initiatives to educate the Muslims came from Napoleon III who had developed a romantic, sentimental attachment for the colonized. Koranic schools were reopened in military territories and numbered about 2,000 in 1963. There were 36 "Arabic-French" primary schools in 1870. A normal school opened in Algiers in 1865 with 20 French and 10 Muslim students. Several collèges were established as well as *médersas* (*madrasas*). In Kabylia, a technical and vocational school opened in 1868.

With the arrival of the Third Republic and the subsequent consolidation of colonialist civil authority, the colonized's education was purposely neglected. In 1882, there were only 16 primary schools open. Religious education was monitored. In 1890, 1.9 percent of the school-age population were in public or private schools. Only 776 students were in public secondary school in 1930. Concurrently at the University of Algiers, there were 92 native students out of a student body of 2,014. By 1954 more than 90 percent of the colonized were illiterate and only one out of 10 Muslim children went to school (q.v. Bibliography; see Charles-Robert Ageron, *Histoire de l'Algérie contemporaine* [1977] and *Histoire* [1979]).

Since independence, Algerian governments have allocated a very high percentage of budget funding toward education (usually about 25 percent). Consider these general changes in school-year enrollments from 1962–1963/1989–1990: Primary 800,000/5,500,000; higher 3,000/227,000 (adapted from EIU, *Country Profile* 1990/1991]). There are eight state universities and the Abd al-Qadir (Abdelkader) Islamic University in Constantine (opened in 1984). This educational commitment is one of the most impressive in the world. Illiteracy has plunged from 90 percent to 48 percent. Nevertheless, many educated Algerians cannot find employment, which has led to discontent and disillusionment.

Primary classes and most of the secondary classes have been Arabized. French is taught as a foreign language. The Arabization Law of December 1990 plans to "Arabize" higher education by the end of the century, but this seems unrealistic (q.v. Arabization) given Berber cultural resistance, recent political upheaval, and the continued use of French as a pragmatic means for technological transfer.

ELECTIONS OF 1948. These were the first elections under the new Statute of Algeria (q.v.), which had been devised largely on lines set by de Gaulle at the Brazzaville Conference during World War II. While the new law was supposed to reward the colonized for their participation in the war against Germany, the elections were so shamefully managed by the governor-general of Algeria that few nationalists were elected. These elections marked the end of a possible decolonization through French constitutional means.

ELECTIONS OF DECEMBER 1991. The first round of this national parliamentary election gave the FIS (q.v.) an astounding 188 seats, just 28 short of a majority in the future session of the *Assemblée Populaire Nationale* (APN). (The FFS [q.v.] gained 26 seats.) Though there were complaints of irregularities, the popular will (47.54 percent of the voters) preferred the FIS over the FLN (q.v.) and other "secular" parties. The inevitable FIS victory in the scheduled January 1992 second round provoked a coup against the administration of President Chadli Benjedid (q.v.) (January 11). The self-installed High Council of State (HCS) (q.v.) then annulled the results of the election and cancelled the second round despite the complaints of the FIS, the FFS, and even the FLN.

ELECTIONS OF JUNE 1990. The local elections of June 12, 1990, were the first free pluralist elections in Algeria's history. They resulted in the Islamist FIS's (q.v.) surprising success as they won 32 of 49 *wilayat* while obtaining 54 percent of the popular vote (28 percent for the ruling FLN [q.v.]). The city councils in all major Algerian cities were also gained by the FIS. In all, 850 out of 1,500 councils were gained by the FIS. Several secular parties decided not to participate in this election (notably the FFS [q.v.]), which resulted in part in a lower registered-voter turnout (60 percentile). Its victory underscored public dissatisfaction with the FLN and the popularity of the FIS's populist Islam.

ELECTIONS OF JUNE 1991. The promised national legislative elections of June 1991 (scheduled for two rounds: June 27 and July 19 runoff) were postponed as a result of violent protests over the electoral process (eleventh hour [April] gerrymandering by the FLN's *Assemblée Nationale Populaire*); these protests subsequently jeopardized Algeria's democratization and especially the FIS's political influence. The FIS called for a general strike on May 25 to protest the electoral law changes and to promote a presidential election. On June 4, police forces tried to dislodge Islamists who had occupied squares in Algiers, which resulted in 17 (official) deaths. On June 5, a state of siege was declared and the elections postponed. Sid Ahmed Ghozali (q.v.) replaced Mouloud Hamrouche (q.v.) as prime minister. A curfew was imposed. With peace restored on June 7, the FIS ended its call for a general strike after receiving assurances from Ghozali of national legislative and presidential elections by the end of 1991. Nevertheless, by the end of the month (June 25) fighting resumed. Abbasi Madani (q.v.) threatened "holy war" unless the state of siege was lifted. This provoked the government's arrest of Madani and his deputy, Ali Benhadj (q.v.) on June 30. The situation calmed and on September 29 the state of siege ended. On October 15, President Chadli Benjedid (q.v.) announced that the first round of national elections would take place in December (q.v. Elections of December 1991).

EMBAREK, DJILALI. Nationalist and unionist. A schoolteacher from El-Eulma, Embarek joined Messali Hadj's (q.v.) PPA and then became a member of the MTLD's (q.v.) central committee. He was treasurer of the MTLD when the French authorities arrested him in November 1954. Freed from prison in April 1955, he joined the FLN (q.v.) and helped create the UGTA (q.v.). He also helped organize the FLN Congress of 1964.

EMIGRANT LABOR. Given the paradoxes of colonialism, its social inequities (e.g., economic dispossession) contradicted by its improvements (health), Algerians who had lost land and competed for scarce and diminishing economic resources found themselves condemned to emigration. These emigrant workers risked tribal dishonor by leaving; however, there was no other choice besides joining the hundreds of thousands of unemployed or underemployed in Algeria. The European settlers regretted this loss of labor but generally ignored the harsh reality that the colonialist system excluded significant native economic participation. Though there were already several thousand Algerians working in France before World War I, their numbers swelled during the war. Besides providing soldiers, France imported about 120,000 Algerians to replace French workers sent to the front.

By 1948, there were 180,000 workers in France. By 1962, their number rose to 400,000. During the War of Independence, the FLN (q.v.) (through the FFFLN) confronted the MNA (q.v.) in an effort to gain the support of the community. On October 17, 1961, a dramatic march of 30,000 emigrants through the heart of Paris publicized their protest over their repression (within the community by French police) and their support of Algerian independence. A brutal suppression left two dead.

Since independence the emigrant community has been targeted with violence especially during times of crises or declining relations between Algeria and France. In September 1973, the Algerian government declared that it would stop emigration to France. Assaults and murders have remained commonplace. Furthermore, the hostility has also been directed against official institutions. French radicals bombed the Algerian Consulate in Marseilles in December 1973 (4 dead, 16 wounded) and gunned down an employee at the *Amicale des Algériens* office in Paris in December 1977.

With the French economy in stagflation during the late 1970s, the emigrant workers were blamed for taking work from the French. Legislation (Bonnet-Stoléru) aimed to provide a payment to the workers to return and threatened the nonrenewal of residence cards. In September 1980 both governments agreed upon a card renewal whereby cards would be renewed and a programmatic method of "reinsertion" with French help was instituted. The emigrant workers have also been allowed to join French unions and have received their support. The population of the Algerian community in France today is approximately 850,000 people.

The emigrant "second generation," or *Beurs*, have become a cultural and political force in France. Suspended between French and Algerian cultures, the *Beurs* have sought justice from France and understanding from Algeria. For example, they have been very active in the struggle against racism in France and have been very critical of Algeria's Arabization Law of 1990 (q.v. Cultural Revolution).

Algeria's hope to "reinsert" the community is illusory given its own economic problems. Many who have returned have had difficulties adapting to Algerian society. This is a particular problem with the youth. Nevertheless, if racism and discrimination continue to increase in France (as disclosed by Jean-Marie Le Pen's nativist *Front National* party) and other European countries (e.g., Germany), Algerians may be forced to return.

ETIENNE, EUGENE (1844–1921). Colonial deputy and senator; French minister. Etienne led the *Parti colonial,* which was a parliamentary bloc that fervently protected the colonial privileges of the settlers. To Etienne, colonialism was equated with the greatness of France.

Etienne was born in Oran and experienced settler frontier life. He moved to Marseilles and became involved with business interests there and in Oran, the city that he represented as a deputy (elected in 1881) in the French National Assembly. Etienne supported the *Code de l'indigénat* (1881) (q.v.), which reinforced his own prejudices toward native Algerians. He opposed the Jonnart (q.v. Clemenceau Reforms) Law of 1919 (q.v.).

Etienne was vice president of the Chamber of Deputies (National Assembly) in 1894, 1895, and 1902–1904. From 1887–1892, he held the position of secretary of state to the Ministry of the Navy and the Colonies. He also was minister of the interior in 1905 and minister of war in 1905–1906; 1913. He was elected to the Senate in 1920.

ETOILE NORD AFRICAINE (North African Star) (ENA). Algerian nationalist organization. This organization was founded in 1925 by members of the French Communist Party (PCF) who wanted to create a North African labor organization. Under the leadership of Messali Hadj (q.v.), the organization eventually evolved into an Algerian nationalist organization. The ENA's objective was to defend "the material, moral, and social interests of North African Muslims." From the beginning, the ENA demanded full independence of all North Africa (including Algeria, Tunisia, and Morocco). The organization was quickly controlled by Algerians, and other nationalities lost interest in it. The French government formally dissolved the ENA in 1929, and many of its members went underground. In 1933, the organization reappeared (*La Glorieuse Etoile Nord-Africaine*) and held a general assembly in France that passed resolutions on the details of independence. In 1934, the ENA was again reorganized under the name of the National Union of North African Muslims.

Messali was imprisoned for a year for "reestablishing a dissolved organization." After his release, he left for Switzerland where he became influenced by the ideas of Chekib (Shakib) Arslan (q.v.). Messali drew away from

Communism and became more closely identified with Pan-Arabism. Despite the initial favorable attitude of the Popular Front Government in allowing him to return to France in 1936, it dissolved the ENA in January 1937. It was succeeded by the PPA (*Parti du Peuple Algérien*) (q.v.), a clearly Algerian group.

EULJ ALI ('EULJ 'ALI; EULDJ ALI; KILIJ ALI). The last and possibly greatest *Beylerbey* (1568–1587). Eulj Ali was taken captive off the Calabrian coast and he converted to Islam, possibly to avenge himself upon a Turk who had abused him. He became a galley officer and then went privateering, serving Hassan Pasha (q.v.) (ibn, or son, of Khair al-Din) and Dragut (q.v.). He distinguished himself during campaigns at Mostaganem (1558) and at Malta (1565).

Eulj Ali was the *Pasha* (governor) of Tripoli before being named *Beylerbey*. He supplied the Morisco rebellion (1568–1571). The *Beylerbey* forced the Hafsids and the Spanish out of Tunis. In the spring of 1571, he participated at the capture of Cyprus from the Venetians. Having fought bravely at the Battle of Lepanto (October 9, 1571), he was made Captain *Pasha*. He delegated (through the *Odjak*) replacements in Algiers while he served the Sultan.

Eulj Ali forced the Spanish from Tunis in 1574 after Don Juan (King Philip's brother) had taken it the year before. He proposed the digging of the Suez Canal as a means to expand Ottoman power in East Africa and toward India. The Captain *Pasha* improved the port of Algiers and modernized the Ottoman fleet using the Algerian corsair as the model warship.

EVIAN ACCORDS. FLN (q.v.)-French accords signed on March 18, 1962, which stipulated a cease-fire and a process for Algerian decolonization. The accords had many chapters. It particularly defined a framework for Algeria's relations with the ex-*métropole* (q.v. Cooperation).

The Evian Accords ensured Algerian political independence while preserving a French presence through ''cooperation,'' which was initially and inevitably neocolonialist as demonstrated by the protection of investments (e.g., hydrocarbons [q.v.]) and the perpetuation of strategic interests (e.g., military bases). They began with a cease-fire, followed by introductory governmental declarations and five chapters complemented by corresponding declarations of guarantees and principles. Chapter I discussed the transition period and described the nature of the interim government, which reserved roles in it for Europeans besides Muslims. This provisional government's task was to organize the self-determination referendum. Algerian internal and external sovereignty was addressed in Chapter II. This chapter also introduced stipulations concerning the Europeans' future role in independent Algeria (detailed in the ''Declaration of Guarantees''). It also explained French-Algerian cooperation. Chapter III dealt with ''military questions.'' Overall, there would be a protracted disengagement from Algeria. Chapter IV asserted that any dispute would be approached by negotiation. According to Chapter V, if Algerian independence with cooperation was adopted, France would immediately recognize the new nation.

The negotiation was arduous. Leading the Algerian team was Belkacem Krim (q.v.). His counterpart was Louis Joxe (q.v.). Krim successfully defended the territorial integrity of Algeria. (The French threatened partition.) He also was able to prevent double-citizenship of the European settlers. Nevertheless, he did receive criticism by the FLN for permitting French military and nuclear bases. Furthermore, French petroleum companies were able to keep their ''Petroleum Code'' and operate quite freely in the Sahara.

Krim and others, including Ben Youssef Ben Khedda (q.v.), believed that the accords represented a ''compromise'' and that its stipulations could be negotiated again. What was important was to gain independence and to stop the violence. The intraelite dispute over the accords contributed to the brief intraelite conflict after the vote for self-determination.

Furthermore, the *Organisation de l'Armée Secrète*'s (OAS) (q.v.) operations and the settlers' reluctance to live in an Algeria governed by the FLN vitiated the stipulations and guarantees designed to protect the French community. The Evian Accords provided a framework for the postcolonial bilateral relationship, but as Ahmed Ben Bella (q.v.) noted in 1962 and even President Valéry Giscard d'Estaing (in February 1978), these agreements became anachronistic.

EXMOUTH EXPEDITION. A naval force brought to Algiers in August 1816 under the command of British Viscount Exmouth (Edward Pellew). When the *Dey* Omar refused to abide by the terms of the Congress of Vienna concerning slavery, Lord Exmouth's fleet effectively bombarded Algiers (August 27). This was done successfully because the British fleet had arrived in the harbor under a flag of truce, placing it in a strategic position to reduce Algerian positions. Though the *Dey* refused to capitulate, he was forced to negotiate. Exmouth dictated terms, including abolition of slavery, freeing of Christian slaves (approximately 1,200), and a 500,000 franc reparation. Janissaries plotted the death of the *Dey* a short time after this humiliation (January 1817).

FACI, SAID (b. 1880). Schoolteacher and moderate critic of French colonialism. Faci acquired his elementary teaching diploma in 1909. He joined the League of the Rights of Men and formed two organizations of teachers in Oran, the *Amicale des Instituteurs* and later in 1921, the *Association des Instituteurs d'Origine Indigère*.

Faci criticized the colonial establishment for preventing easier access to French citizenship. In addition, he advocated a greater role for native teachers in Algerian education. The League of the Rights of Men published Faci's *Le Statut Indigène en Algérie* (1919) and *Le Droit syndical et le statut des fonctionnaires* (1920). In his *Mémoires d'un instituteur algérien d'origine indigène* (Algiers; supplement to *La Voix des humbles*, no. 98, 1931), he described the suspicions of Europeans toward educated natives. In his *L'Algérie sous l'égide de la France* (1936), Faci promoted education for the Muslim masses and viewed native educators as interlocutors within colonial society.

FALAKI, REDA (b. 1920). Writer. Born in Algiers, his real name is Hadj Hamou. He authored *Le Milieu et la marge* (1964) and also distinguished himself as a playwright, as an advocate of Algeria's oral traditions, and as a writer of children's stories.

FAMILY CODE OF 1984. The difficulty in reconciling Western, modernist, and Islamic values in Algerian society was symbolized by the Family Code process. On three other occasions the Family Code had been shelved (1964, 1972, and 1980). It finally passed in 1984. It reinforced traditional Islamic law (*Shari'a*), which palliated Islamist concerns while disappointing feminists (q.v. Women) for its patriarchy (e.g., concerning marriages, divorces, inheritances).

FANON, FRANTZ (1925–1961). Psychiatrist; FLN (q.v.) activist; Third World ideologue. Born in Martinique, Frantz

Fanon was educated in Paris and became a practicing psychiatrist in Algeria (Blida). He sympathized with the FLN and became a contributor and editor to the nationalist newspaper *El-Moudjahid*. Fanon led several FLN diplomatic missions in Africa (e.g., inter-African congresses at Bamako and Cotonou). He was seriously injured along the Moroccan frontier when his vehicle struck a mine. Fanon was stricken with leukemia and died in Washington.

Fanon analyzed the effect of the imposition of colonialism upon the colonized. He perceived a "psychoexistential complex" among his native Antilleans. This complex involved identity and inferiority derived chiefly from economic inequality, racism, and cultural prejudice. During the War of Independence, Fanon applied these ideas and others in his writings. He viewed the violence of the revolution as cathartic because it physically and psychologically destroyed the colonial system. Violence mobilized and united the people. He also warned about the dangers of neocolonialism.

Fanon wrote: *A Dying Colonialism* (1959/1967), *Toward the African Revolution* (1964/1970), *The Wretched of the Earth* (1961/1968), and *Black Skin White Masks* (1952/1967). [Dates are those of original French publications and English editions.] Collectively, Fanon's writings provide a wealth of ideas on colonialism, decolonization, and post-colonialism. The attention given to his ideas on violent decolonization overlooks what Fanon fundamentally strove for: the realization and recognition of human dignity and equality.

FARES, ABDEL RAHMAN (ABDERRAHMANE) (1911–1991). Nationalist; Provisional Executive Council president. Born in Algiers, he eventually graduated from the University of Algiers and became a Muslim notary public. He ran for public office and served on the Algiers Municipal Council and in the Algerian Assembly. He was speaker of the latter body (1953–1956) and supported the "Declaration of the

Sixty-One'' (q.v.). A moderate, he served as an intermediary between the French and the FLN (q.v.) (1956–1961) until the French arrested him. In 1962, he was chosen president of the Algerian Provisional Executive Council, which was charged with facilitating the transition of power from colonial to independent Algeria. Farès tried to reconcile the settler and native communities. Nevertheless, the Provisional Executive's authority was moral rather than military. He established a private legal practice in Algiers in 1962, then was arrested for ''political reasons'' in 1964. He wrote a memoir entitled *La Cruelle vérité* (1982).

FARES, NABILE (b. 1940). Writer and son of Abderrahmane Farès (q.v.). He was an activist for the FLN during the war, but he settled in France after independence. Nabile's writings often express disillusionment with postcolonial Algeria. Among his novels are a trilogy (*Le Champ des oliviers* [1972]; *Mémoire de l'Absent* [1974]; *L'Exil et le désarroi* [1976]); *Yahia, pas de chance* (1970); *La Mort de Salah Baye ou la vie obscure d'un Maghrébin* (1980); and *Un Passager de l'Occident* (1971). His poetry includes *Chants d'histoire et de vie our des roses de sable* (1978) and *L'Etat perdu précédé du discours pratique de l'immigré* (1982).

FATIMID DYNASTY. North African Shi'i dynasty. The name Fatimid refers to Fatima, the wife of Ali, the fourth Caliph. Under the leadership of 'Ubayd ('Ubaid) Allah, an Isma'ili scholar from Syria, a dynasty was established in Tunisia that spread eastward and westward. Most of the propagation and proselytization was done by Abu Abd Allah al-Shi'a, an Isma'ili *da'i*, who converted the Kutama (q.v.), a Berber (q.v.) tribe of Lesser Kabylia (q.v.). The Aghlabid dynasty (q.v.) fell before the strength of the Kutama in 909.

Eventually, 'Ubayd Allah arrived in North Africa and joined (or may have been rescued by) Abu Abd Allah. 'Ubayd Allah proclaimed himself the Mahdi and the *Amir al-Muminin* (Commander of the Faithful). Nevertheless, Abu Abd Allah pressured 'Ubayd Allah to share power and even questioned the Mahdi's administration. On July 31, 911, by the orders of the Mahdi, Abu Abd Allah and his brother were executed.

'Ubayd Allah moved the capital to a new city called Mahdiya (in Tunisia). Fatimid forces reached Morocco and took over Sijilmasa. Expeditions were sent against Ceuta and Melilla and launched across the Mediterranean. Fatimid administration was generally oppressive to the Sunni majority, and this contributed to a great Zenata (q.v.) Berber threat led by the Khariji scholar Abu Yazid (q.v.).

Abu Yazid led a popular revolt that reached the walls of Mahdiya. The Caliph Abu al-Abbas Isma'il al-Mansur (q.v.) finally defeated Abu Yazid, who died from his wounds in 947. Under Caliph al-Mu'izz (r. 953–975) and his effective general Jawhar, Fatimid power was at its height extending westward to Fez, Tangier, and Ceuta. The enduring Fatimid ambition to conquer Egypt was also realized. Al-Mu'izz left for Egypt in 973 after Jawhar had established Fatimid there in 969. The Caliph left the Maghribi provinces to Bulukkin (q.v.) of the Zirid dynasty (q.v.) to govern the Maghrib.

FEDERATION DES ELUS MUSULMANS D'ALGERIE (FEMA). Founded in Constantine by Dr. Mohammed Saleh Bendjelloul (q.v.) during the 1920s, this party soon acquired branches in Oran and in Algiers and its surrounding areas. Its aim was to achieve assimilation for Algerians. Nevertheless, the members were critical of French colonial administration and made numerous demands for reforms. Its aspirations were frustrated by the rejection of the Blum-Viollette legislation (q.v.).

FEDERATION DE FRANCE (FFFLN). The FLN (q.v.) organization in France that attempted to involve the emigrant worker community during the War of Independence.

FEDERATION NATIONALE DES TRAVAILLEURS AGRI-
COLES (FNTA). National Federation of Agricultural Workers that claimed 350,000 members in 1978. It was organized
for wage earners in the agricultural sector who were not well
represented in the UNPA (National Union of Algerian
Peasants), which represented farmers who live from their
own production.

FERAOUN, MOULOUD (1913–1962). Writer. A Kabyle born to
a poor peasant family, Feraoun nonetheless managed to
progress through the French school system and to earn a
degree at the Bouzaréah Normal School (Teachers College).
He became one of the most prolific Algerian authors to write
in the French language. In all of his books, he described
Kabyle life, underscoring the universality of the human
condition. During his life, which was cut short by his murder
by settler extremists, he published three novels, a collection
of essays, and a translation of the poems of a fellow Kabyle,
Si Mohand. His novels are *Le Fils du pauvre* (1950), *La
Terre et le sang* (1953), and *Les Chemins qui montent*
(1957). The essays published in 1954 are entitled *Jours de
Kabylie*. The translation of the poems of Si Mohand
appeared in 1960. Three posthumous works are *Journal
1955–1962* (1962), *Lettres à ses amis* (1969), and an
unfinished novel, *L'Anniversaire* (1972).

FERROUKHI, MOSTEFA (1922–1960). Nationalist; revolutionary. A native of Miliana, Ferroukhi received his secondary
schooling (*madrasa* in Algiers) and joined the PPA (q.v.) in
1942. After World War II, he was a member of the Central
Committee of the MTLD (q.v.) and, in April 1948, he
became a delegate in the Algerian Assembly (q.v. Statute of
Algeria). Along with most of the MTLD leaders, he was
arrested by the French authorities in November 1954 but was
released in April 1955. He then moved to France and then to
Tunis and the FLN (q.v.) in 1957. He was an administrator in

the interior Ministry of the GPRA (q.v.) when named its Ambassador to China. He died in a plane crash near Kiev while on his way to China.

FERRY REPORT. A report made by an investigatory commission of the French Senate under the chairmanship of the statesman Jules Ferry in 1891. Following a trip to Algeria, the commission proposed a greater equity concerning Muslim taxes, a slight increase in Muslim representation on departmental and municipal councils, and a number of reforms of local governments and courts to enhance their sensibilities toward Muslims. In general the report was critical of the colonial administration of Algeria. None of the reforms proposed, however, were immediately implemented (q.v. Clemenceau reforms).

FILALI, ABDALLAH (1913–1957). Messalist loyalist (q.v. Messali Hadj). Born near Collo he lived mostly in Constantine where he was a painter. Filali joined the ENA (q.v.) and was a founding member of the PPA (q.v.). His activity in this party brought him to the attention of French colonial authorities who arrested him in 1937 and condemned him to a five-year prison term. After his release he continued his nationalist activity under the name of ''Mansour.'' He was condemned to death for his role in the Sétif (q.v.) uprising (May 1945). He eluded colonial authorities and became a leader of the MTLD (q.v.) Federation in France. During the War of Independence he worked in the UGTA (q.v.) and supported the MNA (q.v.). Given his attachment to Messali Hadj, he was targeted by the FLN (q.v.) and killed in 1957.

FLATTERS, PAUL (1832–1881). French explorer. Flatters attended St.-Cyr and was a lieutenant in the Third Zouaves. Being an Arabist he served also in the *Bureaux arabes* (q.v.). He wrote *Histoire ancienne du Nord de l'Afrique avant le conquête des Arabes* (1863) and *Histoire de la géographie et géologie de la province de Constantine* (1865). He became associated with the Transsaharian Committee and was charged to explore the possibility of building a railroad into the Sahara. On his second mission into the desert, his group was massacred by the Tuareg (q.v.).

FRANCE (q.v. Introduction; Cooperation; De Gaulle; Emigrant Labor; Hydrocarbons; Mitterrand).

FRANCIS, AHMED (1911–1968). Moderate nationalist; revolutionary. Born in Algiers, Ahmed Francis was educated in French schools and became a medical doctor. He was a member of the UDMA (q.v.) and the Algerian Assembly (q.v. Statute of Algeria), but he subsequently joined the FLN (q.v.) during the War of Independence. He contributed to the internationalization of the war with his service in Scandinavia and Latin America. He was also a member of the CNRA (q.v.). Francis became the minister of finance and economic affairs in the GPRA (q.v.) (1958–1961) and kept this portfolio after independence in Ahmed Ben Bella's (q.v.) first government (1962–1963). He was also a member of the FLN (q.v.) delegation at the Evian Conference (q.v. Evian Accords).

FRANCO (SABIR). Informal language of Algiers during the Regency (q.v.). It is a combination of Arabic, Spanish, Turkish, Italian, and Provençal.

FRAPPART REPORT. This study was produced in 1957, and it complemented the conclusions of other reports (e.g., Maspétiol [q.v.]; Delavignette [q.v.]) concerning Algeria's social and economic condition. It claimed that financial resources were unavailable to raise the standard of living in French Algeria to match that of metropolitan France.

FRENCH COLONIALISM (q.v. Introduction).

FRENCH FOREIGN LEGION. The Legion was established in 1831 by a decree by King Louis Philippe (q.v.). It was headquartered at Sidi-Bel-Abbès where over the years approximately 350,000 Legionnaires were trained and disciplined. The Legion regarded Algeria as its home. While the Legion distinguished itself for its bravery in many of France's modern conflicts, its reputation (and romance) was discredited by open mutiny and refusal to obey directives from Paris during the Algerian War of Independence. The participation of its crack 1st REP (airborne regiment) in the April 1961 coup attempt led to this proud unit's disbanding on orders from President Charles de Gaulle (q.v.).

FRONT DES FORCES SOCIALISTES (FFS). Berber opposition party. Led by Hocine Aït Ahmed (q.v.) the FFS represents essentially Kabyle (q.v.) interests. The FFS was established in 1963 by Aït Ahmed and Mohand ou el Hadj (q.v.). It resisted Ahmed Ben Bella's (q.v.) authoritarianism and eventually incited a Kabyle rebellion against the central government in late 1963. The FFS became ineffective when Mohand ou el Hadj, affected by the conflict along the Algeria-Morocco border (q.v. Border War), decided to reconcile with Ben Bella's government. Aït Ahmed was captured and condemned to death. His sentence was commuted to life imprisonment. In July 1966, he escaped from prison and went into exile in France and Switzerland. He returned to Algeria in December 1989. The FFS was legalized as a result of the new electoral reforms (enacted in 1989).

The FFS's failure to participate actively in local elections in June 1990 (q.v.) was regarded as a political mistake by many observers and contributed to the unanticipated great success of the FIS. It did, however, campaign during the national elections of June and December 1991 (q.v.). After the startling FIS success in December's first round (the FFS won 26 seats), Aït Ahmed tried to rally democratic forces before the second round to impress the expected eventual FIS parliamentary majority that there would be considerable opposition to an Islamist state. The January 1992 overthrow of President Chadli Benjedid (q.v.) and the establishment of the High Council of State (HCS) drew the FFS's protest. It remains in opposition to the HCS.

FRONT ISLAMIQUE DU SALUT (FIS) (Islamic Salvation Front). Leading Islamist party. An Islamist movement had developed in the 1980s and was influenced in several directions. The Islamic Republic of Iran with its anti-West positions had a profound effect. In addition, *Shaykh* Abdelatif Sultani and particularly *Shaykh* Ahmed Sahnoun attracted disaffected youth. Abassi Madani (q.v.), a sociology professor at the University of Algiers, played a particularly influential role. Finally, Mustapha Bouiali (q.v.) organized violent opposition to the FLN (q.v.) establishment. The FIS's history disclosed this contemporary Islamist legacy.

The FIS was organized by Abbasi Madani and Ali Benhadj (q.v.). (*Shaykh* Sahnoun questioned the timing of its formation.) It was legalized on September 12, 1989; the High Council of State (HCS) (q.v.) declared it an illegal party in February 1992. During this period the FIS gained world attention for its Islamist positions, both religious and populist, and especially its astonishing electoral successes (q.v. Elections of June 1990; December 1991). In general, the FIS was very critical of the FLN and also Western values. Its Islamist positions were criticized by women's groups and academics. This movement was quite moderate, however, when compared with the Shi'a in the Mashriq and Iran. The FIS attracted many Algerians, especially the disillusioned, alienated youth. A group within the FIS inspired by Benhadj became much more militant. There were also incidents involving the FIS's own "Islamic police," which monitored Muslim practices.

The FIS claimed to have 3 million members and had been particularly helpful in providing social services such as transportation and health care. It disclosed its political strength during June 1990 elections (q.v.) when it enjoyed spectacular success in regional elections (winning 850 out of 1,541 municipal councils). Though the locally controlled areas by the FIS had some administrative problems, in general, the fear of dramatic and radical change did not take place.

In spite of its electoral success, there was dissension within the movement. Madani was regarded as an *algérianiste*, or a believer that Algeria itself could become an Islamic republic. Benhadj was an *anti-algérianiste* (or a *salafiyiste*) contending that Algeria must become part of a Pan-Islamic community. There were also reports of an undercurrent of opposition to Madani's authoritarian control of the FIS.

The elections of June 1991 (q.v.) were tainted by eleventh hour gerrymandering by the FLN. The FIS called not only for redrawn constituency borders but also for presidential with parliamentary elections. The call for a protest through a general strike failed (in part because FIS's youthful supporters were unemployed). The arrest of Madani and Benhadj on June 30, 1991, after the protracted violence concerning the national electoral process (the leadership of the FIS threatened "holy war") was a severe blow to the FIS. Nevertheless, even without its leaders, the party managed to focus itself quickly before the December elections (it was generally believed that FIS would boycott the rescheduled elections) and gained an impressive victory in the first round (188 out of 232 seats). The prospects of a FIS-controlled government caused the coup against President Chadli Benjedid (q.v.). The replacement of his government by the HCS led to severe repression of the FIS, including the arrest and internment of prominent FIS leaders. (Disturbing reports of conditions in desert internment camps drew international protest.) The declaration on February 9 that the FIS was an illegal party provoked more violent protest between Islamists and police forces. The moderate sentences of Madani and Benhadj (12 years each for sedition) announced on July 15, 1992, have failed to mollify the ''radical'' Muslims. The FIS was also held responsible (televised confessions) for the August 1992 bombing at the Houari Boumedienne (Algiers) Airport that killed nine people. Prime Minister Belaïd Abdesselam (q.v.) has pursued a determined policy to dismantle the FIS's residual infrastructure. A prominent *algérianiste* named Rabah Kebir wants to organize an Islamist government in exile. Algeria remains in a wrenching condition verging on civil war. Indeed the *Mouvement Islamique Armé* (MIA) (q.v.), a militant organization linked to the FIS, has been in conflict with the HCS's security forces (approximately 200 to 400 dead in 1992).

There were other Islamic party competitors to the FIS such as *El Oumma* (The Islamic community) led by Ben Youssef Ben Khedda (q.v.), *El Nahda* (the Renaissance Party) led by Abdallah Djaballah, the *Mouvement pour la Cité Islamique, Hezbollah, Parti d'Unité Arabe Islamique-Démocratique* (PUAID) led by Nourredine Boukrouh, *Hamas* (moderate party) led by Mahfoud Nahnah, and *L'Alliance Islamique nationale.*

FRONT DE LIBERATION NATIONALE (FLN) (National Liberation Front). The FLN was the only legal party in independent Algeria until recent reforms (1989). It was founded by the CRUA (q.v.), which launched the War of Independence (National Liberation). The primary aim in creating the FLN was to gather all nationalists into one organization that would direct the revolution and gain independence for Algeria. In its ''Proclamation'' (q.v.) circulated during the October 31–November 1, 1954 outbreak, the FLN declared its aims to be the establishment of a sovereign Algerian state. By 1956 all major nationalist groups, with the exception of MNA (q.v.) supporters of

Messali Hadj (q.v.), had joined the FLN. Among its members were former supporters of the MTLD (q.v.), UDMA (q.v.), Association of Reformist Algerian Ulama (q.v.), and many Communists (q.v. Algerian Communist Party [PCA]).

At the Soummam Congress of August 1956 (q.v.), the FLN declared itself the sole representative of the Algerian nation. It also created institutions to wage the war against the French (CCE [q.v.]; CNRA [q.v.]). In 1958, the CCE created the GPRA (*Gouvernement Provisoire de la République Algérienne*) (q.v.) whose first president was Ferhat Abbas (q.v.). The FLN also conducted negotiations with the French resulting in the Evian Accords (q.v.).

The FLN was criticized for not mobilizing the people socially and economically. The FLN could pursue only political independence for a variety of reasons. Elite dissension and division stemming from the FLN's heterogeneous (political and ethnic) membership prevented the articulation of a comprehensive ideology, except one on which all concurred: the elimination of French colonialism. The prospect of having hundreds of thousands of European settlers in postcolonial Algeria also qualified ideological development. Furthermore, the Algerian nationalists controlled little Algerian territory, which inhibited the initiation of a genuine complementary social revolution (like that of Amilcar Cabral's *Partido Africano* da *Independêcia da Guiné e Cabo Verde* [PAIGC] in Guinea-Bissau). It can be argued that a national solidarity was achieved in Algerian refugee camps in Morocco and especially Tunisia.

The proclamation of independence (July 1962) that followed final negotiations between France and the FLN at Evian (March) was immediately followed by a power struggle among party leaders, which was won by Ahmed Ben Bella (q.v.) and Houari Boumedienne (q.v.). The FLN retained an important role in the government of the Algerian state through the party's Political Bureau. In 1963 all parties except the FLN were declared illegal. This action and the military takeover (coup) in June 1965 (q.v.) led to the party's political stagnation and corruption. Boumedienne's efforts failed to revivify the party through institutional changes (e.g., Party Secretariat) and political mobilization (e.g., debate over the National Charter [q.v.]). When Chadli Benjedid (q.v.) came to power, he manipulated the membership of the Political Bureau and the Central Committee to eliminate potential rivals. The FLN became more a bureaucracy than an avant-garde political party sensitive to the needs of the people.

After the October 1988 riots (q.v.), Benjedid replaced the unpopular Mohamed Cherif Messaadia (q.v.) with Abdelhamid Mehri (q.v.) as head of the Permanent Secretariat of the Central Committee. Then on November 28–30, 1988, the FLN convened its third Extraordinary Congress where delegates demanded the replacement of the Central Committee (120 to 160 full members and 30 to 40 alternate members) by secret ballot. President Benjedid initiated this action to stimulate reform. The result was that the Central Committee was enlarged to 267 members (but also included anti-Benjedidists such as Yahiaoui [q.v.], Abdesselam [q.v.], Taleb Ibrahimi [q.v.], and Bouteflika [q.v.]), though most of the old members kept their positions. President Benjedid was now regarded as "Head (or President) of the FLN."

The new Constitution (February 1989) (q.v.) and subsequent July legislation ended the FLN's monopoly of power by permitting legal opposition parties. The FLN was shaken by Kasdi Merbah's (q.v.) defection, Rabah Bitat's (q.v.) resignation, and internal disintegration over the course of reform, the declining economy, and the pressures placed upon it by new opposition parties, especially the FIS (q.v.) (given its success in the June 1990 elections [q.v.]). In addition, the FLN remained beset with chronic factionalism. (Merbah's MAJD may be the first of other FLN-splinter parties.) Some observers believed, however, that if the June

1991 elections (q.v.) would have taken place, the FLN would have won them. Yet this interpretation was questionable given the astounding FIS success in the December 1991 elections (q.v.).

In general the FLN has lost its reputation, its moral legitimacy (given the October 1988 violence), and, above all, its social sensibilities (given the blatant privileges enjoyed by party members). In June 1991, President Benjedid resigned as president of the FLN. (He had been criticized by the FIS that he was president of a party not a country.) After the establishment of the Higher Council of State (HCS) (q.v.) the FLN membership seemed split over the issue of supporting or opposing the new government. (The FLN officially opposed the cancellation of elections.) With its technocratic and military links, the FLN remains a powerful organization and influence in Algerian political life. In spite of the criticism leveled against it, and its repudiation in local and national elections, the future of Algeria will still be determined significantly by past and present FLN members.

FURAT, ANAS IBN AL-. Muslim scholar. He influenced the Aghlabid (q.v.) *amirs* and introduced Malikism (q.v.). One of his devout followers was Shanun, a renowned theologian and a strict Maliki.

GAETULIANS (GAETULES). An ancient nomadic people who inhabited the southern slopes of the Atlas range and the Saharan borderlands. This tribe stretched from the Atlantic to southern Tunisia. Their horse-drawn chariots were probably adopted from the Greeks of Cyrenaica. Gaetulian culture has been disclosed by rock engravings in Saharan *wadi* valleys. As cavalry allies of Jugurtha (q.v.), they first fought Rome 111 to 106 B.C. After a major defeat by a Roman army under the command of Lentulus Cossus in A.D. 6, they acknowledged Roman control. Afterward, they served as auxiliaries in the Roman army.

GAISERIC (also GENSERIC) (389–477). Vandal king of North Africa (428–477). He was the son of Goigisebus and a slave. After conquering territory in Lusitania, he led his army into Africa in 429. Aided by the Berbers and the Donatists (q.v.), he conquered much of Numidia (modern Tunisia and eastern Algeria). In 435, he entered into the Treaty of Hippo Regius, establishing an alliance with the Roman Emperor of the West Valentinian III. A second treaty in 442 recognized Gaiseric's sovereignty. In 455, when the usurper Maximus murdered Valentinian, Gaiseric marched on Rome and sacked it. Pope Leo had intervened successfully against Attila in 452, and he tried to limit Gaiseric's activities to looting rather than massacring. Gaiseric returned to North Africa with Valentinian's Empress and two daughters; one of them was Eudoxia who was betrothed to Huneric (q.v.), Gaiseric's son and heir. After an extended period of hostility with the Eastern Roman emperors, Gaiseric concluded a treaty of peace with that empire in 476, whereby the Vandal Kingdom received its formal recognition. Gaiseric's offers of plunder and booty allowed him to exercise considerable influence over Numidian and Mauretanian tribes beyond his direct control. His heretical Arianism against the established Church also permitted Donatism to reassert itself.

GELIMER (GILLIMAR). Last Vandal King of North Africa (520–534). He rose to power over his brother Hilderic (q.v) with the assistance of the army, but refused to acknowledge the Byzantine (q.v.) Emperor Justinian (q.v.). Defeated by Justinian's armies under Belisarius at the Battles of Decimum and Tricamarum in 533, he fled to the protection of the Berbers (q.v.). He was eventually captured by the Byzantines and sent to Constantinople. Shortly afterward, he took up residence in Galatia.

GENERATION OF 1954. This refers to writers who were contemporary to Algeria's decolonization and who used liberation as a theme in their writings. The most prominent members of the "generation" were Yacine Kateb (q.v.), Mohammed Dib (q.v.), Mouloud Mammeri (q.v.), and Mouloud Feraoun (q.v.).

GHANIYA. Important family of Sanhaja Berbers who attempted to restore Almoravid (q.v.) rule to the Maghrib during the twelfth and thirteenth centuries. The name is derived from an Almoravid princess married to the head of the family, Ali bn Yusuf. Two of Ali's grandsons, Ali ibn Ghaniya and Yahya, were involved in campaigns around Bejaïa, Constantine, and Algiers. Their efforts eventually failed given the strength of Almohad (q.v.) forces.

GHERAIEB, ABDELKRIM. President of the *Amicale des Algériens en Europe*; ambassador. Gheraieb was president of the *Amicale* from 1968 to 1978. This period was particularly important because it included the stoppage of Algerian emigration to France and, in particular, heightened violence against the emigrant community, as illustrated by the shocking murder of a caretaker at the *Amicale* in Paris (December 1977). Gheraieb as the *Amicale*'s president was viewed as being in Algeria's second most powerful position in France after the ambassador. He also served as an ambassador to particularly sensitive countries, given his appointments to Iran in 1981 and Lebanon in 1984.

GHOZALI, SID-AHMED (b. 1937). Director-general; ambassador; prime minister. Ghozali was born in Marnia and attended the Ecole des Ponts et Chausées in Paris. He became under secretary of state for public works and then served with distinction as director-general of SONATRACH from 1966 to 1977. He was minister of energy form 1977 to 1979 and then minister of hydraulics for several months (1979). Ghozali lost influence and office with the arrival of the Chadli Benjedid (q.v.) presidency, given his close links with Houari Boumedienne (q.v.), and because of the failure of the El Paso contract (q.v. Hydrocarbons). He was restored to prominence through the Foreign Ministry as ambassador to Belgium. Ghozali served in Kasdi Merbah's (q.v.) cabinet as finance minister and concluded Algeria's first agreement with the International Monetary Fund. In September 1989 Prime Minister Mouloud Hamrouche (q.v.) selected Ghozali to be foreign minister. When violent protests rocked Algeria during the first scheduled national elections (June 1991), President Benjedid selected Ghozali as prime minister. This appointment was viewed in part as a symbolic gesture to the Boumedienne faction as a means to reconcile and unify the FLN (q.v.). Nevertheless, he distanced himself from the Boumedienne faction as he promoted the liberalization of the Algerian economy.

Ghozali was probably aware of plotting against Benjedid, which resulted in the January 1992 coup that inaugurated the High Council of State (HCS) under Mohamed Boudiaf (q.v.). Boudiaf and Ghozali had strained relations, though both agreed upon the need to build an Algerian consensus for political and economic reform. The prime minister announced sweeping economic liberalization plans in February 1992. Given Boudiaf's age and his symbolic presence as president of the HCS, Ghozali appeared well placed for an eventual presidential bid. The assassination of Boudiaf (June 1992) had a significant political and personal effect on Ghozali. He was shaken by the tragic death and was replaced in July as prime minister by Belaïd Abdesselam (q.v.), who had been his patron during the Boumedienne period. He was then appointed Ambassador to France.

GOUVERNEMENT GENERAL DES POSSESSION FRANCAISES DANS LE NORD DE L'AFRIQUE. French administrative system of conquered portions of Algeria that was created on July 22, 1834. At the time, France controlled only the cities Algiers (q.v.), Oran (q.v.), Bejaïa (q.v.), Bône (Annaba [q.v.]), and their immediate hinterlands.

GOUVERNEMENT PROVISOIRE DE LA REPUBLIQUE ALGERIENNE (GPRA) (Provisional Government of the Algerian Republic), 1958–1962 (q.v. Appendices). The GPRA was proclaimed in Cairo on September 19, 1958, by the FLN (q.v.) in response to the arrival of General Charles de Gaulle to power to revitalize the nationalists after suffering severe losses in 1957. The FLN also viewed the GPRA as a means to attract more international attention.

Omar Ouamrane (q.v.), a veteran fighter and comrade of Belkacem Krim (q.v.), has been credited as being an important catalyst to the GPRA's formation after writing a powerful and inspiring memorandum about the need to reinvigorate the nationalist movement. The GPRA's first president was Ferhat Abbas (q.v.), who was followed in August 1961 by Ben Youssef Ben Khedda (q.v.). The GPRA concluded the Evian Accords (q.v.) in March 1962, but soon faced opposition headed by Ahmed Ben Bella (q.v.) and Houari Boumedienne (q.v.) and their Political Bureau (q.v.). The GPRA lost the struggle for postcolonial power in the summer of 1962.

GREKI, ANNA (1931–1966) (Colette Anna Grégoire). Poet. Greki was born in Batna. She became a member of the PCA (q.v. Algerian Communist Party). Greki was arrested in March 1957, then tortured and imprisoned at the infamous Barberousse prison in Algiers. She was sent to an internment camp and then deported in 1958. After the war she returned to Algiers and taught in the Lycée Abdelkader. She died during childbirth.

Greki's poetry is among the best of the war period as disclosed in *Algérie, capitale Alger* (1963; Arabic and French); and the posthumous collection *Temps fort* (1966).

GROUP OF 77. An organization of developing countries (now well over 100 countries) that meet occasionally and lobby the developed world concerning economic issues. The general theme of the group's meetings is an appeal for a new economic order between the developed North and the developing South. Algeria played a leading role in this organization, especially during the Houari Boumedienne (q.v.) presidency.

GROUPE D'ETUDES DES QUESTIONS INDIGENES. Organization formed in the French Chamber of Deputies in 1912 to obtain reforms in the status of Algerian Muslims. It was formed under the leadership of Georges Leygues.

EL-HACHEMI, HAMOUD (d. 1954). Nationalist; revolutionary. Killed early in the War of Independence, El-Hachemi had been active in the PPA (q.v.), the OS (q.v.), the MTLD (q.v.), and the FLN (q.v.). He was an early partisan of armed rebellion, and along with Salah Maïza and Mostefa Ben Boulaïd (q.v.) he tried to reconcile the Centralists and the Messalists (q.v. Messali Hadj) in the MTLD.

AL-HADDAD (EL-HADDAD), SIDI MUHAMMAD (d. 1874). *Muqaddam* of the Rahmaniyya order and a leader of the (Great) Kabyle Revolt of 1871–1872 (q.v.). The *Rahmaniyya* (q.v.) order had resisted French incursions into Kabylia (q.v.) in the 1850s and 1860s. Along with his son al-Aziz (Si Aziz), he joined in the revolt begun by al-Muqrani (q.v.) in 1871. Al-Haddad was captured and imprisoned. He died in an infirmary.

HADDAD, MALEK (1927–1978). Writer. Haddad was born in Constantine and attended secondary school there. He later enrolled at the University of Aix-en-Provence. After a career as a journalist (for the PCA's [q.v. Algerian Communist Party] *Alger républicain*; *Liberté*) and a free-lance writer, he published a number of books. His works include two collections of poetry, *Le Malheur en danger* (1956) and *Ecoute et je t'appelle* (1961), and four novels, *La Dernière impression* (1958), *Je t'offrirai une gazelle* (1959), *L'Elève et la leçon* (1960), and *Le Quai aux fleurs ne répond plus* (1961). All of Haddad's works are clearly marked by the themes of native land, exile, and commitment. Haddad once said: "The French language is my exile," which indicated how colonialism had affected him. He could not write in Arabic.

During the War of Independence, Haddad served the FLN (q.v.) on missions to the USSR, Egypt, and India. After the war he returned to Constantine and was an editor of *Al-Nasr/An-Nasr* (1965–1968) and from April 1968 to 1972 he held the position of director of culture to the Ministry of Information and Culture. He played a prominent role in organizing the First Colloquium on National Culture (May 31–June 3, 1968) and the First Pan-African Cultural Festival in Algiers (July 1969). In 1974 he became secretary of the new *Union des Ecrivains algériens.*

HADDAM, CHEIKH (*Shaykh*) TEDJINI (b. 1921). Minister; ambassador, Rector of Paris Mosque; member of High Council of State (HCS). Tedjini (usually referred to rather than Haddam) was born in Tlemcen (q.v.) and was very well educated. He studied in Tunis and holds doctorates in medicine and theology. He is multilingual (Arabic, French, English, and German). Tedjini has taught at the University of Algiers.

During the War of Indcpendence, he served with the external FLN in Cairo (1956–1957). He presided over the Constitution Committee in 1962 and then began his career as a minister, holding the portfolios of Religious Affairs in 1964 and Health in 1965–1966. Tedjini entered diplomatic service and was ambassador to Tunisia (1970–1975) and Saudi Arabia (1982–1986). In May 1989 he was appointed to head the Paris Mosque, a powerful and influential post. Tedjini has also been president of the Family Planning Committee and was a founding member of the Algerian League of Human Rights. In January 1992, he became a member of the High Council of State (HCS) after the deposal of President Chadli Benjedid (q.v.). The inclusion of the prestigious *Shaykh* in the HCS was probably meant to temper political anxieties.

HADJ ALI, BACHIR (1923–1991) (q.v. Algerian Communist Party [PCA]). PCA secretary-general. Hadj Ali was born in Algiers's Casbah. He became a member of the Communist Party's Central Committee for the Algiers region. In 1948 he became senior editor of *Liberté*, a party newspaper, and gained a seat on the Political Bureau. He also served as interim secretary as a replacement for Amar Ouzegane (q.v.). In 1949 Hadj Ali became secretary-general of the PCA. Arrested before the War of Independence, he negotiated indirectly (through Sadek Hadjerès [q.v.]) an accord with the FLN (q.v.). In 1961, he published an excellent collection of poems entitled *Chants pour le onze décembre*. He also wrote an essay entitled *Notre peuple vaincra* (1961) and published more poetry *Que la joie demeure* (1970). After the Houari Boumedienne (q.v.) coup of 1965, Hadj Ali joined the ORP. He was arrested in 1965 and kept in house arrest until 1971. He then left politics to devote more time to his poetry.

HADJERES, SADEK (b. 1928) (q.v. Algerian Communist Party [PCA]). PCA and PAGS (q.v.) secretary-general; doctor. Hadjères, a Kabyle (q.v.), was born in Larbâa Nath Iratten. He was a member of the *Scouts Musulmans Algériens* of the Association of Reformist *Ulama* (q.v.). He joined the PPA (q.v.) in 1944. Hadjères became an active member of AEMAN as treasurer, then secretary-general, and finally president. After the MTLD's (q.v.) "Berberist crisis" [q.v. MTLD), he joined the PCA in 1950. In 1952 Hadjères became a member of the Central Committee, and in 1955 he rose to the Political Bureau. After the arrest of Bachir Hadj Ali (q.v.), Hadjères became secretary-general of the clandestine PCA. He concluded the agreement with Ramdane Abane (q.v.), which affiliated PCA *combattants de la Libération* to the ALN. Hadjères eventually became the secretary-general of PAGS (q.v.), the PCA's ideological heir. His cousin was General Hachemi Hadjères.

HAMDANI, SMAIL (b.1930). Lawyer; counselor; ambassador. Hamdani was born in Bordj-Bou-Arréridj and attended the University of Algiers and the University of Aix-en-Provence. He became a lawyer and served as chargé d'affaires in Brussels (1963–1964) regarding Algerian-EEC relations. He was then appointed director of juridical consular affairs of the Foreign Ministry (1964–1968). (Concurrently he was a technical counselor for the Ministry of Information.) Hamdani served as counselor, then secretary-general, to the President of the Council of the Revolution (q.v.) (i.e. President Houari Boumedienne [q.v.]) (1968–1977). He became secretary-general of the government and then became counselor to the Presidency of the Republic (i.e., President Chadli Benjedid [q.v.]) (1980–1983) before his selection as ambassador to the Scandinavian countries (1983). In 1984, he was chosen to the important post of Ambassador to Spain (an important LNG customer).

HAMIDOU, RAIS (HAMIDA REIS) (d. 1815). Last great corsair captain of the Regency (q.v.). Son of a simple tailor, he advanced from cabin boy to *raïs* before gaining command of the corsair fleet. His most famous exploits were aboard the *Portekiza*, a Portuguese frigate he dauntlessly captured in 1802. He also commanded the frigate *El Merikana* (The American). Hamida sailed throughout the Mediterranean, raiding along the coasts of Portugal, Sicily, and Naples. He also ventured into the Atlantic. In part, he was able to do this because of Europe's preoccupation with the French Revolutionary and Napoleonic wars. Hamidou was sailing alone when he was engaged by a United States squadron in 1815 (q.v. Decatur) off the coast of Cape de Gata (Gatt). He was killed in the ensuing battle.

HAMMAD, IBN BULUKKIN (BEN BULUGGIN) (eleventh century). Berber (q.v.) leader, founder of the Hammadid (q.v.) dynasty. His father, Bulukkin (q.v.), was the Zirid (q.v.) governor of the Maghrib under Fatimid (q.v.) Caliph al-Mu'izz. Upon the death of Bulukkin, he received the governorship of Ashir. He continued the war against the Zenata (q.v.), raising the siege of Ashir in 1005. When his suzerain attempted to deprive him of the governorship of

Tidjis and Constantine (q.v.), he rebelled and probably declared himself a vassal of the Abbasids (q.v.) (the Fatimids' opponents). The war continued until 1017. The peace treaty led to the division of the Zirid realm as Hammad retained Mila, Tobna, the Zab, Ashir, and lands of the central Maghrib.

HAMMADID DYNASTY. Sanhaja Berber (q.v.) dynasty of the central Maghrib (1014–1152). Founded by Hammad ibn Bulukkin (q.v.), a relative of the Zirids (q.v.) (grandson of Ziri ibn Manad; uncle of the Zirid *amir* Badis [r. 996–1016]), the Hammadid dynasty reached its golden age at the beginning of the twelfth century under the rule of al-Nasir and al-Mansur. Their capital was at Qal'a in the Djebel Maadid north of the Chott el Hodna. By 1017, the Zirids reluctantly recognized Hammadid independence. An active rivalry ensued, which especially weakened the Zirids.

   After becoming suzerain of Algiers (q.v.), Milyana (Miliana), Nigaus, Hamza, and Constantine (q.v.), the Hammadid Amir al-Nasir attempted to extend his empire eastward. After his defeat at Sbeitla in 1064, he regained the offensive and extended his control to the Zab and as far as Wargla (Ouargla). During his reign, he expanded commercial opportunities for Italian traders at Bejaïa (q.v.) (founded by the Hammadids) and indirectly corresponded with Pope Gregory VII. His successor, al-Mansur moved the capital to Bejaïa (q.v.) after Hammadid territory was ravaged by the Banu (Bani) Hilal (q.v.), who had been allies against the Zirids.

   Bejaïa became a cosmopolitan center and Hammadid power was regenerated. Al-Mansur took Tlemcen (q.v.) in 1103–1104 stopping the Almoravid (q.v.) advance. He also recovered Annaba (q.v.) and Constantine. His son al-'Aziz (r. 1104–1121) occupied Djerba (Jerba) and pushed the Arabs from the Hodna. Under Yahya (r. 1122–1152) Hammadid power ended. In 1136 the Genoese plundered

Bejaïa. Compounding this blow, restive Berber tribes challenged the weakened Hammadids. Finally, the Almohads (q.v.) invaded central Maghrib. Yahya surrendered to the Almohads in 1152 and died at Salé (1163).

HAMROUCHE, MOULOUD (b. 1943). Prime minister. Hamrouche served in the ALN (q.v.). In 1979 he was appointed chief of protocol (1979–1984), secretary-general of the government (1984–1986), and then secretary-general of the Presidency of Chadli Benjedid (q.v.). He was selected by Benjedid to replace Kasdi Merbah (q.v.) as prime minister in September 1989. Hamrouche was charged with accelerating political, economic, and social reforms. This also meant reorganizing the FLN (q.v.) and neutralizing the influence of older members. His government received a serious blow as a result of the Islamist FIS's (q.v.) popularity and success in the local elections of June 1990 (q.v.). A year later, unrest before the June 1991 national legislative elections (q.v.) forced President Benjedid to replace Hamrouche with Sid Ahmed Ghozali (q.v.). Hamrouche has remained a leading figure in the FLN.

HARATIN. Berber-Negroid people of the Sahara. The Haratin have been called the "Black Berbers." They usually performed agricultural tasks as sharecroppers at Saharan oases. They speak Arabic.

HARBI, MOHAMMED (b. 1933). Nationalist; journalist. Harbi became a Messalist (q.v. Messali Hadj) as a teenager, serving in the PPA-MTLD (q.v.). He held the position of secretary-general of the *Association des Etudiants nord-africains* (AENA) in 1954. During the War of Independence, he joined the FLN (q.v.) and served in its *Fédération de France* (FFFLN), an organization that aimed to politicize the emigrant worker population. In 1961 he became the GPRA's ambassador to Guinea and acted as a consultant to the Evian negotiations during that same year. He also became secretary-general of the Foreign Ministry (1961–1962).

Harbi joined Ahmed Ben Bella's (q.v.) government as an adviser to the president and was editor of the FLN's *Révolution africaine* (1963–1964). He also contributed to the composition of the Charter of Algiers (q.v.). Harbi opposed Colonel Houari Boumedienne's (q.v.) coup, resulting in a five-year prison term without being brought to trial. He was then placed under house arrest until he was allowed to leave for France in 1973.

While in exile, Harbi produced valuable works on Algerian history and nationalism, though it is important to keep in mind the author's historical relativism (*Aux origines du FLN: Le Populisme révolutionnaire en Algérie* [1975]; *Le FLN: Mirage et réalité, des origines à la prise du pouvoir 1945–1962* [1980]). He also edited a book of documents on the revolution (many from his personal collection), which is entitled *Les Archives de la Révolution algérienne* (1981).

HARKIS. Algerians who were loyal to France during the War of Independence. The word is derived from *haraka* (to move; derived noun is *harakat,* meaning military enterprise or operation). The French often mobilized collaborating native units during the colonial period. For example, they were deployed against Abd al-Qadir (q.v.) and even sent to the Rif War. An important rationale for General Maurice Challe's (q.v.) participation in the April 1961 revolt against the government was his fear that loyal Algerians were being betrayed. Many *harkis* perished in retributions after the War of Independence and suffered, too, in detention camps in spite of protective stipulations in the Evian Accords (q.v.). Those who managed to arrive in France found themselves victims of discrimination. They were often confused with emigrant workers rather than as French citizens who risked their lives, families, and homes to maintain French rule in Algeria. Many of the *harkis* were sent to live in remote relocation camps and stayed there for years. Among the most prominent *harkis* and an advocate for their rights was the Bachaga Benaissa Said Boualam (q.v.). In order to publicize their plight and express their frustration, *harkis* went on hunger strikes in the 1970s and even kidnapped Algerian workers. Brahim Sadouni, a *harki*, walked from Rouen to Monte Cassino from May to July 1987 and was eventually received in December by Prime Minister Jacques Chirac.

During his November 1983 visit to France, President Benjedid declared that "Algeria is not vengeful" and said that *harki* children would be welcome, but he acknowledged that adults posed security problems. After France issued a stamp in the late 1980s commemorating *harki* service, Algeria announced that mail with that particular postage attached would be returned.

Like the *Beurs* (q.v. emigrant labor), the young people are suspended between their Algerian and French backgrounds. Their exasperation included violent protests in 1991. The *harkis* want to realize the promise of integration within French society. There are approximately 450,000 French Muslims.

HAROUN, MOHAMED ALI (b. 1927?). Lawyer; minister. Haroun was born in Birmandreis and served with the FLN (q.v.) during the War of Independence. After the war, he pursued a legal career (he is a doctor of law) and was a lawyer in the Supreme Court. Haroun became the minister of human rights in 1991. Haroun became a member of the High Council of State (HCS) (q.v.) in January 1992. Like his fellow member Haddam Tedjini (q.v.), Haroun's presence on the HSC, given his human rights background, appeared to reduce fears concerning the new government's intentions.

HASAN AGHA (HASSAN/HASSEN AGHA) (1536–1543/44?/ 49?). *Khalifa* of Khayr al-Din (q.v.) in Algiers (q.v.). Born in Sardinia, Hasan was taken prisoner by Khayr al-Din and placed among his eunuchs. When Khayr al-Din was summoned to Constantinople in 1536 by Sultan Suleiman (the Magnificent), he placed Hasan in control of the Regency (q.v.). Hasan launched strikes into Spain to protect the persecuted Muslim population. This led to the retributive attack on Algiers by Charles V (q.v.) in 1541, which was an utter failure. Hasan extended Turkish power to Biskra (q.v.) and the Ziban and continued his conflict with Spain by assaulting its North African enclaves (e.g., Mers el-Kébir). Both sides also confronted one another over Tlemcen (q.v.) and Mostaganem. By the time of his death, Hasan succeeded in securing and strengthening the Regency. Some sources relate that he lived quietly as a private citizen until 1549 after falling from power in disgrace.

HASAN BABA (d. 1683). Corsair captain. Hasan Baba took part in the revolt of 1671 that replaced power of *aghas* with *deys*. When his father-in-law, the *Dey* Hajj Muhammad, fled to Tripoli upon learning of the approaching French fleet, Hasan Baba seized power (1682). He withstood the bombardment (q.v. Algiers) by Admiral Duquesne's ships from August 26 to September 12. When Duquesne returned in 1683 to renew the assault, Hasan Baba agreed to negotiate and turned over hostages, among them his rival Husayn *raïs* (''Mezzomorto''/''Mezzo Morto'') (q.v.). When Husayn was allowed to return to shore to expedite an indemnity settlement, he plotted with other *raïs,* which led to the murder of Hasan. Hasan was succeeded as *Dey* by Husayn.

HASAN BEY. *Bey* of Oran (1817–1831). Prior to becoming *bey*, he had served as an army cook and merchant. As *bey*, he kept Abd al-Qadir (q.v.) and his father under house arrest at Oran from 1824 to 1826. Unlike Ahmad *Bey* (q.v.) or *Dey* Husayn (q.v.), Hasan did not organize a military resistance when the French took over the city in 1831. Hasan moved to Algiers and then to Alexandria. He died in Mecca.

HASSAN CORSO (HASSEN) (sixteenth century). Regency (q.v.) leader. Hassan was of Corsican heritage and a popular and effective Turkish commander. He distinguished himself in campaigns in western Algeria against the Moroccans and Spanish. He recaptured Mostaganem and also installed a permanent Turkish governor in Tlemcen (q.v.). Hassan nearly took Oran (q.v.) from the Spanish, but he was ordered to withdraw by the Sultan, who needed Algerian support in the eastern Mediterranean.

Hassan briefly headed the Regency (1556–1557) after the death of Salah *Raïs* (q.v.). When Istanbul sent a new *Beylerbey*, Tekerli, Janissaries forbade the new appointee to enter Algiers. This was an indication of their support for Hassan Corso. Nevertheless, Tekerli conspired with the *raïs* and members of the *Ojak* and managed to enter Algiers. Hassan was captured and impaled at the Bab Azoun gate. Tekerli himself was soon assassinated by members of the *Ojaq*.

HASSAN PASHA (HASSEN PASHA; HASSAN IBN KHAYR AL-DIN) (d. 1572). *Khalifa* of Algiers (1544–1546; *Beylerbey* 1546–1551; 1557–1561; 1562–1567). Hassan Pasha was the son of Khayr al-Din (q.v.). Hassan organized two campaigns (1544; 1546) to take Tlemcen (q.v.) from the influence of the Spanish. Upon the death of his father, Hassan became *Beylerbey*. He engaged the Moroccans after their seizure of Tlemcen (q.v.) (1550/1551). He retook the city in 1552. As a result of intrigues, he was summoned to Constantinople in 1552 but was sent back in 1557. He returned to defeat the Moroccans at Tlemcen (1557) and devastated the Spanish in battle on August 26, 1558, relieving the siege of Mostaganem. In an effort to gain Turkish control over Kabylia (q.v.), he successfully enrolled Kabyles (q.v.) against the Moroccans (after a politically strategic marriage). Further efforts were delayed again by intrigues as Hassan was seized by Janissaries and returned to Istanbul in chains (1561).

Returning to Algiers the following year, he reestablished himself. He failed to dislodge the Spanish from Oran (q.v.) and Mers el-Kébir in April 1567. The Sultan called him to service in the continuing siege of Malta, and in 1567, like his father, he took command of the Ottoman fleet with the title of Captain Pasha. He left the Regency to the very competent Eulj Ali (q.v.).

HASSAN (HASSEN) VENEZIANO (VENETIANO). Regency (q.v.) raïs. Hassan was a lieutenant of Eulj Ali (q.v.). He was named Veneziano because he had been a ship's writer on a Venetian vessel seized by Dragut (q.v.). Miguel de Cervantes, the author of *Don Quixote*, *Man of Glass*, and so on, was his slave and provided a vivid description of the Regency (q.v.) leader. Hassan ruled the Regency as *Pasha* in 1577 to 1580 and then later controlled the *ta'ifa* of the corsairs from 1582 to 1588, during which time he was actual ruler of Algiers (q.v.). He was named Captain Pasha of the Ottoman fleet after the death of Eulj Ali.

HASSAN IBN AL-NU'MAN AL-GHASSANI. Umayyad governor. Hassan recaptured Carthage from the Byzantines in 698 and defeated al-Kahina (q.v.) in 702. He then organized *Ifriqiya*.

HIGH COUNCIL OF STATE (HIGH STATE COUNCIL; HIGHER STATE COUNCIL/SUPREME STATE COUNCIL) (HCS) (q.v. Introduction). Government established in January 1992. After forcing the resignation of President Chadli Benjedid (q.v), a High Security Council soon named itself the High Council of State (HCS). Though a collective executive (q.v. Appendices), it does have a president. As of this writing, General Khaled Nezzar (q.v.), commander of the military, was the most powerful member in the HCS.

Its first President was Mohamed Boudiaf (q.v.), who served from January until his assassination in June 1992. He was succeeded by Ali Kafi (q.v.). Under Boudiaf, a consultative rather than legislative *Conseil Consultatif National* (CCN) was inaugurated in April. The HCS has faced the determined opposition of alienated Islamists, frustrated by the HCS's cancellation of national elections (q.v. Elections of December 1991; *Front Islamique du Salut*), which would have given the FIS power. That frustration has resulted in arrests, internment camps, and violence. In addition, the HCS faces the opposition of political parties. It has also been critical to the press, which continues as of this writing to exercise a tempered freedom. The HCS has expressed its desire to conduct elections in a secure political environment. Today that wish seems wistful given the wrenching political conditions of contemporary Algeria.

HILDERIC (463-533?). A Vandal (q.v.) king of North Africa (523–530). He was half Roman (by Eudoxia, q.v. Gaiseric; Huneric) and apparently spent much of his youth in Constantinople. Upon his accession to the throne, he extended religious freedom to those Christians who his predecessors had persecuted. This contributed to contentious relations with Theodoric the Ostrogoth. Theodoric's death prevented the launching of a military expedition against the Vandals. Hilderic also tried to keep close relations with the Eastern Roman (Byzantine) Emperor Justinian (q.v.), whom he knew personally. His reign divided the Vandal state and the court, and his family was upset over the exchange of expensive gifts to Justinian. Hilderic was deposed by the Vandal army in May 530 and succeeded by Gelimer.

HIPPO REGIUS (q.v. Annaba).

HISTORIC LEADERS (CHIEFS). Name applied to the nine nationalists who headed the CRUA and who were most closely associated with the outbreak of the War of Independence (National Liberation) in November 1954. The group was divided into three external members—Ahmed Ben Bella (q.v.), Hocine Aït Ahmed (q.v.), and Mohammed Khider (q.v.)—who were to supply the internal members, taking positions of political and military leadership in Algeria itself—Mohamed Boudiaf (q.v.), Mostefa Ben Boulaïd (q.v.), Mourad Didouche (q.v.), Belkacem Krim (q.v.), Rabah Bitat (q.v.), and Larbi Ben M'Hidi (q.v.). There is some argument among scholars concerning the decisive importance of the "Historic Leaders" in launching the revolution. Another interpretation is that the honor should go to the Committee of Twenty-two, since the core of the CRUA (q.v.) was this Committee.

HOUHOU, DJAMEL EDDINE (b. 1934). Diplomat; minister. Houhou was the longtime director of French Affairs at the Foreign Ministry from the crucial years 1962–1971. This period saw the initiation and implementation of cooperation (q.v.) policies. He then served as Ambassador to Canada (1971–1974) and to Egypt (1974–1977). He was appointed minister of youth and sports (1977–1982). He also became a member of the FLN's Central Committee (1979). During the height of French-Algerian "codevelopment" under Mitterrand (q.v.), Houhou served as ambassador in Paris (1982–1984) before becoming minister of health in 1984.

HOUHOU, REDA (1911–1956). Writer. Born near Biskra (q.v.), Houhou was the son of a pious and traditional family. He joined the Association of Reformist *Ulama* (q.v.) after World War II. In 1956, he was taken hostage by the French authorities in Constantine (q.v.) after the assassination of the police chief and was shot by the colonialist commando group, the "Red Hand." Houhou's works include *The Beauty of Mecca* (1947), *With Hakim's Ass* (1953), *The Inspiring Woman* (1954), and *Human Types* (1955). Houhou was a keen observer of life in Algeria and was a critic of colonialism.

HUNERIC (HUNNERIC) (d. 484). Vandal (q.v.) king of North Africa (477–484). He was the eldest son of Gaiseric (q.v.). Sent to the court of the Roman emperor of the West as a hostage (435), he was married to the daughter of Emperor Valentinian III in 455. During his reign, he led the defense against marauding Berbers (q.v.) and suppressed a revolt in the Aurès (q.v.), which became a chronic threat to the Vandal kings. Arianism was championed, and Catholics were often persecuted severely.

AL-HUSAYN BEN AL-HUSAYN (1765–1838). Last *Dey* of Algiers (1818–1830). Born in Izmir, Husayn was well educated. He served as tribute collector for the Regency (q.v.) before his elevation. Surviving assassination attempts by Janissaries and local rebellions during his reign, he was able to establish relative calm by the late 1820s. He also sent a fleet to participate in the unsuccessful suppression of the Greek Revolution. He built two mosques in the Casbah and rebuilt the Jami Safir mosque. His trouble largely resulted from his encounters with European governments in which he refused to compromise the honor of the Regency (q.v.). For example, Husayn ignored the decision by the Congress of Aix-la-Chapelle (1819), which called for the abolition of privateering. His expulsion of the British consul led to the bombardment of Algiers by a British fleet in June 1824. Poor relations with France concerning a commercial debt owed to the Regency was compounded by the *Dey*'s striking or tapping the French consul Pierre Deval with a fly whisk in April 1827. This led to a blockade of the Algerian coast by a French fleet (q.v. Introduction; Charles X). Discussions between France and the Regency failed to settle differences. King Charles X decided in 1830 to dispatch an expedition, which also served as a diversion from his unpopular domestic policies. After the defeat of the *Dey*'s forces, Husayn capitulated on July 5 and left for Italy. He eventually settled and died in Alexandria.

HUSAYN PASHA, HADJIDJI (known as "MEZZOMORTO")
(d. 1701). Algerian *raïs*; *dey*. Mezzomorto may have been
born in Majorca, but he first appears as a famous corsair
commander in 1674. At the time of the French bombardment
of Algiers (1683), he served as a hostage from the *Dey* to the
French. Upon his return to Algiers, he led a rebellion against
Dey Hasan Baba (q.v.), had him executed, and succeeded
him. In 1684 he negotiated a peace with the French.
Hostilities were soon renewed, and the French again
bombarded Algiers in 1688. This time Husayn responded by
conducting a series of raids along the French coasts and
marauding French shipping. Before receiving the appointment as Captain Pasha of the Ottoman fleet in 1689, internal
strife forced him to flee from Algiers to Tunis. He later
refitted and strengthened the Ottoman fleet.

HYDROCARBONS (q.v. Appendices). This is Algeria's most
strategic and wealthy sector. Large natural gas and oil fields
were discovered by French companies from 1954 to 1956,
especially at Hassi R'Mel and Hassi Messaoud. This was an
important find for France politically and psychologically
(given the prestige of the Anglo-American Cartel). The
promise of hydrocarbon wealth provided a very powerful
rationale for holding on to Algeria. For example, the
Organisation Commune des Régions Sahariennes (OCRS)
was formed in January 1957, which represented a French
condominium plan to share the Sahara's wealth with
bordering states. The FLN (q.v.) also suggested that it would
pursue a similar strategy with its neighbors. (Since the Arab
Maghrib Union [q.v.] [AMU]; [q.v. Maghrib Unity], this is
being realized, e.g., the planned gas trunk line to Morocco.)

The Evian Accords secured French hydrocarbon interests
by assuring (1) the continuation of colonial Petroleum Code
with recent modifications, which gave the companies full
freedom of their transfer flows; and (2) the promotion of the
use of French francs in all hydrocarbon financial matters.

With their position entrenched, the companies continued to expand the volume of production. The perpetuation of French privileges was challenged by the elaboration and evolution of an Algerian hydrocarbons policy aiming at the nationalization of the sector. In December 1963, SON-ATRACH, a state enterprise, was established to build a third pipeline (independent of the oil companies' consortium plan). Algeria conducted its first independent exploration in 1965.

On July 29, 1965, the Algiers Accord was signed between the French and Algerian governments. The French companies kept their concessions and their control (though modified by ASCOOP, see below). Algeria's royalties were computed at $2.08/barrel fob Bougie (Bejaïa [q.v.]). This gave Algeria an opportunity to plan its revenues by insulating it from the caprice of the world petroleum market. Algeria was also able to tax a greater percentage of the profits. The accord featured the innovative *Association Coopérative* (ASCOOP). It was a partnership between an Algerian state company (SONATRACH) and a French one (eventually ERAP). Both companies would explore and exploit the sector together with the French state enterprise financing 60 percent of the research costs. Another imaginative idea included in the accord was a new financial aid arrangement. An *Organisme de Coopération Industrielle* (OCI) was inaugurated that would operate as a partnership to stimulate Algeria's industrialization. In addition, Algeria's Supreme Court would play a role (not final) concerning arbitration. The natural gas package gave Algeria a marketing monopoly (though it paid production costs from French wells) and a 50 percent shared interest of a joint liquefaction enterprise. France also offered itself as a purchaser (satisfactory accord reached in 1967). Since Algerian planners projected (like former French ones; *Perspectives décennales* [q.v.]; Constantine Plan [q.v.]) natural gas fueling Algeria's industrialization, these stipulations were very well received.

Algeria regarded the Algiers Accord as another stage toward territorial recovery and economic liberation. It seemed to promise a "naturalization" rather than a disruptive nationalization of the sector. It also committed France, Algeria's most important economic furnisher and client, to continue a privileged bilateral cooperation (q.v.).

In 1967 Algeria bought out British Petroleum's remaining interests and, as a result of the Arab-Israeli Six-Day War of June 1967, slapped an embargo on the United States and the United Kingdom. A few months later, five American companies were nationalized. In 1968 Getty Oil negotiated an accord that gave Algeria 51 percent of its concessions.

In 1969 Algeria and France began negotiating new fiscal arrangements. Algeria advised the concessionaires to raise the posted petroleum price to $2.65/barrel. This was a protracted negotiation that eventually called into question the entire bilateral relationship. On February 24, 1971, President Boumedienne declared the nationalization (51 percent) of French interests in the Sahara. Production was stopped and technicians were removed from the field. The French companies came to satisfactory terms with Algeria by the end of the year. The nationalization of French concessions (rhetorically, "the battle of oil") was viewed by the Algerian government as marking the economic liberation of Algeria.

Algeria easily diversified its oil markets, particularly as a result of the Oil Embargo of 1973 as West Germany and the United States became important importers. Algeria especially benefited from OPEC price escalations, which produced unimagined revenues. Algeria's crude (among the world's "sweetest"/lightest, thereby reducing refining costs) sold as high as $40/barrel in 1981 and even reached $45/barrel on the Rotterdam spot market. The collapse of prices in the mid-1980s dropped Algeria crude to $12/barrel, which reverberated throughout the entire economy and contributed to the October 1988 (q.v.) rioting. Algeria also permitted greater foreign investment and profit opportunities concerning petroleum exploration and production (Investment Law of 1986). In 1980 crude oil sales produced 61 percent of Algeria's hydrocarbon export earnings, but this dropped to 25 percent for 1983, given oil price reduction and the growth in LNG (liquefied natural gas) sales.

At first, both French and Algerian planners valued petroleum over natural gas. This was due in part to existing energy markets and operating systems and the technical problem of natural gas recovery and delivery. In the short-term, oil was easier to exploit and more profitable. Natural gas liquefaction processes were just beginning to come on line (e.g., the *Compagnie Algérienne de Methane Liquide* [CAMEL] at Arzew in 1964).

In 1969 El Paso Corporation signed a contract with SONATRACH for the annual delivery of 10 billion m^3 for 25 years to the United States, which strengthened Algeria's resolve while bolstering its confidence during the negotiations with the French during 1969 to 1971. Algeria's VALHYD (*Valorisation des Hydrocarbures*) Plan of 1978, produced with the collaboration of American Bechtel consultants, profiled oil and gas production and Algeria's future development. It underscored how Boumedienne's state-building period was linked to hydrocarbons production and receipts. Interest rates, overruns, and debts led to the reformulation of gas pricing. A new gas policy was especially articulated by SONATRACH'S Nordine Aït Laoussine (now Minister of Energy since June 1991), who argued that LNG prices should be equivalent to competing energies. The decision to equate gas with oil prices was made in 1979.

Consumer reluctance to subscribe to the new formulation created great pressures on Algeria. The El Paso contract was jeopardized. Though El Paso had provided great technical assistance at Arzew, and Algeria benefited internationally from this relationship, the American corporation found the pricing principle uneconomical. This contract dissipated in 1981. In February 1980 negotiations began with *Gaz de France* (GDF), which balked at Algerian insistence of parity prices. A major contract in April 1981 with Belgium's Distrigaz provided a pricing formula calculated not solely on Algerian crude but a "basket" of crudes that Belgium imported. In February 1982, France agreed on a similar agreement in an accord for the delivery of 9.1 billion m^3 annually, which featured the French government's subsidy of 13.5 percent of the price because of anticipated contracts with Algeria. This innovative accord was reminiscent of the Algiers Accord of 1965 and symbolized President François Mitterrand's (q.v.) implementation of "codevelopment." In 1983, the Trans-Mediterranean pipeline began pumping natural gas to Italy.

The energy parity policy was a good risk as long as prices remained inelastic and high. The drop in oil prices in the mid-1980s and, by linkage, the drop in LNG prices, weakened the Algerian economy. Algeria's clients (e.g., Distrigaz and Spain's Enagas) wanted to renegotiate contracts. From $5.11/MMBtu in 1982, France paid about $2.00/MMBtu in 1987. The mutually satisfying January 12, 1989, LNG accord set the price at $2.30/MMBtu. Furthermore, both sides agreed to participate in joint cooperation projects, several of which have been realized.

This sector was especially affected by Benjedid's policies of decentralization. SONATRACH was "restructured" into smaller enterprises. Algeria lifted 33 million metric tons of oil in 1988. Its gross production of natural gas was 105.6 billion m^3 of natural gas in 1987. Algeria's gas reserves are estimated as the seventh largest in the world. There is reluctance today by foreign companies to invest in the sector, in spite of more attractive terms offered by the Algerian government (1986 legislation), given the domestic distress and violence.

IBADISM (AL-IBADIYYA; ABADIYYA, IBADA). An early movement of dissent in North African Islam relating directly to Kharijism (q.v.). The sect was named after Abd Allah ibn Ibad (or Abad) al-Murri al-Tamimim. A *shaykh* from Basra, Salama ibn Said, was the first to preach Ibadi doctrines in the Maghrib at Qayrawan. This led to the establishment of an Ibadi state in Tripolitania and the occupation of Qayrawan in 758. Eventually the Ibadi state extended from Barka to the land of the Kutama (q.v.) under the imamate of Abu al-Khattab. An Abbasid (q.v.) Army from Egypt was dispatched against the Ibadis and defeated them at the Battle of Tawargha in 761. The remaining Ibadi forces fled to Tahert (Tagdempt) where Abd al-Rahman ibn Rustam, a former Ibadi governor of Qayrawan, established a new Ibadi capital and (q.v. Rustamid) dynasty. Under this imam's two successors, Ibadism reached its zenith. By the end of the eighth century, the imamate of Tahert reached from Tlemcen (q.v.) to Tripoli. The Ibadi state survived until 909 when it was finally crushed by the armies of Abu Abd Allah al-Shi'i, who founded the Fatimid (q.v) state. The Ibadis then moved into the Sahara. Major Ibadite centers today are at Ouargla (Wargla) and the M'zab (q.v.) in Saharan Algeria.

IBN also see Ben.

IBN BADIS, ABD AL-HAMID B. AL-MUSTAFA B. MAKKI (q.v. Ben Badis).

IBN BATTUTA, ABU ABDALLAH (1325–1368). Traveler; jurist. Born in Tangier where he studied Islamic law, Ibn Battuta set out in 1325 to make the *hajj* to Mecca. On his way, he stayed in the Abd al-Wadid (q.v.) capital of Tlemcen (q.v.) for a short time before proceeding to Miliana, Algiers (q.v.), and then to Hafsid-controlled Bejaïa (q.v.). He also visited Constantine (q.v.) and Annaba. After finally reaching Mecca, Ibn Battuta went on journeys that would take him to

South and East Asia. On his way back to Tangier he stopped in Tenès and Tlemcen (q.v.). His last great venture was to Mali. Ibn Battuta's recollections (*Rihla*) provide valuable information concerning the fourteenth-century Maghrib.

IBN KHALDUN, WALI AL-DIN ABD AL-RAHMAN B. MUHAMMAD B. MUHAMMAD B. ALI BAKR MUHAMMAD B. AL-HASAN (1332–1406). Historian; "sociologist"; philosopher. Ibn Khaldun was born in Tunis. The Maranid invasion provided him with a number of theological and literary instructors during his early years. In 1349, an attack of Black Death took his parents, which had a traumatic effect on his life. Shortly thereafter he left for Fez, where he became a court functionary. Following an attack on the area by the *amir* of Constantine (q.v.), Ibn Khaldun began a series of circuitous moves around the area. He returned to Fez in 1354 as part of the sultan's secretariat. For his court intrigues, he was imprisoned (1357–1358). With the death of the sultan, Ibn Khaldun became court poet of his successor. From 1362 until 1368 he was at the courts of Granada and Bejaïa (q.v.). Moving to Biskra (q.v.), he withdrew from politics and attempted to become a man of letters. He then moved to Tlemcen (q.v.) in 1375, but shortly thereafter went into refuge in a fortress near Frenda. There he stayed for four years and did much reflecting over his ideas. He returned to Tunis in 1378 to begin a new career as teacher and scholar. As a result of a conspiracy against him, he fled to Cairo in 1382. From this new home he continued his career as teacher, traveler, and scholar until his death.

He is best known for two works, his *Ibar*, or *Universal History*, and his *Muqaddima*, or *Introduction*. His ideas on tribal cohesion and consciousness, *asabiyya* (q.v.), or "collective interest" (Charles-André Julien's [q.v.] interpretation of the word), the rise and fall of dynasties, and the effect of rural-city conflict are particularly admired.

IBN TASHFIN, YUSUF (d. 1106) (q.v. Almoravids). Almoravid leader. He was a founder of the Almoravid Empire and extended its territory. Ibn Tashfin founded Marrakesh in 1062, which became the Almoravid capital. He invaded Spain in 1086 and controlled territory as far as Toledo. In the East he moved into Algeria taking Tlemcen (Ibn Tashfin is credited with the founding of modern Tlemcen [q.v.]), Oran (q.v.), and Algiers (q.v.). Ibn Tashfin ordered the construction of some of the most notable mosques in North Africa (e.g., Great Mosques of Tlemcen and of Algiers).

IBN TUMART (c. 1080–c. 1130). Spiritual leader of the Almohads (q.v.); nicknamed "the Torch." He was born in Igillaz, a village in the northern anti-Atlas, to the Hargha of the Masmuda (Zenata [q.v.]) Berbers). There is historiographical controversy concerning his education. Ibn Tumart may have gone to Spain where he may have been influenced by the ideas of Ibn Hazm (d. 1064), who emphasized the Qur'an, tradition (*sunna*), and general consensus (*ijma*) as juridical sources. Traveling eastward (c. 1105–1110), Ibn Tumart continued his studies, probably at Baghdad, and may have gone to Damascus. It is not certain if he met his contemporary, the renowned scholar Abu Hamid al-Ghazali. He was highly influenced by the ideas of al-Ash'ari (873–935), the founder of orthodox scholasticism. On his way back to the Maghrib, Ibn Tumart stopped at an Ash'ari(te) study center in Alexandria. His Orthodoxy and social criticism provoked controversy at Bejaïa (q.v.), the Hammadid (q.v.) capital. At Mallal near Bejaïa, he chose a young scholar and Zenata Berber, Abd al-Mu'min (q.v.), to be his student and companion.

Ibn Tumart taught strict adherence to the Qur'an and the Sunna. He emphasized the "oneness" or unity of God (*tawhid*), and his followers would be called "Unitarians," or the al-Muwahhidun or "Almohads" (Spanish corruption of the Arabic word). He challenged the Maliki(te) (q.v. Malikism) use of their own secondary juridical works instead of relying upon Qur'an and the Sunna. He also condemned the use of personal opinion (*ray*) in Malikite jurisprudence. Unlike other theologians, Ibn Tumart aimed to proselytize and propagate his ideas (articulated in Berber [q.v.] besides Arabic). His political doctrine included Shi'a (q.v.) ideas of the Mahdi and the sinless Imam. At Marrakesh he probably met the Almoravid ruler Ali ibn Yusuf, a devout Maliki. Ibn Tumart's agitation against Malikism, which was adhered to fervently by the Almoravids (q.v.), finally forced him to flee to his ancestral home.

After several years of preaching and praying, tribesmen recognized him as Imam. When he received their oath, he called himself the Mahdi. In order to keep unity, he led a hierarchy that was based on Berber tribal organization and confederation (e.g., councils and assemblies). Ibn Tumart felt strong enough to initiate attacks against the Almoravids. According to sources, his death was kept a secret for several years until Abd al-Mu'min could secure his succession as *Amir al-Mu'minin* (Commander of the Faithful). It seems, however, that given the closeness of the two men, and the Mahdi's chosen deputy, that his succession was anticipated by the Berber tribes. Abd al-Mu'min would embark upon many conquests, consequently unifying the Maghrib from the Atlantic to *Ifriqiya*.

IBN UTHMAN, MUHAMMAD (q.v. Ben Othman).

AL-IBRAHIMI, BACHIR (1889–1965). Born in Bejaïa (q.v.), al-Ibrahimi became a leading companion of Abd al-Hamid Ben Badis (q.v.) and his successor. He was a well-known orator of the Association of Reformist Algerian Ulama (q.v.). He achieved a great reputation as an Arabic and Islamic scholar while contributing numerous articles to his association's various journals (q.v. Literature in Arabic). Al-

Ibrahimi was the father of the statesman, Ahmed Taleb-Ibrahimi (q.v.).

IFRAN (IFREN). Zenata (q.v.) Berber (q.v.) tribe. A very powerful group within the Zenata, the Ifran were located in eastern Algeria but eventually spread westward. They played a significant role in resisting the Arab conquest and also in the revolts of the ninth century.

IMACHE, AMAR (1895–1960). Nationalist. As an emigrant in France, Imache became involved in the ENA (q.v.) and became editor of its paper, *El-Ouma*. He was renowned as a polemicist in Arabic, French, and Berber. Arrested in 1934, he was incarcerated with Messali Hadj (q.v.). Imache eventually broke with Messali, accusing him of promoting a "personality cult." In 1947 he attempted to organize another nationalist party called the *Parti de l'Unité algérienne*. Failing to mobilize enough interest in it, he joined Ferhat Abbas's (q.v.) UDMA (q.v.).

IMALAYEN, FATIMA ZOHRA (q.v. Assia Djebar).

INDUSTRIALIZATION (q.v. State Plans). Beginning after World War II, French colonial authorities realized that there was a need to promote industrialization in Algeria, given shortages of commodities. Furthermore, the "galloping" Muslim birthrate portended an economic as well as political nightmare and necessitated the generation of hundreds of thousands of jobs. Modest industrializing efforts were undertaken until the War of Independence when France provided impressive study and massive aid toward the development of a second sector. This was disclosed by the *Perspective décennales* (q.v.) and the Constantine Plan (q.v.).

In part influenced by its socialism, the FLN accelerated these industrializing efforts through the development of hydrocarbons (already projected by the French) (q.v.). The model pursued was called "industrializing industries" and was based on using hydrocarbons as a catalytic multiplier (influenced by Professor Gérard Destanne de Bernis's ideas). This was viewed in the First and Second Four-Year Plans (1970–1977) where the second sector received most of the allocations. Though the two Five-Year Plans (1980–1989) distinguished themselves by placing significant attention on the first and third sectors, the second was not neglected. The First Five-Year Plan aimed to complete industrial projects of the Four-Year Plans.

Steelworks are located in Algiers and especially at the Hadjar complex near Annaba. Trucks, refrigerators, televisions, textiles, cement, fertilizers, plastics, clothing, shoes, cigarettes, matches, and paper are manufactured nationally. Algeria plans to assemble its own automobiles jointly with European companies (Fiat; Peugeot) in the 1990s.

A general complaint concerning industrialization has been the concentration of capital and resources resulting in an ultramodern sector that is not labor intensive, thereby exasperating the under- and unemployment problem.

INTEGRATION. This was the policy articulated by Governor-General Jacques Soustelle (q.v.). It called for the political, administrative, and economic integration of Algeria with France. It was not meant to be an authentic assimilation as Soustelle did not call for social and cultural integration because that would threaten Muslim identity (and that of the European settlers [q.v. *pieds-noirs*]).

Though the policy relieved the *pieds-noirs,* who feared abandonment, its logical conclusion was the democratization of Algeria, another threat to the settlers' political predominance. The policy was abandoned after Soustelle left office.

INTERMINISTERIAL COMMITTEE OF WAR. The first GPRA (q.v.) was reorganized at the Tripoli meeting of January

1961. The government remained that had been appointed in September 1958 with the following changes: Belkacem Krim (q.v.) became foreign minister, and Krim, Abdelhafid Boussouf (q.v.), and Lakhdar Ben Tobbal (q.v.) constituted the Interministerial Committee of War, which was in charge of coordinating the military effort in Algeria and of acquiring supplies to the internal leaders. This committee was eliminated at the August 1961 GPRA meeting.

IRATEN. A Berber (q.v.) tribal group of Great Kabylia (q.v.). Throughout the Turkish period, they continued to be independent until subdued by the French in 1857. They revolted unsuccessfully in the great Kabyle uprising of 1871–1872 (q.v.).

ISLAMIC JIHAD OF SHEIKH SADIQ AL MOUNDIRI. A military Islamist opposition group. On August 29, 1985, it raided police barracks near Blida, killing one officer. In addition, it claimed responsibility for an attack on the Algerian Embassy in Beirut. Other attacks near Blida were made in October and November. The group claimed to have attacked a police station in Oran as well. Islamist violence in the 1980s was also symbolized by Mustapha Bouiali (q.v.). The appeal of politicized, populist Islam contributed to the emergence of the *Front Islamique du Salut* (FIS) (q.v.).

ISSAD, HASSAN (b. 1896). Political organizer; labor leader. Along with Hadj Ali Abdelkader (q.v.), he was a founder of the ENA (q.v.) and served on its Central Committee. Issad had also been active in leading workers in various organizations created by the PCF (French Communist Party) and its labor group, the CGTU (*Confédération Générale du Travail Unitaire*).

JAZAIRY, IDRISS (b. 1936). Counselor; ambassador. Jazairy received an excellent education in public policy. He attended the Ecole Nationale d'Administration (ENA) in Paris and earned Master's degrees from Oxford University (political science) and Harvard University (public administration). From 1963 to 1970, he was director of economic, cultural, and social affairs in the Foreign Ministry. He then served from 1971 to 1977 as counselor of economics and international cooperation affairs to President Houari Boumedienne (q.v.). He was an assistant secretary-general of the Ministry of Foreign Affairs from 1977 to 1979. Concurrently he presided over the United Nations General Assembly's Committee on North-South Dialogue (1978–1979). He then served as ambassador to Belgium, Luxemburg, and the European Community (1979–1982). He became a roving ambassador for the Ministry of Foreign Affairs concerning international economics issues in 1982 before being tabbed as president of the *Fonds International de Développement Agricole* (FIDA) (International Fund for Agricultural Development) in 1984.

JEUNES ALGERIENS (q.v. Young Algerians).

JEWS. The Jews of Algeria predate the Arab and Muslim conquest. Jewish communities played prominent political and commercial roles throughout the history of Algeria. One of the most famous resistants to the Arab invasion was al-Kahina (q.v.), who headed an apparently Judeo-Berber tribe, the Jarawa.

   After the Arab conquest, Jewish communities existed within the Berber states (q.v. Rustamids, Hammadids, Zirids) and maintained contacts with their religious compatriots in the Maghrib and in Spain. There was a significant Jewish cultural and commercial presence in cities such as Tahert, Qal'a, Bejaïa (q.v.), Tlemcen (q.v.), and Algiers (q.v.). When persecutions in Spain intensified in the late fourteenth and fifteenth century, many Jewish immigrants arrived in Algeria. The Andalusians were highly cultured when compared with the Maghribi Jews. This created tensions, but it also enriched North African Jewry.

Jews also played significant political roles. Abu al-Faraj led a Berber revolt against the Zirids. He was captured and executed (989). Christian Spanish kings often employed Jews as ambassadors throughout the Maghrib. Nevertheless, Spanish incursions in the sixteenth century along the North African coast (e.g., Oran [q.v.] and Bejaïa) were catastrophic for Jews (e.g., properties destroyed; enslavement).

Despite these upheavals, the Jewish communities persisted and even prospered. Relations among Berbers, Arabs, and Jews were generally good. Occasional violence did occur. There is an example of a *marabout* from Blida who not only stopped violence against Jews but also had properties returned.

The Turks discriminated against Arabs, Berbers, and particularly Jews (targeted with special taxes). Nevertheless, the Regency's (q.v.) leaders often used Jews for diplomatic and financial assistance. Naphtali Busnach (Bushnaq) became Mustafa *Dey*'s (1798–1805) chief adviser. Busnach's assassination in 1805 provoked a murderous outburst against the Jews in Algiers. The debts owed (7 to 8 million francs) by the French government to the Busnach and Bakri families and their associates were a cause of the French expedition of 1830.

At the time of the French conquest there were 30,000 Jews in Algeria. Like the Muslims, the Jews faced the French threat of cultural assimilation. Hebrew presses and schools were established; nevertheless, many Jews were assimilated. They gained the right of naturalization in 1865 and became French citizens by the Crémieux Decree (q.v.) of 1870. (This applied to most Jews except those in the South, whose legal status was unclear.) The granting of citizenship, a privilege in colonial society, contributed to an increasingly virulent anti-Semitism, especially among European settlers as witnessed by attacks in Tlemcen (1881), Algiers (1882, especially 1897–1898), Oran (1883), Sétif (1883) (q.v.), and Mostaganem (1897). This violent climate was aggravated by the Dreyfus Affair. There was also a significant Muslim outburst of anti-Semitism in Constantine (1934).

France's defeat in 1940 and the establishment of the Vichy (q.v.) government was a disaster to the 117,646 Jews living in Algeria. The Crémieux Decree was abrogated, producing great suffering but also the mobilization of Jewish resistance. Ironically, even after the Allies ended Algeria's Vichy administration, the Crémieux Decree was not restored and systematic discrimination continued in spite of the protests of Charles de Gaulle's (q.v.) Free French. Finally, the Decree was reinstated on October 20, 1943.

The terrible experience during World War II led to the inauguration of the *Fédération des Commmunautés Israélites d'Algérie* to protect the community. A new crisis emerged, however, with the rise of militant Muslim nationalism and finally the War of Independence. The FLN (q.v.) urged Jews to support Algerian independence and promised toleration, citing the injustices committed against them by the colonial establishment. Jews were sympathetic toward the nationalists. Nevertheless, many Jews identified culturally with France, which left them torn. In February 1958, two members of the Jewish Agency were killed. The Muslim desecration of the Great Synagogue in December 1960 and of the Jewish cemetery in Oran increased anxieties and fears. Symbolizing the difficult position of the community were the publicized killings of William Lévy, the Socialist Party's secretary-general for Algiers, by the OAS and of his son by the ALN (q.v.). This insecurity led to another Jewish "diaspora," this time to France (70,000) and Israel (5,000). Repatriation/expatriation was aided greatly by the United Jewish Social Fund.

After independence, the situation became increasingly difficult for the Jews who remained. While Ahmed Ben Bella's government had proper relations with the community (despite Ben Bella's Nasserist affinities), the situation deteriorated with the Houari Boumedienne (q.v.) era. Boumedienne was an ardent Arab nationalist and a staunch supporter of the Palestine Liberation Organization (PLO). Jews lost civil rights and as a consequence of the Arab-Israeli June 1967 War, synagogues and other Jewish buildings were defaced. All the synagogues except one (pillaged eventually in 1977) were converted into mosques. By 1970 there were less than 1,000 Jews left. There is still a small community in Algeria, the vestige of a great historical legacy.

Among Algerian-born Jews who have particularly distinguished themselves are Jacques Derrida (q.v.), Annie Cohen-Solal, and Bernard-Henri Lévy.

AL-JILALI, ABDERRAHMAN (b. 1906). Historian. Al-Jilali was a member of the Association of Reformist *Ulama* (q.v.). His *General History of Algeria* (1954) was written in Arabic and strove to develop a historical and national consciousness. Al-Jilali symbolized how Abd al-Hamid Ben Badis's (q.v.) influence created a cultural nationalism.

JONNART, CHARLES CELESTIN (1857–1927). Governor-general. Jonnart served as a deputy, senator, and diplomat for the Third Republic. He particularly distinguished himself in Algerian affairs. He served multiple terms as governor-general (q.v. Appendices) and promoted the founding of the University of Algiers (1909). He was reform oriented and encouraged agricultural and artisan production. Georges Clemenceau (q.v. Clemenceau Reforms) viewed Jonnart as an ideological ally. Both men tried to enact substantial reform in post-World War I Algeria (q.v. Jonnart Law). Their reforming efforts resulted in some changes but not enough to satisfy impatient Young Algerians (q.v.) and especially Emir Khaled (q.v.).

JONNART LAW OF FEBRUARY 1919 (q.v. Clemenceau Reforms). Named after Governor-General Charles Jonnart (q.v.), this was a reform bill in favor of Muslims and intended as a reward for Algerian participation in World War I. It created an electorate of some 425,000 Algerians who had not opted for French citizenship but who voted in a separate second electorate (i.e., a quasi-citizenship), the first being reserved for European settlers and those few Algerians who had become naturalized Frenchmen. It did not allow naturalization with Muslim status (i.e., preservation of personal status under Muslim law). Access to the second electoral group was granted to those Algerian men who, by virtue of economic position, education, or relatively long service in French institutions, had been most affected by the French presence in Algeria. Specifically, the second electorate included licensed merchants, school certificate holders, civil employees, landowners, and veterans. Voters were granted immunity from the *Code de l'Indigénat* (q.v.). They could elect their own representatives, but within severely limited bounds: Not more than one-third of municipal councilmen in local councils or one-fourth on lesser councils could be elected by the second electorate. There was no change, however, in the makeup of that peculiar institution of colonial Algeria, the *Délégation financières* (q.v.). This law was significant because it created a large body of Algerians who could vote and who soon became politically aware, resulting in political groups such as the moderate *Fédération des Elus Musulmans* party. It was also viewed as being too moderate and too restrictive by the incipient nationalist elite (q.v. Young Algerians; Emir Khaled) because the minority colonialist population's predominance remained institutionally and politically protected.

JOXE, LOUIS (1901–1991). French Evian Accords (q.v.) negotiator. Joxe had a distinguished public service as an ambassador, deputy, and minister. In Algerian history, he played a crucial role as the minister of state in charge of Algerian affairs (1960–1962). Joxe was a (Charles) de Gaulle (q.v.) loyalist who accepted the unenviable task of dealing with the wrenching decolonization of Algeria. He was charged to be chief negotiator of the Evian Accords. Joxe perceived his primary diplomatic objective as the protection of the European community. The arduous discussions led to detailed stipulations listing guarantees to the *pieds-noirs,* which were quickly anachronistic, given the anarchic events in Algeria (q.v. *Organisation de l'Armée Secrète* [OAS]). Joxe had said that another difficulty was the FLN as an organization: How much authority and legitimacy did it possess? Joxe handled his difficult tasks professionally and earned the respect of his Algerian counterparts.

JUBA I; JUBA II (d. A.D. 19?) (q.v. Numidia). Numidian kings. Juba I died in 46 B.C. as a supporter of the Roman general and statesman Pompey. His son Juba II became an illustrious client of Rome (q.v.). Juba II was brought to Rome by the victorious Caesar and grew up in his household and that of his nephew, Octavian (later Augustus). Juba became Romanized and Hellenized, even writing books in Greek. He was especially a patron of the arts. He married the daughter of Antony and Cleopatra, Cleopatra Selene, in 29 B.C. They renamed Cherchell (q.v.) as Iol Caesarea in honor of Augustus, and it became a celebrated capital of Roman culture and arts. Juba's second capital was at Volubilis in Mauretania (Morocco). Juba's kingdom relied upon Roman military assistance. Juba's loyalty resulted in a gradual Romanization of the area and, with that, prosperity and an enriched civilization.

JUGURTHA (d. 104 B.C.). King of Numidia (118–106 B.C.). He was the illegitimate son of Mastanabal and grandson of King Masinissa (q.v.). After his father's death, he was raised by his uncle Micipsa with his cousin and principal rival,

Adherbal. His uncle sent him to command a Numidian force in Spain under Scipio Africanus Minor in 134 B.C., where he distinguished himself and made many Roman friends. Upon his uncle's death in 118 B.C., three cousins ruled: Adherbal, Hiempsal, and Jugurtha. Civil war broke out when Rome decided to give Adherbal eastern Numidia. The ambitious Jugurtha gained the upper hand. When Adherbal took refuge in the fortress of Cirta (q.v. Constantine) in 112, Jugurtha laid siege, which eventually led to a massacre of the inhabitants, including a number of Italian merchants; this event provoked Roman hostility. After the Roman Senate sent an army to Numidia under consul Bestia, a temporary peace was declared. Shortly thereafter the conflict resumed, and the Roman army suffered a major defeat at Suthul. A conciliatory peace was concluded by the Romans in 109, which created a furor in Rome. A new army was sent to Numidia under Quintus Metellus (109–106). Marius, in particular, and Sulla also played significant roles in this conflict. Jugurtha was finally defeated in a pitched battle on the Muthul River in 106 B.C. He was betrayed by his father-in-law, King Bocchus of Mauretania (q.v.), and later captured in an ambush and sent as a prisoner to Rome, where he died under mysterious circumstances. Jugurtha's resistance to Rome was inspirational to the FLN (q.v.) in its struggle against the French.

JULIEN, CHARLES-ANDRE (1891–1991) (q.v. Bibliography). French historian. Julien's *Histoire de l'Afrique du Nord* (1931) was an objective work that especially contradicted the colonialist historical interpretations of Algerian history as presented during the centenary celebrations of French colonialism in Algeria. He also played an important role in the formulation and promotion of the Blum-Viollette legislation (q.v.). Julien has been honored by the French, Moroccan, and Tunisian governments. He was a *Conseiller de l'Union Française* (1947–1958). The *Histoire de l'Algérie contemporaine: La Conquête et les débuts de la colonisation (1827–1871)* (1964) was another monumental historiographic contribution.

JUSTINIAN (483-565) (r. 527–565). Byzantine (q.v.) emperor. Justinian ordered the conquest of the Vandal (q.v.) kingdom, which General Belisarius achieved and "reincorporated" into the (Eastern) Roman Empire in 533–534. The invasion force had 500 ships with 30,000 sailors, an army of 16,000, and 6,000 horses. The Byzantines had learned new cavalry tactics from their campaigns against the Persians, which they applied against the Vandals. Belisarius kept the invaders under strict discipline, which encouraged public support. Though the Byzantines were outnumbered, Gelimer (q.v.) was decisively defeated in September 533. After the disintegration of the Vandals, the Byzantines also faced the pressure of regional Berber (q.v.) tribesmen. The Byzantines established fortresses in eastern Algeria. Justinian also tried to repair the infrastructure of his North African conquest. The Byzantines, like the Vandals, appreciated Berber military prowess. They mustered North African levies and deployed them to support Justinian's other military operations. A cultural consequence was the reassertion of the establishment (i.e., traditional Catholic/Orthodox) Church at the expense of Donatists (q.v. Donatism), Arians, Jews (q.v.), and pagans.

KABYLE REVOLT OF 1871–1872 (GREAT KABYLE RE-
VOLT). Kabylia (q.v.) with its history of independence
became even more restive with the arrival of the French to
the region in the 1850s. Subsequent conflict (q.v. Kabyles)
dislocated the area socially and economically and provoked
great resentment. In January 1871, native troops in Kabylia
resisted deployment to France. Concurrently, Muhammad
al-Hajj al-Muqrani (q.v.), a leading Kabyle notable and a
bachaga, wanted to assert more autonomy from the French
administration. The condescending refusal of his proposal by
French authorities instigated his summoning of a war council
in March. Al-Muqrani's initiative received the prestigious
support of Sidi Muhammad al-Haddad (q.v.), the *muqaddam*
of the Rahmaniyya order. (His son al-Aziz [Si Aziz] also
played an important role.) The "Great Revolt" (proclaimed
as a *jihad*) began in April. Approximately 150,000 Kabyles
joined in the insurrection, which threatened the entire
colonial establishment. From eastern Algeria the struggle
against the French reached Algiers (q.v.) and Cherchell
(q.v.). Al-Muqrani, who assumed the title of *Amir al-
Mujahidin*, was killed in May, but his brother, Bu Masraq
(q.v.) replaced him. The French Army slowly regained the
initiative by late 1871. Bu Masraq was captured in June
1872, ending the rebellion. Besides suffering great loss of
life, the Muslims of eastern Algeria lost more land (574,000
hectares expropriated by 1875) and were punished, too, with
indemnities (36,500,000 francs).

KABYLES (q.v. Kabylia). Prominent Berber (q.v.) group. The
Kabyles (from the Arabic *qabila* [tribe]) are Berbers
inhabiting the mountainous regions east of Algiers (q.v.) and
west of Sétif (q.v.) from the Mediterranean Sea to the
southern slopes of the Djudjura mountains. There is also a
large Kabyle population in Algiers. In Kabylia itself, most of
these Berbers are agriculturalists, although population pressure has forced many Kabyles to emigrate where jobs and

incomes have been traditionally available, primarily Algiers and France. Kabyle villages are generally administered by a *jama'a,* which is an assembly of adult males where decisions are reached by consensus. Kabyles rule themselves according to their customary law, which is complemented by Islamic jurisprudence. Practically all Kabyle villages are divided into competing political groups known as *çoffs* (*soffs*). But because the jama'a is governed by consensus and because the lesser *çoffs* in one village are generally allied to the dominant *çoff* in another nearby village, the potential for violence is generally slight. Women do not have a direct voice in the public affairs of Kabyle society, which is patrilineal. Within the family circle they can, however, achieve considerable power, particularly if they have sons. Women generally dress in loose and brightly colored cotton garments, wear heavy silver jewelry, and cover their heads with silk scarfs. Men wear flowing robes, woolen burnooses, and skull caps, or *chechias.*

The Kabyles and their Berber brethren provided constant harassment to conquerors (q.v. Introduction). The French began "controlling" Kabylia in the 1850s after confronting the resistances of Bu Baghla (q.v.), Lalla Fatima (q.v.), and Bu Renan (q.v.). Nevertheless, in April 1871 the Kabyles rose against the French (q.v. Kabyle Revolt of 1871–1872) led by Muhammad al-Hajj al-Muqrani (q.v.), *Shaykh* Sidi Muhammad al-Haddad (q.v.), *muqaddam* of the Rahmaniyya (q.v.) order, and his son al-Aziz (Si Aziz). The entire French colonial establishment was threatened. The suppression of their "Great Revolt" led to vast expropriation and, given the subsequent lack of subsistence compounded by population growth, eventually to the expatriation of Kabyles to France as emigrant workers (q.v. Emigrant Labor).

During the War of Independence, Kabyles played prominent roles (e.g., Belkacem Krim [q.v.], Ramdane Abane [q.v.], Aït Hamouda [Amirouche (q.v.)], Hocine Aït Ahmed [q.v.], and Ben Youssef Ben Khedda [q.v.]). Kabyles also contributed culturally toward the development of an ethnic and national identity (e.g., Jean Amrouche [q.v.], Marguerite Taos-Amrouche [q.v.], Mouloud Feraoun [q.v.], Malek Ouary [q.v.] and Mouloud Mammeri [q.v.]. Kasdi Merbah (q.v.), Mohammed Seddik Ben Yahia (q.v.), Belaïd Abdesselam (q.v.), and Nordine Aït Laoussine (q.v. Hydrocarbons) are among the many Kabyles who have distinguished themselves in postcolonial Algeria.

Kabyles revolted in 1963–1964 against the central government and were restive again dating from the "Berber Spring" of 1980 when violence broke out in protest of Arabization and the repression of Kabyle culture. Not surprisingly, Kabyles have voiced their opposition to the December 1990 Arabization Law (q.v. Arabization). The recent political liberalization has resulted in the emergence of Kabyle parties (e.g., FFS [q.v.], MCB, RCD). The inability of Kabyle leaders to unite has sapped a potentially powerful political bloc.

KABYLIA (q.v. Kabyles). Mountainous region of the Tell (Atlas) in eastern Algeria. The term is sometimes used to identify the entire range of Algerian mountains east of Algiers (q.v.) from the coast to Tunisia. Kabylia is divided into several distinct areas, the most prominent of which is Great Kabylia, east and southeast of Algiers, extending to Bejaïa (q.v.), including the impressive Djudjura range. Lesser Kabylia stretches from Bejaïa to Jijel including the Babor Mountains. Little is known of the history of Kabylia before the sixteenth century, except as a region of persistent resistance to conquest. Even with strong states adjacent to this area, control over the region was nominal.

During the Turkish occupation Kabyle political and administrative institutions remained intact, though occasionally a *Dey* possessed the acumen to assert his authority (e.g., Muhammad ibn Uthman [1766–1791]). The area was temporarily under French control from 1860 until 1871 after the suppression of Bu Baghla (q.v.), Lalla Fatima (q.v.), Bu Renan (q.v.), and adherents of the Rahmaniyya (q.v.) order. Following the suppression of the Kabyles' "Great Revolt" of 1871 (q.v.), much of Kabylia was sequestered for European colonization. During the War of Independence, Kabylia was one of the main insurgent regions. After the war it remained rebellious (1963–1964) against the central government. The Kabyles remain proud and protective of their heritage. The city of Tizi Ouzou (100,749 [1983]) is its cultural center.

KADDACHE, MAHFOUD (b. 1913). Historian. Kaddache's historiography has been internationally recognized and admired. He has been a professor at the University of Algiers and has served the *Centre National d'Etudes Historiques* (National Center of Historical Studies). Among his works are *La Vie politique à Alger de 1919 à 1939* (1972); *L'Algérie dans l'Antiquité* (1972); *L'Emir Abdelkader* (1974); *Récits de feu* (1976); *L'Algérie médiévale* (1982); and especially *Histoire du nationalisme algérien: Question nationale et politique algérienne*, 2 vols. (1980).

"KADDURA AL-DJAZAIRI" (ABU ABU ALLAH MUHAM-MED BEN SAID) (d. 1687). *Mufti*. Kaddura was of Tunisan origin but moved to Algeria. He is reputed to have been the most learned *mufti* of his age in Algeria.

KAFI, ALI (b. 1928?). Nationalist; ambassador; president of the High Council of State (HCS) (q.v.). Kafi was born to a peasant family in El Harrouch near Skikda (formerly Philippeville). He became an Arabic teacher. Kafi partici-pated in the Messalist (q.v. Messali Hadj) PPA (q.v.) and MTLD (q.v.). He joined the ALN (q.v.), attended the Soummam Conference (q.v.), and headed *Wilaya* II. A dauntless soldier, Kafi crossed the treacherous Morice Line (q.v.) twice.

After independence, Kafi served in the diplomatic corps (until 1975), distinguishing himself as an ambassador to Egypt, Syria, Lebanon, Libya, and Tunisia. He was also a member of the FLN's (q.v.) Central Committee (beginning in 1975), which played an important role in the selection of Chadli Benjedid (q.v.) as president. In November 1990, Kafi became secretary-general of the *Organisation National des Moudjahidins* (Veterans), an association affiliated with the FLN. Kafi became dissatisfied, however, with the FLN establishment and gravitated politically toward what could be called the Sid Ahmed Ghozali (q.v.) group. Kafi supported the overthrow of President Benjedid in January 1992 and became a member of the High Council of State. He was a staunch supporter of President Mohamed Boudiaf (q.v.). After Boudiaf's assassination (June 1992), Kafi was selected to be his successor as president of the HCS. Kafi seemed initially more willing to open up toward the opposition. Nevertheless, under Prime Minister Belaïd Abdesselam (q.v.), the government has pursued a determined policy to crush the Islamist movement. In addition, political and civil liberties have been curtailed.

AL-KAHINA. Berber (q.v.) leader. This Berber leader distinguished herself in resisting the Arab invasion in the Aurès (q.v.) region after Kusayla's (q.v.) defeat and death (686). Her name means "the prophetess." She led the Jerawa (Djarawa) tribe of apparently Jewish (q.v. Jews) Berbers against the Arab invaders. Her campaigns featured a stunning success at the Meskiana River. The Ummayad (q.v.) Caliph Abd al-Malik reinforced the strength of Hasan ibn al Nu'man al-Ghassani's army, which finally defeated the Aurès Berbers. The noble al-Kahina died during combat in 702.

KAID (QAID), AHMED (1927–1978) (Major Slimane). Revolutionary; minister. Kaid was born near Tiaret and attended primary school there. He was eventually enrolled in the French military school at Hussein-Dey, then in the Normal School in Algiers. Although he joined the FLN (q.v.) after the start of the War of Independence, his political activism to that point had been in the moderate UDMA (q.v.). He rose to assistant chief of staff of the ALN (q.v.) during the war and also served on the CNRA (q.v.). He sided with the Ahmed Ben Bella (q.v.)-Houari Boumedienne (q.v.) faction (also known as the Political Bureau [q.v.] or Tlemcen group) in the summer of 1962. He was elected to the National Assembly in 1962 and became minister of tourism in 1963. After a public disagreement with Ben Bella, he resigned from the government in late 1964; he kept his seat, however, on the Central Committee of the FLN. After the Boumedienne coup of June 1965, he served as spokesman of the Council of the Revolution (q.v.). Thereafter, he served as minister for finance until December 1967, at which time he became head of the FLN. He resigned from this position in 1972, rebuking the party's bureaucracy. He also reproved the Agrarian Revolution (q.v.). In March 1976 he publicly criticized the Boumedienne government at a news conference in France. Afterward, he lived in Switzerland and Morocco. Though it was reported that Kaid died of a heart attack, there was suspicion about his death given his anti-Boumedienne position. It was reported that many thousands attended his funeral at Tiaret.

KATEB, MUSTAPHA (d. 1989). Playwright. Kateb was one of the greatest figures in modern Algerian theater. He wrote 15 plays including *El Kahina* (1953). He served under the impresario Mahieddine Bachtarzi. He began his own company in 1940 and eventually became the director of an FLN theater group during the War of Independence. His greatest achievement was the establishment of *L'Institut National d'Art Dramatique et Choréographique*. He also was the director of the Algerian National Theater.

KATEB, YACINE (1929–1989). Novelist; playwright; poet. Kateb was one of Algeria's most renowned writers. He was born in Constantine. He was expelled from school after participating in the 1945 Sétif (q.v.) uprising. He then worked as a reporter for *Alger Républicain*. In 1951 he went to France and labored as an agricultural hand (with Malek Haddad [q.v]), an electrician's aide, and an unskilled worker. He met Bertolt Brecht in 1954. During the War of Independence, he stayed out of Algeria.

Kateb's most famous literary work was the novel *Nedjma* (Star), which was first published in 1956. Written in French, this novel has been translated into several languages. *Nedjma* is a pageant of literary style and historical significance. Its most profound theme is the search for and expression of personal and national identity. It is a masterwork involving history, autobiography, and poetry. This novel was complemented by *Le Polygone étoilé* (1966), which illustrated the author's disillusionment with independence.

A versatile writer in French and Arabic, Kateb also published a collection of poems *Soliloques* (1946) and wrote a number of plays such as *Le Cercle des représailles* (1959) and *Mohammed, prends ta valise* (in Arabic; 1971). Though Kateb was accused of supporting the authoritarian "Colonels," he was also very critical of the Algerian government concerning the October 1988 rioting. He was awarded in 1987 the *Grand Prix national français des lettres*.

A freethinker, he opposed the neo-revivalist Islam and especially its consequences upon women. He supported Berber rights. In 1985, he declared that he was "neither Muslim nor Arab, but Algerian" (*Le Monde*, October 31, 1989). Kateb viewed Algeria as a pluralistic culture. He could not reconcile himself to independent Algeria or colonial Algeria. His denunciation of the bloody repression of the October 1988 demonstrations related to what must have been a brutal personal irony—a reminder of Sétif 1945 (q.v.).

KESSOUS, MOHAMMED-AZIZ (1903–1965). Moderate nationalist. Kessous's father was a *caïd* and his grandfather was a *raïs*. He collaborated with Dr. Mohammed Saleh Bendjelloul (q.v.) in the founding of the *Fédération des Elus*'s newspaper, *L'Entente franco-musulmane* in 1935. In the same year he published *La Vérité sur le malaise algérien*, which examined social and political problems in Algeria in relation to integration.

Kessous also founded with Ferhat Abbas (q.v.) the newspaper *Egalité* in 1944, where he assumed the position of editor-in-chief. In 1949, this newspaper became *La République algérienne*. Kessous became a member of the French National Assembly. He stayed in France during the War of Independence.

KHALAF (KHELAF/KHELEF), ABDALLAH (q.v. Kasdi Merbah).

KHALDI, ABDELAZIZ (1917–1972). Reformer. Khaldi authored *Le Probléme algérien devant la conscience démocratique* (1946), which underscored the need of the French government to implement meaningful reform in Algeria.

KHALED (KHALID) BEN EL-HACHEMI (1875–1936). Nationalist. "Emir Khaled" is sometimes considered the "founder of the Algerian nationalist movement." A grandson of Abd al-Qadir (q.v.), he was born in Damascus, Syria, and grew up there before his father's move to Algeria in 1892. Khaled began his French education at the famed Lycée Louis-le-Grand in Paris in 1892 and was admitted to St. Cyr the following year. By 1908 he had been promoted to the rank of captain, the highest rank an Algerian could attain in the French Army. He resigned in 1910, but returned after receiving the rank of *Chevalier* of the Legion of Honor in 1914. He served in the army during World War I. In 1918 he lobbied to have the democratic ideals of the Paris Peace Conference applied to Algeria.

At first attracted to the Young Algerians (q.v.), he broke with them over the issue of the abandonment of Muslim status (in the acquisition of French citizenship). He proposed instead French citizenship with Muslim status, the cessation of foreign (i.e., European) immigration to Algeria, abolition of the *communes mixtes* (q.v.), compulsory education in both Arabic and French, and equal representation (European/Algerian) in assemblies. Upon this platform he entered the 1919 municipal elections in Algiers. His efforts to promote his ideas through his French language publication, *Ikdam*, provoked hostility. He was forced to leave Algeria in 1923. As war broke out between the French and the Rifs in neighboring Morocco (Khaled was sympathetic toward Abd al-Krim), he moved from Paris to Alexandria. He was accused in 1925 of conspiring against the French. As a result of the charge, he challenged the French consul to a duel whereupon the French ambassador demanded his extradition. He returned to Syria where he died in January 1936.

KHAMMAR, ABULQASIM (Abulqasim/Abu al-Qasim) (b. 1931). Poet. Born at Biskra (q.v.), Khammar used free verse in *Leaves* (1967) and disclosed an early attempt to break from nationalist poetry toward more universal themes.

KHARIJISM (KHARIJITES; KHAREDJITES) (q.v. Rustamids, M'zab). Kharijism is a separatist Islamic sect represented in Algeria today by the M'zabites (q.v.) who inhabit seven cities established by their ancestors in the Sahara around Gharadaia. This movement began as a violent reaction to the Caliph Ali's decision of arbitration at the Battle of Siffin in 659. A group of his supporters were disillusioned that Ali did not have God decide the outcome of this crucial battle in the history of the Caliphate and Islam. This resulted in a schismatic and rebellious sect. Though Ali persecuted the Khariji(tes), they eventually assassinated the Caliph.

The word stems from the verb *kharaja*, meaning to leave or exit. The Khariji(te)s believed that leaders who failed to uphold religious and moral standards had to be removed from their positions. It was also egalitarian, contending that any Muslim demonstrating the requisite qualities of faithful commitment could become a caliph regardless of social position. Ibadism (q.v.) and Sufriyism (q.v.) were Khariji sects that particularly influenced the independent-minded Berbers (q.v.). Kharijism provided a rationale for rebellion.

KHATIB, YOUCEF (b. 1932). Revolutionary. Born in Ech-Chlef, he was a member of the UGEMA and a second-year medical student when the student union called for a general strike in 1956. He joined the ALN (q.v.), served as a doctor, and rose to the position of head of medical services in *Wilaya* IV. Promoted to the rank of major in 1961, and then to the rank of colonel in 1962, he took command of the *Wilaya* and fought against the external troops of Houari Boumedienne (q.v.) during the immediate postwar power struggle. Thereafter, he left the army to renew his medical studies. He was a deputy in the National Assembly, and a member of the Political Bureau of the FLN until the coup of June 1965 and then of its Secretariat until 1967.

KHAYR AL-DIN (also spelled KHAIR AL-DIN, also known as BARBAROSSA [Red Beard]) (c. 1483 [1466?]-1546). Most famous Turkish *ra'is* and *Beylerbey* of Algiers (q.v.), who set up Turkish *ra'is*-Janissary state (q.v. Regency) in Algeria. He gained renown as a pirate under the command of his brother Aruj (q.v.). When his brother undertook a fatal expedition against Tlemcen (q.v.), he appointed Khayr as governor of Algiers. After word of Aruj's death arrived, Khayr was chosen by his fellow *ra'is* to succeed him.

Finding himself beset by uprisings, he paid homage to the powerful Ottoman Sultan Selim I. This was politically astute because the Sultan bestowed Khayr with the titles of *pasha* and *beylerbey*, sent him 2,000 men with artillery, and gave him authority to recruit volunteers. Upon the arrival of these forces, Khayr immediately proceeded to secure his position. In addition, he was able to repel a Spanish force under Ugo de Moncade (1519). Khayr was defeated, however, by a Hafsid (Tunisian) army in Kabylia (q.v.). He was forced to flee to Djidjelli and to abandon Algiers temporarily. From his base at Djidjelli, Khayr began to regain territory from the Hafsids. He seized Collo (1521), Annaba (q.v.) (1522), Constantine (q.v.), and finally reoccupied Algiers in 1525. In 1529 he reduced the Spanish fortress of Peñon and used its ramparts and other materials to construct a breakwater (200-yard jetty) and to develop a naval base. In 1533, Khayr was called to Constantin-ople and promoted to Captain Pasha (High Admiral) of the Ottoman fleet by Sultan Suleiman the Magnificent.

In 1534, he took his revenge upon the Hafsids by plundering Tunis. Charles V's (q.v.) forces managed to seize Tunis in 1535. Khayr attacked Mahon, taking booty and 6,000 captives. He then directed his attention to his responsibilities of the Ottoman fleet until his death. He was interned in the mosque at Büyük Dere.

KHEIREDINE (KHEIRIDDINE), MOHAMED (CHEIKH [*Shaykh*]). A member of the Association of Reformist Ulama (q.v.), Kheiredine supported the Manifesto of the Algerian People (q.v.). During the War of Independence (q.v.) he served as FLN (q.v.) representative in Rabat. He was also a member of the CNRA (q.v.). After the war Kheiredine was a deputy (1962–64) in the National Assembly. He was also an owner of a plastics plant near Algiers. In 1976, he signed a Manifesto (q.v. ''New Appeal to the Algerian People'') along with Ferhat Abbas (q.v.), Ben Youssef Ben Khedda (q.v.), and Hocine Lahouel (q.v) that was critical of Houari

Boumedienne's (q.v.) government and policies. Like the other signatories, he was placed under house arrest and his factory was expropriated by the state. President Benjedid (q.v.) later released Kheiredine and returned his property.

KHELEF (KHALLAF), ABDELAZIZ (b. 1943). Technocrat; minister. Khelef served with SONELGAZ (Algeria's natural gas state enterprise) in its economics division (1968). He became the director-general of planning and industrial development (1972–1977). This was an exciting, dynamic period during Houari Boumedienne's (q.v.) ambitious state-building (q.v. State Plans). Khelef then became secretary-general of the Ministry of Light Industry (1977–1979). He was also selected to the FLN's (q.v.) Central Committee (1979). Under President Chadli Benjedid (q.v.), Khelef served as minister of commerce (1980–1986) and then as minister of finance (1986–1988). He then became secretary of state for Maghrib Affairs in 1989, an important position given the establishment of the Arab Maghrib Union (AMU) (q.v. Maghrib Unity).

KHEMISTI, MOHAMED (1930–1963). Foreign minister. Khemisti (like Ahmed Ben Bella [q.v.]) was a native of Marnia. He served as secretary to Abderrahmane Farès (q.v.), president of the Provisional Executive in 1962. Khemisti helped facilitate the transfer of power from the Provisional Executive to Ben Bella. He was named foreign minister in Ben Bella's first cabinet. Khemisti viewed the neocolonial condition with France as a temporary strategic expedient until Algeria developed itself. Khemisti also believed that Algeria should develop a strong solidarity with the Third World. He was assassinated on April 11, 1963. His wife has played a significant role as a feminist (q.v. Women).

KHIDER, MOHAMMED BEN YOUSSEF (1912–1967). "Historic Leader" (q.v.); revolutionary; FLN (q.v.) secretary-general. The son of a poor family from Biskra (q.v.), Khider was born in Algiers (q.v.) and eventually became a bus driver/fare collector. He joined Messali Hadj's (q.v.) ENA, then his PPA (q.v.). He campaigned and was elected deputy for Algiers in 1946, but he went into exile in Cairo after his car, without his knowledge, was used in the OS (q.v.)-organized 1950 holdup of the Oran post office. A partisan of armed rebellion, he tried to reconcile Messalists and Centralists when the MTLD (q.v.) split into two factions. Along with others he also helped organize the FLN, earning him the title of "historic leader." Khider was involved with initial contacts between the French government and the FLN in 1956. Nevertheless, the French authorities seized Khider along with Ahmed Ben Bella (q.v.), Mohamed Boudiaf (q.v.), Hocine Aït Ahmed (q.v.), and Mostefa Lacheraf (q.v.) in the infamous hijacking of an Air Maroc airplane on October 22, 1956. He was elected to the CNRA (q.v.) while in prison, and in 1962 he supported Ben Bella and became secretary-general of the FLN. He later disagreed with Ben Bella about the role of the party and of the army in independent Algeria. Thereupon, he resigned and went into exile, but he deposited a significant sum of party funds in Switzerland, which Algeria has tried to recover. Khider became an opponent of Houari Boumedienne (q.v.) and was assassinated in Madrid.

KILIJ ALI (q.v. Eulj Ali).

KIOUANE, ABDERRAHMANE. Nationalist; revolutionary. A lawyer and PPA (q.v.) activist, he attained a variety of leadership positions within the MTLD (q.v.) (especially on Central Committee). Although he worked for Jacques Chevallier (q.v.), the mayor of Algiers (q.v.) when the War of Independence broke out, he was arrested in November 1954, then freed in March 1955. After his release, he was a partisan of internal autonomy, not of independence. This position caused him to be attacked in various FLN (q.v.) tracts. He eventually joined the FLN and was appointed the GPRA's (q.v.) ambassador to China in 1961.

KREA (Cachin), HENRI (b. 1933). Writer; poet. Kréa was born in Algiers (q.v.) and was the son of a mixed marriage (his mother was Algerian, his father European). He published one novel, *Djamal*, in 1961, and some plays including *Le Séisme* (1958) (whose subject is Jugurtha [q.v.]) and *Théâtre Algérien* (1962). He is renowned as a poet of the revolution as viewed in *Liberté première* (1957); *La Révolution et la poésie sont une seule et même chose* (1957, 1960); and *La Conjuration des égaux* (1964). Other collections include *Poèmes en forme de vestige* (1967) and *Tombeau de Jugurtha* (1968). Kréa chose to live in France after Algeria became independent.

KRIM, BELKACEM (1922–1970). "Historic leader" (q.v.); GPRA (q.v.) minister. Belkacem Krim, a Kabyle (q.v.), was born near Dra-el-Mizan and began his adult life as an employee of the Mirabeau mixed commune (q.v. *communes mixtes*). In 1945 he joined the PPA (q.v.) as well as the OS (q.v.). From 1947 on, following the assassination of a forest ranger, he was always on the run from French authorities. He was twice condemned to death, in *absentia* (1947 and 1950). In 1954 he became the sixth internal leader of the CRUA (q.v.)-FLN and is regarded as one of the "historic leaders." He commanded the Kabylia *wilaya*. After the Soummam Congress (q.v.), Krim reluctantly opposed his fellow Kabyle, Ramdane Abane (q.v.). He left Algeria after the Battle of Algiers (q.v.) to join the "external" delegation of the FLN. During the GPRA years, he served as war minister, vice president of the Council of Ministers (1958), foreign minister (1960), and minister of the interior (1961). He headed the FLN negotiating team, which concluded the Evian Accords (q.v.), and was the chief opponent of Ahmed

Ben Bella (q.v.) immediately after independence was achieved (1962). He stayed out of politics from 1963 to 1965. He was accused of plotting against Houari Boumedienne (q.v.) and was again condemned to death in *absentia,* this time ironically by the Algerian courts. In 1969 he organized the *Mouvement Démocratique de Renouveau Algérien.* Krim was assassinated in Frankfurt, probably by Algerian security agents.

KUSAYLA BEN LEMZEM AL-AWRABI (KOCEILA; KUSAILA; KASILA) (d. 686). Berber chief of the Awraba tribe who resisted Arab conquest of the Maghrib. Kusayla, allied with Byzantine (q.v.) forces, temporarily withstood Arab incursions into the Aurès (q.v.) region. He distinguished himself at Tahoudha in 683 with the defeat of 'Uqba ibn Nafi (q.v.). This allowed Kusayla to occupy Qayrawan and to control *Ifriqiya* for several years. The resolute Umayyad Caliph Abd al-Malik then dispatched Zuhair ibn Qais and an army to the West, which destroyed Kusayla and his allies at Membs near Qayrawan in 686.

KUTAMA (KOTOMA; KITAMA). Berber (q.v.) tribe. At the time of the introduction of Islam to the Maghrib, the Kutama occupied all the land between the Aurès (q.v.) and the Mediterranean. They converted to Shi'ism (q.v.) and provided invaluable service especially as soldiers to the Fatimids (q.v.). After the departure of the Caliph al-Mu'izz for Egypt, the Kutama gradually lost their political significance, especially since the vast majority of their fellow Muslims were Sunni (q.v. Sunnism). By the late nineteenth century, the Kutama had practically disappeared.

LACHERAF, MOSTEFA (b. 1917). Nationalist; essayist; minister; ambassador. Lacheraf received an excellent education and eventually taught at the Lycées at Mostaganem and then at Louis-le-Grand in Paris. He participated in the PPA (q.v.) and the MTLD (q.v.). He left the MTLD in 1952 and later joined the FLN (q.v.) in 1954. He was captured along with Ahmed Ben Bella (q.v.), Hocine Aït Hocine (q.v.), Mohamed Boudiaf (q.v.), and Mohammed Khider (q.v.) in the infamous French skyjacking of an Air Maroc plane in October 1956. Lacheraf managed to escape from a clinic in 1961.

Lacheraf helped draft the Tripoli Program (q.v.). He was appointed ambassador to Argentina (1965) and later Mexico (1974, 1979). He was an adviser to President Houari Boumedienne (q.v.), especially concerning cultural affairs. Boumedienne appointed him as minister of national education in April 1977. Lacheraf's tenure in this position was quite controversial. He questioned rapid Arabization (q.v.), the keystone of the Cultural Revolution (q.v.), and contended that Algeria should pursue a more pragmatic and programmatic approach to language (bilingualism). In 1982, President Chadli Benjedid (q.v.) selected Lacheraf as Algeria's permanent delegate to UNESCO in Paris. His most famous written work is *L'Algérie: Nation et société* (1965, 1969). He also studied oral tradition in *Chanson des jeunes filles arabes* (1953).

LAHOUEL, HOCINE (b. 1917). Nationalist; revolutionary. Lahouel attended high school at Skikda and joined the ENA (q.v.) in 1930. He was an early leader of the PPA (q.v.) and was an editor of *El Ouma*. Lahouel was arrested in 1937 and released two years later. He was torn between supporting the OS's (q.v.) insurrectionary tactics and the MTLD's electoral pursuits. He became secretary-general of the MTLD (q.v.) in 1950 and was a prominent Centralist (i.e., the MTLD's Central Committee) in the MTLD split. He joined the FLN (q.v.) in 1955 and represented this organization in Indonesia and in Pakistan. Thereafter he refused all political positions (though he was asked to play a diplomatic role in Latin America). In 1965 he became president of the National Textile Society. In 1976 Lahouel cosigned with Ferhat Abbas (q.v.), Ben Youssef Ben Khedda (q.v.), and Cheikh Kheiredine (q.v.) an anti-Boumedienne manifesto entitled ''New Appeal to the Algerian People'' (q.v.). He was placed under house arrest until President Benjedid released him.

LAID AL-KHALIFA, MOHAMMED (AL KHALIFA, MO-HAMED LAID). (1904-1979). Poet; educator. Born at Aïn Beïda near Constantine, he received a traditional education, attended the University of Zitouna in Tunis, and taught in private schools and in Arabic (not French) colonial schools in Algeria. A member of the Association of Algerian *Ulama* (q.v.), Laïd al-Khalifa was put under house arrest in 1954 at the outbreak of the War of Independence. In 1966, he was awarded the Union of Algerian Writers' literary prize. He influenced most of the Algerian Arabic language poets during the interwar years (q.v. Literature in Arabic).

LAKHDAR, REBBAH. Nationalist; revolutionary; unionist. A member of the PPA (q.v.) and a prominent MTLD (q.v.) leader, Lakhdar joined the FLN (q.v.). He was also a businessman who once owned a café and then significantly an electronics store (radio antennas). His store served as a storing place for arms and a contacts point for the revolution-aries. After a meeting at his store attended by Ramdane Abane (q.v.), Ben Youssef Ben Khedda (q.v.), and others, Lakhdar asked Mufdi Zakaria (q.v.) to compose a national anthem (''Kassaman''). Under the auspices of the FLN, Lakhdar founded the *Union Générale des Commercants Algériens* in 1956. He was arrested and tortured that same year. After independence he was elected a deputy in 1964. He eventually retired from political activity.

LALLA FATIMA (FATHMA) (fl. 1850s). *Marabout* who resisted the French. In the tradition of al-Kahina (q.v.) this woman continued Berber (q.v. Kabyles) resistance against the French after the death of Bu Baghla (q.v.). She was finally captured in July 1857.

LAPERRINE, HENRI (1860–1920). French officer. A graduate of St.-Cyr and classmate and friend of Charles de Foucauld (q.v.), Laperrine "pacified" the Sahara through the inauguration of mobile native Saharan troops. He also secured a peace treaty with the Ahaggar Tuareg (q.v.) in 1905. When the Sahara became restive during World War I, Laperrine was called back from the Western Front and restored order. He died in an air crash.

LAVIGERIE, CHARLES MARTIAL ALLEMAND (1825–1892). Archbishop, then Cardinal; founder of the Society of Missionaries of Africa ("White Fathers"). Lavigerie was very well educated and eventually held an associate professorship in ecclesiastical history at the Sorbonne. In 1867 Lavigerie, then serving as Bishop of Nancy, was sent to Algeria. This gave him an opportunity to pursue his interest in missionary work.

    With some difficulty he gained approval for his apostolate from the French government. He established the Order of White Fathers, which was conceived as apostolic and Ignatian in character. The White Fathers administered orphanages and asylums, schools, and hospitals. A complementary Missionary Sisters of Our Lady of Africa was founded in 1869.

    The White Fathers pursued their mission especially in Kabylia (q.v.) and the Sahara. In 1878 Lavigerie extended the White Fathers' work into equatorial Africa. Archbishop Lavigerie was elevated to a Cardinal in 1881. Three years later he became the first Primate of the newly restored See of Carthage.

LEBJAOUI, MOHAMED (b. 1926). Nationalist; revolutionary; dissident; writer; poet. Born in Algiers, Lebjaoui was a prosperous middle-class Algerian merchant who was also a friend of Albert Camus (q.v.). He joined the FLN secretly in 1955. He became a member of the first CNRA and contributed to the Soummam Platform (q.v.). He then headed the FLN's *Fédération de France* (FFFLN) (q.v.). Lebjaoui was captured and incarcerated at the infamous Santé prison. He became disenchanted with Houari Boumedienne (q.v.) and founded the dissident OCRA and then the *Mouvement Algerién des Forces Populaires et de l'Armée pour la Démocratie et l'Union Maghrébine.* His written works include: *Vérités sur la Révolution algérienne* (1970); *Bataille d'Alger ou bataille d'Algérie* (1972); *Au nom de l'Algérie* (1976); *Un morceau de lune et une étoile couleur de sang* (poetry, 1975); and *Sous le bras, mon soleil* (poetry, 1982).

LEKHIFIF (pseud.) (q.v. FILALI, ABDALLAH).

LITERATURE BY ALGERIANS (IN ARABIC). Algeria possesses a distinguished Arabic literary heritage. Cultural centers such as Qal'a, Bejaïa (q.v.), Ouargla, Constantine (q.v.), Algiers (q.v.), and Tlemcen (q.v.) produced notable literary and scholarly achievements. Ibn Hani al-Andalusi (d. 973) was a famous poet from Msila. Ibn Rashiq (d. 1063), also from Msila, was the official poet of al-Mu'izz (q.v.) in Qayrawan (Kairouan). The writings of Abu Zakariya (d. 1078) of Ouargla have been especially valuable to historians concerning the history of the Ibadis. Abu Zakariya's work was complemented by al-Wargalani (d. 1174) of the M'zab. In the twelfth century Ibn al-Faqqun (Ben Lefgoun) was a distinguished poet, and al-Khatib (Ibn Qanfud/Qonfoud) (d. 1197) was a noted historian in Constantine. Abu Madyan (Sidi Bou Mediene/Medin) (d. 1197) was a renowned teacher in Tlemcen. Al- Ghobrini (d. 1315) described the impressive array of scholars in Tlemcen during the thirteenth century. Tlemcen was the home of the poet Ibn Khamis (d. 1308), the historian of the Abd al-Wadid dynasty, al-Tanasi (d. 1493), and the theologian al-Sanusi (d. 1490). Other important intellectuals of Tlemcen include the judicial scholar, al-Wansharishi (d. 1508), the biographer, Ibn Maryam al-Maliti (d. 1605), and the historian of Andalusia, al-Maqqari (d. 1632). The renowned theologian Abd al-Rahman al-Tha'alibi (d. 1470) (q.v.) lived in Algiers. The brilliant Ibn Khaldun (d. 1406) (q.v.) lived in several Algerian cities before resettling in his native Tunis. Two noteworthy writers during the Regency were al-Warthilani (d. 1780), who recounted his voyage to Mecca, and al-Tilimsani (died c. 1779), who described military affairs.

Though most famous for his resistance against the French, the Amir Abd al-Qadir (q.v.) also wrote about religious and scientific issues besides military affairs. Shaykh Atfiyech (1818–1914) wrote an admired Qur'anic commentary and was a scholar of Islamic jurisprudence. Al-Hafnawi (1852–1942) researched and publicized Algeria's literary past. His efforts were continued by Mohammed Bencheneb (q.v.) and Saadeddine Bencheneb (q.v.). Other important Arabic contributors were Ibn al-Khodja Mostafa (1865–1915), who wrote a *Treatise on the Rights of Women* (1895), and the linguistic works of Belkacem Ben Sédira (1846–1901). Arabic was particularly promoted by the Association of Reformist *Ulama* led by the *Shaykh* Abd al-Hamid Ben Badis (q.v.). Ben Badis's influence was widespread and continues to be influential in contemporary Algeria. Ben Badis's work was continued by Bachir al-Ibrahimi (q.v.). Mubarak al-Mili (q.v.), Abderrahman al-Jilali (q.v.), and Tawfiq al-Madani (q.v.) contributed prominent historical works. Important modern poets/novelists/playwrights include Mohammed Laïd al-Khalifa (q.v.) and Moufdi Zakaria (q.v.), Reda Houhou (q.v.), Abd al-Hamid Ben Haddouga (q.v.), Tahar Wattar (q.v.), Kateb Yacine (q.v.), Salah Kharfi (b. 1932), Abdallah Cheriet (b. 1933), Mohammed-Lakhdar Abdalqadir al-Sayhi (q.v. Saihi), Abulqasim Khammar (q.v.), Abdallah Rakibi, Mohammed Siddiq Mabrouka Boussaha (b. 1944), Mohammed Saïd Zahiri (d. 1956),

Mohammed Mouni, Zohor Ouanisi (Ounissi) (b. 1936), Ahlam Mosteghanemi (b. 1953), Rashid Ksentini (1887–1944), Mahieddine Bachetarzi (b. 1896), and Mustapha Kateb (q.v.). Algeria's admirable modern Arabic literary production should be enhanced by the determined emphasis on Arabization.

LITERATURE BY ALGERIANS (IN FRENCH) (q.v. Gabriel Audisio, Isabelle Eberhardt, Louis Bertrand, Jean Pomier, and Albert Camus). The first Algerian-written novel in French was Mohammed Ben Chérif's *Ahmed Ben Mostapha, goumier* (1920), followed by Hadj Hamou's *Zohra, la femme du mineur* (1925). These works were the products of assimilated Algerian writers. Indeed, Algerian writers proved that they could be as exact in syntax and creative in imagination as the colonizing French. This was epitomized by the works of Jean Amrouche (q.v.).

The next generation of Algerian writers sought liberation and national identity (though Amrouche and others, e.g., Mohammed Chérif Sahli [q.v.], also researched cultural identity). This can be seen in the works of Kateb Yacine (q.v.), Mohammed Dib (q.v.), Mouloud Mammeri (q.v.), Assia Djebar (q.v.), Leïla Sebbar (q.v.) (concerning the immigrant community), Malek Haddad (q.v.), Mouloud Feraoun (q.v.), and Rachid Mimouni (q.v.). In poetry, Henri Kréa (q.v.), Jean Sénac (q.v.), Anna Greki (q.v.), Bachir Hadj Ali (q.v.), and Boualem Khalfa were particularly prominent. Many of these same literary figures expressed disillusionment with the loss of traditional values and life-styles and even in the illusory promises of the revolution. This can also be seen in the works of Mourad Bourbonne (q.v.), Rachid Boudjedra (q.v.), Nabile Farès (q.v.), Mouloud Achour (q.v.), and in the poetry of Noureddine Aba (q.v.) and Ahmed Azeggagh (q.v.). Boudjema Bouhada (b. 1942) has distinguished himself as a playwright.

In spite of Arabization, Algerian writers still find French to be an excellent means of expression. Very few of these works have been translated into English (e.g., Kateb, *Nedjma;* Djebar, *Fantasia: An Algerian Cavalcade; A Sister to Scheherazade; Women of Algiers in Their Apartment;* and Mimouni, *The Honor of the Tribe*).

LITERATURE BY ALGERIANS (IN LATIN). Roman Algeria distinguished itself by its literary figures. The stoic Marcus Cornelius Fronto (110?–180?) from Cirta (Constantine [q.v.]) was a tutor of Marcus Aurelius and was a proponent of older, simpler styles of Latin. Lucius Apuleius (Appuleius) (second century) from Madaure (M'Daourouch) was the author of *Metamorphoses* and especially the *Golden Ass,* the adventures of a man transformed into an ass before Isis returns him to human form. Marcus Minucius Felix (third century) from Thélepe (Tébessa) was a Christian convert who authored the dialogue *Octavius,* which is known as the earliest Christian work written in Latin. Optat from Mila distinguished himself in the fourth century. The most renowned figure was Augustine (q.v.) from Thagaste (Souk Ahras), the Bishop of Hippo (Annaba), and author of *Confessions* and *The City of God.*

LOI CADRE. French enabling act. This legislation, passed by the National Assembly in June 1956, created the procedures through which colonies could opt for internal autonomy. The act also established universal suffrage and single electorates in the colonies.

A *loi-cadre* was tailored for Algeria during the brief premiership (May–October 1957) of Maurice Bourgès-Manoury. The premier with the assistance of Robert Lacoste drafted the administrative plan. Under its provisions Algeria would be divided into autonomous territories linked by a federal organ. France would still manage economic and foreign affairs. The single electoral college increased Muslim political participation but also recognized ethnic particularism (e.g., the Kabyles [q.v.]), which aimed at sapping the strength of Algerian nationalism.

The implementation of the *loi-cadre* could only have been achieved in a period of peace and only if France could assert its political authority over colonialist protest. That was never to be. The National Assembly repudiated the *loi-cadre* and with it, the short-lived Bourgès-Manoury government. Though a redrafted *loi-cadre* eventually passed, the extension of European settler (*pied-noir* [q.v.]) power in the planned territorial assemblies diluted its political effectiveness.

MACTA (MAKTA, MACHTA), BATTLE OF. Abd al-Qadir's (q.v.) victory on June 28, 1835, over the French forces under General Camille-Alphonse Trézel. The column of 2,000 French troops marching toward Arzew was attacked from the hills by a large Algerian force. The French sustained heavy casualties. Trézel was soon replaced by General Thomas-Robert Bugeaud (q.v.).

AL-MADANI, ABASSI (b. 1931). Founder and leader of the *Front Islamique du Salut* (FIS) (q.v.). Madani began his Qur'anic education before the War of Independence. He participated in a bomb attack against Radio Algiers during the war, which resulted in a seven-year imprisonment. After the war he went to England to study and earned a doctorate. He became a professor of education at the University of Algiers. Provoked by his frequent criticisms of Algeria's "un-Islamic" educational system, the Algerian government detained him for 18 months (released in 1984).

Abassi and his deputy, Ali Benhadj (q.v.), founded the FIS, which received legal status in September 1989. His leadership was not distinguished by his theology or oratory (unlike Benhadj). He did communicate his ideas simply (e.g., "Neither Charter nor Constitution . . . only the Qur'an"), which is reminiscent of *Shaykh* Abd al-Hamid Ben Badis's (q.v.) aphorisms. The FIS effectively presented populist positions and especially targeted the FLN's (q.v.) corruption, which appealed to the disillusioned younger generation. The FIS also was very well organized, though there was some apparent discontent over his authoritarian control over the movement (i.e., a "personality cult"). In addition, the FIS appeared split ideologically. One group has favored a "national" movement chiefly aiming toward establishing an Islamist state in Algeria (*Algérianistes*). Another group has preferred to attach the Algerian movement to international Islamism (*Salafistes*). Madani adhered primarily to the *Algérianiste* position.

The success of the FIS in the local of elections of June 1990 (q.v.) gave Madani worldwide attention and illustrated the effectiveness of his message and organization. His generally moderate image was tainted, however, during the violent protests that postponed the national elections of June 1991 (q.v.) and led to his arrest on June 30. Madani had called for a "holy war" (June 28) against the Army and demanded that the state of siege be lifted (declared on June 5). He was finally sentenced in July 1992 to a generally recognized moderate 12-year imprisonment.

The FIS's dramatic success in the first round of the rescheduled elections in December 1991 (q.v.), even with Madani and Benhadj detained, underscored the party's effective organization. Though that election was cancelled by the High Council of State (q.v.), which also later declared the FIS illegal (February), Islamist opposition continues, but it is expressed today in bullets rather than ballots.

AL-MADANI, TAWFIQ (Tewfik) (1899–1983). Member of the Association of Reformist *Ulama* (q.v.); historian; minister; ambassador. Al-Madani contributed profoundly toward reviving and promoting Arabic study (especially historiography) and culture in Algeria. His works include *Book of Algeria* (1931), an introduction to the country for the youth, which was implicitly nationalist. He also published *The War of Three Hundred Years Between Algeria and Spain* (1968). Al-Madani wrote the play *Hannibal* (1950). He was also the editor-in-chief of *El-Basaïr*.

Besides his literary contribution, al-Madani played an impressive political role. He helped organize the Neo-*Destour* Party in Tunisia. He became secretary-general of the Association of Reformist *Ulama* (1952). Soon after the war began, the *Ulama* joined the FLN (q.v.). Al-Madani became a member of the external delegation (1956) and was later chosen minister of cultural affairs (1958) in the GPRA (q.v.). He served as minister for *Habous* (Religious Foundations) in

Ahmed Ben Bella's (q.v.) first two governments. Al-Madani also served his country as ambassador to Iraq and Pakistan before retiring to devote himself to historical studies and in particular the *Centre National d'Etudes Historiques* (National Center of Historical Studies). His posthumous *Memoires de Combat* was published in 1989.

MAGHRAWA. A prominent confederation of Berber tribes in the Zanata group. They originally led a nomadic existence in the area between the Chélif valley and the mountains of the Madyuna.

MAGHRIB UNITY (q.v. Morocco; Tunisia). An enduring ideal shared by Maghrib states to integrate themselves into some type of unity. Competing nationalisms prevented the tangible realization of Maghrib unity until the 1980s when President Chadli Benjedid (q.v.) resolutely pursued it by concluding accords with Tunisia and Mauritania in 1983. Despite severe differences and broken relations with Morocco over the Western Sahara (q.v.), Benjedid and King Hassan II met in 1983 and 1987, which marginally improved the bilateral relationship; but continuing contacts led finally to a diplomatic restoration in 1988. Algiers's aspiration to solve the Western Saharan War within the framework of a Great Maghrib framework was underscored when Morocco and POLISARIO (q.v.) consented to a U.N.-promoted peace proposal in August 1988. Though a final settlement to the Saharan War was not reached (a self-determination referendum expected to take place before the end of 1991 never occurred), the positive regional actions and achievements contributed to the creation in February 1989 of the Arab Maghrib Union (q.v.) dedicated to regional cooperation and integration. Its member states, Algeria, Morocco, Tunisia, Mauritania, and Libya, have been collaborating economically, culturally, and to a lesser degree, politically. The immediate aim, as of this writing, is the creation of a customs union. Nevertheless, political instability, especially in Algeria, has impeded integration initiatives, as well as the unresolved Western Saharan conflict.

MAHSAS, ALI (b. 1923). Nationalist; revolutionary; minister. Born in Boudouaou, Mahsas joined the PPA (q.v.) in 1942 and became a member of its Central Committee in 1946. He was also a member of the OS (q.v.) and, along with Ahmed Ben Bella (q.v.), was imprisoned for his activities in that clandestine organization. He escaped with Ben Bella from prison in 1952 and then settled in France. As editor of *L'Algérie libre*, he urged MTLD (q.v.) members to follow neither of the two splinter groups, the Centralists or the Messalists (q.v. Messali Hadj). Because he also saw the CRUA (q.v.) as agents of the Centralists, he was not invited to meet with Mohamed Boudiaf (q.v.), Ben M'Hidi (q.v.), Ben Bella (q.v.), Mustafa Ben Boulaïd (q.v.), and Mourad Didouche (q.v.) at their Bern meeting in spring 1954. In fact, Mahsas did not join the revolutionary forces until after the outbreak of the War of Independence. He left France to join the FLN (q.v.) in Cairo in 1955. He opposed the decisions of the Soummam Congress (q.v.) and was subsequently arrested in Tunisia on orders from Amar Ouamrane (q.v.). He escaped and spent the last years of the war in Germany.

After independence, Mahsas served in various official positions, the most important of which was minister of agriculture and agrarian reform (1963–1966), which was concurrent with the *autogestion* (q.v.) period. He was also a member of the Political Bureau and the Central Committee of the FLN. Mahsas supported the Houari Boumedienne (q.v.) coup of June 1965, which deposed Ben Bella. In the next year, however, he left Algeria and briefly joined the OCRA. He then opted for a life of exile in France, though maintaining an interest in Algerian affairs. This was seen in his participation in an organization called the *Rassemblement National pour la Démocratie et la Révolution*. He returned to Algeria in 1979. He was involved in the recent development of opposition parties since the October 1988 riots (q.v.) and has played a leading role in the *Union des Forces Démocratiques* (UFD).

Mahsas authored *L'Autogestion en Algérie* (1976); and *Le Mouvement révolutionnaire en Algérie, de la 1re Guerre mondiale à 1954* (1979).

MAISON DE LA CULTURE D'ALGER. A PCA club that organized political discussions, a small theatrical group, and other social, political, and cultural activities. The Maison de la Culture d'Alger sponsored a small periodical, *La Jeune méditerrannée*.

MAISON-CARREE MUTINY (January 25, 1941). This can be viewed as the first rebellion in the Algerian nationalists' struggle for independence, which occurred when 800 Muslim infantry and Spahis mutinied (owing to the discrimination and deprivations to which they were subjected) and killed their French officers and NCOs. Seizing arms from a nearby armory, the mutineers fought the French army and police for 15 days before being suppressed. Leaders of the mutineers, Muslim NCOs, were observed raising the index fingers of their right hands toward Heaven, representing the Muslim unity and purity. The gesture also symbolized jihad, as well as Messali Hadj's (q.v.) nationalist cause.

MALEK, REDA (REDHA; RIDA) (b. 1931). FLN (q.v.) ideologue; ambassador; minister; president of the *Conseil Consultatif National* (CCN) (q.v.); member of the High Council of State (HCS) (q.v.). Malek served as director of *El-Moudjahid* during the War of Independence and participated in the Evian negotiations (spokesman for the Algerian delegation). He was a co-writer of the Tripoli Program (q.v.). Though he served briefly as minister of information and culture (1978), Malek had a distinguished career as a diplomat serving in Belgrade, Paris, Moscow, Washington (during the Iranian hostage crisis), and London. He was removed, however, from the FLN's Central Committee by President Chadli Benjedid (q.v.). Malek left retirement to serve on and subsequently preside over the CCN. He was chosen to serve on the HCS itself following the elevation of Ali Kafi (q.v.) to the presidency after Mohamed Boudiaf's assassination (q.v.) (June 1992). In February 1993, Prime Minister Belaïd Abdesselam (q.v.) appointed Malek as a foreign minister. In August, the HCS replaced Abdesselam with Malek.

MALIKISM. The dominant Islamic juridical school in Algeria and the Maghrib. Named after Malik ibn Anas (q.v.). Malikism is based primarily on the Medinan community; it is against general consensus (*ijma*), private opinion (*ray*), and analogy (*qiyas*). Its rigidity was protested by the renowned theologian al-Ghazali (1058–1112).

MAMMERI, MOULOUD (1917–1989). Novelist; poet. Mammeri was born in Taourirt-Mimoun in Great Kabylia (q.v.) and earned the reputation as one of Algeria's greatest literary figures during the era of decolonization. He wrote in French, but he also promoted Berber culture (especially poetry). The Algerian government intervened in 1980 when Mammeri planned a program concerning Kabyle culture. This provoked rioting (q.v. Kabyles).

Mammeri attended the Lycée Bugeaud and the Lycée Louis-le-Grand. He intended to enroll in the Ecole Normale Supérieure but World War II broke out. Eventually Mammeri became a professor at the University of Algiers and director of the Center of Anthropological, Prehistoric, and Ethnographic Research.

Mammeri's literary contributions describe the difficulties in reconciling native (especially Kabyle) and French culture. His novels are *La Colline oubliée* (1952); *Le Sommeil du juste* (1955); *L'Opium et le bâton* (1965), one of the best novels concerning the war; and *La Traversée* (1982), which discloses his own disillusionment with independent Algeria. His works concerning Berber culture are distinguished by

Les Isefra, poèmes de Si Mohand ou Mhand (1969); *Poèmes kabyles anciens* (1980); *Machaho!* (1980); and *Tellem chaho!* (1980). He was also an accomplished playwright (*Le Banquet, précédé de La mort absurde des Aztèques* [1973] and *Le Foehn* [1982]). Mammeri died in an automobile accident.

MANIFESTO OF THE ALGERIAN PEOPLE. Proclamation of February 10, 1943, concluding that the Europeans and the Algerians were distinct ''without common soul.'' It demanded specific reforms such as the condemnation and end of colonialism and of the exploitation of the Algerian people by France. It called for the right of self-determination and a constitution for Algeria guaranteeing absolute liberty and equality. The document was signed by Ferhat Abbas (who was most responsible for it), Dr. Mohammed Saleh Bendjelloul, and other moderate leaders. While the document made sweeping demands, it did not specifically propose what the future relationship would be between France and Algeria. The Manifesto was presented to Governor-General Peyrouton on March 31, 1943, who viewed it as a framework for future reform. This conciliatory position was meant, in part, to persuade Muslims to join Allied forces against the Axis powers. A later document, the *Additif*, was attached (May) to the Manifesto and was much more specific in demands. The Manifesto was the first major document to speak of a sovereign Algerian nation and an Algerian state. It disclosed, too, how the moderate nationalists had moved toward more radical positions since the Blum-Viollette legislation (q.v.). The Manifesto was rejected by the colonial authorities, but it did persuade the French to implement changes such as the Ordinance of March 7, 1944 (q.v.).

AL-MANSUR (reign 984-996). Zirid (q.v.) ruler. Al-Mansur freed himself from the Fatimids (q.v.) and defeated the Kutama (q.v.). This instability allowed the Zenata (q.v.) to secure themselves in the western Maghrib.

AL-MANSUR (d. 1104). Hammadid (q.v.) ruler. He succeeded his father, al-Nasir, in 1088 and moved the capital to Bejaïa in an effort to protect it from nomadic attacks (e.g., Banu Hilal [q.v.]). Al-Mansur found himself faced with the combined opposition of the Zenata and the Almoravids (q.v.). After the fall of Ashir, the traditional stronghold of his family, al-Mansur raised an army and defeated both the Almoravids and the Zenata, whom he drove into the mountains of Kabylia (q.v.). He also defeated the Banu Hilal.

AL-MANSUR ISMA'IL, ABU TAHIR/ABU AL-'ABBAS (r. 946–953). Fatimid (q.v.) caliph. As third caliph, he came to power during the time that Abu Yazid (q.v.) was threatening the Fatimids. He finally defeated the Khariji (q.v. Kharijism) leader and later his son, thereby resecuring the Fatimid control of *Ifriqiya* (including eastern Algeria). The Caliph also built up the Fatimid navy, which had notable successes against the Byzantines. Al-Mansur moved the capital from al-Mahdiya to al-Mansuriya (947). He died suddenly at the age of thirty-nine.

MARCH DECREES (q.v. Introduction; Agriculture; *Autogestion*).

MARGUERITTE AFFAIR. An incident in the department of Oran in the spring of 1901. A Muslim preacher named Yacoub (Yakub) incited his followers to take over the settlement of Margueritte. As a result, the subprefect was held prisoner, French property was looted, and a rural policemen and five Europeans were killed. The incident sparked lively debate on the floor of the French Chamber of Deputies concerning its origins and drew attention to the conflicting colonial theories of assimilation (q.v.) and association (q.v.). The immediate result was an extension of disciplinary commissions, the *Tribunaux répressifs indigènes*. For the succeeding decade, the affair served a public admission that the Algerian Muslim had been injuriously ignored. It also reminded the colonial establishment of the explosive potential of the oppressed colonized population.

MASINISSA (MASSINISSA) (240?-148 B.C.). Masinissa was the King of Numidia (q.v.) (eastern Algeria). He succeeded his father Gala as chief of the Eastern Numidian Massyli (Masaesyli) c. 208 B.C. At first, he was allied with the Carthaginians. His rival, Syphax of Siga (q.v.), ruler of the western Numidian Massyli, overthrew him with Carthaginian assistance. Masinissa allied himself with the Romans, aided Scipio in his victory over Hannibal and Syphax at Zama in 202 B.C., and was rewarded with all of Numidia.

Masinissa established his capital at Cirta (Constantine [q.v.]) and strengthened his kingdom with a formidable army and navy during his reign. He promoted agriculture and commerce (apparently a genuinely "money economy," i.e., coins were struck for general use besides for symbolic or commemorative reasons). His seizures of Carthaginian territory were achieved with the implicit support of Rome, which still feared the still prosperous but defenseless Carthage. In 154 B.C., Masinissa expropriated the fertile territory less than 100 miles from Carthage. The Carthaginians, fearing more Massyli incursions, attempted to ally with the Mauretanians and Libyans. At the age of eighty-eight, Masinissa was victorious over the Carthaginians in 150 B.C. The old king now entertained ambitions of taking over Carthage.

Rome did not want to see another powerful state established across the Mediterranean. That fear, compounded by the pathological fear of Carthage heightened by Cato's oratory (*Delenda est Carthago*—"Carthage must be destroyed!"), resulted in an expedition to take over Carthage. A three-year war culminated in the brutal carnage of Carthage in 146 B.C. Rome established itself in North Africa. Masinissa died during the siege of Carthage.

Masinissa's kingdom and his personal dynamism was highly regarded by Algerian nationalists. It was also used as another argument to repudiate colonialist efforts denying a past Algerian sovereignty. Masinissa received admiring attention in the "enriched" National Charter of January 1986 (q.v.).

MASPETIOL REPORT OF 1955. A study of the financial relationship between Algeria and France issued in June 1955. The report revealed that most Algerian Muslims had an average income of $45/year. Only 50,000 Muslims earned as much as $502/year. Conversely, no European earned less than $240/year. The minuscule graduation of taxes, the report concluded, also operated to the advantage of the wealthy Europeans. These disclosures staggered and embarrassed Paris. Citing the enormous stagnation and underdevelopment, the report recommended an annual increase in public expenditure of 15 billion AF (*Anciens Francs*) a year, reaching 150 billion AF in 1962.

MASSYLI (MASAESYLI; MASSYLE). This was one of the powerful tribes of northern Algeria. The eventual kingdom of the Massyli ranged more than 500 miles to the west of Cape Bougaroun, north of Constantine. The Massyli had two capitals: Siga and, most famous, Cirta (Constantine [q.v.]). This was the tribe of Masinissa (q.v.).

MAURETANIA ("LAND OF THE MAURI [BERBERS]"). The ancient Latin name for an area of North Africa bounded on the east by Algiers, on the south by the Atlas mountains, and on the west by the Atlantic Ocean. The land was composed of tribal federations by at least the fourth century B.C. At first, the Mauretanians were pastoralists, but by the time the Romans conquered the region, the society was markedly sedentary, particularly as noted by its wheat production. Little is known of its history prior to 108 B.C. when Bocchus I emerged as an ambitious ruler over the tribal chiefs. He cooperated with the Numidians against the Romans and received territorial compensations. In 106 B.C., Bocchus turned to the Romans (symbolically delivering to them Jugurtha [q.v.], his son-in-law) and thereby secured Roman recognition of his control as far east as the Chélif River. Around 80 B.C. the Bogud dynasty appeared, and by 50 B.C. the kingdom was divided along the Muluccha River, the east under the rule of Bocchus II and the west of Bogud II. As a result of Bogud's support of Antony in the Roman civil war, the victorious Octavian awarded both kingdoms to Bocchus. Upon the end of the dynasty in 25 B.C., Emperor Augustus awarded both kingdoms to the Numidian prince Juba II. His successor Ptolemaeus was executed by Caligula in A.D. 39, and the two kingdoms became Roman provinces under the titles of Mauretania Tingitana and Mauretania Caesariensis. The first major uprising of the Kabyles of Mauretania Caesariensis occurred in 259, and the areas east of Algiers continued to be under the control of local chieftains. In 289, the Transstagnensis nomads also rebelled. As a result, Rome largely abandoned Mauretania Caesariensis west of the Chélif. When the Vandals invaded Mauretania in 429, the collapse of Roman authority was complete.

MECILI, ALI (d. 1987). Close colleague of Hocine Aït Ahmed (q.v.); lawyer. Mécili, a Kabyle (q.v.), was the son of an *instituteur* (teacher/teaching aid/instructor) who joined the ALN as a teenager. After the war he joined Aït Ahmed's FFS (q.v.) in opposition to the government of Ahmed Ben Bella (q.v.). He was arrested along with Aït Ahmed. Mécili moved to France and studied law at Aix-en-Provence. Ironically, he became renowned for his defense of the expulsion from France of 13 Ben Bellists in 1986. The forty-seven-year-old lawyer was murdered in April 1987. Aït Ahmed attributed Mécili's death to the Algerian governmental agents. Mécili was regarded as an advocate of democracy in Algeria.

MEDEGHRI, AHMED (1934–1974). Minister. Born in Oran, Medeghri was a schoolteacher before the War of Independence. During the war he served with FLN (q.v.) representatives in Morocco and became a major in Houari Boumedienne's (q.v.) external army in Morocco. After the war he was a prefect, a deputy in the National Assembly, and then minister of the interior under Ahmed Ben Bella (q.v.). This latter position became highly controversial when Medeghri, a staunch Boumedienne loyalist, resigned in protest (July 1964) over Ben Bella's decision to have prefects report directly to the president. His resignation heightened the tension between Boumedienne and Ben Bella and contributed to the coup of June 1965. After Boumedienne seized power, Medeghri returned as minister of the interior, a post he held until his death as a result of a car accident. This powerful minister was said to have become disenchanted with Boumedienne. The reported cause of his death (automobile accident) was viewed as suspicious.

MEHRI, ABDELHAMID (b. 1926). Nationalist; revolutionary; minister; ambassador; head of FLN (q.v.). Mehri came from a very poor family, but he disclosed an excellent aptitude for scholarship, especially in Arabic literature (attended the University of Zitouna [Tunis]). He served with the (PPA-) MTLD (q.v. Messali Hadj). In 1953 he served on the Central Committee of the MTLD. In 1954 he resisted an appeal from the CRUA (q.v.) to be its spokesman. Mehri was arrested in 1954 and released a year later.

He joined the FLN serving as its representative in Damascus in 1955. In 1956 he was elected to the CNRA (q.v.) and the CCE (q.v.) in 1957. Having an interest in Maghribi affairs that predated the outbreak of the revolution (Mohamed Boudiaf [q.v.] had introduced him to Moroccan nationalists; Mehri also had served as a Messalist liaison with the Tunisian Neo-*Destour* party), he became the GPRA's (q.v.) minister of North African affairs in 1958. He was appointed the minister of social and cultural affairs (1960–1961) in the second GPRA. After the war he become the director of the Ecole Normale at Bouzaréah.

After Colonel Houari Boumedienne's (q.v.) coup of June 1965 (q.v.), he returned to politics and served in several positions: secretary-general of the Ministry of Primary and Secondary Education (1970–1977); FLN Central Committee (1979); minister of information and culture (1979); FLN Political Bureau (1984); and ambassador to France (1984). After the restoration of relations with Rabat, he became ambassador to Morocco (1988). He was then called back to Algiers after the October Riots (q.v.) and made head of the FLN secretariat, replacing Mohamed Cherif Messaadia (q.v.). Mehri and the FLN endured humiliating electoral losses (q.v. Elections of 1990; 1991). Though the FLN protested the High Council of State's (HCS) (q.v.) cancellation of national legislative elections, it remains divided concerning support of the HCS's policies.

MELOUZA (MELOUZA MASSACRE). A town north of the Sahara that was the site of an ALN (q.v.) assault on May 28, 1957, that resulted in the death of approximately 300 civilians who were suspected to be supporters of Messali Hadj (q.v.) and Mohamed Bellounis (q.v.). The French publicized the atrocity internationally to disparage the FLN (q.v.).

MELUN CONFERENCE (JUNE 25–29, 1960). Preliminary though premature discussions between GPRA (q.v.) and French government. After President Charles de Gaulle (q.v.) announced on June 14, 1960 that he would be willing to speak to "leaders of the insurrection," the GPRA dispatched Mohammed Ben Yahia (q.v.) and Ahmed Boumendjel (q.v.). The two FLN representatives were quartered in Melun. The French demanded a cease-fire before serious negotiations. The Algerians refused and asked for discussions with a French official at the ministerial level. This was not offered by de Gaulle. The discussions ended quickly. The short-lived conference benefited the GPRA because it provided positive international publicity. The talks were conducted courteously and were actually an important step toward more substantial discussions the following year and finally those of February-March 1962 culminating in the Evian Accords (q.v.).

MENDJLI, ALI (b. 1922). Nationalist; revolutionary; president of the National Assembly. Born near Skikda, Mendjli was a member of the MTLD (q.v.) and then joined the FLN (q.v.). He campaigned in Kabylia (q.v.) in the ALN (q.v.) and along the Algerian-Tunisian border. He was elected to the CNRA (q.v.) (1959). Mendjli was attached to the Algerian negotiating team. His mission was to observe for Houari Boumedienne (q.v.). After the war he served as a deputy in the National Assembly and was elevated to its vice presidency. As a member of the Political Bureau (1964), he reportedly urged an acceleration in nationalizations. Mendjli was close to both Ahmed Ben Bella (q.v.) and Boumedienne, but he apparently was not part of the Colonel's plot to overthrow the president. After the coup of June 1965 (q.v.), he held the title of president of the National Assembly, but it no longer convened.

MERBAH, KASDI (Abdallah Khalaf/Khalef/Khelef) (1938–1993). Security chief; prime minister. Merbah was director of military security from 1962 and planned the FLN (q.v.) Congress, which confirmed Chadli Benjedid (q.v.) as president in 1979. He became a cabinet member in 1980 and held the agriculture portfolio from January 1984 to February 1988. He played an important role in dismantling the socialist sector and privatizing it. In February 1988 he became minister of health.

Merbah was regarded as one of the most effective leaders within the FLN. He was appointed prime minister after the October 1988 riots (q.v.). He protested the rapid pace of reform and was unable to stem rising prices, which led to his dismissal on September 9, 1989, which he considered unconstitutional. He averted a national crisis by stepping down. He remained an active member of the Central Committee before establishing the *Mouvement Algérien pour la Justice et le Développement* (MAJD). His repudiation of the FLN was regarded as a serious blow to the party.

MERBAH, MOULAY (b. 1913). Messalist (q.v. Messali Hadj). Merbah joined the PPA (q.v.) in 1944. He became a member of the Central Committee of the MTLD (q.v.) in 1951 and a member of its Political Bureau in 1954. During the War of Independence he served the MNA (q.v.) in Europe and at the United Nations. After the war he was secretary-general of the PPA (q.v.), which had been reformed in 1962. He resigned after Messali Hadj (q.v.) hesitated in calling for a general meeting of the organization. In October 1962, he unsuccessfully attempted to reconcile with the FLN's (q.v.) Political Bureau. He was arrested and then freed. He then became a lawyer in Médéa.

MESSAADIA, MOHAMED CHERIF (b. 1924). Revolutionary; FLN (q.v.) party leader. Messaadia was a student at the University of Zitouna, Tunis. During the War of Independence, Messaadia was implicated in the ''plot of the colonels.'' Excused by the special court appointed to try the plotters, he was one of several young officers sent to open a southern front that would operate from Mali and Niger. This was an attempt by the ALN (q.v.) to outmaneuver the Morice Line (1960) (q.v.) (fortifications along the Algerian-Tunisian border). He was a deputy of the Constituent National Assembly and then the National Assembly. He became a member of the Central Committee of the FLN in 1964 and held a series of functions within the party. Messaadia became minister of veterans (*Moudjahidine*) (1979–1980). He then was chosen by President Chadli Benjedid (q.v.) to head the FLN Permanent Secretariat. This was an unpopular choice among the party, given Messaadia's rather undistinguished and bureaucratic career. Messaadia also became a member of the Political Bureau (1981). He was replaced on October 30, 1988, by Abdelhamid Mehri (q.v.) in order to revitalize the FLN after that month's rioting. He later associated with an anti-Benjedidist faction within the FLN.

MESSALI (Mesli) HADJ (1898–1974). Paramount nationalist. Messali was born in Tlemcen (q.v.) and was the son of a shoemaker. In his youth he was influenced by the Darqawa (q.v.) brotherhood. Before becoming Algeria's chief nationalist figure, Messali served in the French Army, enrolled in Arabic classes at French higher institutions, and worked a variety of jobs. Messali joined the *Etoile Nord-Africaine* (ENA) (q.v.) and quickly replaced Hadj Ali Abdelkader (q.v.) as the organization's leader in 1926. He attended the Brussels Congress in 1927, where he met Jawaharlal Nehru, Achmed Sukarno, and Ho Chi Minh. The ENA was dissolved in November 1929.

While in temporary exile in Switzerland, he met *Shaykh* Arslan (q.v.), an early spokesman for Pan-Islamic and Pan-Arabic ideologies. He regenerated the ENA (*La Glorieuse Etoile Nord-Africaine*) in 1933, but it became clearly an Algerian nationalist movement and no longer subscribed to communist internationalism. The objective was establishment of an Arab independent Algerian state. Messali supported the Popular Front until disagreement with the Blum government over colonial issues led him to separate himself and the ENA from the French Left. The Popular Front disbanded the ENA in January 1937. In March 1937 he launched the *Parti du Peuple Algérien* (PPA) (q.v.).

Messali opposed the Blum-Viollette legislation (q.v.) and was opposed to the moderate Algerian Muslim Congress (q.v.). It seemed too moderate. Nevertheless, Messali Hadj's influence forced political rivals and parties (e.g., Abd al-Hamid Ben Badis [q.v.], Ferhat Abbas [q.v.], Mohammed Saleh Bendjelloul [q.v.], and the PCA [q.v. Algerian Communist Party]) to become more radical. Because of his political views and activities, Messali was arrested in 1941 and sentenced to hard labor. He was forced to reside in southern Algeria, then transferred to Brazzaville in Central Africa. At the end of World War II, he was amnestied and returned to Algeria. He accepted leadership of the *Amis du Manifeste et de Liberté* (AML) (q.v.) organized by Abbas, and for a brief period it appeared that the Algerian nationalist movement had attained unity and solidarity. The arrest of Messali and deportation proceedings contributed to the outbreak at Sétif (q.v.) and Guelma in May 1945.

Messali then founded the *Mouvement pour le Triomphe des Libertés Démocratiques* (MTLD) (q.v.) to replace the PPA, which had been outlawed by the French authorities (though the PPA continued secretly within his new political framework, thus the occasional designation of PPA-MTLD). Younger members of the movement pressured a reluctant Messali to accelerate his demands for Algerian independence. Messali's ambivalence led to the formation of the *Organisation Spéciale* (OS) (q.v.) in 1947 and finally in 1954 the *Comité Révolutionnaire d'Unité et d'Action* (CRUA) (q.v.) and the *Front de Libération Nationale* (FLN) (q.v.). The MTLD also endured the "Berberist Crisis" (q.v.) in 1949. This was caused by Kabyles (q.v.) who protested the emphasis on Arabism within the movement. They also questioned Messali's authoritarian control. In 1953–1954, the MTLD split between "Centralists" and "Messalists." The "Centralists" (from the Central Committee of the MTLD), like the OS, wanted immediate action to liberate the country.

The events of November 1954 eclipsed Messali, and he became less effective as the War of Independence progressed. He tried to compete with the FLN by organizing in December 1954 the *Mouvement National Algérien* (MNA) (q.v.), but his time had passed. Indeed, the FLN and MNA conducted ruthless operations against each other (q.v. Mohammed Bellounis; Mélouza). It was a tragic dimension of the War of Independence. An effort to regenerate the PPA immediately after the war was rejected by the ruling FLN.

Messali Hadj was still in exile, ironically from independent Algeria, when he died in France. He was buried in his native Tlemcen in 1974. *Les Mémoires de Messali Hadj* was published in 1982.

MESSIMY, ADOLPHE (1869–1935). Assimilationist (q.v. Assimilation) French republican politician and military specialist. While in the military, Messimy rose to the rank of captain of light cavalry. He then served in the French Chamber as a deputy from the department of the Seine. During the pre-World War I years, he supported full use of Algerian troops in the French Army. In 1912, Messimy presented a report to the Chamber proposing a series of reforms of the *Code de l'indigénat* (q.v.), an expansion of the number of Muslim seats in Algerian assemblies, and an easier naturalization process for Algerians who could demonstrate French language proficiency or French professional training. He continued to press for similar reforms through 1914. Messimy returned to military service with the outbreak of World War I.

MEZERNA, AHMED (1907–1982). Nationalist. A member of the PNR (*Parti National Révolutionnaire*), an Algerian pre-ENA (q.v.) organization linked to the French Communist Party (PCF), Mezerna eventually became a leading supporter of Messali Hadj (q.v.). He joined the ENA and its successor, the PPA. In 1938 he was made secretary of the Algiers Federation of the PPA. Repeatedly arrested and condemned by the French colonial authorities, he remained a Messalist leader during World War II. Mezerna played an important role in organizing the May 1945 protests (q.v. Sétif), which subsequently led to his imprisonment (1945–1946). Along with Jellouli Farès of the Tunisian Neo-*Destour* party and Mehdi Ben Barka of the Moroccan *Istiqlal* party, Mezerna lobbied the United Nations for North African independence. As a loyal supporter, he sided with Messali during the MTLD split and was in Cairo for negotiations with the CRUA (q.v.) when the War of Independence broke out on October 31–November 1, 1954. In July 1955, he was arrested by Egyptian authorities, apparently at the request of the FLN leaders who did not trust his Messalist past.

MICIPSA (d. 118 B.C.). King of Numidia (q.v.) (148–118). Eldest son of Masinissa, he shared power with his brothers Mastanbal and Gulusa until he overpowered them both. He furnished the Roman armies in North Africa with grain and troops. He also promoted a greater Roman commercial presence within his realm. Micipsa adopted Jugurtha (q.v.), his nephew, as a co-successor (along with Adherbal).

AL MILI, MUBARAK (1897–1945). Member of the Association of Reformist *Ulama* (q.v.); historian. Born in El-Milia in Lesser (Little) Kabylia (q.v.), he wrote in Arabic and viewed history (like Tawfiq al-Madani [q.v.]) as a means to develop consciousness and national identity. His most important book was *History of Algeria in the Past and in the Present* (1931).

MIMOUNI, RACHID (b. 1945). Writer. Mimouni, a specialist in economics and development, is one of contemporary Algeria's leading new novelists. His works consider the contradictions concerning the promise and reality of independence. His novels include *Printemps n'en sera que plus beau* (1978); *Fleuve détourné* (1982); *Tombéza* (1984); and *L'Honneur de la tribu* (1989) (translated into English as *Honor of the Tribe*).

MINING. Algeria is mineral-rich. Along the Tunisian border, iron ore is mined at Ouenza and Bou Khadra and phosphates at Djebel Kouif and especially Djebel Onk. In 1988, 3.1 million metric tons of high-grade iron ore and 1.2 million metric tons of phosphates were produced. There is also modest mercury, lead, and zinc production. Coal is mined near the Moroccan border at Kénadsa southwest of Béchar. A very rich but unexploited deposit of iron ore is at Gara Djebilet, southwest of Tindouf, in the far west along the border with Mali. The Ahaggar Mountains hold uranium.

MITTERRAND, FRANÇOIS (b. 1916). Fourth Republic minister; president of Fifth Republic. As minister of interior in the Mendès-France government, Mitterrand reported to the premier in October 1954 his concern over conditions in Algeria. After the revolution began a month later, Mitterrand affirmed that "Algeria is France" and soon introduced a series of reforms. The "Mitterrand Plan" addressed social economic needs such as land reclamation and equitable salaries. Mitterrand extended democracy by instituting women's suffrage. His efforts to make the Statute of Algeria (q.v.) more liberal angered anxious *pieds-noirs* (q.v.). Under the Faure government, Mitterrand served as minister of justice. This was a difficult period as torture was used systematically in Algeria. Mitterrand is credited with tempering its abuses and intervening in other cases.

As head of the French Socialist Party during the Fifth Republic, Mitterrand visited Algiers in 1976. This trip was done in part to reconcile his controversial past with independent Algeria. He called for a "redress" (*redressement*) in French-Algerian relations during that period of bilateral difficulties (especially over commercial imbalances and the war in Western Sahara [q.v.]).

After becoming president in 1981, Mitterrand pursued a "redress," resulting in numerous accords of "co-development" highlighted by the February 1982 LNG accord (q.v. Hydrocarbon Sector). He hosted President Chadli Benjedid's (q.v.) state visit in November 1983. Relations declined in late 1984, but revived especially after the October 1988 riots (q.v.). France provided political, financial, and economic assistance to the beleaguered Benjedid government. It also continued financial support (February-March 1992) to the High Council of State (HCS). Mitterrand's government has generally pursued a "wait-and-see'' policy concerning the difficult current situation in Algeria. Most recently, it seems ready to resume a more ''normal'' cooperation (q.v.).

MOHAMMEDI, SAID (b. 1912). Soldier; revolutionary. Mohammedi fought in the French Army, then in the *Wehrmacht* (German Army). The Germans parachuted him into Tunisia in 1944 and he was captured by French troops and subsequently imprisoned. He joined the ALN (q.v.) and commanded *Wilaya* III. He was appointed to the CNRA (q.v.) and became minister of state in the GPRA (q.v.). He was vice president in Ahmed Ben Bella's (q.v.) second and third governments. He was close to Houari Boumedienne, but he apparently was not among the plotters of the coup of June 1965 (q.v.).

MONIS PROJECT. Proposal submitted before the French Chamber of Deputies in 1911. Actually prepared by Governor-General Jonnart (q.v.), it called for a renewal of the powers of local Algerian officials in the *communes mixtes* (q.v.) for seven years, but reduced the extent of their jurisdiction. It rivaled the Rozet project submitted in 1909. Both proposals were seen as attacks on the *Code de l'indigénat* (q.v.).

MORCELI, NOUREDDINE (b. 1970). Athlete. Morceli was born in Ténès. Along with his compatriot, Hassiba Boulmerka (q.v.), he won the 1,500 meters in the 1991 World Championships. This was the first time that a country produced two champions in the same event. Morceli also holds the indoor world record in the 1,500 meters (3:32.84). Though he was the favorite at the Barcelona Olympics (1992), he was boxed in during the 1,500 meters and failed to earn the expected gold medal. After the Olympics, he soon, however, reestablished his athletic dominance in his event. Morceli is a devout Muslim. He nonetheless has supported Boulmerka, who has been denounced by conservative Muslim clerics for her athletic career. Morceli like Boulmerka is a recipient of the Order of Merit.

MORICE LINE. Name given to a barrier erected along the Tunisian border in 1957 by the French under the direction of the French Defense minister, André Morice. It was intended to restrict the flow of supplies and troops from Tunisia to the ALN (q.v.) and also to defend the highway and rail system from Bône (Annaba [q.v.]) to Tebessa. Set about 40 kilometers from the Tunisian border, it was approximately 450 kilometers in length. It consisted of two rows of electrified (5,000 volts) barbed wire on either side of a roadway and was set off by fields of antipersonnel mine-fields. In 1959 the line was doubled in the north from Soux-Ahras to Cape Roux and in the center in front of the minefields. It was highly effective separating the internal from the external ALN.

MOROCCO. Algeria and Morocco have had a very close, if not a mutual history especially seen during the periods of the Almoravids (q.v.) and the Almohads (q.v.). The Moroccan Marinid dynasty competed with the Algerian Abd al-Wadids (q.v.). During Abd al-Qadir's (q.v.) resistance to the French, the Sultanate gave assistance to the Amir until the Battle of Isly (1844), resulting in the Treaty of Tangiers between France and Morocco. The Sultanate also influenced the prominent Awlad Sidi Shaykh (q.v.) in western Algeria.

During the colonial period, the respective administrations argued over the frontiers between the two territories. As Algeria neared independence, Ferhat Abbas (q.v.) negotiated an agreement with Rabat in July 1961, calling for a final border delineation after the War of Independence. This was done, in part, to prevent Morocco from concluding a frontier settlement with the French.

After Algeria attained independence, Morocco waited for the fulfillment of this agreement. President Ahmed Ben Bella (q.v.) declared, however, that the western border was permanent. When his government was shaken by the Kabyle (q.v.) revolt of October-November 1963, Morocco seized frontier posts. The ''Border War'' (q.v.) was short-lived, but it underscored that the fraternal feelings during the War of Independence were over.

Relations warmed after Houari Boumedienne (q.v.) came to power. King Hassan attended the OAU summit in Algiers in 1968. Summit meetings in January 1969 in Morocco and in May 1970 in Algeria led to the establishment of commissions to settle outstanding bilateral contentions, especially the border problem. On June 15, 1972, two conventions were signed that called for the recognition of the present border and the mutual exploitation of the iron deposits at Gara Djebilet. Though Morocco refrained, Algeria ratified the conventions in 1973.

The decolonization of the Spanish Sahara produced more problems. Algerian actions seemed paradoxical. Apparently Foreign Minister Abdelaziz Bouteflika (q.v.) was willing to accept a partition of the Spanish Sahara between Morocco and Mauritania as long as the 1972 conventions were ratified. Hassan seemed very pleased with this proposal. When Bouteflika returned to Algiers, President Boumedienne reportedly rejected his foreign minister's actions. When the Madrid Accords of November 1975 divided the Spanish Sahara between Morocco and Mauritania, Algeria gave the POLISARIO (q.v.), the Sahrawi liberation organization, massive support. Boumedienne probably felt he had been betrayed by King Hassan. Formal relations broke as a result of the crisis and conflict.

As the War in Western Sahara continued, President Chadli Benjedid (q.v.) and King Hassan met in 1983, which achieved little. From 1984 to 1986, Morocco and Libya agreed to be allies (Oujda Treaty). This was a counterpoise to President Chadli Benjedid's (q.v.) 1983 accords with Mauritania (pulled out of Western Sahara in 1979 [q.v. Algiers Agreement]) and Tunisia. Benjedid and Hassan met again in 1987. In May 1988 relations were renewed. Then in February 1989, the Arab Maghrib Union (q.v. Maghrib Unity) was signed promising further regional cooperation if not collaboration (e.g., plans for a natural gas trunk line to Morocco). In

March 1989, Morocco ratified the 1972 conventions. Morocco has kept a particularly anxious watch on Algeria's domestic developments since the October 1988 riots (q.v.).

MOULAY, ABDELKADER (1924?–1971). Soldier. Moulay was born into a well-to-do family in Oran province and received a very good French education. He joined the army and in an 18-year career, he reached the rank of major. Moulay, along with several other Algerians, deserted in 1958 and reached Morocco. He remained with the external ALN (q.v.). After independence he was the chief of the Cabinet of the Ministry of Defense and a member of the General Staff. He eventually was appointed secretary-general of the Ministry of National Defense. He died in a helicopter accident.

MOUVEMENT ISLAMIQUE ARME (MIA). Militant Islamist organization. The MIA has pursued a violent campaign against the HCS (q.v.) government (q.v.) (200 to 400 soldiers and policemen died during 1992). The MIA's recognized leader is Abdelkader Chebouti.

MOUVEMENT NATIONALISTE ALGERIEN (MNA). The MTLD was reorganized by Messali Hadj (q.v.) as the MNA in December 1954, one month after the beginning of the War of Independence. In order to seize the revolutionary initiative from the FLN (q.v.), the MNA also initiated guerrilla operations.

Though both the FLN and the MNA had much in common, repeated efforts to unite the two organizations failed, leading to interelite violence. As French forces laid back to observe the nationalist carnage in Algeria and France, MNA and ALN units conducted ferocious attacks on each other. The fratricidal violence was symbolized by the ALN's atrocious massacre of MNA sympathizers (300 dead) at Mélouza (q.v.) in May 1957. Though the MNA military and political threat became inconsequential, especially after the Mohammed Bellounis (q.v.) affair, the FLN continued its campaign against it and any other nationalist group that questioned its legitimacy.

MOUVEMENT POUR LE TRIOMPHE DES LIBERTES DE-MOCRATIQUES (MTLD; PPA-MTLD). This party was organized by Messali Hadj after the Sétif uprising (q.v.) as a successor party to the banned *Parti du Peuple Algérien* (PPA). The PPA continued to operate secretly, though within a new Messalist framework (thereby the occasional designation of PPA-MTLD). The MTLD acted as the electoral party, while the PPA continued to pursue purely nationalist objectives. Impatient younger members in the MTLD were permitted to form the paramilitary *Organisation Spéciale* (OS) (q.v.) in 1947 (suppressed in 1950). Concurrently, the "Berberist Crisis" (q.v.) arose in which Berber members questioned the emphasis on Arabism and also Messali's authoritarianism. The Messalist movement became em-broiled among legalists, Berbers, and revolutionaries. In 1953, the MTLD split as "Centralists" (of the Central Committee) demanded an immediate preparation for revolu-tion. They were opposed by the "Messalists." Eventually, a third group broke from the intraelite conflict and formed the *Comité Révolutionnaire d'Unité et d'Action* (CRUA) (q.v.) and subsequently the *Front de Libération Nationale* (FLN). The MTLD was itself outlawed in 1954, after the outbreak of revolution, at which time Messali Hadj organized the *Mouvement Nationaliste Algérien* (q.v.) as a competitor to the FLN.

MUHI AL-DIN, BEN MUSTAFA (1757–1833). Father of Abd al-Qadir (q.v.); head of the Qadiriyya (q.v.) brotherhood in Algeria. Muhi al-Din assisted the Moroccan penetration of Oran province from 1830 to 1832 and served as the Moroccan sultan's *khalifa* in Tlemcen (1831) and Oran province (1832). He also began resistance against the French. Because of his advanced age, he contended that his son should be elected as his successor as Commander of the

Believers. This was done and Abd al-Qadir eventually became a great national hero.

AL-MU'IZZ (r. 1016–1062) Zirid *amir*. He loosened ties with Cairo, which was done in part because of his Sunni subjects. In a symbolic gesture to assert his independence from the Fatimids (q.v.), he proclaimed the suzerainty of the Abbasids of Baghdad. The Fatimids (q.v.) were particularly annoyed by this rebellious *amir* and forced the Banu Hilal (q.v.) and Banu Sulaym westward, which would have significant consequences in the history of Algeria (i.e., cultural Arabization).

AL-MUQRANI, MUHAMMAD AL-HAJJ (EL-MOKRANI, MOHAMED) (d. 1871). Principal leader of the (Great) Kabyle Revolt (q.v.) of 1870–1871. Al-Muqrani was a *Bachaga* who was a favorite among French officers. Nevertheless, he resented the reduction of his own administrative prerogatives. Al-Muqrani favored a traditional feudal, aristocratic political system in Algeria. The condescending attitude by the colonial authorities (along with France's military disasters against the Germans) convinced al-Muqrani to rebel. He hoped to rally other tribal chiefs and notables to his side (e.g., Ben Ali Chérif). He summoned a war council in March 1871. His initiative received the prestigious support of *Shaykh* Sidi Muhammad al-Haddad (q.v.), the *muqaddam* of the Rahmaniyya (q.v.), and his son Si Aziz. The revolt began in April, swept through eastern Algeria, and eventually reached Algiers and Cherchell. Al-Muqrani was killed in battle in May 1871. His brother Bu Masraq (q.v.) carried on the fight until his capture in June 1872. The consequences of this war included the disastrous colonial expropriation of Kabyle land, leaving the indigenous population severely distressed.

M'ZAB. Plateau area in the Sahara where the Ibadi (q.v. Ibadism) M'zabi (Mozabites) (q.v.) live. Despite the hot and dry climate, the M'zab is watered by an underground river. This has led to the building of Ghardaïa and complementary oases towns (Melika, Beni Isguen, Bou Noura, and El Atteuf). The M'zab is renown for its groves of date palms.

M'ZABI (M'ZABITES/MOZABITES/MIZABIS). Ibadi (q.v. Ibadism) Berbers (q.v.) living in the M'zab (around Ghardaia) in the central Sahara. They are famous as shrewd businessmen and renowned cultivators of dates at their Saharan oases. The M'zabi settled in this area after the fall of the Rustamid dynasty (q.v.) at Tahert to the Fatimids (q.v.). The Ibadis were driven to Sedrata and finally into the Sahara. The M'zabis speak their own Berber dialect. On occasion there has still been sectarian strife (e.g., July 1990 between Malikis and Ibadis).

NABI, BELKACEM (b. 1929). Engineer; minister. Nabi played a significant role in Algeria's hydrocarbons sector (q.v.). He was president of Algeria's holdings of SN REPAL (oil company) (1965–1967). (SN REPAL was a French company that was eventually incorporated into ERAP.) From 1970 to 1974 he was the governor (*wali*) of the Tlemcen *wilayat* before becoming an adviser to the presidency (1974–1979). He was appointed minister of energy and petrochemical industries (1979) and was the principal spokesman of the new price parity policy (oil=gas). Nabi reportedly remarked at one point: "A therm is a therm." Nabi had to endure the loss of the El Paso contract but secured new contracts with European partners (Belgium, France, United Kingdom, Spain, Italy). The Trans-Mediterranean gas line was also put into operation. As long as oil prices remained high, Algeria enjoyed fabulous export receipts. The price precipitously fell during the mid-1980s. Nabi left the Ministry of Energy in 1988.

NAPOLEON III (1808–1873). French president; emperor; Arabophile. During his regime, Napoleon III had a particular interest in Algeria. Sensitive to settler demands and protests against the military's "rule of the sabre," he inaugurated a Ministry of Algeria and Colonies (1858–1860) under Prince (Jerome) Napoleon. The goal was to assimilate the indigenous population by reorganizing (Jerome used the word "dislocation") social and economic structures and replacing Islamic law with French law. The military was particularly aware of the danger of implementing these measures and lobbied the emperor. Napoleon III visited in 1860 and ended the Ministry. The Imperial Government tried to impede rural colonization. In his famous February 6, 1863, letter, he considered Algeria an "Arab kingdom" rather than a colony. The *Sénatus-consulte* of April 22, 1863 (q.v.), aimed at protecting tribal lands, but it introduced European property standards. This initiative actually led to the eventual selling of tribal lands. The Emperor believed that Algerians should be able to achieve full citizenship without compromising their personal (Muslim) status (this also applied to Jews). This was underscored by the *Sénatus-consulte* of July 14, 1865, which gave Muslims "subject" status. It also called for greater opportunities for Muslims in the French administration and military. Nevertheless, full naturalization could still not occur unless an individual repudiated Muslim status. Very few Muslims opted for full French citizenship.

Napoleon's concern for the colonized was also disclosed in education. He permitted the reopening of higher Muslim educational centers (*madrasas; médérsas*), the inauguration of "Arabic-French" primary and secondary schools, and a technical school in Kabylia. His perspective toward Algeria may have been romantic, but if his good intentions were conscientiously applied, Algeria would not have endured such a severe colonialism.

NASR-EDDINE (q.v. Etienne Dinet).

NATIONAL CHARTER OF 1976. This was produced by the FLN (q.v.) as a means to define the Algerian state. It was highly theoretical and was an excellent expression of how the Houari Boumedienne (q.v.) government envisioned the Algeria of the future as socialist, centralist, and Muslim. It underscored that "socialism, in Algeria, is an irreversible movement." It confidently asserted that Algeria was a Muslim state and linked socialist state-building to the "Islamic values which are a fundamental constitutive element of the personality of the Algerian people" rather than to a "materialist metaphysic" or a "dogmatic foreign conception." The Charter reiterated the aim "to consolidate national independence" by liquidating all forms of imperialist or neocolonialist influence. The Charter (composed of seven chapters) was in the rhetorical tradition of the Tripoli Program (q.v.) and the Charter of Algiers (q.v.). What distinguished this document was the Boumedienne government's decision to allow public discussion. The Charter was complemented by a Constitution of 1976 (q.v.).

NATIONAL CHARTER OF 1986 (REVISED). President Chadli Benjedid (q.v.) authorized a revision or "enrichment" of the National Charter. The changes were more stylistic than substantive. It was also written in a simpler language. What was particularly significant was a survey of Algerian history that included the contributions of the previously taboo names of Messali Hadj (q.v.) and Ferhat Abbas (q.v.). It placed greater emphasis on complementing socialism with the private sector and emphasized the guiding role of Islam. In a referendum on January 16, it received 98.37 percent approval with a turnout of 95.9 percent (both figures were controversial).

NATIONAL REVOLUTIONARY COUNCIL (q.v. Council of the Revolution).

NAVAL BATTLE OF MERS-EL KEBIR (or ORAN, July 3, 1940). Following the French defeat in June 1940, a portion of the French fleet took refuge at the Algerian port of Mers el-Kébir, near Oran. The British feared that this formidable force (two battle cruisers; two battleships; eight cruisers, destroyers, and submarines) would fall into the hands of the Nazis. After a muddled negotiation, the British gave the French admiral an ultimatum to sail for Britain or scuttle his ships. It was rejected. The British fired on the French, inflicting some 1,400 casualties, contending that this controversial action was done to prevent the French from joining the Germans (though Vichy had already taken adequate measures to keep it out of the Axis's hands). This tragic incident particularly aggravated relations between the British government and Charles de Gaulle's (q.v.) Free French movement.

NAVARRO, PEDRO (1460?–1528). Spanish soldier. Navarro commanded the expedition, including Cardinal Ximenes de Cisneros (q.v.), that captured Oran in 1509. In 1510, Navarro also captured Bejaïa. Navarro built the Penñon fort which dominated the harbor at Algiers in order to enforce provisions of a 1510 treaty which contained the Algerian recognition of Ferdinand of Spain as sovereign over areas of Maghrib. Navarro symbolized the crusading spirit of the Spanish *reconquista,* which carried a Spanish presence to the Maghribi littoral.

NEKKACHE, MOHAMMED-SEGHIR. Nationalist; revolutionary; minister. Nekkache was an Algerian surgeon who was active in the MTLD (q.v.) before the revolution. He served as medical officer attached to the General Staff of the ALN (q.v.) during the War of Independence. He held portfolios in several of Ahmed Ben Bella's (q.v.) cabinets: minister of health (1962), minister of social affairs (1963), and minister of health, veterans, and social affairs (1964). He was also a member of the FLN's (q.v.) Central Committee and Political Bureau. Nekkache opposed Colonel Houari Boumedienne's (q.v.) coup and was arrested in 1965. He was held in house arrest at Touggourt from 1969 to 1971. Nekkache was amnestied in 1983.

"NEW APPEAL TO THE ALGERIAN PEOPLE." Opposition manifesto. This document appeared in 1976 and called for democratic institutions in Algeria, reconciliation with Morocco over the decolonization of the Spanish Sahara (q.v. Western Sahara), and Maghrib unity (q.v.). It was signed by Ferhat Abbas (q.v.), Hocine Lahouel (q.v.), Ben Youssef Ben Khedda (q.v.), and Mohamed Kheiredine (q.v.).

NEZZAR (Nazzar), KHALED (b. 1937?). Major general. Nezzar served with the French Army before joining the ALN (q.v.). He was stationed along the contentious Moroccan border in 1963 (q.v. Border War). In 1967 he commanded the Algerian battalion sent to Egypt as a result of the June Arab-Israeli War. He studied at the Ecole supérieure de Guerre in France in 1975. He was appointed to the Central Committee of the FLN (q.v.) in 1979. In 1984 Nezzar was promoted to general and became the assistant chief of staff; he commanded the Army itself in 1986. Nezzar was responsible for the suppression of the October 1988 riots (q.v.). Nezzar gained particular attention in July 1990 when he was appointed minister of defense. This portfolio had been held by the president. With the prospect of the *Front Islamique du Salut* (FIS) (q.v.) taking over the government as a consequence of national elections (q.v. December 1991 elections), Nezzar played a most prominent role in the deposal of President Chadli Benjedid (q.v.) in January 1992. He subsequently became recognized as the most powerful figure within the High Council of State (HCS) (q.v.). He survived an assassination attempt (car bomb) in February, 1993.

NUMIDIA. The ancient kingdom of eastern Algeria. Numidia and its capital, Cirta (q.v. Constantine), gained particular prominence during the reign of Masinissa (q.v.) and Jugurtha (q.v.). After Jugurtha's defeat by Rome in 106 B.C., Mauretania (q.v.) annexed western Numidia. Numidian kings became involved in the late Republic's power struggles, weakening Numidia further. Juba II (q.v.) was a pure client who eventually left Numidia to "rule" Mauretania. Numidia and Mauretania were soon integrated into the Empire.

NUSAYR, MUSA IBN. Arab governor and conqueror. He became governor of *Ifriqiya* (c. 705) and finally integrated the North African coast to the Umayyad Caliphate. His Berber ally, Tariq ibn Ziyad, crossed the straits of Gibraltar (*Jabal* al-Tariq [mountain of Tariq]). After Tariq took over the Visigothic capital of Toledo, Nusayr joined him. By the time that both men were called back to Syria in 714, Spain (al-Andalus) was also under the control of the Umayyads.

OCCUPATION RESTREINTE. Official French policy in Algeria until 1840, whereby the French could occupy only the major towns of the Algerian hinterland, and exercise control over the remainder through native or Turkish rulers. The policy was formulated in 1834.

OCHIALY (q.v. Eulj Ali).

OCTOBER RIOTS (EVENTS, DESTABILIZATION) OF 1988 (q.v. Introduction). There are multiple reasons for the riots, which resulted tragically in heavy casualties. (Official statistics claim that 161 people were killed [other accounts claim between 200 and 500 dead], 154 wounded, and 3,743 detained. These numbers have been challenged. There was an estimated $250 million of property damage.) The precipitous drop of oil prices, which are linked to Algeria's LNG's contracts, had a severe manifold effect upon the economy, affecting, for example, food subsidies and the prices of basic commodities. This economic disaster exacerbated chronic unemployment (20 to 30 percent). The growing austerity contrasted with the privileges held by FLN (q.v.) bureaucrats. These frustrations drew many youths, who could not relate to the revolutionary platitudes of the older generation, toward Islamist leaders. Algerians also resented their government's support of the USSR's invasion of Afghanistan, a Muslim country.

A series of industrial strikes in late September and early October created tensions. Then on October 4, in the Bab al-Oued district of Algiers (q.v.), youths set fire to police cars and government buildings. On October 5, more assaults continued to destroy vehicles and properties. Algerians began calling these violent demonstrations an *intifada* (referring to the continuing Palestinian uprising [since December 1987]) against the government, a bitter irony given the government's longtime support of the PLO. Rioting spread to Constantine (q.v.) and Sétif (q.v.).

On October 6, with the police unable to handle the situation, the government declared a state of siege and troops were called out, receiving sporadic armed attacks. Schools were closed down and foreign television crews were not allowed to report. On October 7 (Friday, the Muslim Sabbath), Islamists in Algiers, such as Ali Benhadj (q.v.) in Belcourt and Imam Abdelmalkek in Hydra discouraged the violence while attempting to coordinate demonstrations. Other Islamists throughout the country seemed to be encouraging demonstrations in other parts of the country.

On October 8, violence spread to Oran (q.v.), Annaba (q.v.), Mostaganem, and Blida targeting the FLN ruling establishment. Chronically restive Kabylia (q.v.) began rumbling. On October 9, a communiqué from a "Movement for Algerian Renewal" called for the disbanding of the FLN. Concurrently, fighting continued in Algiers where soldiers opened fire on crowds. President Chadli Benjedid (q.v.) appeared on television on October 10 promising reform. On October 11, violence ended, and the government lifted the state of siege on October 12.

The results of the October Riots were democratic reforms culminating in a new Constitution in February 1989 (q.v.) and the end of the FLN's monopoly of power (July 1989 legislation) as opposition parties were allowed to organize. The riots indicated that the FLN had lost touch with political and social realities; in particular, the FLN's revolutionary socialist discourse meant little to the rising expectations of an increasingly exasperated youth. The "Events of October" represent a seminal period in Algeria's postcolonial history.

EL-OKBI, TAYEB (q.v. Tayyib al-Uqbi).

ORAL TRADITION. This is an important source of Algerian heritage. Poets would recite specific histories and cultural traditions. Among the most famous of these poets were Ibn Triki and Ibn Amsaïb (d. 1768) of Tlemcen (q.v.); Sidi Ben Ali of Algiers (q.v.) in the seventeenth century; Sidi Lakhdar

Ben Khlouf of the Mostaganem region in the sixteenth century; Si Abd al-Qadir (concerning the conquest of Algiers); Abdallah Ben Keriou (d. 1921) of Laghouat; Mohammed Ben Sahla (end of the nineteenth century) of Tlemcen; and Mohammed Ben Kheir (d. 1889), a celebrant of the resistance of the Awlad (Ouled) Sidi Shaykh (Cheikh) (q.v.) tribal confederation of western Algeria. The great Kabyle (q.v.) poet Si Mohand ou-Mhand (q.v.) is another important example of this tradition. Mouloud Feraoun (q.v.), Mouloud Mammeri (q.v.), Jean Amrouche (q.v.), Marguerite Taos-Amrouche (q.v.), and Malek Ouary (q.v.) presented collections of Berber oral literature.

The contemporary popularity of *raï* (q.v.) singing, a type of social and political protest fusing traditional music and modern pop/rock, has added a new dimension to the oral tradition.

ORAN (Wahran). Oran was founded in the tenth century by Andalusians and became a base for the Umayyads (q.v.) before its takeover by the Fatimids (q.v.). It prospered under the Almohads (q.v.) and the Abd al-Wadids (q.v.). Pedro Navarro (q.v.) seized the city in 1509. Over the centuries it was fought over by the Spanish and the Turks. The Turks seized it in 1708 but lost the city to the Spanish in 1732. Finally the Turks took it in 1791 when the Spanish left after the devastating earthquake of 1790. During the colonial period, the port was particularly developed and a *Ville Nouvelle* (''New City'') built. Unlike other colonial cities, most of the city's population was European. As a result of decolonization, 300,000 Europeans left the city.

Oran has its own university (established in 1965), and it remains an important port. The region around Oran (Oranais) is renown for its agricultural production. Its population was recorded as 663,504 in 1983.

ORDINANCE OF 7 MARCH 1944. A reform initiative by General Charles de Gaulle (q.v.). This reform by de Gaulle, who headed the *Comité Française de Libération Nationale* (CFLN), increased native representation in local assemblies and permitted full citizenship for 50,000 to 60,000 Muslims without loss of their Muslim status (approximately 65,000 Algerians took advantage of this naturalization). Historians wonder if the terrible War of Independence could have been averted if this reform could have been initiated 10 years earlier (as in the Blum-Viollette Bill [q.v.]). The *Code de l'Indigénat* (q.v.) was also abolished. While enhancing de Gaulle's prestige, the reform was viewed by Algerian nationalists as too little too late.

O'REILLY, ALEXANDER (1722?–1794). Spanish general. Born in Ireland, O'Reilly began a career as a soldier of fortune. He entered Spanish service at first, and then in 1757 he joined the Austrian army. In 1759 he served with the French before returning to the Spanish military. As a colonel, he campaigned against Portugal in 1762 and instructed Prussian methods to the Spanish army. In 1763 he was promoted to general.

O'Reilly was selected to command a Spanish expedition against Algiers in 1775, which provoked much jealousy among Spanish officer corps. With 40 ships of the line and 350 other vessels, and with 30,000 troops, he carried out a combined land and sea assault on Algiers, which failed (at the cost of 4,000 casualties). He returned to Spain, still in favor with Charles III, and remained so until Charles's death in 1788. O'Reilly's expedition was the last combined land-sea assault on Algiers during the Regency (q.v.).

ORGANISATION DE L'ARMEE SECRETE (OAS). Paramilitary settler force. The OAS developed from earlier settler organizations (i.e., *Front National Français; Front de l'Algérie Française* [FAF]). The OAS was established to prevent the decolonization of Algeria. Led by Generals Raoul Salan and Edmond Jouhaud, though they often could not control all of its actions, the OAS terrorized France besides Algeria. Significant other members included Roger Degueldre and Pierre Sergent. Its operations severely impeded Paris's control of events.

As the Evian Accords (q.v.) were being concluded, OAS units created havoc. It threatened the political positions of both the Gaullist government and the FLN (q.v.) and ironically contributed to greater cooperation between both sides. It was blamed for creating the conditions that forced the panicked "exodus" of *pieds-noirs* (q.v.) from Algeria, though the fear of nationalist retribution from the consequences of colonialism was also a powerful motivation. Before signing its own accord with the FLN in June, the OAS's operations became more nihilistic. Its most destructive "scorched earth" tactic was the burning of the University of Algiers's library. The OAS was also involved in the unsuccessful attempt to assassinate President de Gaulle in August 1962.

ORGANISATION SPECIALE (OS). Paramilitary organization affiliated with the MTLD (q.v.) formed shortly after the passage of the Algerian Statute of 1947. From 1947 until 1950, it accumulated military stores, provided military training, and prepared plans for violent insurrection. To finance these activities, one group robbed the Oran Post Office in 1948. In 1950, however, the French police successfully began suppressing its activities and arrested prominent members. The Central Committee on the OS met and agreed to dissolve. Nevertheless, the OS experience proved very valuable to the young nationalists. Many of its members (e.g., Ahmed Ben Bella [q.v.], Hocine Aït Ahmed [q.v.], and so on) became leaders of the revolution. In addition, the emergence of the OS was symptomatic of a growing generational disillusionment with the older nationalist elite symbolized by the venerable Messali Hadj (q.v.).

OUAMRANE, AMAR (1919–1981). Nationalist; revolutionary. Ouamrane, a Kabyle (q.v.), served in the French military with distinction in World War II and was decorated. He also became a committed member of the PPA (q.v.) and attempted to politicize his fellow soldiers. He tried to muster an insurrection among a group of Algerian sharpshooters (*Tirailleurs algériens*) in order to support the PPA protests at Cherchell in May 1945. He was condemned to death but amnestied in 1946. Ouamrane went underground in 1947. When the MTLD (q.v.) splintered, he at first sided with Messali Hadj (q.v.). After the outbreak of the revolution in November 1954, he was Belkacem Krim's (q.v.) assistant, then commanding colonel of *Wilaya* IV. He is credited with enlisting Ramdane Abane (q.v.). Ouamrane was a member of the CNRA (q.v.) from October 1956. He eventually broke with Krim and supported Ahmed Ben Bella (q.v.). Ouamrane was a deputy in the Constituent Assembly (1962) and then retired from public office.

OUARY, MALEK (b. 1916). Writer; poet. As a Kabyle (q.v.) (and like Jean Amrouche [q.v.], a Christian), Ouary had always been interested in his ancestors' oral traditions (q.v.). He published translations entitled *Collier d'épreuves* (1955) and *Poèmes et chants de Kabylie* (1972). He also wrote the novels *Le Grain dans la meule* (1956) and *La Montagne aux chacals* (1981).

OUATTAR (OUETTAR, WATTAR), TAHAR (q.v. Wattar, Tahar).

OU EL-HADJ, MOHAND (Mokrane Belhadj/Benhadj [?]) (b. 1912). ALN (q.v.) colonel; Kabyle (q.v.) resistant. Before the revolution, Ou el-Hadj had been a landowner and merchant. He joined the ALN in late 1955. By 1958, he had became military assistant to the commander of *Wilaya* III. The following year he commanded the *Wilaya.* He was promoted to colonel in 1960 and remained in command of the *Wilaya* until after independence was attained. During the summer of 1962, he sided with the GPRA (q.v.) and fought against the troops of the Tlemcen (q.v.) (Ahmed Ben Bella [q.v.]-Houari Boumedienne [q.v.]) group. After Ben Bella came to power, Ou el-Hadj remained in command of the Kabylia (q.v.) region. He was elected a deputy to the National Assembly. In 1963, he joined Hocine Aït Ahmed's (q.v.) FFS (q.v.) opposition party in revolt against the central government, but he rallied to the government when the Border War (q.v.) with Morocco broke out. In April 1964, he was named to the Political Bureau. He joined the Boumedienne coup against Ben Bella and became a member of the FLN (q.v.) secretariat during the summer of 1965. In 1967, he joined, however, the anti-Boumedienne coup attempt engineered by Tahar Zbiri (q.v.). Its failure effectively ended Ou el-Hadj's political influence and career.

OUJDA GROUP. The Oujda group represented Houari Boumedienne's (q.v.) closest colleagues in the Political Bureau (q.v.). The name comes from a Moroccan city that headquartered external ALN forces. The group included Chérif Belkacem, Abdelaziz Bouteflika (q.v.), Ahmed Kaid (q.v.), Ahmed Medeghri (q.v.), and Mohamed Tayebi (q.v.).

OU-MHAND, SI MOHAND (q.v. Si Mohand).

OUSSEDIK, AMAR (OMAR) (Si Tayeb) (b. 1920). Messalist; Marxist; revolutionary; ambassador. A member of the (PPA-) MTLD, then the PCA (q.v. Algerian Communist Party), after it encouraged native Algerians to join, Oussedik eventually joined the FLN (q.v.). He was political chief of *Wilaya* IV He served in the CNRA (q.v.) (1957–1962) and was a secretary of state of the GPRA (q.v.). Oussedik was a friend of Frantz Fanon (q.v.) and an advocate of his ideas. He distinguished himself as an ambassador. During the War of Independence, he led an important FLN mission to Conakry (1960) and accompanied Ben Youssef Ben Khedda (q.v.) to the People's Republic of China. After the war, he continued his diplomatic career in the foreign service, holding ambassador posts in Belgium, the Soviet Union, India, and Italy.

OUZEGANE, AMAR (OMAR) (1910–1981). PCA (q.v. Algerian Communist Party) leader; journalist; minister. As a member of the Young Communists, Ouzegane founded *L'Oeil des PTTA,* a clandestine journal (he was a postal telegraph clerk). In 1934 he was the editor of the Algiers Communist Party's publication, *La Lutte sociale.* He also promoted communication between European and Muslim intellectuals (including Albert Camus's [q.v.] participation). In 1945 he was the first secretary of the PCA and also became the first Muslim deputy. His growing nationalist interests led to his expulsion from the PCA in 1948. Ouzegane also asserted that Islam complemented progressive political and social policies.

During the War of Independence, Ouzegane was both a militant and a theoretician for the FLN. He helped edit the Soummam Platform (q.v.). He was arrested in 1957.

After independence, he served as minister of agriculture and agrarian reform (1962–1963), as a minister of state (1963–1964), and also minister of tourism. He helped in the preparation of the Tripoli Program (q.v.) and began his position as editor of *La Révolution africaine* in 1968. Ouzegane emphasized the compatibility of Islam with socialism. He is the author of a book, *Le Meilleur combat* (1962).

NOTE: Consult the Glossary for other political parties. Since the official end of Algeria as a one-party state (Constitution of February 1989), approximately 60 political parties were organized (not all certified by the government.)

PARTI DE L'AVANT-GARDE SOCIALISTE (PAGS). This is the successor to the Algerian Communist Party (PCA) organized in 1966, which had been tolerated by the ruling FLN government. After the October Riots (q.v.) the PAGS became a legalized opposition party with Sadek Hadjères (q.v.) as its secretary-general.

PARTI DE LA REVOLUTION SOCIALISTE (PRS). An opposition movement founded by Mohamed Boudiaf (q.v.). During the summer of 1964, the PRS joined with the remnants of Hocine Aït Ahmed's (q.v.) FFS (q.v.) to form the *Comité National pour la Défense de la Révolution* (CNDR) (q.v.). Among the members of the CNDR, besides Boudiaf and Aït Ahmed, were Mohammed Ben Ahmed (Si Moussa) Moussa Hassani, and Mohammed Chaabani (q.v.)—all leaders who disagreed with Ahmed Ben Bella (q.v.). The members of the CNDR were expelled from the FLN (q.v.) on July 4, 1964.

PARTI DU PEUPLE ALGERIEN (PPA). A Messalist (q.v. Messali Hadj) party. The PPA succeeded the *Etoile Nord-Africaine* (ENA) (q.v.). Though it shared the ENA's objectives of an independent Algeria, it was a purely nationalist movement rather than internationalist (i.e., like the initially Maghribi-oriented ENA). The PPA was replaced ostensibly in 1946 by the *Mouvement pour le Triomphe des Libertés Démocratiques* (MTLD) (q.v.), though it continued to operate secretly within the new post-Sétif (q.v.) Messalist framework (thus the occasional PPA-MTLD designation). Efforts to revive the party at independence were not permitted by the FLN. Mohammed Mechaoui, a nephew of Messali Hadj, attempted to have the PPA certified as an opposition party as a consequence of the 1989 political reforms, but the application was denied.

PARTI SOCIAL DEMOCRATE. A legalized opposition party (August 16, 1989) as result of the Constitution of 1989 (q.v.) and the July 1989 legislation. Led by Ajrit Abderrahmane, this organization supports "economic centrism."

"PEACE OF THE BRAVE" (q.v. Introduction). A call for a cease-fire by Charles de Gaulle (q.v.) on October 23, 1958. The GPRA (q.v.) rejected this initiative, thereby signaling to de Gaulle its intent to pursue its objective of complete independence from France.

EL PENON. Formerly a rocky projection in the harbor of Algiers. The Spanish built a fortress there (q.v. Algiers; Pedro Navarro), which was reduced and demolished by Khayr al-Din (q.v.), who used the wreckage to improve and fortify Algiers's harbor.

PERSPECTIVES DECENNALES. A plan prepared by the Fourth Republic for the development of Algeria. The *Perspectives décennales* was disclosed in February 1958. This plan concluded that drastic measures were necessary to ensure Algeria's social and economic development. The agricultural sector, traditionally guarded by the colonial *colonat,* was relatively ignored. Instead "nonagricultural activities" would receive more attention. The objectives of the *Perspectives* were to provide jobs, to raise the standard of living, and to exploit natural resources (especially the recent natural gas and oil discoveries [q.v. Hydrocarbons]).

According to French planners, these goals could be attained through the rapid industrialization of Algeria and by continued extraction of its hydrocarbon wealth in the Sahara. The expected need of 50,000 technicians also ensured a French presence. The *Perspectives* projected 875,000 new jobs (552,000 in the industrial sector alone). According to

René Gendarme (q.v. Bibliography), one fault of this plan was that it neglected training (*formation*) of the work force. The *Perspectives* influenced the development and elaboration of the Constantine Plan (q.v.) of October 1958.

The *Perspectives*'s reliance upon the development of the hydrocarbon sector providing a multiplier effect throughout the economy would be adopted by Algerian planners after independence.

PIED-NOIR (*Colon*). Term for the European settlers of Algeria. The name, meaning "black foot," may have been coined by the native Muslims' description of the settlers' shoes. At first, the term *pied-noir* related an urban settler while *colon* referred to a rural settler. Today, *pied-noir* implies all European settlers of French Algeria (extended to include former French North Africa).

The decision to permit the colonization to Algeria introduced European settlers. Though France occasionally dispatched social and political misfits to Algeria. *pieds-noirs* were also victims of European economic distress (e.g., phylloxera blight of 1880) and political upheaval. Algeria became a "melting pot" of European nationalities, and the settlers often related their experience to the much admired American model. By 1954, approximately half of the *pieds-noirs* (total population 1,029,000) were not of French origin.

The *pieds-noirs* received their French identity from colonialism and many idealized their "Frenchness." They knew, however, that their own very existence as a minority was threatened by the Muslims. This resulted in a garrison mentality and opposition to change and reform, which weakened their dominant position.

Three powerful *pied-noir* families (*grands colons*) were: the Borgeauds, the Schiaffinos, and the Blachettes. The Borgeaud family possessed the mansion of La Trappe, with its very productive land used for viticulture. This family owned the popular Bastos brand of cigarettes and had interests in practically all of Algeria's economy. Henri

Borgeaud was a conservative senator during the time of the War of Independence. The Schiaffino family controlled shipping and amassed a huge fortune. Like Henri Borgeaud, Laurent Schiaffino was a senator and very conservative. The Blachette family owned huge fields of alfalfa in the Oranais (region of Oran [q.v.]). Georges Blachette was a deputy and, unlike his fellow *grands colons,* he was a liberal.

During the tumultuous period culminating in the end of French Algeria, hundreds of thousands of fearful *pieds-noirs* fled Algeria leaving land and property vacant, which was expropriated by the Algerian government (q.v. *autogestion*). (About 90 percent had left by the end of 1962.) French authorities were unprepared for the massive *pied-noir* "exodus" (*exode*). Repatriated *pieds-noirs* have organized associations that have lobbied the French government for indemnities to compensate their losses as a consequence of decolonization.

The *pieds-noirs* have enriched France economically (e.g., viticulture on Corsica) and culturally. They have been often unfairly stereotyped (as racist) by the metropolitan French. Many *pieds-noirs* return to visit Algeria. During his state visit to France, President Chadli Benjedid (q.v.) offered them a warm invitation; hostile acts visiting *pieds-noirs* occurred, however, in 1990. These were extraordinary given the usual cordiality and hospitality accorded to the former colonials.

Pieds-noirs have distinguished themselves in a variety of professions. Among Europeans born in Algeria are Albert Camus (q.v.), Yves Saint-Laurent, and members of the Marciano family ("Guess" fashions).

POLISARIO (*Fronte Popular para Liberación de Saguia el Hamra y Río de Oro*); Popular Front for the Liberation of Saguia el Hamra and Río de Oro (q.v. Western Sahara; Introduction; Morocco). The Sahrawi (q.v.) organization dedicated toward the legitimate, internationally recognized self-determination of the ex-Spanish Sahara. The POLISARIO was formed on May 10, 1973. It has been supported by Algiers since 1975, especially since the Madrid Accords of November 14, 1975, which partitioned the ex-Spanish Sahara between Morocco and Mauritania. On February 27, 1976, the POLISARIO announced the creation of the Arab Sahrawi Democratic Republic (SADR), which through the years received considerable international recognition, especially through the diplomatic efforts of Algeria. Algeria's logistical support of the POLISARIO's military operations particularly alienated Morocco (q.v.) and relations were broken. The Algiers Agreement of 1979 (q.v.) resulted in Mauritania's recognition of the SADR.

The impetus toward Maghrib unity (q.v.) improved regional relations, and both Morocco and the POLISARIO agreed to a U.N.-sponsored framework in 1991 to resolve the conflict through a self-determination process. Progress continued in 1991, including a cease-fire negotiation. A self-determination vote was projected for late 1991 or early 1992. Nevertheless, problems over who could vote remained unresolved. In February-March 1993 (as of this writing) the Security Council again has attempted to negotiate a self-determination referendum framework amenable to all parties.

Algeria's contemporary instability has weakened the POLISARIO's position. Indeed, during the October 1988 riots (q.v.), the POLISARIO's offices were reportedly targeted by rioters signaling that monies allocated to the Sahrawis would be better served at home.

POLITICAL BUREAU (Tlemcen Group). Established by Ahmed Ben Bella (q.v.), Mohammed Khider (q.v.), and Rabah Bitat (q.v.) with the powerful support of Houari Boumedienne (q.v.) in opposition to the GPRA (q.v.). The Political Bureau and its supporters took over power from the GPRA after the brief intraelite civil war during the summer of 1962. Ben Bella tried to rule through this body rather than through the regular FLN (q.v.) organization, a practice that quickly led to disagreement with Khider, who eventually resigned from the government and went into exile with the FLN funds. The Political Bureau remained an institution within the FLN.

Under President Chadli Benjedid, (q.v.) it became more of an advisory group to the presidency.

POMIER, JEAN (1886–1977). Writer. Born in Toulouse, Pomier arrived in Algiers in 1910. Included by Jean Déjeux (q.v. Bibliography) among the *Algérianistes* (e.g., Robert Randau [1873–1950], Louis Lecoq [1885–1932], and Charles Hagel [1882–1938]), Pomier encouraged the publication of assimilated Algerians. He is most renowned as the editor of *Afrique,* the bulletin of the *Association des Ecrivains algériens,* which began publication in 1924. Pomier resigned as editor in 1955 and then left Algeria for France in 1957. Pomier's writings in *Afrique* influenced a generation of Algerian writers. A collection of his poems, *A cause d'Alger,* was published in 1966.

PROCLAMATION OF 19 JUNE 1965. This document proclaimed the beginning of Colonel Houari Boumedienne's (q.v.) regime after the coup that deposed President Ahmed Ben Bella (q.v.). The proclamation declared that there was a need for a "revolutionary readjustment" (i.e., an end to Ben Bella's government). It called for "a socialism which conforms to the specific realities of the country" rather than a "circumstantial, publicity-seeking socialism."

PROCLAMATION OF 1 NOVEMBER 1954. The document heralding the War of Independence. The FLN (q.v.), proclaiming, too, its own existence, projected its goal as the "restoration of the Algerian state" and the "preservation of all fundamental freedoms." It claimed that it would use "every means until the realization of our goal." This included the "internationalization" of the revolution. Though the goal was independence from France, "French cultural and economic interests will be respected." It aimed for relations based on "equality and mutual respect."

Though the FLN suffered from intraelite struggles, it remained united concerning these objectives.

QADIRIYYA (Qadiriyah). Prominent religious order, or brotherhood, of which Abd al-Qadir (q.v.) was a leader. The *Qadiriyya* gained a foothold in the Maghrib (especially in western Algeria) in the fifteenth century, particularly as a consequence of the arrival of refugees from Andalusia. It was founded by Abd al-Qadir al-Jilani (q.v.) in the twelfth century. *Qadiriyya* affiliates demanded strict adherence to Islam. It has been regarded as an aristocratic brotherhood compared with its chief rival, the *Tijaniyya* (q.v.).

RADJEFF, BELKACEM (b. 1909). Nationalist. A native of Kabylia (q.v.), Radjeff emigrated to France in search of work. In May 1933 he became a treasurer of Messali Hadj's (q.v.) ENA (q.v.) and was arrested in 1934 and sent to prison (released in 1936). He was on the Central Committee of the MTLD (q.v.), but refused to side with either the Messalists or Centralists. After independence he worked on behalf of war orphans.

RAHAL, MOHAMMED BEN (1856–1928). Young Algerian (q.v.). Born in Nedroma of a family noted for its *marabouts*, he received his father's permission to attend the Collège Impérial at Algiers. He replaced his father as *Agha* of Trara in 1878 and served that year as a member of the Algerian delegation at the International Exposition at Paris. He resigned as *caïd* in 1884 to expand his scientific studies. He was one of two Muslims consulted by the French senatorial investigative committee in 1891. In 1912 he was a member of the Young Algerian delegation to Paris. He served as a *conseiller-général* in 1903 and as a *délégué financier* (q.v. *Délégations financières*) in 1920. In later years he discarded much of his earlier French orientation.

RAHMANIYYA. A religious order founded in the eighteenth century and named for Muhammad bn Abd al-Rahman al-Gushtuli al-Djurdjuri al-Azhari Abu Kabrain (al-Qubrayn), a Kabyle (q.v.) from the Djurdjura region, who studied at al-Azhar in Cairo. The brotherhood became particularly influential in eastern and southeastern Algeria. A branch of the order called the Khalwatiya promised special privileges in the afterlife to its members. The two founding *zawaya* are located in the Djurdjura and near Algiers. Though the order was initially nonpolitical, members became anti-French during the period of French incursions in Kabylia (q.v.). The Muqaddam Sidi Muhammad al-Haddad (q.v.) joined al-Muqrani (q.v.) and proclaimed a jihad against the French on April 8, 1871 (q.v.

Kabyle Revolt 1871–1872). That effort failed; al-Haddad surrendered to the French in July and his *zawiya* was closed. By 1900, the order included about 150,000 members and 170 *zawaya*.

RAÏ (RAI; RAY; RAYY). A popular style of Maghribi music reminiscent of American folk and rap. The name comes from the Arabic words for "opinion" and "vision." Rai has been used as a protest vehicle. Chab Khaled, an Algerian, is regarded as the "King of Rai."

RAMDANE, ABANE (q.v. Ramdane Abane).

RANDON COMMISSION. A commission established by decree of May 5, 1869, to study the political organization of Algeria. The commission's report, issued in 1870, proposed neither the end of military institutions nor a federative form of autonomy. These proposals reaffirmed the Second Empire's reservations concerning settler control of Algeria. The commission was presided over by Marshal Jacques-Louis Randon, a former governor-general of Algeria.

REGENCY. Name for the Turkish state in North Africa (sixteenth to nineteenth centuries). This was established by the Barbarossa brothers (Aruj [q.v.] and Khayr al-Din [q.v.]). It was ruled by *Beylerbeys*, *Pashas*, *Aghas*, and *Deys*. The institution that often determined who would lead the state was the *Ojaq*, a council of Janissaries. Besides the Janissaries, the *ra'is* (*raïs*), or captains of the corsairs, also had an influential role. Both groups competed politically, with the *ojaq* usually dominating the *ta'ifa* (*taïfa*) (the organization of corsair captains) until 1671. Piracy against the infidel was pursued for religious, political, and economic reasons. It should be noted that these rationales were similar to those of European and later American privateers. The Regency especially attracted Christian converts from the eastern Mediterranean and the Balkans.

Though the Regency technically was under the suzerainty of the Ottoman Sultan, it eventually acted as an autonomous state. It was especially powerful in the sixteenth and seventeenth centuries. The Regency was ruled by *Beylerbeys* (to 1587), *Pashas* (to 1659), *Aghas* (to 1671), then *Deys* (to 1830). Of the 30 deys who succeeded one another between 1671 and 1818, 14 were assassinated. The *Dey*'s power was limited by his council (*Divan*), usually dominated by the military.

The Algiers province belonged to the *Dey* (*dar al-sultan*). The remaining three provinces (*beyliks*) were ruled by *Beys* (western *beylik* at Mazouna, Mascara [from 1710] and Oran [from 1792]; the central, or Titteri, *beylik*, with Médéa as its seat of government; and the eastern or Constantine *beylik*). *Beys* were practically independent, though they had to deliver customs dues to the *Dey* every three years. The *Beys* used collaborating *makhzan* tribes to collect taxes from subject tribes (*rayah*). Turkish troops were also stationed in the provinces. The Kabyles (q.v.) and nomadic tribes generally maintained their independence and posed constant military threats.

Though the Regency's wealth was determined significantly by its institutionalized piracy, it had other economic resources. The Algerian littoral and the plains of the hinterland remained very productive. Indeed, debts over grain shipments to France during the French Revolution contributed to the fall of the Regency in 1830. The production of the artisans of Algiers was also admired. The wealth of the rulers resulted, too, in impressive mosques and public works.

The Regency's piracy provoked numerous attacks (q.v. Algiers). Among the most famous were those conducted by England, France, and Spain. England and France used bombardments to intimidate the Turks (who called themselves "Algerians"). Spain and the Regency waged war for approximately 250 years. Charles V (q.v.) mounted an invasion, which was a spectacular failure in 1541. Another assault was attempted in 1775 (q.v. Alexander O'Reilly). Oran was also fought over. In 1708 the Turks displaced the Spanish, who recovered the enclave in 1732. After the disastrous earthquake of 1790, Oran was finally ceded in 1791 to the Turks. The Regency received annual tribute from many nations. Among them were the United States, Holland, Portugal, the Kingdom of Naples, Sweden, Norway, and Denmark, as well as England, France, and Spain.

The Regency's weakness was exploited during the early nineteenth century. Restive sufi orders (e.g., *Tijaniyya* [q.v.]; *Qadiriyya* [q.v.]) commenced active opposition against the Turks (especially in the West). The Americans succeeded in imposing conditions on Algiers in 1815 (q.v. Decatur; Barbary Wars). Lord Exmouth's expedition (1816) (q.v.) reinforced the will of the Congress (or Concert) of European countries. Finally, the deterioration of French-Regency relations (q.v. Charles X; Introduction) led to the blockade and then invasion of Algeria, which deposed Husayn *Dey* (q.v.), ending a remarkable North African state.

ROME. Rome's presence in North Africa directly related to the Punic Wars. After the destruction of Carthage (146 B.C.) (later rebuilt) and the termination of the Jugurthine War (q.v. Jugurtha) in 106 B.C., Rome began to administer North Africa directly. The Romans used their legions (i.e., the Third Augustan [q.v.]) to build roads, ports, aqueducts, and baths. Roman expeditions reached into the Sahara (such as that of Lucius Bulbus in 19 B.C.). The Maghrib was a granary for Rome. Olives and viticulture were also part of the economy. Among the prominent "Algerian" cities: Pomaria (Tlemcen [q.v.]), Cartennas (Ténès), Tipasa, Icosium (Algiers [q.v.]), Calama (Guelma), Sitifis (Sétif [q.v.]), Rusicade (Skikda), Cirta (Constantine [q.v.]), Thagaste (Souk Ahras), Thamugadi (Timgad), Igilgili (Jijel), Iol Caesarea (Cherchell [q.v.]), and Hippo Regius (Annaba [q.v.]).

North Africa was particularly attractive to veterans. Roman cities in Algeria featured mosaics, baths, theaters.

The great ruins at Timgad and Djemila, for example, demonstrated the Roman planned city. The Romans probably introduced the camel to Numidia from their eastern provinces. The Roman administration did face chronic Berber (q.v.) revolts (e.g., Tacfarinas [q.v.] [17–24]; Faraxen [253–262]; Firmus [373–475]; Gildon). As the Empire began its decline in the third and fourth centuries, the prosperous North African colonies' accustomed high standard of living suffered. Christianity was viewed as a means of dissent and conversion occurred quickly. After Constantine's Edict of Milan (313), which established Christian toleration, the African Church suffered a schism known as Donatism (q.v.; q.v. Augustine). This also weakened Rome's political authority, expediting the Vandal (q.v.) takeover in the early fifth century.

RUSTUMID DYNASTY (c. 776–910). A dynasty of Ibadi (q.v. Ibadism) Khariji(te)s (q.v. Kharijism) located at Tahert (Tahart; Tadgempt). The first Rustumid imam was the Persian Abd al-Rahman ibn Rustum, who became governor of Qayrawan at the time of its capture by the Kharijites in 758. When the town was recaptured by the Arabs three years later, he fled westward and established his headquarters at Tahert. In 776, the imamate was conferred on him. At its height, the state stretched from Tlemcen (q.v.) to Tripoli. Like the Abd al-Wadid (q.v.) dynasty several centuries later, the Rustumids faced dangerous forces on the East (Aghlabids [q.v.]; Fatimids [q.v.]) and in the West (Idrisids). Given the religious demands of Kharijite society, the imamate government was constantly faced by the threat of schism and rebellion. This weakened the imam's authority and in 911 Fatimid (Shi'i [q.v. Shi'ism]) troops captured Tahert.

SAADI, YACEF (b. 1928). ALN urban guerrilla. A baker's son, Saadi joined the PPA (q.v.) and then the OS (q.v.). He was arrested in Paris in 1953 but released on grounds of insufficient evidence. In 1956 he helped organize what would be the Battle of Algiers (q.v.).

Saadi became the ALN leader of this campaign, which struck terror throughout the city. Using attractive Algerian women who could pose as "Europeans" to deliver explosive devices, the French resorted to calling in "paras" from the *bled*. The Battle of Algiers attracted worldwide attention.

Arrested in 1957 (with Zohra Drif [q.v.]), he was condemned to death. He was released in 1962. Subsequently he married Djamila Bouhired (q.v.) and became associated with the Ahmed Ben Bella (q.v.)-Boumedienne (q.v.) (Tlemcen [q.v.]) group. Saadi presented an oral memoir of his activities in *Souvenirs de la bataille d'Alger* (1962) and published *La Bataille d'Alger* (1982). He also played himself in the classic film, *The Battle of Algiers* (1965) (q.v. Cinema).

SAFIR, EL BOUDALI (twentieth century). Writer. Safir, with Emmanuel Roblès, and others founded *Forge* (1946–1947), a literary journal that published Algerian authors. With the assistance of authors such as Mohammed Dib (q.v.) and Albert Camus (q.v.), he was also one of the organizers of *Soleil* (1950–1952).

SAHARA (q.v. Algerian Sahara)

SAHLI, MOHAMMED CHERIF. Writer; ambassador. Sahli works have reflected a historical search to affirm an Algerian identity as seen in works such as *Le Message de Yougourtha* (1947); *Abdelkader, chevalier de la foi;* and *Décoloniser l'histoire; Introduction à l'histoire du Maghreb*. Sahli also served as Ambassador to Czechoslovakia.

SAHNOUN, MOHAMED (b. 1931). Diplomat. Sahnoun received an excellent education. He attended the Lycée français de

Constantine before studying at the Faculté de droit et des Sciences économiques in Paris, and New York University. Sahnoun participated in the War of Independence. He was director of the Africa, Asia, and Latin American affairs of the Foreign Ministry from 1962 to 1963 and director of Political Affairs in 1964. He also served as deputy secretary-general of the Organization of African Unity (1964–1965). Sahnoun has served with distinction as ambassador in critical posts. From 1975 to 1979, he was ambassador to the Federal Republic of Germany. In 1979, he became ambassador to France and participated decisively in the negotiation of the September 1980 agreement concerning emigrant labor (q.v.). He also played an important role concerning the Algerian mediation of the American hostage crisis with Iran (1979–1981). He became ambassador to the United States in 1984 and organized the presidential summit meeting in 1985 between Chadli Benjedid (q.v.) and Ronald Reagan (1985). When Abdelhamid Mehri (q.v.) was called to Algiers to lead the FLN (q.v.) after the October 1988 "events" (q.v.), Sahnoun replaced him in Rabat. A friend of United Nations Secretary-General Boutros Boutros-Ghali, Sahnoun became the chief U.N. representative charged with the most difficult task of pacifying war-torn Somalia and providing food for its starving people. Sahnoun's efforts were admired internationally, but he resigned in frustration (November 1992) because of the lack of international support. His resignation drew greater attention to the region and eventually the intervention of U.N.-backed troops.

SAHRAWI (Sahraoui, Saharawi) (q.v. POLISARIO, Western Sahara).

SAID, ABID (1933–1967). ALN (q.v.)/ANP (q.v.) officer. Saïd served in the War of Independence as an operations officer. After independence, he served with Colonel Tahar Zbiri (q.v.) in the Fifth Military region. He succeeded Zbiri in 1963 and commanded operations against the FFS (q.v.) in Kabylia (q.v. Hocine Aït Ahmed). Alienated later by Colonel

Houari Boumedienne (q.v.) and loyal to Zbiri, this able soldier participated in the attempted coup in 1967. Evidently, its failure led to his suicide.

SAIHI, MUHAMMED LAKHDAR ABDELKADER (b. 1933). Poet. The poetry of Saihi, who composes in Arabic, has dealt with the Sétif (q.v.) riots of May 1945, the War of Independence, agrarian reform, and bureaucratic excess.

SAKIET SIDI YOUSSEF. This was a Tunisian village bombed on February 8, 1958, by French forces during the War of Independence resulting in 80 fatalities including women and children. The international outrage and Félix Gaillard's government accepting the "good offices" of the Americans and British to settle French-Tunisian grievances upset the politicized Army, which recalled the Suez fiasco. The Gaillard government fell in April, and in May 1958 the military and settlers overthrew the Fourth Republic (q.v. Introduction) and called for Charles de Gaulle (q.v.) to assume power.

SALAFIYYA. Orthodox reformist movement in Islam generally following in the spirit of Muhammad Abduh's (q.v.) teachings. In Algeria, adherents were particularly intent on attacking maraboutic brotherhoods as well as the Young Algerians (q.v.), who were influenced by French culture and who appeared to want to become French. The Salafiyya movement emphasized a return to religious sources and the customs of the *salaf,* or the pious predecessors of early Islam. Salafiyya ideas were publicized in the weekly newspaper *Du-L-Faqar,* edited by Ibn al-Mansur al-Sanragi. Abd al-Halin ibn Smaya taught Salafiyya ideas at the Algiers *Madrasa.* The Salafiyya movement inspired the formation by *Shaykh* Abd al-Hamid Ben Badis (q.v.) of the Association of Reformist *Ulama* (q.v.).

SALAH RAIS (d. 1556). *Beylerbey.* An Egyptian who had a distinguished naval career with the Ottomans (and the

Barbarossas), he succeeded Hassan Pasha (q.v.) as *Beylerbey* in 1552. His reign was noted for extending Turkish domination into the interior. He forced the *qa'ids* of Touggourt and Ouargla to pay tribute. Biskra (q.v.) came under Turkish control. He captured Fez in 1553, but was unable to keep it. He captured Bejaïa (q.v.) from the Spanish, which was their second most important Algerian enclave (after Oran [q.v.]). The *Beylerbey* died of the plague as he marched on Oran.

SALLUST (86–c. 35 B.C.). A Roman official and historian. Sallust held a governorship in Africa and other official posts during the late Republic. He supported Julius Caesar and opposed Cicero. His history entitled the *Jugurthine War* (112–105 B.C.) surveys the difficulties the Romans had in suppressing Jugurtha (q.v.) and the Numidians. It also provides historians with valuable descriptions of North African politics, cultures, and values.

SANHAJA. A large confederation of Berber (q.v.) tribes. The Sanhaja were generally desert or pastoral Berbers and included three main tribes: the Lamtuna (Lemtouna), Giuddala, and Massufa. They reached the height of their influence from the tenth to twelfth centuries given the rise of the Zirid (q.v.) and Almoravid (q.v.) dynasties. They usually fought against the Zenata (q.v.) Berbers. Sanhaja power diminished with the rise of the Zenata Almohad (q.v.) dynasty.

SANUSIYYA MOVEMENT. A sufi order/brotherhood. Its founder was Muhammad Ali ibn al-Sanusi (1787–1859) who was born in Algeria. Sanusi called for Muslim unity and questioned *ulama* legal interpretations. The Sanusiyya became a strong missionary and reformist movement in Libya where a determined effort was made to unify tribes. The Sanusis resisted Italian colonialism. After World War II, the head of the Sanusis (Sayyid Idris) became King of Libya.

SAOUT AL-ARAB (q. v. Salah Boubnider).

SEBBAR, LEÏLA (b. 1941). Writer. Sebbar was born in Algeria but moved to France. Her father was Algerian and her mother French. Her writings describe the difficulties reconciling her identity and those of other *Beurs,* or ''second generation'' (q.v. Emigrant Labor), suspended between two powerful cultures. Her literary contribution includes the novels: *Fatima ou les Algériennes au square* (1981); *Shérazade, brune, frisée, les yeux verts* (1982); *Parle mon fils, parle à ta mère* (1984); and *Les Carnets de Shérazade* (1985).

SENAC, JEAN (1926–1973). Poet. Sénac was born in *Oranie* (the region of Oran). His background was French and Spanish. Sénac opposed colonialism and became poetically engaged in the liberation of «Mère Algérie» while living in France and Spain. In October 1962 he was an adviser to the Ministry of Education. In 1963 he helped found the *Union des Ecrivains algériens.* His tragic murder in Algiers has remained unsolved.

    Sénac not only distinguished himself as a poet, but he promoted the poetry of others. Among his works are: *Poèmes* (1954); *Matinale de mon peuple* (1961); *Avant-Corps, précédé de Poèmes iliaques et suivi du Diwan du Noûn* (Paris 1968); and *Anthologie de la nouvelle poésie algérienne* (1971). There have also been posthumous publications (e.g. *Le mythe du sperme* [1984]; *Alchimies (lettres à l'adolescent)* [1987]

SENATUS-CONSULTES OF 22 APRIL 1863 AND 14 JULY 1865 (q.v. Introduction). Proclamations by Napoleon III (q.v.) in 1863 and 1865. The *Sénatus-Consultes* collectively reflected the French Emperor's Algerian sensibility and naïveté. The 1863 *Sénatus-Consulte* declared that communal and permanently occupied Algerian lands would be protected from sequestering. This meant the recognition of

Muslim property rights, but this was to be institutionalized by identifying, delimiting, dividing, and subdividing Muslim lands among tribes and family clans (*duwar*). Ironically, the introduction of Western property standards resulted in the eventual selling of tribal lands. French "subject" status was conferred upon the Muslims by the *Sénatus-Consulte* of 1865. While Muslims were officially allowed to participate in the administration and military, they could not become full French citizens unless they abandoned their Islamic civil legal status. Very few of the colonized were willing to qualify their personal position as Muslims. (There were only about 2,000 full French Muslim citizens before World War I.)

SETIF (Sitif). City southwest of Constantine. Sétif is located on the ruins of the Roman city of Sitifis, the capital of the province *Mauretania Sitifiensi*. Nearby is the battle site where the Almohads (q.v.) defeated the Banu Hilal (q.v.) in 1152. The city declined during the period of the Turkish domination following the sixteenth century.

Sétif is renowned in modern Algerian history as the site of an event that had a significant influence on the development of Algerian nationalism. On May 8, 1945, a victory in Europe celebration was planned in Sétif. Nationalists were upset over the concurrent deportation proceedings of Messali Hadj (q.v.). During the parade nationalist placards appeared (some demanding the release of Messali Hadj). Demonstrators also unfurled the green and white flag that had been Abd al-Qadir's (q.v.) banner. When colonial authorities tried to seize these placards and flags, the crowd went wild. Shots were fired, apparently by the police. Algerians broke up into mobs that swarmed the streets and attacked Europeans. Before the day was over, nearly 100 Europeans had been killed. The French reaction was swift and brutal. Before the reprisals subsided, possibly 50,000 Algerians had died. (The Tubert Report claimed that between 1,020 and 1,300 were killed; between 5,000 and 10,000 is generally held to be accurate.) Of the more than 4,500 arrests, only 2,000 were ever brought to trial; 151 were sentenced to death, and 28 were actually executed. There was also violence in nearby Guelma.

The AML (*Amis du Manifeste et de la Liberté*) (q.v.) was blamed for the upheaval. The united nationalist movement soon lost its cohesion, though it was beginning to fracture before this tragedy, given the increasingly influential presence of PPA (q.v.) militants. The uprising particularly politicized the younger Muslim generation. The growth of radical nationalism among the younger elite quickly led to the War of National Liberation that broke out in November 1954.

Sétif's population was recorded at 186,978 in 1983.

AL-SHADILI, ABUL-HASAN (d. 1258). *Sufi* founder of Shadiliyya movement (*tariqa*). Born in the Moroccan Rif, al-Shadili journeyed to the Mashriq and eventually returned to the Maghrib, establishing himself in Tunisia. Shadiliyya adherents were subject to the religious authority of a spiritual governor, or leader, (*wali*). The movement spread throughout the Maghrib (q.v. Suhailiyya).

SHARSHAL (q.v. Cherchell).

SHI'ISM. An Islamic sect. Like Kharijism (q.v.), Shi'ism involved the figure the Caliph Ali. Unlike the Khariji, the Shi'ites (Shi'a) supported Ali and believed that he and his descendants should hold the Caliphate. Shi'ism includes the doctrine of the ''Hidden Imam'' (especially adhered to by the followers of the Twelfth Imam [Muhammad al-Muntazar] known as ''Twelvers'') and the *Mahdi*, a divine ''rightly guided leader'' who would bring justice to the world.

North African history has been influenced significantly by the Isma'ilis (''Seveners'' who follow Isma'il, the Seventh Imam). The Fatimid dynasty (q.v.) was an Isma'ili dynasty. The concept of the *Mahdi* played an important role in the

Almohad (q.v. Ibn Tumart) movement. The vast majority of Algerians follow Sunnism (q.v.).

SI ABDELKADER EL-MALI (q.v. Abdelaziz Bouteflika).

SI AHMED (q.v. Ahmed Draia).

"SI MAISUM" (title given to Muhammad Ben Ahmad) (c. 1820–1883). Algerian leader of the Shadhili Order. Born among the Gahrib tribe (between Bogari and Miliana), he received his formal training at Maouma, a center of Islamic studies. He returned to his tribesmen and established mosques at Kuran and Fikh. After visiting the shrine of Abd al-Rahman al-Tha'libi (q.v.), he became interested in the Shadhili Order. Shortly after joining, he was appointed a *shaykh*. The French offered him the directorship of a *madrasa* in Algiers (q.v.), but he declined. Si Maisum remained on good terms with the French.

SI MOHAND OU-MHAND (1845?–1907). Kabyle (q.v.) poet. Most of Si Mohand's work was oral (q.v. Oral Tradition), but it was later collected and translated by Mouloud Feraoun (q.v.) and Mouloud Mammeri (q.v.). Si Mohand has been called the "Kabyle Verlaine."

SI OTHMANE (q.v. Bouhadjar Benhaddou).

SI SALAH (q.v. Mohammed Zamoum).

SI TAYEB (q.v. Omar Oussedik).

SONATRACH (q.v. Hydrocarbons).

SOUIDANI, BAOUJEMAA (BOUDJEMAA) (1922–1956). Nationalist; revolutionary. Souidani was Rabah Bitat's (q.v.) second in command for the region of Algiers (q.v.) during the first two years of the War of Independence. He had been a member of the PPA (q.v.), of the OS (q.v.), and of the Committee of Twenty-Two (q.v.). After the uprising of 1945 (q.v. Sétif), he was particularly interested in buying and dealing weapons, which resulted in an 18-month sentence in 1949. Out of prison, he participated in the holdup of the Oran post office, later killed a French police inspector, and lived underground in Boufarik until the outbreak of the revolution in November 1954. He was killed while on his way to talk to a French journalist, Robert Barrat.

SOUIYAH, HOUARI (b. 1915). Nationalist; revolutionary. Souiyah was a businessman from Oran who was a member of the MTLD's (q.v.) central committee in 1954. He sided with the ''Centralist'' group against Messali Hajj (q.v.) as the party split. Like other prominent MTLD members, Souiyah was arrested by the French in November 1954. After his release in April 1955, he joined the ALN (q.v.) in Oran region. After independence, he was appointed prefect in Oran, was elected to the National Assembly, and became a member of the Central Committee of the FLN (q.v.). He held no official position after Houari Boumedienne's (q.v.) coup of June 1965 (q.v.).

SOUMMAM CONGRESS. FLN (q.v.) meeting held in the Soummam Valley during August and September 1956. This Congress had ''internal'' representatives from all of the revolutionary war zones but none from the so-called ''external'' delegation (q.v. Ahmed Ben Bella). The primary leader was the dynamic Ramdane Abane (q.v.). Delegates affirmed the primacy of internal leaders and blamed external leaders for failing to supply enough weapons to support the continuing struggle against the French. This heightened intraelite tensions. The Congress affirmed collegiality or group decisions and the primacy of the political arm of the FLN over the military.

The Soummam Congress created the parliamentary *Conseil National de la Révolution Algérienne* (CNRA) (q.v.) and the executive *Comité de Coordination et d'Exécution* (CCE) (q.v.). The CCE made decisions between meetings of the full CNRA. The Soummam Platform reasserted the FLN's objectives as declared in the Proclamation of November 1 (q.v.). It also stated that the agricultural sector would receive special attention after independence. At Soummam, the decision was made to bring the war to Algiers (q.v. Battle of Algiers).

SOUSTELLE, JACQUES (1912–1990). Governor-general during the War of Independence. Soustelle was an anthropologist of pre-Columbian societies and a Gaullist who was appointed governor-general of Algeria in 1955 by Premier Pierre-Mendès France. Soustelle's liberal reputation preceded him, and he received a chilly welcome in Algiers by the increasingly worried settlers. Soustelle comforted them by asserting that Algeria was part of France and that this would be cemented by a policy of complete "integration" (q.v.). Of course, that realization threatened the settlers' position, too, because implicitly this meant the projected political democratization of Algeria. Soustelle intensified social and economic improvements highlighted by the creation of the *Sections d'Administrative Spéciales* (SAS). Nevertheless, the FLN-instigated massacre of settlers (*pieds-noirs* [q.v.]) at Philippeville (Skikda) in August 1955 shocked this sensitive man, resulting in arbitrary retribution ("collective responsibility"). Consequently, he became a staunch adherent of French Algeria.

When it was announced by the Guy Mollet government that he was to be replaced, Soustelle was given a rousing farewell. He came back to Algeria in 1958 when de Gaulle took over and served briefly in his government. Soustelle's advocacy of French Algeria and opposition to de Gaulle's policies eventually drew him toward conspiratorial rebellion.

Soustelle was later pardoned, and he served as a senator from Lyons. He continued his anthropology (a member of the *Académie française* since 1983), but he always maintained that France had lost a great opportunity in Algeria. It is doubtful if this well-intentioned man's policy of integration would have been accepted by both colonial and metropolitan France.

SPECIAL COMMISSION OF 1830 (AFRICAN COMMISSION). This group was dispatched by King Louis-Philippe (q.v.) in 1830 to assist him in deciding what to do with the conquest of Algiers and littoral areas. In December 1833, the Special Commission was enlarged and it became known as the "African Commission."

The commission's report generally concluded that France needed to maintain its presence. It argued that it would be an "act of weakness" to withdraw. It considered the "military and maritime" advantages of Algeria's geostrategic position. The commission considered the beneficent potential of France's "civilizing mission." It applied the familiar imperialist rationale that "markets are becoming rare." Above all, the commission recognized that the French population found this enterprise popular. This convinced Louis-Philippe to endorse colonization in 1834.

STATE PLANS (q.v. Appendices; Hydrocarbons; Introduction). Houari Boumedienne's (q.v.) regime initiated economic planning. Algeria implemented a Three-Year (Pre-) Plan (1967–1969) and two Four-Year Plans (1970–1977) to establish an industrial base. The general strategy was to build "industrializing industries" to act as economic multipliers. Monies were particularly allocated toward hydrocarbons and manufacturing industries. The implementation of these plans were complemented by the growth of technocrats to manage new state enterprises. Boumedienne's socialist state-building resulted in a highly centralized state capitalism. The rise in energy prices reaching unanticipated heights caused, however, global diseconomies that eventually affected producers like Algeria with regard to the cost of capital investment. A criticism of this type of development with its consequential ultramodern industries was that it was not labor-intensive, thus failing to address effectively the country's massive under- and unemployment. In addition, concentrated attention and expenditure in the second sector left the first and third sectors relatively neglected.

Chadli Benjedid's (q.v.) two Five-Year Plans (1980–1989) attempted to correct these "intersectoral imbalances." The First Five-Year Plan (1980–1984) aimed to complete the projects of the Four-Year Plans, but also aspired to coordinate sector integration, thereby creating a greater balance in economic development. This plan devoted greater attention to agriculture and infrastructure and reduced the accelerated capital-intensive heavy industrialization of Boumedienne's plans. The Second Five-Year Plan (1985–1989) complemented the first as it targeted the elimination of the vertical and horizontal state monopolies, thereby continuing economic decentralization. The Second Five-Year Plan continued the quest for a stronger internal economy through developing sectoral integration in preparation for the "after petroleum" period. Algeria also aspired to stimulate transfers of technology. In early 1988, an effort was made to stimulate the state sector as many of its companies were transformed into competitive *Entreprises Publiques Economiques* (EPE) with independent boards of directors owned by independent trust monies. If unsuccessful, the EPEs would be threatened with liquidation. The realization of state planning objectives in the 1980s was impeded by the precipitate drop in petroleum prices and, after the October 1988 riots (q.v.), political instability.

The riots discredited the FLN (q.v.) politically and economically. Liberalization of the economy accelerated the deconstruction of the statist Boumedienne system. In 1990 the state monopoly over foreign trade ended. Foreign investment was offered more generous terms (Algeria's investment codes had been restrictive). Then for the first time Algeria negotiated an agreement with the International Monetary Fund. In February 1992, Prime Minister Sid

Ahmed Ghozali (q.v.) called for more liberal economic reform. His successor, Belaïd Abdesselam (q.v.), has braked liberalization and has called for severe austerity. He also favors more control over foreign investment. Algeria's future planning will be qualified by its compounding international debt ($25 billion in 1992), its collapsing economy, and its enduring political crisis.

STATUTE OF ALGERIA (ORGANIC STATUTE) (1947). An act of the French National Assembly that created an Algerian Assembly of 120 members based on the two-college system, 60 of whom were to be Muslims. The purpose was to give Algeria more local autonomy, though the Assembly had little actual power. European settlers generally opposed the change and demanded and received a strong (and historically amenable) governor-general to assure themselves continued control over the colonial administration.

The statute gave all Muslims French citizenship, but it kept separate electoral colleges. In general the new system failed to satisfy intractable *pieds-noirs* (q.v.) and impatient Algerian nationalists. Elections were fixed to ensure a malleable Muslim representation in the Assembly. Nationalists also criticized the voting system, which was heavily weighted to protect and perpetuate the settlers' power. After their initial participation in the process, elections were boycotted (especially by the Messalists [q.v. Messali Hadj]) while others explored revolutionary alternatives (e.g., OS [q.v.]; CRUA [q.v.]).

SUFRIYISM. A major branch of the Kharijis (q.v. Kharijism) said to have been founded because of its members' opposition to the sanctioning of the murder of one's adversaries and their families. The Sufriyyi also rejected the idea that non-Khariji Muslims could be regarded as pagans. They appeared in the Maghrib in the eighth century and eventually allied themselves with the Ibadis (q.v. Ibadism) and were absorbed into their ranks.

SUHAILIYYA. An Algerian branch of the Shadiliyya (q.v. Abul-Hasan al-Shadili) religious order, established in the nineteenth century.

SUNNISM. The Orthodox Islamic sect. The vast majority of Algerians are Sunni (Sunnites) and follow the doctrines of Malikism (q.v.). Besides the Qur'an, the Sunnis emphasize the customs of Muhammad's time and the practices of the Prophet (*sunna*) as recorded in reports (*hadith*). The interpretations of the *sunna* and the *hadith* in relation to the Qur'an contributed to the development of different Sunni schools of law such as the Maliki.

SYPHAX (d. 203 B.C.). King of the Massyli of western Numidia. At first an ally of Rome, he then supported Carthage following his marriage to Sophonisbe. Scipio fought him, won, and took him to Rome as part of his triumphal parade. Syphax's rival was Masinissa (q.v.), an ally of Scipio's, who then annexed Syphax's kingdom.

TACFARINAS (d. A.D. 24). At one time a Roman auxiliary, Tacfarinas led a Numidian revolt for eight years. He survived three Roman victories before falling in battle at Auzia against the Roman proconsul Dolabella.

TAFNA, TREATY OF (20 May 1837) (q.v. Introduction). A highly significant peace agreement between the *Amir* Abd al Qadir (q.v.) and General Thomas-Robert Bugeaud (q.v.). The Treaty's stipulations disclosed that the French interpreted the *Amir*'s territory as sovereign, underscoring the idea of an Algerian statehood. It also stipulated that Abd al-Qadir could purchase arms. Given the expedient negotiation and the conflicting ambitions of the *Amir* and the French, the treaty was in effect for only two years.

TALEB IBRAHIMI, AHMED (b. 1932). Minister; medical doctor; son of the *Shaykh* Bachir Ibrahimi (q.v.). Taleb Ibrahimi was elected president of the UGEMA in 1955 and served in the FLN's *Fédération de France* (FFFLN) before being arrested in February 1957. He was imprisoned in the infamous Santé but released in 1961. He served in the GPRA's (q.v.) delegation to the United Nations in December 1962.

Taleb Ibrahimi was arrested in June 1964 for associating with "counterrevolutionaries," but he was released in January 1965. In July 1965 he was appointed minister of national education, and in July 1970 he became minister of information and culture. After the death of President Houari Boumedienne (q.v.), he served as counselor minister to President Chadli Benjedid (q.v.). After the tragic death in 1982 of Mohamed Ben Yahia (q.v.), Taleb Ibrahimi became the foreign minister. He served in this position until the formation of the Kasdi Merbah (q.v.) cabinet of November 9, 1988. A year later he became a member of the enlarged Central Committee of the FLN. Taleb Ibrahimi became a critic of Benjedid's policies. After the establishment of the High Council of State (q.v.), Taleb Ibrahimi was viewed as a possible choice for prime minister before the selection of Belaïd Abdesselam (q.v.) in July 1992. He is apparently esteemed by the military and technocratic elite.

He is the author of *Lettres de prison* (1966) and *De la décolonisation à la Révolution culturelle* (1973). The latter work surveys the development of official Algerian cultural policy. In the early 1980s Taleb Ibrahimi urged a greater appreciation of Algeria's pluralist cultural heritage.

TALEB, MUHAMMAD (1917–1952). Nationalist. Taleb was a leading Messalist (q.v. Messali Hadj) serving in the ENA (q.v.) and the PPA (q.v.). He was a founder of *L'Action algérienne*, the underground PPA newspaper published in 1944 to 1945. He supported the AML (q.v.) and was on the MTLD (q.v.) Central Committee. It was reported that at his funeral 5,000 mourners sang the PPA anthem.

TAOS-AMROUCHE, MARGUERITE (q.v. Amrouche, Marie-Louise) (1913–1976). Kabyle (q.v.) author and sister of Jean Amrouche (q.v.). Educated in France, she settled there permanently in 1945. Publishing under the name of Marguerite-Taos Amrouche, she was the author of two novels, *Jacinthe noire*, which first appeared in 1947 and was reedited in 1972, and *La Rue des tambourins,* published in 1960. She also edited a collection of Kabyle poems and tales entitled *Le Grain magique,* which appeared in 1966. She promoted Berber culture through literature, radio broadcasts, and records.

TASSILI N'AJJER. The site of remarkable prehistoric cave artistry (thousands of illustrations) that indicates how the Sahara supported a neolithic herding culture. These "frescoes" are highlighted by paintings of hunters, cattle herders, horsemen, and chariots. The paintings' ages range from 5500 B.C.–A.D. 100. The site was particularly studied and analyzed by Henri Lhote in the 1950s. It is one of the world's greatest sites of prehistoric art.

TAYEBI, MOHAMED (b. 1918) (nom de guerre, Si [Commandant] Larbi, also used by Ben Redjem Larbi). Nationalist; revolutionary; ambassador; minister. A native of Sidi-Bel-Abbès, he was a merchant who became a member of the PPA (q.v.) and the OS (q.v.). He headed zone III in *Wilaya* V during the War of Independence. He then served as a deputy in the National Assembly, ambassador to Cuba (1963) and Brazil (1964). He also became director general of national security. He was a member of the Council of the Revolution (q.v.) and the secretariat of the FLN (q.v.). He became minister of agriculture and agrarian reform in 1968. In 1980 he served as secretary-general of the government.

TEDJINI, CHEIKH *(Shaykh)* HADDAM (q.v. HADDAM, CHEIKH [*Shaykh*] TEDJINI).

TEMAM (Temmam), ABDELMALEK (d. 1977). Nationalist; revolutionary. A member of the PPA (q.v.), he did not act openly because he was employed by the French colonial administration. As a member of the Central Committee of the MTLD (q.v.), he sided against Messali Hadj (q.v.) in the party split of 1954, but he joined the FLN (q.v.) in May 1955 and worked on *El-Moudjahid*. He was a member of the CNRA (q.v.). Arrested in 1957, he spent the balance of the war in prison. Released in 1962, he participated in the drafting of the Tripoli Program (q.v.). He also served on committees that prepared the FLN Congresses of 1962 and 1964. He then became the director of the Algerian National Bank (BNA).

AL-THA'LIBI, ABD AL-RAHMAN BN MUHAMMAD BN MAKLUF AL-JA'FARI AL-JAZARIRI (1386–1468). Sidi Abd al-Rahman al-Tha'libi was one of the most famous citizens of Algiers. He is famous for his scholarship, saintliness, and especially his commentary of the Qur'an.

THIRD AUGUSTAN LEGION (q.v. Rome). This Roman military unit was garrisoned in North Africa and provided security and acted, too, as a work force. At first recruited from Gaul, legionaries were later raised in North Africa. For about 400 years, the Third Augustan was the only legion permanently assigned to North Africa. It was composed of about 5,000 to 6,000 men. It was complemented by non-Roman auxiliaries, creating a total force of about 20,000 to 25,000.

THRASAMUND (d. 523). Vandal king. He was a successor and nephew of Huneric (q.v.). Though an Arian, he did not persecute establishment (Catholic) Christians to the extent that his uncle did. He was cultivated and tried to keep good relations with the Byzantines (q.v.). Byzantine relations with traditional Christians were nonetheless a constant threat to his power. He married Amalfrida, the sister of Theodoric the Ostrogoth. Thrasamund faced marauding tribesmen from Mauretania (q.v.), Tripolitania, as well as Numidia (q.v.).

TIFINAGH (TAFINAGH). Tuareg (q.v.) alphabet or writing system that is similar to ancient Egyptian hieroglyphics or Phoenician script.

TIJANIYYA. An Islamic Sufi brotherhood founded by Ahmad bn Muhammad al-Tijani in 1781. It spread from the border area of Algeria and Morocco eastward and also southward into the Sahara and West Africa (influencing the famous West African jihad of al-Hajj Umar in the nineteenth century). It was more egalitarian than other brotherhoods and particularly rivaled the Qadiriyya (q.v.).

TLEMCEN (Tilimsan). Very historic city of northwestern Algeria. The site has been inhabited since prehistoric times, probably due to its location as a watering spot (Berber word *tilmas* meaning ''spring''). Little is known of its history until the eighth century, when Idris I of Fez built a mosque at that location. Thereafter Tlemcen (q.v.) served as a Muslim provincial capital of importance. The modern city was established by the Almoravid (q.v.) Yusuf ibn Tashfin (q.v.) near the end of the eleventh century and was expanded by the Almohads (q.v.) during the following century. Under the Almoravids, it served as a theological and legal training center (q.v. Literature in Arabic). It has several famous mosques such as the "Great Mosque." During the thirteenth and fourteenth centuries, Tlemcen grew as a religious center and commercial hub for the region while serving as the capital of the Abd al-Wadid dynasty (q.v.). It prospered, too, under Marinid control. Because of its commercial and cultural significance, it remained an object of aggression by the Turks and Spaniards during the first half of the sixteenth century. The Turks finally secured possession of it in 1555. During the period of Turkish occupation the city fell into decline. From 1830 to 1833, it came under the suzerainty of the Sultan of Morocco. The French under Governor-General Thomas-Robert Bugeaud (qv.) took control over it in 1842, and it became a *commune de plein exercise* (q.v.). In 1858 it became an arrondissement (district) capital. During 1956 the city was practically besieged by a section of the ALN (q.v.) forces. After the administrative reform of 1958, it became the capital of a department of the same name. It is located on Algeria's main east-west railroad and highway. The name of the city was given in 1962 to the "Tlemcen group," or the Ahmed Ben Bella (q.v.)-Houari Boumedienne (q.v.) faction that opposed the GPRA (q.v.).

The population was recorded as 146,089 in 1983.

TRANSPORTATION. In the late 1980s there were more than 100,000 kilometers (62,000 miles) of national roads including the Trans-Saharan highway. Railways (3,900 kilometers/ 2,418 miles of track) provide passenger service and especially transport coal, lead, zinc, and iron ore to the coast. The government wants to expand this network to exploit the country's considerable national mineral wealth. The Algiers Métro is projected to be running during the 1990s. Air Algérie is the national airline and operates internationally from four airports (Algiers, Oran, Annaba, and Constantine). Algeria's national fleet features ferries and LNG tankers. A construction of a new port has begun at Djendjen near Jijel. Algiers's port is also projected for modernization.

TRIPOLI PROGRAM. FLN (q.v.) document. This document was the product of the last meeting of the wartime FLN before intraelite rivalry broke out in violence. The Tripoli Program was presented in June 1962. It criticized the Evian Accords (q.v.) (and by inference the elite who negotiated it) and its neocolonial character. It asserted that a "People's Democratic Revolution" would lead the postcolonial "ideological combat." It proclaimed a "socialist option" for Algeria's future development. Heavily imbued with Marxism, the program declared that the quest for democracy necessitated class conflict and economic transformation. It also projected the nationalization of foreign interests in Algeria ("the recovery of natural resources"). Emphasizing the first sector, it also proposed classic socialist models of state farms and cooperatives. Clearly, the Tripoli Program viewed the decolonization of the economic sectors, including ending the economic duality (e.g., modern and traditional) and repairing the devastation caused by colonialism, as complementing Algeria's revolutionary political image. The co-writers of the Tripoli Program included Mohammed Ben Yahia (q.v.), Mostefa Lacheraf (q.v.), Redha Malek (q.v.), and Mohammed Harbi (q.v.).

TUAREG or TOUAREG [singular: TARGUI]. A Saharan nomadic people located in Algeria at the Ahaggar (Hoggar) Mountains and the Adjjer Plateau of the Sahara. Their nomadism particularly traverses the Algeria-Niger border. These Berbers (q.v.) are distinguished by the men wearing veils and not the women. Their Berber language is known as *Tamahaq* and their alphabet *Tifinagh* (q.v.). The Tuareg maintain many of their ancestral customs to the exclusion of Islamic tenets. For example, they practice a number of matriarchal principles in family matters and uphold a caste system.

The 1968 to 1974 severe drought forced many of the Tuareg to cities, abandoning their pastoralist profession. In addition, relentless modernization has also penetrated the Sahara, threatening Tuareg ancient practices and customs. The Tuareg response recently (early 1990s) has been a violent one. In Mali, Tuareg have demanded an independent state and, in Niger, some type of federal accommodation in order to preserve their imperiled identity.

TUNISIA. Historically, Tunisia has been a staging ground for invasions of Algeria. The Carthaginians (q.v. Carthage) penetrated eastern Algeria. The rise of the Numidia (q.v.) reciprocated by advancing eastward and participated under Masinissa (q.v.) in the eventual downfall of Carthage.

Tunisia was known as *Ifriqiya* during the time of the Arab conquest. The Arabs settled in Qayrawan and planned further expansion westward. The Aghlabids (q.v.) spread their power westward to Algeria as did their successors, the Fatimids (q.v.). Tunisia along with the rest of the Maghrib came under the Almohads (q.v.). The Hafsids, like the Marinids, and Algerian Abd al-Wadids (q.v.), broke free from Almohad control. The Hafsids usually controlled sections of eastern Algeria. With the slow decline of the Hafsids, the Spanish and Turks vied for control. In 1574 the Turks took over. In the 1600s the Tunisian *beylik,* like the Algerian Regency (q.v.), operated independently though officially still under the suzerainty of the Sultan. The Husaynid dynasty was established in 1705.

The French took over Tunisia in 1881 and made it (like Morocco later) a protectorate (unlike Algeria, which was assimilated as part of France). A Young Tunisian movement (influenced the Young Algerians [q.v.]) led to a Destour, then Neo-Destour Movement (Tawfiq al-Madani [q.v.] was a cofounder) headed by Habib Bourguiba. Bourguiba led the country to autonomy in 1954 and full independence in 1956.

During the Algerian War of Independence, the FLN (q.v.) and the ALN (q.v.) were given political and military havens. President Bourguiba's efforts to mediate the conflict failed. The French air strike at Sakiet Sidi Youssef (q.v.), Tunisia, contributed to the fall of the Fourth Republic. The Tunisian effort to force the French from their Bizerte base ended in bloodshed in 1961. Bourguiba had hoped to alter the border in order to share the hydrocarbon wealth located in eastern Algeria. The FLN's determination to maintain colonial borders (q.v. Evian Accords; Morocco) prevented any demarcation change.

After Algeria attained its independence, Bourguiba observed how France tolerated nationalizations. His effort to nationalize French land resulted in a harsh French response, which soured relations for years. Algeria's ideological radicalism seemed also threatening and even enveloping after Muammar Qaddafi came to power in Libya in 1969.

In January 1980, Libyan-trained Tunisian commandos attacked Gafsa in southern Tunisia. This force had been permitted unofficially to maneuver through Algeria. This resulted in President Chadli Benjedid's (q.v.) condemnation of the Gafsa operation and initiated a period in which Algeria tried to assure the Tunisians of its goodwill. The result was an accord in 1983 that became a cornerstone in the pursuit of Maghrib Unity (q.v.).

Relations with Algeria continued to be close after Zine el-Abidene Ben Ali gently removed the aged Bourguiba from power in November 1987. President Ben Ali found himself, like President Benjedid, confronted by political Islamism. He was less willing, however, to pursue a democratic course. He applauded the arrival of the High Council of State (q.v.) and its subsequent suppression of the FIS (q.v.).

'UBAYD ('UBAID) ALLAH (q.v. Fatimids; Shi'ism).

'UKBA IBN NAFI ('OKBA/'UQBA BEN NAFI BEN ABD KAIS AL-KURASHI AL-FIHRI) (d. 683). Famous Arab general in the early conquest of the Maghrib. He was a maternal nephew of Amir Ibn al-As, the Arab conqueror of Egypt, who gave him command in *Ifriqiya* (663). 'Ukba founded the stronghold of al-Qayrawan (al-Kairouan) in 670. The areas he conquered remained dependencies of Egypt. In 675, 'Okba was replaced by Abu al-Mujahir. The Caliph eventually returned 'Ukba to his governorship of *Ifriqiya* in 682. This time he led armies into the Zab and in Tahart, where
he succeeded in gaining tribute for the Umayyads (q.v.). There is historiographical dispute of how far his expedition to the West extended. His reaching the Atlantic Ocean was probably legendary. Charles-André Julien (q.v.) contended that he reached central Algeria. 'Ukba was not able to consolidate his gains by occupying the countryside. He was overwhelmed at the Battle of Tahudha (Thabudeos) by Berbers and Greeks under the command of Kusayla (q.v.).

UMAYYAD DYNASTY (661–750). Arab dynasty. This Arab dynasty with its capital at Damascus extended its power westward into North Africa, Andalusia (Iberian peninsula), and southern France. The Arabs, after having initial difficulties conquering the Maghrib given the defense of Berber (q.v. Kusayla; al-Kahina) and Byzantine (q.v.) forces, finally were able to establish themselves along the littoral (q.v. Musa Ibn Nusayr). The expansion of the Arabs was also culturally highly significant given the introduction of Islam and the Arabic language. The Umayyads managed to keep the Arab empire's integrity. After they were overthrown by the Abbasid (q.v.) coalition, the empire became fragmented. In North Africa there were the developments of powerful independent Arab dynasties (q.v. Aghlabids; Fatimids).

UNION DEMOCRATIQUE DU MANIFESTE ALGERIEN (UDMA). A liberal party formed by Ferhat Abbas (q.v.) in 1946 after the failure of the *Amis du Manifeste et de la Liberté* (AML) (q.v.). As with all of Abbas's efforts before he joined the FLN (q.v.), this party sought to solve Algerian problems peaceably within the French system. For example, it campaigned in local elections under the flawed framework of the Statute of Algeria (q.v.).

After the War of Independence broke out, the FLN targeted the UDMA with terrorism (symbolized by the assassination of Abbas's nephew in August 1955). The UDMA already had doubts of France's ability to reconcile the national aspirations of the Algerian people with that of colonialism. By the end of 1955, the party's political base had eroded. In April 1956 Abbas joined FLN cadres in Cairo and eventually presided over the GPRA (q.v.) (1958–1961).

UNION DES ECRIVAINS ALGERIENS. The Union of Algerian Writers was first created in October 1963. This group became inert in 1967 when Jean Sénac (q.v.), the organization's secretary-general, resigned. Brought to life again in January 1974 (q.v. Malek Haddad), it is essentially composed of Arabophone authors. It was one of a dozen professional unions controlled by the FLN (q.v.).

UNION GENERALE DES TRAVAILLEURS ALGERIENS (UGTA). Algerian labor union. the UGTA was founded in 1956 as a means to exercise Algerian labor power and promote worker "national" solidarity. The UGTA lost its autonomy when it was taken over by the FLN (q.v.) in 1963. Nevertheless, strikes occasionally occurred and were endured by the Government. Since the liberalization as a consequence of the October 1988 riots, Algerian workers have become much more assertive.

AL-UQBI, TAYYIB (EL OQBI, TAYEB) (1888–1960). Influential member of the *Ulama*. Born near Biskra, al-Uqbi was an eloquent, impulsive, and polemical public speaker who was a member of Abd al-Hamid Ben Badis's (q.v.) Association of Reformist Algerian *Ulama* (q.v.). He had lived in the Hijaz and was influenced by the Wahhabi movement. He broke with the *Ulama* in the mid-1930s. Al-Uqbi was charged by colonialist authorities with having instigated the murder of the Grand Mufti of the Malekite (Maliki) rite in Algiers in 1936. This resulted in a lengthy litigation, but al-Uqbi was eventually cleared of the crime.

VANDALS (q.v. Gaiseric; Gelimer; Hilderic; Huneric; Thrasamund). Collective name for a group of Teutonic tribes that occupied the area of Algeria in the fifth and sixth centuries. In 428 the Vandals invaded North Africa under the leadership of Gaiseric. By May 430, only three Roman cities had not fallen to them: Carthage (q.v.), Hippo (q.v. Annaba), and Cirta (q.v. Constantine). In January 435, Gaiseric signed a treaty with Emperor Valentinian III, whereby the emperor retained Carthage and its province, and the other six provinces were surrendered to the Vandals. In October 439, Gaiseric attacked Carthage and captured it. From their North African kingdom, the Vandals sailed to Italy and sacked Rome in 455. The Vandals occupied North Africa for 94 years. They settled along the coast and the immediate hinterland. The Berbers remained independent, though they were actively recruited for the Vandal armies.

Pursuing his objective to restore the Roman Empire, the ambitious Byzantine Emperor Justinian (q.v.) commanded Belisarius to lead an expedition against the Vandals. Meeting little resistance, the Byzantines entered Carthage on September 14, 533. After the subsequent Battle of Tricamarum, Gelimer, the Vandal ruler, was routed and forced to flee to the mountains, where he eventually surrendered. After a minor revolt in 536, the Vandals disappeared from Algerian history.

VICHY ALGERIA (June 1940 to November 8, 1942). Following the signature of the armistice with the Axis in June 1940, the European settlers (q.v. *pieds-noirs*) of Algeria enthusiastically rallied behind Marshal Philippe Pétain's government located at Vichy. The halfhearted European resistance was short-lived once the settlers realized that the armistice did not endanger either their personal or business interests or their control over the Muslim majority. The settlers were allowed to form fascist and ultranationalist organizations. The Vichy government banned political parties and imprisoned European and Muslim leaders and began a systematic persecution of Jews (q.v.) (e.g., the abrogation of the Crémieux Decree [q.v.] and the implementation of anti-Semitic laws). Increased collaboration eventually led to the formation of small European and Jewish resistance units, which conspired with the Americans to facilitate the invasions of Algeria and Morocco in November 1942.

Although the Muslims supported the Third Republic's war effort (in sharp contrast to the *colons*, who saw little reason to die for Danzig), as "subjects" and not citizens, it made little difference to them who governed Algeria. Catering at the same time to the European minority, the Vichy administration deprived the Muslim population of many of their prewar advantages and rights. Although some Muslims supported the pro-Nazi *Parti Populaire Français* and the *Parti Populaire Algérien*, Muslim resistance to the Vichy regime came from members of the Algerian Communist Party (PCA) (q.v.) (whose secretaries, Kaddour Belkaim, Ali Rabiah, and Ahmed Smaili, were assassinated or executed by the Vichy government) and from members of the French-educated *évolués*, such as Ferhat Abbas (q.v.). Vichy, however, rejected Abbas's repeated attempts to gain equality and citizenship for the Muslims, which prompted him to change his political goals from that of cooperation to autonomy.

Economically, Algeria was exploited to meet demands by Vichy France and the Nazis. Algeria provided supplies for General Erwin Rommel's *Afrika Korps* in Libya. (Vichy successfully resisted German efforts to obtain French North African military collaboration [the Paris Protocols].) Nevertheless, the Vichy government also realized Algeria's economic vulnerability without its secure trans-Mediterranean commercial network. Projects were outlined to promote rapid industrialization. The Martin Law (*loi Martin*) aimed at providing Muslims with irrigated and expropriated lands, but it was never implemented.

Paradoxically, given the ideals of the Atlantic Charter, Vichy's policies in Algeria were supported indirectly by the

United States government, which agreed to supply food and fuel to stem the North African disintegrating economy. In return the Americans were granted the right to place a dozen American vice-consuls in North Africa for intelligence operations (the Weygand-Murphy Agreement). The Americans made little effort to work with Algerian nationalists. Even after the success of the Allied invasion, some of the Vichy legislation remained temporarily in place (q.v. Jews). It is the general historiographic consensus that General Charles de Gaulle (q.v.) never forgot settler collaboration with Vichy and that this affected his sensibilities concerning their plight during Algeria's decolonization.

VIEUX TURBANS (Old Turbans). Early twentieth-century Islamist group. The *Vieux Turbans* defended traditional Islam, the *Ulama*, and especially the *Shari‘a* and its juridical system from a variety of colonial threats (e.g., the imposition of French civil law on Muslims). They were particularly critical of the assimilationist Young Algerians (q.v.). One of the most prominent *Vieux Turbans* was M'hamed Ben Rahal (q.v.). These Islamists can be viewed as forerunners of the Association of Reformist *Ulama* (q.v.).

WAR OF INDEPENDENCE (NATIONAL LIBERATION; ALGERIAN WAR) (1954–1962) q.v. Introduction.

WARNIER LAW OF 1873 (q.v. Sénatus-consultes). Act of French government, which effectively removed control over land from the Muslim communities. Under its provisions, communal tribal lands were made available for sale (approximately 310,000 hectares). Once sold, land would remain under French land codes and could not return to Muslim property law even if purchased by a Muslim. The law resulted in the eviction of Muslims from the fertile coasts to the hinterlands and condemned thousands economically to meager self-subsistence by farming poor land or by pursuing migrant labor. The Warnier Law and its legal complement of April 22, 1887 (redrew [i.e., restricted] communal property lines), were the fundamental measures resulting in the expropriation of 1,750,000 hectares (excluding the territory taken before and after the Great Kabyle Revolt of 1871–1872 [q.v.]).

WATTAR (OUETTAR), TAHAR (TAHIR) (b. 1936). Writer; poet; and playwright. Born near Sedrata, Wattar was the editor of an Arabic journal entitled *Al-Sha'ab al-thaqafi* (*Ash Shab ath thaqafi*) (*Cultural People*). He became highly influential in Arabic literary circles. Among his novels (written in Arabic) are *Smoke from My Heart* (1961), *The Ace* (1974), and *The Earthquake* (1974).

WESTERN SAHARA. Ex-Spanish Sahara. The controversial decolonization, or technically "de-administration," of Spanish Sahara by the Madrid Accords of November 1975 effectively partitioned the territory between Morocco and Mauritania. After having misunderstood or miscalculated Moroccan ambitions (q.v. Morocco), Algeria began supporting logistically and diplomatically the Sahrawi liberation organization POLISARIO (q.v.) and, since February 27, 1976, the Sahrawi Arab Democratic Republic (SADR).

Algeria's objective has been the realization of an internationally recognized authentic national self-determination. The development of Maghribi cooperation (q.v. Maghrib Unity) has helped reconcile Algeria with Morocco. The anticipated United Nations national self-determination referendum for late 1991 or early 1992 has not taken place. A resolution remains problematic as of this writing primarily because of difficulties defining and identifying legitimate Sahrawi voters for the referendum.

WOMEN IN ALGERIA. Women comprise 52 percent of Algeria's population and make up just below 10 percent of the active work force. About the same number of women receive schooling as men, though this varies in some regions. In general, more women are illiterate than men given the very few educational opportunities before independence. (In 1982 the total percentage of literate people [fifteen years and older] was at 44.7 percent with 57.3 percent males and *31.7 percent* females). In Algeria's history women have played a very important role. While there are the examples of the renowned al-Kahina (q.v.) and the lesser known Lalla Fatima (q.v.), women have traditionally had important and influential roles in Berber societies. During the War of Independence, women played a highly significant role (q.v. Battle of Algiers). Frantz Fanon (q.v.) especially described how their efforts would result in a new, more egalitarian position in independent Algeria's society. As Fadéla M'Rabet, David C. Gordon, and Peter R. Knauss, among others (q.v. Bibliography), have disclosed, this promise was frustrated by traditional patriarchy.

Nevertheless, women did pursue social and political equality. Ten women were elected to National Assembly. One of the deputies, Fatima Khemisti, the wife of slain Foreign Minister Mohamed Khemisti (q.v.), succeeded in passing her bill that raised the female minimum eligible age of marriage to sixteen. Women were also granted constitutional equality. Concurrently the *Union Nationale des*

Femmes Algériennes (UNFA) was organized and eventually integrated into and thereby monitored by the FLN. The National Charter of 1976 (q.v.) underscored the positive role played by women during the revolution and the need for their social "emancipation." Nine women became deputies in the *Assemblée Populaire Nationale* (APN).

Algerian feminists were mobilized with the Family Code legislation (q.v.) of the 1980s. From October 1981 to January 1982, feminists demonstrated against the code's patriarchal stipulations. Among the protesters were some of the heroines of the revolution, including Zohra Drif (q.v.), Djamila Bouhired (q.v.), and Fettouma Ouzegane. Meriem Benmihoub, a prominent lawyer, has also played an important role during this period and in the development of Algerian feminism. These extraordinary demonstrations succeeded in having the government reconsider the code. Nevertheless, in 1984 the Family Code (q.v.) was passed, which repudiated demands concerning monogamy, equal inheritance, equal age at marriage, equal divorce rights, and the end of forms of paternalism. In general, the Family Code viewed women as under the guardianship of men.

The emergence of the Islamist FIS heightened feminist concerns. New women's groups have been formed such as the Algiers Association for the Emancipation of Women and Independent Association for the Triumph of Women's Rights. Human rights groups, i.e., the LADH and LADDH (Algerian League of the Defense of Human Rights), have also supported women's emancipation. Collectively, these groups' foremost objective is to change mentalities. That challenge is quite difficult given the Islamist movement, which is symbolized by the wearing of traditional Muslim clothing. For example, the FIS mayor of Annaba fired an office secretary because she refused to wear a veil at work. Yasmina Belkacem, a renowned revolutionary heroine who lost both legs while carrying a bomb during the War of Independence, was challenged by a young university man who questioned her revolutionary reputation because she was wearing slacks. She responded: "If we [women] had not fought . . . you would be a bootblack in the streets of Algiers in order to earn something to buy a morsel of bread" (*Le Nouvel observateur* [international], no. 1273 [1989]: 59).

There have been women parliamentarians and especially women ministers (q.v. Appendices) (Zohor Ounissi, a sociologist and former editor of *El Djazaira*; and Nafissa Lalliam and Leila Aglaoui in Sid Ahmed Ghozali's 1991 government). Meriem Zerdani has recently become a minister counselor in Prime Minister Belaïd Abdesselam's (q.v.) government. While the vast majority of Algerian women are not actively involved in women's rights movements, feminist activities have attracted worldwide attention as have the literary contributions of women such as Assia Djebar (q.v.) and Leïla Sebbar (q.v.).

XIMENES (JIMENEZ) DE CISNEROS, FRANCISCO (1437–1517). Spanish Cardinal (1507); statesman. Cardinal Ximenes was a fervent Catholic prelate with political ambitions. After the expulsion of the Moriscos and their settling in the Maghrib, he urged the Spanish government to establish itself on the North African coast, in part to preempt Morisco and Muslim retribution.

In 1505 Mers el-Kébir was taken after corsairs had attacked Alicante, Elche, and Malaga earlier in the year. Under Pedro Navarro (q.v.), Oran (q.v.) was taken in 1509. The Cardinal accompanied this expedition in which 4,000 Muslims were massacred and 8,000 were taken prisoner. The Cardinal consecrated two mosques as Catholic churches, founded a hospital for the wounded, established two monastic houses, and named an inquisitor. The Spanish also took Bejaïa (q.v.) in 1511.

YACINE, KATEB (q.v. KATEB YACINE)

YAGHMORASAN IBN ZIYAN (r. 1235–83). A Zenata leader who established the Abd al-Wadids (Ziyanids) (q.v.).

YAHIA, ABDELNNOUR ALI. Minister; lawyer; chairman of the Algerian League of the Defense of Human Rights (LADDH). Yahia was attracted to Messali Hadj's (q.v.) PPA (q.v.) and MTLD (q.v.). and was imprisoned during the war. Like other Kabyles (q.v.), he became alienated in 1949 as a consequence of the Berberist crisis (q.v.). He joined the FLN (q.v.) in early 1955 and was a founder of the UGTA (q.v.). He was arrested in May 1956 and kept in house arrest until 1961. Yahia supported Hocine Aït Ahmed (q.v.) and Mohand Ou el-Hadj (q.v.) during the Kabyle insurrection of 1963–1964.

After reconciling with the political establishment, he acceded to the Central Committee in April 1964. Yahia served as minister of public works in 1965–1966 and agriculture 1966–1967. He left government office to become a lawyer. Yahia eventually served the Court of Appeals and Supreme Court. He has championed human (especially Berber) rights in Algeria. He was detained from October 1983 to May 1984 and from July 1985 to June 1986. In a courageous act, a petition containing 2,700 names demanding Yahia's release was given to the Ministry of Justice in January 1984. In June 1985 he founded with others the LADDH. It became an affiliated member of the International Federation of Human Rights in December 1986.

YAHIAOUI, MOHAMMED SALAH. Officer; FLN (q.v.) party leader. By the end of the War of Independence, which he spent fighting in *Wilaya* I, Yahiaoui had risen to the rank of captain. He served briefly in the FLN hierarchy, but returned to the ANP (q.v.) as assistant director of the Military Academy at Cherchell (q.v.). In late 1965, he was named commander of the Third Military Region (Béchar/Colomb-

Bechar). As FLN party coordinator, he was a member of the Political Bureau of the FLN and gave one of the keynote speeches at the 4th Party Congress. Yahiaoui favored "pure and hard" socialism. It was this Congress, however, that rejected Yahiaoui and selected Chadli Benjedid (q.v.) as secretary-general of the FLN and sole candidate for the country's presidential elections of February 1979. Surprisingly, Benjedid included his rival in the new Political Bureau of June 29, 1979. Nevertheless, in 1980 Mohamed Cherif Messaadia (q.v.), who was also eased out of the Political Bureau, replaced Yahiaoui as party coordinator. Yahiaoui returned to the Central Committee in 1989. Yahiaoui was prominently active among the anti-Benjedid faction of the FLN, which included Messaadia (q.v.), Ahmed Taleb Ibrahimi (q.v.), Abdelaziz Bouteflika (q.v.), and Boualem Benhamouda (q.v.).

YASIN 'ABD ALLAH IBN YASIN (q.v. Almoravids).

YAZID, M'HAMMED (b. 1923). Nationalist; diplomat. Yazid's father and grandfather served in the French Army. Yazid attended the lycée at Blida. He became a PPA (q.v.) activist who was also secretary-general of the AEMAN in 1946–1947. He was on the Central Committee of the PPA(-MTLD [q.v.]) when he was arrested in 1948 and sentenced to two years in prison and 10 years of exile from Algeria. In France during the early 1950s, he lived a clandestine existence under the name of Zoubir. He was removed from party duties on Messali Hajj's (q.v.) insistence, presumably because he was too conciliatory with respect to the PCF (French Communist Party). He naturally became a strong Centralist in the MTLD split. On November 1, 1954, he was in Cairo where he immediately joined the FLN.

Yazid and Hocine Aït Ahmed (q.v.) were "unofficial delegates" to the famous Bandung Conference in April 1955. Yazid became the FLN's representative in New York along with Abdelkader Chanderli (q.v.). He also served as minister of information in the GPRA (q.v.) (1958–1962). After independence, he was a deputy in the National Assembly. He served as ambassador in Lebanon (1971–1979) and in 1981 assumed the position of director of the office of the Arab League in Paris. Yazid was then tabbed to be director of the *Institut d'Etudes Stratégiques Globales* (INESG).

YOUNG ALGERIANS (JEUNES ALGERIENS). Muslim reformers. The Young Algerians were a group of Muslims in the early 1900s who shared a French cultural and political orientation. They sought limited political reform within French Algeria, using the model of the Young Tunisian movement. Their position was symbolized by a delegation of nine under the leadership of Dr. Belkacem Ben Thami (q.v.), which arrived in Paris in June 1912 (another had been sent in 1908 [q.v. Clemenceau Reforms]). It presented a manifesto to the French government calling for the abolition of the *Code de l'indigénat*, (q.v.), equity of taxation, increased representation in Algerian local assemblies, representation for Muslims in some French assemblies, more educational opportunities for natives, and automatic French citizenship for conscripts with honorable discharges. The group's call in 1912 for immediate representation of non-French Algerians in Paris was opposed on all sides of the French political scene. In 1913 Ben Thami along with Omar Bouderba and Emir Khaled (q.v.), the grandson of Abd al-Qadir (q.v.), formed the *Union franco-algérienne* as a vehicle to promote Young Algerian positions. By the beginning of World War I, the group numbered about 1,000, mostly professionals. Their primary goal in the prewar period was to gain compulsory military service for Muslims in the belief that political rights would follow. The group split in 1919 over reaction to the Clemenceau reforms (q.v.) (Jonnart Law [q.v.]). Those remaining in the group suffered electoral defeat at the hands of Emir Khaled (q.v.) and grew increasingly isolated and politically anachronistic given the rise of nationalism.

Prominent Young Algerians also included Fekar Ben Ali and especially Chérif Benhabylès, the author of *L'Algérie française vue par un indigène.*

ZAB. Region of Algeria, an area around Biskra (q.v.), measuring 125 miles east-west and 40 miles north-south, from the Sahara to the southern Atlas. Hardly occupied by the Romans, the area suffered from the Arabic invasions of the eleventh and twelfth centuries. From the sixteenth to the eighteenth centuries, the area was controlled by the Bu Okkaz family. Rivalry between this family and the Ben Gana clan continued from the end of that period until the French occupation in 1844.

ZAHIRI, MOHAMMED SAID (d. 1956). Arabophone novelist. Zahiri wrote a number of moralistic novels such as *Customs among Algerian Women* (1931), which defended the use of the veil, and *Visiting Sidi Abed* (1933), which attacked maraboutism. His work can be considered anticolonial.

ZAHOUANE, MOHAMMED (b. 1913). Diplomat. Zahouane was educated at the Lycée in Constantine, at the Sorbonne, and at New York University. After Algerian independence was achieved, he served as director of African, Asian, and Latin American affairs at the Foreign Ministry (1962–1963), then as director of Political Affairs (1964) in the same ministry. He was a delegate to the United Nations' General Assembly (1964–1965), then assistant secretary-general in the Organization of African Unity. He authored *Economic and Social Aspects of the Algerian Revolution* (1962).

ZAKARIA, MOUFDI (1909–1977). Poet; lyricist; nationalist. Born in the M'zab (q.v.), he began publishing poems in Arabic in 1925. He was a prominent militant in the ENA (q.v.) and served in the PPA (q.v.). Zakaria composed the ENA's anthem. He was editor-in-chief of *Ech Chaab* and was arrested in August 1937 after the second edition was published. He was released before the outbreak of World War II and served in the clandestine PPA. He cooperated with Ferhat Abbas (q.v.), in editing the ''Manifesto of the Algerian People.'' He supported the MTLD (q.v.) but did not take sides in its internal divisions. Upon the request of Rebbah Lakhdar (q.v.), he composed "Kassaman" in April 1955, which became the national anthem of Algeria. He was arrested in 1956. After the War of Independence, Zakaria left politics to handle his business affairs. He opposed Houari Boumedienne's (q.v.) government and died in Tunis.

ZAMOUM, MOHAMMED (SI SALAH) (1928–1961). ALN (q.v.) commander. A Kabyle and son of a schoolteacher, Zamoum joined the OS (q.v.). He was arrested during the crackdown of that organization and tortured. After his release he played an important role in Kabylia (with Belkacem Krim [q.v] and Amar Ouamrane [q.v.]), planning and preparing for the War of Independence in Kabylia. Now called Si Salah, he succeeded Si M'hammed (Colonel Ahmed Bougarra/ Bouguerra) as the head of *Wilaya* IV. He was a member of the CNRA (q.v.). Col. Houari Boumedienne (q.v.) named Si Salah as an adjutant in the General Staff in the west. Instead of accepting this position, he undertook the perilous journey to Tunisia to plead for logistical support for the "interior" *mujahidin*.

Frustrated by the lack of support from the GPRA (q.v.) and the exterior ALN, Si Salah, backed by the *Wilaya* IV council, made contact with the French and proposed a cease-fire based on the "Peace of the Brave" (q.v.). In one of the most dramatic moments of the War of Liberation, Si Salah secretly met President Charles de Gaulle (q.v.) in Paris in June 1960. Permitted a safe conduct back to Kabylia (q.v.), Si Salah eventually was executed by orders of Boumedienne. The former interpretation of his death was that he was killed by the French while attempting to reach Tunisia.

ZAYANID (Ziyanid) DYNASTY (q.v. Abd al-Wadids).

ZBIRI, TAHAR (born c. 1930). ALN/ANP officer. Born in the Annaba (q.v.) region, he began working as a miner at the age of sixteen. Zbiri became a member of (PPA-)MTLD (q.v.). He was an armed participant in an ALN (q.v.) attack on Guelma on November 1, 1954. In 1955 he was captured and imprisoned, but he escaped (with Mostefa Ben Boulaïd [q.v.]). Zbiri served in the Aurès and became a member of the CNRA (q.v.) in 1959. He broke through the Morice Line (q.v.) in 1960 to take command of *Wilaya* I. He was promoted to colonel in 1961 and sided with the Ahmed Ben Bella (q.v.)-Houari Boumedienne (q.v.) (Tlemcen) group in the violent intraelite conflict (June-August) of 1962. Although he was Ben Bella's (q.v.) chief of staff of the ANP (q.v.), he supported Vice President Boumedienne during the coup of June 19, 1965, and personally arrested President Ben Bella. Remaining chief of staff but losing operational control under Boumedienne, Zbiri became alienated over the lack of attention given to former members of the internal ALN within the APN. In December 1967, he attempted a coup against Boumedienne. It failed and Zbiri was arrested and exiled (a notable difference compared with Colonel Mohamed Chaabani's fate [q.v.]). Zbiri was given a complete pardon in October 1980 by President Benjedid (q.v.), and he returned to Algeria. Zbiri became a member of an anti-Benjedid faction linked to Boumediennists after the October 1988 riots (q.v.).

ZENATA. One of the two great confederations of Berbers (q.v.) (the other being the Sanhaja [q.v.]). The Zenata were more sedentary than the Sanhaja. They reached their height of power and influence under the Almohad dynasty (q.v.).

ZENATI, RABAH (1877–1952). Writer; assimilationist. Zenati became a naturalized Frenchman in 1903 and became a teacher. He served in World War I in the Zouaves. Along with Saïd Faci (q.v.) and others he founded the journal *La Voix des humbles* in 1922. In 1929, he founded *La Voix indigène* in Constantine (q.v.), which was renamed in 1947 *La Voix libre*.

Zenati wrote *Le Problème algérien vu par un Indigène* (1938), which called for complete assimilation.

ZEROUAL, LIAMINE (LAMINE) (b. 1941). Officer; ambassador; minister of defense; president. Zeroual was born in Batna and joined the ALN (q.v.) at the age of sixteen. He continued his military career after the War of Independence and attended military schools in Moscow and Paris. After heading Algerian military institutions and commands, he was promoted to general in 1988 and was appointed commander of land forces. He resigned in 1989 after disagreements with President Chadli Benjedid (q.v.) and defense minister Khaled Nezzar (q.v.). In 1990, he was named Ambassador to Romania, but he left this post before the end of the year and retired. Nevertheless, in July 1993 he accepted the defense portfolio replacing Nezzar. In January 1994, Zeroual was selected to be ''President of the State'' by the HCS (q.v.). As of this writing he aspires for reconciliation and dialogue with the Islamists in an effort to end the internecine strife that has claimed approximately 4,000 Algerian lives.

ZIGHOUT, YOUSSEF (d. 1956). ALN commander. A blacksmith, Zighout was a member of the PPA (q.v.), the OS (q.v.), the CRUA (q.v.), and the FLN (q.v.). He was Mourad Didouche's (q.v.) assistant in the North-Constantinois region (*Wilaya* II). After Didouche's death, he succeeded him as commander. Along with Lakhdar Ben Tobbal (q.v.), Zighout played a decisive role in planning what would be the Philippeville massacres (August 20, 1955), an uprising by Algerians against Europeans. The atrocities committed by the ALN (q.v.) consequently incited bloody French retributions, which succeeded in demonstrating to Algeria, France, and the world that the FLN was determined to destroy colonialism by any means. Zighout was killed soon after the Soummam Conference (q.v.).

ZIRID (Zeirid) DYNASTY. Berber (q.v.) dynasty. Yusuf ibn Ziri ibn Manad (d. 971) and his Sanhaja (q.v.) Berbers had helped the Fatimids (q.v.) against the Ibadi (Kharijite) (q.v. Kharijism) Abu Yazid (q.v.) and the Zenata (q.v.) west of Tiaret. He constructed his capital at Ashir in the Titteri Mountain region. From this vantage point, he strengthened his position by sending his son Bulukkin (q.v.) to secure Algiers (q.v.), Médéa, and Miliana. When the Fatimids left for Egypt, the Zirids were entrusted as their provincial governors (taking the title *amir*) of the Maghrib.

Bulukkin (r. 973–984) (q.v.) particularly increased Zirid power. By 980, he had taken over Morocco but withdrew before fortified Ceuta (reminiscent of past Fatimid enterprises). Under the Amir al-Mansur (r. 984–996), the Zirids began to assert their independence from the Fatimids, who responded by inciting their longtime Kutama (q.v.) allies to revolt. After the suppression of the Kutama, Zirid power was never the same. Another Sanhaja group, the Hammadid dynasty (q.v.), established itself at Qal'a early in the eleventh century and challenged the Zirids. When al-Mui'zz (r. 1016–1062) (q.v.) decisively broke with the Fatimids, the Caliph in Cairo dispatched the marauding Banu Hillal (q.v.) and Banu Sulaym to the East, which forced the Zirids into Mahdiya, which became their redoubt. (The Hammadids subsequently left Qal'a for Bejaïa.) Weakened by internal dissensions, and its struggles against nomadic Arabs and rival Sanhaja Berbers, the Zirid state was gradually taken over by the forces of the Norman Roger II by 1150.

ZIYANIDS (Zayanids) (q.v. Abd al-Wadids).

FRENCH GOVERNORS IN COLONIAL ALGERIA

GOVERNORS

Louis-Auguste-Victor de Bourmont*	1830
Bertrand Clauzel*	1830–1831
Pierre Bethezène*	1831–1832
Anne-Jean-Marie-René Savary*	1832–1833
Théophile Voirol*	1833–1834
Jean-Baptiste Drouet**	1834–1835
Bertrand Clauzel**	1835–1837
Charles-Marie Denys Daumrémont**	1837
Sylvain-Charles Valée**	1837–1841

GOVERNOR-GENERALS

Thomas-Robert Bugeaud*	1841–1847
Louis-Christophe de la Lomorcière (La Morcière)	interim
Marie-Alphonse Bedeau	1847
Henri-Eugène-Philippe-Louis d'Orléans (d'Aumale)	1847–1848
Louis-Eugène Cavaignac	1848
Nicholas-Anne-Théodule Changarnier	1848
Gerald-Stanislas Marey Monge	1848
Viala Charon	1848–1850
Alphonse-Henri d'Hautpol	1850–1851

*Served under the title Commander-in-Chief of the Army of Africa.
**Served under the title Governor-General of French Possessions in North Africa.

Aimable-Jean-Jacques Pelissier	1851
Jean-Louis-César-Alexandre Randon	1851–1858

MINISTERS

Napoléon-Joseph-Charles-Paul Bonaparte	1858–1859
Justin-Napoléon de Chasseloup-Laubat	1859–1860

GOVERNOR-GENERALS

Aimable-Jean-Jacques Pelissier	1860–1864
Edouard-Charles de Martimprey	1864
Marie-Edme-Patrice-Maurice de MacMahon	1864–1870
François-Louis-Alfred Durrieu	1870
Jean-Walsin Esterhazy	1870
Alexandre-Charles-Auguste du Bouzet	1870–1871
Arsène-Mathurin-Louis-Marie Lambert	1871
Louis-Henri de Gueydon	1871–1873
Antoine-Eugène-Alfred Chanzy	1873–1879
Jules-Philippe-Louis-Albert Grévy	1879–1881
Louis Tirman	1881–1891
Jules-Martin Cambon	1891–1897
Lozé (named but refused post)	
Louis Lépine	1897–1898
Edouard-Julien Laferrière	1898–1900
Célestin-Auguste-Charles Jonnart	1900–1901
Charles Lutaud	1911–1918
Célestin-Auguste-Charles Jonnart	1918–1919
Jean-Baptiste-Eugène Abel	1919–1921
Jules-Joseph-Théodore Steeg	1921–1925
Henri Dubief	1925
Maurice Viollette	1925–1927
Pierre-Louis Bordes	1927–1930
Jules-Gaston-Henri Carde	1930–1935
Georges Le Beau	1935–1940

Jean-Charles Abrial	1940–1941
Yves-Charles Châtel	1941–1943
Bernard-Marcel Peyrouton	1943
Georges-Albert-Julien Catroux	1943–1944
Yves Chataigneau	1944–1948
Marcel-Edmond Naegelen	1948–1951
Roger-Etienne-Joseph Leonard	1951–1955
Jacques-Emile Soustelle	1955–1956

RESIDENT MINISTERS

| Georges-Albert-Julien Catroux | 1956 |
| Robert Lacoste | 1956–1958 |

DELEGATES-GENERAL

Raoul Salan	1958
Paul-Albert-Louis Delouvrier	1958–1960
Jean Morin	1960–1962
Christian Fouchet	1962

Based on lists in David P. Henige, *Colonial Governors from the Fifteenth Century to the Present* (Madison: University of Wisconsin Press, 1970); Charles-André Julien, *Histoire de l'Algérie contemporaine: La Conquête et les débuts de la colonisation (1827–1871)*, vol. 1 (Paris: Presses Universitaires de France [PUF], 1964); Charles-Robert Ageron, *Les Algériens musulmans et la France (1871–1919)* (Paris: PUF, 1968); and Charles-Robert Ageron, *Histoire de l'Algérie contemporain: De l'insurrection de 1871 au déclenchement de la guerre de libération (1954)* vol. 2 (Paris: PUF, 1979).

REVOLUTIONARY ORGANIZATIONS AND NATIONAL GOVERNMENTS

CRUA Members

(Algiers, April 1954)

"Historic Leaders"

Hocine Aït Ahmed
Ahmed Ben Bella
Mustefa Ben Boulaïd
Mohamed Larbi Ben M'Hidi
Rabah Bitat
Mohamed Boudiaf
Mourad Didouche
Mohammed Khider
Belkacem Krim

Membership of the Committee of Twenty-Two

Mokhtar Badji
Abdelkader (Kobus) (?) Belhadj
Athmane Belouizdad
Ramdane Ben Abdelmalek
Hadj (?) Ben Alla
Mostepha Benaouda
Mustapha Ben Boulaïd*
Larbi Ben M'Hidi*
Lakhdar Ben Tobbal

Rabah Bitat*
Zoubir Bouadjadj
Said Bouali
Ahmed Bouchaib
Mohamed Boudiaf*
Abdelhafid Boussouf
Mourad Didouche*
Ali Mellah
Mohammed Merzoubui
Mohammed Nechati
Boudjemaa Suidani
Yousef Zighout

Names followed by (?) are members about whom there may be some question. Names followed by * are the ''historic leaders'' (q.v.); see CRUA list above.

Members of the First CNRA (August 1956)

FULL MEMBERS	ALTERNATE MEMBERS
Ramdane Abane*	Mostepha Amar Benaouda
Ferhat Abbas	Lakhdar Ben Tobbal*
Hocine Aït Ahmed	Mohammed Ben Yahia
Ahmed Ben Bella	Abdelhafid Boussouf
Mustafa Ben Boulaïd	Mahmoud Cherif*
Ben Youssef Ben Khedda	Bachir Chihani
Larbi Ben M'Hidi	Slimane Dhilès (?)
Rabah Bitat	Ahmed Francis
Mohamed Boudiaf	Idir Aissat (?)
Saad Dahlab	Mohammed Lebjaoui (?)
Mohammed Khider	Ahmad Mahsas
Belkacem Krim*	Abdelhamid Mehri
Lamine Debaghine	Ali Mellah*

Tawfiq al-Madani
Amar Ouamrane*
M'Hammed Yazid
Youssef Zighout*

Brahim Mezhoudi*
Said Mohammedi*
Abdelmalek Temmam
Tayeb Thaalbi

Names followed by (?) are men who, according to William B. Quandt (*Revolution and Political Leadership* [Cambridge: MIT Press, 1969], 288), were probably members but whose membership has not been established beyond the shadow of a doubt. Names followed by (*) are those who attended the Soummam Congress that elected members to the CNRA.

CCE Members
(Cairo, September 1957)

Ramdane Abane
Ferhat Abbas
Lakhdar Ben Tobbal
Abdelhafid Boussouf
Mahmoud Cherif
Lamine Debbaghine
Belkacem Krim
Abdelhafid Mehri
Amar Ouamrane

First GPRA Members
(September 1958)

Ferhat Abbas, President
Belkacem Krim, Vice President in Charge of Armed Forces

Vice Presidents who were in French prisons at the time:
Hocine Aït Ahmed
Ahmed Ben Bella
Rabah Bitat
Mohamed Boudiaf
Mohammed Khider

Lamine Debbagine, Minister for Foreign Affairs
Mahmoud Cherif, Minister for Arms and Supplies
Lakhdar Ben Tobbal, Minister of the Interior
Abdelhafid Boussouf, Minister for Liaisons
and Communications
Abdelhamid Mehri, Minister for North African Affairs
Ahmed Francis, Minister for Economic Affairs and Finance
M'Hammed Yazid, Minister for Information
Ben Youssef Ben Khedda, Minister for Social Affairs
Tawfiq al-Madani, Minister for Cultural Affairs

Secretaries of State:
Lamine Khène
Omar Oussedik
Moustefa Stambouli

Second GPRA
(Tripoli, January 1960)

Membership was the same as the First GPRA,
but with the following changes:

Belkacem Krim, added Ministry of Foreign Affairs
to his other duties
Abdelhamid Mehri, Minister for Social and Cultural Affairs
Said Mohammedi, Minister of State

Removed from the First GPRA were:

Lamine Debbaghine (Foreign Affairs)
Mahmoud Cherif (Arms and Supplies)
Tawfiq al-Madani (Cultural Affairs)

Resigned from the First GPRA:

Ben Youssef Ben Khedda (Social Affairs)

Third GPRA
(August 1961)

Ben Youssef Ben Khedda, President and Minister for Finance
Belkacem Krim, Vice President and Minister of the Interior
*Ahmed Ben Bella, Vice President
*Mohamed Boudiaf, Vice President
*Hocine Aït Ahmed, Minister of State
Lakhdar Ben Tobbal, Minister of State
*Rabah Bitat, Minister of State
*Mohammed Khider, Minister of State
Said Mohammedi, Minister of State
Abdelhafid Boussouf, Minister for Armaments
and General Liaisons
M'Hammed Yazid, Minister for Information
Saad Dahlab, Minister of Foreign Affairs

*Honorary members who were actually in French prisons
between 1958 and 1962.

Ben Bella's First Government (September 1962)

Ahmed Ben Bella, President
Rabah Bitat, Vice President
Amar Bentoumi, Minister of Justice
Ahmed Medeghri, Minister of Interior
Houari Boumedienne, Minister of National Defense
Mohammed Khemisti, Minister of Foreign Affairs
Ahmed Francis, Minister of Finance
Amar Ouzegane, Minister of Agriculture
Mohammed Khobsi, Minister of Commerce
Laroussi Khelifa, Minister of Industry and Energy
Ahmed Boumendjel, Minister of Reconstruction,
    Public Works
Bachir Boumaza, Minister of Work and Social Affairs
Abderrahmane Benhamida, Minister of Education
Mohammed Nekkache, Minister of Health

Said Mohammedi, Minister of War Veterans
Abdelaziz Bouteflika, Minister of Youth and Sports
Tawfiq al-Madani, Minister of Religious Foundations (*Habous*)
Mohammed Hadj Hamou, Minister of Information
Mohammed Hassani, Minister of Posts and Telecommunications

Ben Bella's Second Government (September 1963)

Ahmed Ben Bella, President
Houari Boumedienne, Vice President and Minister of Defense
Said Mohammedi, Vice President
Amar Ouzegane, Minister of State
Mohammed Hadj Smain, Minister of Justice
Ahmed Medeghri, Minister of Interior
Abdelaziz Bouteflika, Minister of Foreign Affairs
Bahir Boumaza, Minister of Economy
Ahmed Mahsas, Minister of Agriculture
Ahmed Boumendjel, Minister of Reconstruction
Mohammed Nekkache, Minister of Social Affairs
Cherif Belkacem, Minister of National Orientation
Tawfiq al-Madani, Minister of Religious Foundations
Abdelkader Zaibek, Minister of Posts and Telecommunications
Ahmed Kaid, Minister of Tourism
Sadek Batel, Undersecretary, Youth Sports

Ben Bella's Third Government (December 1964)

Ahmed Ben Bella, President, Minister of Finance, Information,
   and Interior
Houari Boumedienne, Vice President and Minister of Defense
Said Mohammedi, Vice President
Abderrahmane Cherif, Minister Delegated to Presidency
Mohammed Bedjaoui, Minister of Justice
Abdelaziz Bouteflika, Minister of Foreign Affairs
Ahmed Mahsas, Minister of Agriculture
Nourredine Delleci, Minister of Commerce
Bachir Boumaza, Minister of Industry and Energy

Mohammed Hadj Smain, Minister of Reconstruction and Housing
Safi Boudissa, Minister of Work
Mohammed Nekkache, Minister of Health, War Veterans, and Social Affairs
Cherif Belkacem, Minister of Education
Sadek Batel, Minister of Youth and Sports
Tedjini Haddam, Minister of Religious Foundations
Abdelkader Zaibek, Minister of Posts and Telecommunications
Said Amrani, Minister of Administrative Reform
Amar Ouzegane, Minister of Tourism
Sid Ahmed Ghozali, Undersecretary for Public Works

Members of the Political Bureau of the FLN Before the Boumedienne Coup of 1965

FIRST POLITICAL BUREAU (AUGUST 1962)

Ahmed Ben Bella, President
Mohammed Khider, Secretary-General of the FLN
Rabah Bitat, Vice President
Hadj Ben Alla, Vice President of Assembly
Said Mohammedi, Minister of War Veterans

SECOND POLITICAL BUREAU (APRIL 1964)

Ahmed Ben Bella, President
Hadj Ben Alla, President of the Assembly
Said Mohammedi, Vice President
Houari Boumedienne, Vice President and Minister of Defense
Ali Mendjli, Vice President of Assembly
Mohand Ou el Hadj, Member
Ahmed Mahsas, Minister of Agriculture
Omar Benmahjoub, Deputy
Mohammed Nekkache, Minister of Social Affairs
Abdelaziz Bouteflika, Minister of Foreign Affairs
Bachir Boumaza, Minister of National Economy
Ahmed Medeghri, Minister of Interior

Tahar Zbiri, Chief of Staff of ANP
Mohamed Chaabani, Commander Fifth Military Region
Aït al Hocine, President of Amicale in France
Hocine Zahouance, Member
Khatib Youssef, Deputy

First Boumedienne Cabinet (July 1965)

Houari Boumedienne, President and Minister of Defense
Rabah Bitat, Minister of State
Ahmed Medeghri, Minister of the Interior
Abdelaziz Bouteflika, Minister of Foreign Affairs
Ahmed Kaid, Minister of Finance
Belaid Abdesselam, Minister of Industry and Energy
Ali Mahsas, Minister of Agriculture
Nourredine Delleci, Minister of Commerce
Mohamed Bedjaoui, Minister of Justice
Ahmed Taleb, Minister of Education
Tedjimi Haddam, Minister of Public Health
Abdelaziz Zerdani, Minister of Labor and Social Affairs
Abdennour Ali Yahia, Minister of Public Works
Mohamed Hadj Smain, Minister of Reconstruction and Housing
Boualem Benhamouda, Minister of *Mujahidin* (Veterans)
Abdelkrim Ben Mahmoud, Minister of Youth and Sports
Larbi Saadouni, Minister of Religious Affairs
Abdelkader Zaibek, Minister of Postal and Telecommunications
    Services
Bachir Boumaza, Minister of Information
Abdelaziz Maaoui, Minister of Tourism

CHANGES IN BOUMEDIENNE'S FIRST CABINET:

Smain was dismissed April 5, 1966. Reconstruction and Housing
    Ministry was merged with Public Works.
Mahsas was dismissed September 22, 1966. Ali Yahia replaced him
    at the Ministry of Agriculture two days later and was himself

replaced at Public Works by Lamine Khène.

Boumaza fled Algeria on October 8, 1966. Mohamed Ben Yahia replaced him as Minister of Information on October 24, 1966.

Zerdani and Ali Yahia resigned December 15, 1967. On March 7, 1968, Zerdani was replaced by Mohamed Said Mazouzi at the Ministry of Labor and Social Affairs, while Mohamed Tayebi took over for Ali Yahia as Minister of Agriculture.

Cabinet Changes, 1965–1978

1966: Bitat, Minister of Transportation

1967: Ali Yahia, Minister of Agriculture; Mohamed Seddik Ben Yahia, Minister of Information; Khène, Minister of Public Works

1970: Belkacem, Minister of Finance; Tayebi, Minister of Agriculture; Yaker Layachi, Minister of Commerce; Mohamed Said Mazouzi, Minister of Labor and Social Affairs

1973: Belkacem, Minister of State; Bitat, Minister of Transportation; Smail Mahroug, Minister of Finance; Ben Yahia, Minister of Higher Education and Scientific Research; Ahmed Taleb-Ibrahimi, Minister of Information and Culture; Benhamouda, Minister of Justice; Boumedienne, Minister of National Defense; Said Ait Messaoudene, Minister of Post and Telecommunications; Abdelkrim Benmahmoud, Minister of Primary and Secondary Education; Omar Boudjellab, Minister of Public Health and Population; Zaibek, Minister of Public Works; Mouloud Kassim, Minister of Traditional Education and Religious Affairs; Mahmoud Guennez, Minister of War Veterans; Abdallah Fadel, Minister of Youth and Sports; Kamel Abdallah Khodja, Secretary of State for Planning; Abdallah Arbaoui, Secretary of State for Water and Irrigation

1975: Mohamed Ben Ahmed Abdelghani, Minister of Interior

Boumedienne Cabinet, 1978

Mohammed Hadj Yala, Minister of Commerce
Mostefa Lacheraf, Minister of Education

Sid Ahmed Ghozali, Minister of Energy and Petrochemistry
Mohamed Seddik Ben Yahia, Minister of Finance
Mohamed Liassine, Minister of Heavy Industry
Abdellatif Rahal, Minister of Higher Education
Abdelmadjid Aochiche, Minister of Housing and Construction
Redha Malek, Minister of Information and Culture
Abdelmalek Benhabyles, Minister of Justice
Mohammed Amir, Minister of Labor
Belaid Abdesselam, Minister of Light Industry
Mohamed Zerguini, Minister of Postal Services and Communi-
cations
Said Ait Messaoudene, Minister of Public Health
Boualem Benhamouda, Minister of Public Works
Abdelghani Akbi, Minister of Tourism

Members of the Political Bureau of the FLN (1979)

Chadli Benjedid
Rabah Bitat
Abdelaziz Bouteflika
Abdallah Belhouchet
Ahmed Draia
Ahmed Bencherif
Mohamed Salah Yahiaoui
Larbi Tayebi
Djilali Affane

Mohamed Ben Ahmed Abdel-
ghani
Belaid Abdesselam
Boualem Benhamouda
Mohamed Said Mazouzi
Mohamed Seddik Ben Yahia
Mohamed Amir
Kasdi Merbah
Ahmed Taleb-Ibrahimi

Benjedid Government (March 8, 1979)

Chadli Benjedid, President of the Republic and Secretary-General
of the Party
Mohamed Ben Ahmed Abdelghani, Prime Minister, Ministry of
Interior
Abdelaziz Bouteflika, Minister, Adviser to the President
Ahmed Taleb-Ibrahimi, Minister, Adviser to the President
Abdelmalek Benhabyles, Secretary-General of the Presidency
Mohamed Seddik Ben Yahia, Minister of Foreign Affairs

Salim Saadi, Minister of Agriculture and Agrarian Reform
Sid Ahmed Ghozali, Minister of Hydraulics
Ahmed Ali Ghazali, Minister of Public Works
Belkacem Nabi, Minister of Energy and Petrochemical Industry
Said Ait-Messaoudène, Minister of Light Industries
Mohamed Liassine, Minister of Heavy Industry
Mohammed Hadj Yala, Minister of Finance
Abdelhamid Brahimi, Minister of Planning and National Development
Abderazak Bouhara, Minister of Health
Rafik Abdelhak Brerhri, Minister of Higher Education and Scientific Research
Mohamed Kharroubi, Minister of Education
Mouloud Oumeziane, Minister of Labor and Vocational Training
Abdelghani Akbi, Minister of Commerce
Mohamed Zerguini, Minister of Post and Telecommunications
Abdelmadjid Aouchiche, Minister of Housing, Construction, and Urban Development
Mohamed Cherif Messaadia, Minister for War Veterans
Boualem Baki, Minister for Religous Affairs
Djamal Houhou, Minister for Sports
Abdelmadjid Allahoum, Tourism Ministry
Salak Goudjil, Transportation Ministry
Lahcene Soufi, Minister of Justice
Abdelhamid Mehri, Minister of Information and Culture
Ahmed Houhat, Secretary of State for Fisheries
Brahim Brahimi, Secretary of State for Forestry and Reforestation
Smail Hamdani, Secretary-General of the Government

Benjedid Government (July 15, 1980)

Chadli Benjedid, President and Secretary-General of the Party (FLN)
Ahmed Taleb Ibrahimi, Minister Counselor to the President
Boualem Benhamouda, Interior
Mohammed Seddik Ben Yahia, Foreign Affairs

Selim Saadi, Agriculture and Agrarian Revolution
Brahim Brahimi, Irrigation
Mohammed Kourtbi, Public Works
Belkacem Nabi, Energy and Petrochemicals
Said Ait Messaoudène, Light Industry
Mohammed Liassine, Heavy Industry
Mohammed Hadj Yalla, Finance
Abdelhamid Brahimi, Planning and Organization of National
    Territory
Abderrazak Bouhara, Health
Rafik Abdelhak Brerhri, Higher Education and Scientific Re-
    search
Mohammed Kharroubi, Secondary and Primary Education
Mouloud Oumeziane, Labor and Vocational Cadres
Abdelaziz Khallaf, Commerce
Adennour Bekka, Posts and Telecommunications
Ahmed Ali Ghazali, Housing, Construction, and Town Planning
Bakhti Nemiche, Ex-Servicemen (*Mujahidin*)
Abderahman Chiban, Religious Affairs
Djamel Houhou, Youth and Sport
Abdelmajid Allahoum, Tourism
Salah Goudjil, Transport
Boualem Baki, Justice
Boualem Bessaiah, Information and Culture

SECRETARIES OF STATE

Mohammed Tayebi Larbi, Secretary-General to the Government
Ahmed Ben Frikka, Maritime Fishing
Mohammed Rouighi, Woods and Afforestation
Mohammed Larbi Ould Khalifa, Culture and Folklore
Hajj Slimane Cherif, Secondary and Technical Education
Mohammed Narbi, Vocational Training
Ali Oubuzar, Foreign Trade

Benjedid Government (January 12, 1982)

Chadli Benjedid, President and Secretary-General of the Party (FLN)
Mohammed Ben Ahmed Abdelghani, Prime Minister
Ahmed Taleb Ibrahimi, Minister Counselor to the President
Mohammed Hadj Yalla, Interior
Boualem Benhamouda, Finance
Mohammed Seddik Ben Yahia, Foreign Affairs
Boualem Baki, Justice
Selim Saadi, Agriculture and Agrarian Affairs
Brahim Brahimi, Irrigation
Mohammed Kourtbi, Public Works
Belkacem Nabi, Energy and Petrochemicals
Said Ait Messaoudène, Light Industry
Kasdi Merbah, Heavy Industry
Abdelhamid Brahimi, Planning and Organization of National Territory
Abderrazak Bouhara, Health
Rafik Abdelhak Brerhri, Higher Education and Scientific Research
Mohammed Cherif Kharroubi, Secondary and Primary Education
Mouloud Oumeziane, Labor and Vocational Cadres
Abdelaziz Khallaf, Commerce
Bachir Rouis, Posts and Telecommunications
Adennour Bekka, Youth and Sports
Ahmed Ali Ghazali, Housing Construction and Town Planning
Bakhti Nemiche, Ex-Servicemen
Abderahman Chiban, Religious Affairs
Abdelmajid Allahoum, Tourism
Salah Goudjil, Transport
Boualem Bessaiah, Information
Abdelmajid Meziane, Culture
Mohammed Nabi, Vocational Training

SECRETARIES OF STATE

Ahmed Ben Frikka, Maritime Fighting and Transport
Mohammed Larbi Ould Khalifa, Secondary and Technical Education
Ali Oubuzar, Foreign Trade
Mohammed Rouighi, Woods and Afforestation
Z'Hor Ounissi, Social Affairs
Jalloul Khatib, Secretary of State to the Prime Minister for Civil Service and Administrative Reform

Benjedid Government (January 22, 1984)

Chadli Benjedid, President and Secretary-General of the Party (FLN)
Abdelhamid Brahimi, Prime Minister
Ahmed Taleb Ibrahimi, Foreign Affairs
Mohammed Hadj Yalla, Interior
Boualem Benhamouda, Finance
Boualem Baki, Justice
Abdallah Khalaf, Agriculture and Fisheries
Bachir Rouis, Information
Boualem Bessaiah, Posts and Telecommunications
Belkacem Nabi, Energy and Petrochemical Industries
Salah Goudjil, Transport
Selim Saadi, Heavy Industry
Zaytuni Masudi, Light Industry
Mohammed Rouighi, Irrigation, Environment and Forestry
Abdelaziz Khallaf, Commerce
Mohammed Cherif Kharroubi, National Education
Rafik Abdelhak Brerhri, Higher Education
Mohammed Nabi, Vocational Training and Labor
Kamel Boushama, Youth and Sports
Djamel Houhou, Health

Z'Hor Ounissi, Social Protection
Bakhti Nemiche, Ex-Servicemen
Ahmed Ben Fariha, Public Works
Abdelrahman Belayyat, Housing and Construction
Abderahman Chiban, Religious Affairs
Abdelmajid Meziane, Culture and Tourism
Ali Oubuzar, Planning and Organization of National Territory

Benjedid Government (February 19, 1986)

Chadli Benjedid, President and Secretary-General
    of the Party (FLN)
Abdelhamid Brahimi, Prime Minister
Ahmed Taleb Ibrahimi, Foreign Affairs
Mohammed Hadj Yalla, Interior
Abdelaziz Khallaf, Finance
Mohammed Cherif Kharroubi, Justice
Abdallah Khalaf, Agriculture and Fisheries
Rachid Benyelles, Transport
Bachir Rouis, Information
Mostefa Benamar, Trade
Abdelmalek Nourani, Housing Construction and Regional Devel-
    opment
Boualem Bessaiah, Culture and Tourism
Belkacem Nabi, Energy and Petrochemical Industries
Fayçal Boudraa, Heavy Industry
Z'Hor Ounissi, National Education
Rafik Abdelhak Brerhri, Higher Education
Mohammed Rouighi, Irrigation, Environment, and Forestry
Aboubakr Belkaid, Labor and Vocational Training
Zaytuni Masudi, Light Industry
Mohammed Djeghaba, War Veterans
Ali Oubuzar, Planning
Mostefa Benzaza, Posts and Telecommunications
Djamel Houhou, Health
Ahmed Ben Fariha, Public Works

Boualem Baki, Religious Affairs
Mohammed Nabi, Social Affairs
Kamel Boushama, Youth and Sports
Mohammed Ben Ahmed Abdelghani, Minister-Counselor
to the Presidency
Mohammed Salah Mohammed, Secretary-General
to the Government

Benjedid Government (November 9, 1988)

Chadli Benjedid, President and Secretary-General of the Party
(FLN)
Kasdi Merbah, Prime Minister
Boualem Bessaieh, Foreign Affairs
Aboubakr Belkaid, Interior and Environment
Boualem Baki, Religious Affairs
Mohamed Djeghaba, War Veterans
Ali Benflis, Justice
Mohamed Nabi, Labor and Social Affairs
El-Hadi Khediri, Transport
Mohamed Ali Amar, Information and Culture
Sid Ahmed Ghozali, Finance
Mourad Medelci, Commerce
Ahmed Benfreha, Hydraulics, Forestry, and Fishing
Nourredine Kadra, Agriculture
Aissa Abdellaoui, Public Works
Nadir Ben Matti, Construction, Housing, and Regional Develop-
ment
Mohamed Tahar Bouzghoub, Light Industry
Salim Saadi, Heavy Industry
Saddek Boussena, Energy and Petrochemical Industries
Messaoud Zitouni, Public Health
Abdelhamid Aberkane, Higher Education
Slimane Chikh, Education and Training
Cherif Rahmani, Youth and Sports
Yacine Fergani, Posts and Telecommunications

Benjedid Government (September 16, 1989)

Chadli Benjedid, President and Secretary-General
  of the Party (FLN)
Mouloud Hamrouche, Prime Minister
Sid Ahmed Ghozali, Foreign Affairs
Mohammed Saleh Mohammedi, Interior
Said Chibane, Religious Affairs
Ghazi Hidouci, Economy
Mohamed el-Mili Brahimi, Education
Abdelkader Boudjemaa, Youth
Ali Benflis, Justice
Mohamed Ghrib, Social Affairs
Hassan Kahlouche, Industry
Cherif Rahmani, Equipment
Sadek Boussena, Mines
El-Hadi Khediri, Transport
Abdelkader Bendaoud, Agriculture
Akli Kheddis, Public Health
Hamid Sidi Said, Posts and Telecommunications
Benali Henni, Minister Delegate for Local Authorities
Abdessalem Ali-Rachedi, Minister Delegate for Universities
Abdennour Keramane, Minister Delegate for Professional Train-
  ing
Smail Goumeziane, Minister Delegate for the Organization of
  Commerce
Amar Kara Mohamed, Minister Delegate for Employment
Abdelaziz Khallaf, Secretary of State for Maghrib Affairs
Ahmed Medjouda, Secretary-General of the Government

Benjedid Government (June 18, 1991)

Chadli Benjedid, President
Sid Ahmed Ghozali, Prime Minister
Khaled Nezzar, Defense
Lakhdar Brahimi, Foreign Affairs

Aboubakr Belkaïd, Parliamentary and Association Relations
Abdelatif Rahal, Interior and Local Collectivities
Ali Benflis, Justice
Hocine Benissad, Economy
Nordine Aït Lahoussine, Energy
Ali Benmohamed, Education
Mohamed Salah Mentouri, Labor and Social Affairs
Abdenour Keramane, Industry and Mining
Mohamed Serradj, Postal and Telecommunications
Brahim Chibout, Veterans
Chikh Bouamrane, Communication and Culture
M'Hamed Benredouane, Religious Affairs
Nafissa Lalliam, Health
Djillali Liabes, Universities
Mourad Belguedj, Transportation
Mohamed Elyes Mesli, Agriculture
Mustapha Herrati, Equipping and Housing
Mohamed Boumahrat, Professional Training and Employment
Ali Haroun, Minister Delegate of Rights of Man
Cherif Hadj Slimane, Minister Delegate of Research, Technology,
    and Development
Abdlemadjid Tebboune, Minister Delegate of Local Collectivities
Ali Benouari, Minister Delegate of the Treasury
Mourad Medlici, Minister Delegate of the Budget
Ahmed Fodil Bey, Minister Delegate of Commerce
Lakhdar Bayou, Minister Delegate of Small and Medium Industry
Kamel Leulmi, Secretary-General of the Government

Government of Algeria (July 19, 1992)

HIGH COUNCIL OF STATE (EXECUTIVE)

Ali Kafi, President (replaced the assassinated Mohamed Boudiaf)
Major General Khaled Nezzar, Redha Malek (replaced Ali Kafi;
    Malek also elected President of CCN in April 1992), Tidjani
    Haddam, Ali Haroun, Members

Belaïd Abdesselam, Prime Minister and Minister of the Economy
Khaled Nezzar, Defense
Lakhdar Brahimi, Foreign Affairs
Messaoud Aït Chaalal, Councillor to the Prime Minister
Abdelmadjid Mahi-Bahi, Justice
Mohamed Hardi, Interior and Local Collectivities
Ahmed Djebbar, Education
Abdennour Keramane, Industry and Mines
Brahim Chibout, Veterans
Mohamed Elias Mesli, Agriculture
Sassi Lamouri, Religious Affairs
Farouk Tebbal, Habitat
Mohammed Seghir Babès, Health and Population
Mâamar Benguerba, Labor and Social Affairs
Djelloul Baghli, Professional Training
Abdelouahab Bakelli, Tourism and Handicrafts
Hamraoui Habib Chawki, Culture and Communication
Abdelkader Khamri, Youth and Sports
Tahar Allan, Postal and Telecommunications
Mokhtar Meherzi, Transportation
Hacen Mefti, Energy
Mokdad Sifi, Equipment
Ahmed Benbitour, Finance

MINISTER DELEGATES

Tahar Hamdi, Commerce
Ali Brahiti, Budget
M'Hammed Tolba, Interior, charged with public security, Director General of the National Security Police

Kamel Leulmi, Secretary-General of the Government

NAME CHANGES OF SELECTED CITIES AND SITES SINCE INDEPENDENCE

Alma: Bou Douaou
Aumale: Sour el-Ghozlane
Bône: Annaba
Bougie: Bejaïa
Castiglione: Bou-Ismail
Colomb-Béchar: Béchar
Fort de l'Eau: Bordj El-Kiffan
Fort Flatters: Zaouiet el-Kahla
Fort National: Larba Nath Iratten
Inkermann: Oued Riov
LaCalle: El-Kala
Lambèse: Tazoult
Lamorcière: Ouled Mimoun
Maison Carrée: El-Harrache
Marengo: Hadjout
Margueritte: Ain Torki
Nemours: Ghazaouat
Orléansville: El-Asnam: Ech-Chlef
Palestro: Lakhdaria
Philippeville: Skikda
St. Arnaud: El-Eulma
St. Cloud: Gdeyel
St. Denis du Sig: Sig
Trézel: Sougheur

SELECTIVE LIST OF NEWSPAPERS AND JOURNALS

Note: Since the 1989 liberalization, 150 new dailies, weeklies, and magazines appeared. This list includes some of those publications.

L'Action algérienne. Underground PPA (q.v.) publication.

L'Afrique latine. Louis Bertrand's (q.v.) journal.

Alger républicain. Leading French-language Communist (q.v. Algerian Communist Party) newspaper of colonial Algeria. The paper championed Muslim interests, assuring it a faithful readership even among moderates. The best-known editors and contributors were Henri Alleg, Boualem Khalfa, and Isaac Nahori. It has recently reappeared as an independent publication as a result of the relaxation of press censorship.

Algérie actualité. Weekly published by the Ministry of Information; became much more independent during the 1980s, especially under editor Kamel Belkacem, who was even censored in May 1989.

Algérie libre. (PPA-)MTLD (q.v.) bimonthly.

L'Algérien en Europe. Publication of the Amicale des Algériens en Europe.

Attakadoum. (*Al-Taqqadum*/Progress) Bilingual publication (1923–1931); associated with Young Algerians.

L'Avenir. RCD newspaper.

Al-Badil. MDA French-Arabic newspaper.

Al-Balagh al-Djazai'iri. Publication of Abu al-Abbas al-Alawi (q.v.), a prominent sufi scholar.

Al-Basa'ir. Religious journal in Arabic of the Association of Algerian Reformist Ulama (q.v.) from 1936 to 1939; 1947 to 1956.

Du-l-Faqar. (*Dhou-'l-Fiqâr*) Arabic-language weekly expounding ideas of reformist Muhammad Abduh (q.v.).

Ech Chaab. See *al-Sha'ab.*

Ech Chihab. See *al-Shihab.*

Coopération. (*Hebdo-Coopération*) Newspaper of the European community (q.v. *pieds-noirs*) in the immediate postcolonial period which was in print for several years.

Dépeche Algérienne. Conservative newspaper owned by the *pied-noir* Schiaffino family.

Al-Djazair. (*L'Algérien*) Publication of the Emigration Algérienne en France et en Europe.

El-Djeich. Monthly magazine of the ANP (q.v.).

Al Djezair al Joum (*Youm*). Representative of the new freedoms in Algeria's printed media, this paper was particularly critical of the High Council of State's (HCS) (q.v.) decision to cancel elections and was suspended in August 1992.

Echo d'Alger. Very conservative newspaper that closed down after the April 1961 military-settler revolt; its owner was Alain de Sérigny, a powerful *pied-noir* (q.v.).

Echo d'Oran. Prominent colonialist newspaper.

Egalité. Newspaper presenting the views of Ferhat Abbas (q.v.) and the Amis du Manifeste (q.v. AML).

L'Entente Franco-Musulman. Publication of Muslims who were given the vote during the colonial period

El-Forkane. A French language publication of the FIS (q.v.) begun in January 1991 and banned in August 1991

El-Hack. (*Al-Haqq*) Young Algerian (q.v.) newspaper of Oran.

Horizons 2000. An evening newspaper which began on 1 October 1985 which illustrated growing official tolerance toward freedom of the press.

Al-Hurriya. PCA (q.v. Algerian Communist Party) newspaper suppressed in 1962.

Al-Ihlas. Newspaper of the anti-reformist Association of Algerian Sunnite Ulama, 1932–39.

L'Ikdam. Young Algerian (q.v.) French language newspaper formed in 1919 when two earlier papers, *L'Islam* and *Le Rachidi* combined; it was also associated with the Emir Khaled (q.v.).

L'Ikdam nord-africain. Publication of the ENA (q.v.).

Al-Islah. Reformist Muslim journal published in Biskra from 1927 to 1930; 1940. Its director was Tayeb Uqbi (q.v.). Though poorly funded and appearing irregularly, it encouraged successor journals and generally reflected the opinion of the Association of Reformist Ulama (q.v.).

L'Islam. Small French-language newspaper or newsletter representing Young Algerian (q.v.) interests and tolerated by the French authorities even during World War I because it supported the French war effort. In 1919, *L'Islam* joined forces with a similar publication, *Le Rachidi*, and became *L'Ikdam*. Because of the fairly liberal attitude of the French government after the war, *L'Ikdam* became a more effective voice for Algerian demands.

Al-Jazair. Arabic-language newspaper of the MTLD (q.v.). It published half as many copies as *L'Algérie libre.*

Le Jeune indépendant. New liberal newspaper.

La Jeune méditerrannée. Short-lived periodical founded in May 1937 as a house organ for the ''Maison de la culture d'Alger (q.v.),'' a Communist (q.v. Algerian Communist Party [PCA]) discussion group. Albert Camus (q.v.) edited *La Jeune Méditerrannée* shortly before he resigned from the PCA.

Journal d'Alger. A relatively moderate newspaper owned by the *pied-noir* (q.v.) Blachette family.

Al-Jumhuriyah. Contemporary Arabic daily published in Oran by the Ministry of Information.

El-Khabar. Largest contemporary Arabic daily.

Libre Algérie. FFS newspaper.

La Lutte sociale. Communist (q.v. Algerian Communist Party [PCA]) newspaper published in 1932 and after. It was in French with occasional Arabic translations of French articles.

Al-Maghrib al-'arabi. Communist (q.v. Algerian Communist Party [PCA]) publication.

Al-Man'ar. MTLD (q.v.) publication; also a review advocating the ideas of Muhammad Abduh (q.v.).

El-Massa. (*Al-Masa*) An evening paper launched on October 1, 1985, demonstrating growing official toleration of the press.

Le Matin. Algiers newspaper on the left that was suspended in August 1992 by the HCS (q.v.) government.

El-Moudjahid. The newspaper of the FLN (q.v.); it began publishing in 1956 in Algiers and then continued operations from Rabat and in Tunis.

El-Moundiq. The FIS's (q.v.) newspaper (in Arabic); banned by the government in August 1991.

Al-Muntaqid. (*Le Censeur*) Weekly publication (Constantine) of *Shaykh* Abd al-Hamid Ben Badis (q.v.).

Al-Nasr. Arabic daily published in Constantine by the Ministry of Information.

La Nation. French-language newspaper published in Algiers that was particularly accusatory toward the government concerning the death of President Mohamed Boudiaf (q.v.). It is close to the FLN (q.v.) and was forced by the HCS (q.v.) government to suspend operations in August 1992.

Le Nouvel Hebdo. A new newspaper that began publication as a result of governmental liberalization concerning printed media.

El-Ouma. French publication of the ENA (q.v.), then the PPA (q.v.).

Le Peuple. FLN (q.v.) French-language newspaper.

Al-Raiat al-Hamra. Irregular Communist publication in French and Arabic addressed to workers in France.

La République algérienne. The UDMA's (q.v.) weekly French-language newspaper.

Révolution africaine. Algiers weekly journal of the FLN (q.v.).

Révolution à l'Université. Publication of the UGEMA-UNEA.

Révolution et Travail. Publication of the UGTA (q.v.)

Es-Sahafa. Satirical weekly.

Al-Sha'ab. Weekly publication of PPA (q.v.) and now an Arabic daily published by the FLN.

Al-Shihab. (*Le Météore*) Weekly, then monthly publication of the Association of Reformist *Ulama* (q.v.).

Le Soir d'Algérie. New independent newspaper.

La Voix des humbles. Antireformist monthly review (appearing from 1922 to 1933) published in Oran and later Constantine by the Association of Teachers of Native Algerian Origin (OAIOIA); founded by Rabah Zenati (q.v.).

La Voix indigène. Later known as *La Voix libre*, founded by Rabah Zenati (q.v.), it was an antireformist Muslim Algerian newspaper published in Constantine from 1929 until 1940 and from 1946 to 1952. It defended the doctrine of assimilation and was associated with Dr. Mohammed Saleh Bendjelloul (q.v.).

Al-Watan. Arabic-language newspaper representing the views of the UDMA (q.v.). It was quickly forced to cease publication because of financial problems. Now it is a politically independent newspaper.

FOREIGN TRADE (CUSTOMS BASIS)
(Millions of U.S. dollars)
(International Bank for Reconstruction/World Bank)

	Value of Exports, fob	Value of Imports, cif
1967	724	639
1968	830	815
1969	934	1,009
1970	1,009	1,257
1971	857	1,227
1972	1,306	1,492
1973	1,906	2,259
1974	4,260	4,036
1975	4,291	5,974
1976	4,972	5,307
1977	5,809	7,102
1978	6,126	8,667
1979	9,863	8,407
1980	13,871	10,525
1981	14,396	11,302
1982	13,144	10,679
1983	12,583	10,332
1984	12,795	10,263
1985	13,034	9,814
1986	8,066	9,234
1987 (est.)	9,242	9,263

Export/Import

	Nonfuel Primary Products	Fuels	Manufactures
1967	134/214	563/10	26/415
1968	177/195	589/13	64/607
1969	230/208	632/16	72/785
1970	232/233	709/27	68/998
1971	142/263	641/43	73/922
1972	159/347	1,080/34	67/1,112

1973	263/473	1,582/36	62/1,749
1974	234/1,040	3,941/60	86/2,936
1975	233/1,520	3,964/102	94/4,353
1976	274/1,109	4,654/84	44/4,113
1977	195/1,520	5,557/97	38/5,485
1978	206/1,726	5,885/130	35/6,812
1979	184/1,878	9,640/165	40/6,364
1980	194/2,708	13,628/259	49/7,548
1981	204/2,865	14,124/230	68/8,207
1982	148/2,658	12,908/165	89/7,856
1983	104/2,728	12,365/214	114/7,390
1984	118/2,536	12,549/211	129/7,516
1985	105/3,050	12,827/184	103/6,579
1986	89/2,540	7,870/274	107/6,420
1987 (est.)	119/2,292	8,986/347	137/6,625

EXPORTS AND IMPORTS
(IMF, *Direction of Trade Statistics;* in millions $US)

EXPORTS	1982	1983	1984	1985	1986	1987	1988
World	11.5	13.0	13.0	12.8	7.43	8.61	8.21
Industrial nations	10.6	11.7	11.7	11.0	6.82	7.85	7.21
Developing nations	734	1.25	1.15	1.43	524	696	954
France	3.51	3.86	3.64	3.83	1.60	1.90	1.13
Germany	697	576	385	440	235	354	840
Italy	1.74	1.36	2.31	2.86	1.48	1.32	1.45
Japan	344	255	87	133	95	126	283
Netherlands	1.50	1.17	1.53	1.18	1.06	1.30	517
Spain	605	634	439	763	425	375	414
UK	206	138	185	225	85	137	257
USA	1.70	2.86	2.77	1.28	1.29	1.65	1.79
IMPORTS							
World	10.8	10.4	10.5	9.84	9.23	7.04	8.05
Industrial nations	8.92	8.47	8.57	8.37	7.74	5.58	6.56

Developing							
nations	1.46	1.58	1.61	1.35	1.38	1.32	1.32
France	2.25	2.44	2.42	2.56	2.21	1.61	1.72
Germany	1.49	1.16	1.10	1.11	1.02	739	863
Italy	727	852	903	1.08	1.19	787	889
Japan	786	624	838	570	420	274	241
Netherlands	262	273	260	285	275	206	294
Spain	804	723	452	135	423	321	398
UK	377	339	355	297	234	148	169
USA	816	625	581	643	711	495	806

Algerian Dinars per US dollars
(Annual Average Conversion Factors)
(IMF, *International Financial Statistics*)

1967	1968	1969	1970	1971	1972	1973	1974	1975	1976	1977
4.94	4.94	4.94	4.94	4.91	4.48	3.96	4.18	3.94	4.16	4.14

1978	1979	1980	1981	1982	1983	1984	1985	1986	1987	1988
3.96	3.85	3.83	4.31	4.59	4.78	4.98	5.02	4.70	4.85	5.91

1989	1990	1991
7.60	8.95	18.47

Gross Domestic Product
(Rounded in Billions of Dinars [DA])
(IMF, *International Financial Statistics*)

1967	1968	1969	1970	1971	1972	1973	1974	1975	1976	1977
16.0	19.0	20.0	23.0	23.0	27.0	32.0	56.0	62.0	74.0	87.0

1978	1979	1980	1981	1982	1983	1984	1985	1986	1987	1988
105	128	162	191	208	234	264	292	297	313	320 (est.)

Investment as Percent of GDP
(IMF, *International Financial Statistics*)

1967	1968	1969	1970	1971	1972	1973	1974	1975	1976	1977
19.9	25.3	29.8	36.0	36.3	40.2	44.5	45.3	50.2	46.3	51.0

1978	1979	1980	1981	1982	1983	1984	1985	1986	1987	1988
52.6	42.3	39.1	37.0	37.3	37.6	36.4	33.9	32.4	30.3	30.7

Recent GDP Statistics
(Compiled by Economist Intelligence Unit,
Algeria: Country Report, nos. 1; 4 [1992])

GDP at current DA (*Dinars algériens*):

1987	1988	1989	1990	1991	1992*
305.5	317.0	497.0	735.0	735.0	1.039*

*December 31, 1992, 22.13 DA=$1.00

STATE INVESTMENT PLANS
(Adopted *Algérie informations,* numéro hors-série [July 1982])

	1967–1969	1970–1973	1974–1977	1980–1984
Agriculture	1.869	4.140	12.005	47.100
Industry	5.400	12.400	48.000	154.500
Infrastructure	1.537	2.307	15.521	
economic				37.900
social				16.300
Education	1.039	3.310	9.947	
Education-*formation*				42.200

1984–1989 Five-Year Plan (selected sectors)
(Economist Intelligence Unit, *Algeria: Country Profile, 1988–1989,*
citing Ministry of Planning)

	DA billions	% of total
Agriculture and hydraulics	79.0	14.4
Industry	174.2	31.6
Project implementation	19.0	3.5
Transport	15.0	2.7
Economic infrastructure	45.5	8.3
Social infrastructure	149.5	27.2

Selected Ministries' Budgetary Allocations
(Total Budget [in thousands of DA] 65,500,000)
(*Annuaire de l'Afrique du Nord,* 1988)

Thousands of DA

Presidency of the Republic	700,000
Defense	6,084,400

Foreign Affairs	831,061
Interior	7,762,808
Religious Affairs	49,000
Agriculture	445,800
Transportation	326,811
Justice	676,000
Higher Education	3,432,000
Finances	1,660,000
Labor and Social Affairs	1,802,503
Education and Formation	17,081,001
Public Health	3,872,000
Veterans (Mujahidin)	3,151,255

HYDROCARBONS PRODUCTION

PETROLEUM (rounded in thousand metric tons; *UN Industrial Statistics Yearbook*)

1979	1980	1981	1982	1983	1984	1985	1986	1987	1988
53.7	47.3	36.9	33.5	31.3	32.4	31.3	31.3	33.0	33.2

NATURAL GAS (rounded in bn m^3; Economist Intelligence Unit, *Algeria,* citing Cedigaz; *Financial Times International Gas Report*)

	1981	1982	1983	1984	1985	1986
Gross Production	65.4	82.1	85.3	91.3	90.1	97.4
Marketed Production	21.9	26.7	35.6	38.5	35.5	40.0

Recent Natural Gas Production Statistics
(official estimated bn m^3)
(Compiled by Economist Intelligence Unit,
Algeria: Country Report, nos. 1; 4 [1992])

1987	1988	1989	1990
111.5	112.6	99.9	106.0

A SELECTIVE BIBLIOGRAPHY

Researchers commencing historical studies of Algeria face several challenges: (1) publications have emphasized the modern period, e.g., colonialism, the War of Independence, and independent Algeria (which underscores the need for more precolonial/pre-Regency [ancient and medieval] studies); (2) given the intensity of its modern history, biases have influenced scholarship; and (3) most of the published work is in French (with a slowly growing production in Arabic), which poses both language and accessibility problems. This essay emphasizes literature that has been published in English but also mentions prominent French contributions (in addition, q.v. Literature in Arabic). Its purpose is to provide general rather than comprehensive assistance. The reader is also invited to review the bibliography compiled in the first edition of the *Historical Dictionary of Algeria*.

Abbreviations/acronyms for this bibliography:
MERIP: Middle East Research & Information Project
OPU: Office des Publications Universaires
PUF: Presses Universitaires de France
SNED: Société Nationale d'Edition et de Diffusion

Bibliographical, Biographical, Historiographical, and General Research Sources
  For years Richard Lawless has provided invaluable service to Algerian studies, especially as a bibliographer. See *A Bibliography of Works on Algeria Published in English Since 1954* (Durham, England: University of Durham, 1972); *Algeria: Volume 19* (Oxford, Santa Barbara: Clio Press, 1980); and *Algerian*

Bibliography: English Language Publications, 1830–1973 (London, New York: Bowker; University of Durham, 1976). A recent work that includes bibliographies of bibliographies is Michel Maynadies's *Bibliographies algérienne: Répertoire des sources documentaires relatives à l'Algérie* (Algiers: OPU, 1989). Other useful bibliographic sources are M. Bouayed, *Dix ans de production intellectuelle en Algérie* (Algiers: Bibliothèque nationale, 1984); and Jean-Claude Vatin, ed., "Elements pour une bibliographie d'ensemble sur l'Algérie d'aujourd'hui," *Revue Algérienne des sciences juridiques, économiques, et politiques* 5 (March 1968): 167–278. The *Bibliographie d'Algérie* (1964–) produced by Algiers's Bibliothèque Nationale is valuable but usually available only in libraries with specialized Arab and/ or African collections. For earlier works see Robert Lambert Playfair, *A Bibliography of Algeria from the Expedition of Charles V in 1541 to 1887* (London: Royal Geographical Society, Supplementary Papers, part 2), 127–430; and *Supplement to the Bibiliography of Algeria from the Earliest Times to 1895* (London: Murray, 1898).

David E. Gardinier furnishes substantial coverage of Algeria in "Decolonization in French, Belgian, and Portuguese Africa: A Bibliographical Essay," in Prosser Gifford and William Roger Louis, eds., *The Transfer of Power in Africa: Decolonization, 1940–1960* (New Haven: Yale University Press, 1982), 515–566; and Gifford and Louis, eds., *Decolonization and African Independence: The Transfers of Power, 1960–1980* (New Haven: Yale University Press, 1989), 573–635.

Bibliographies are also found in the *Middle East Journal* (includes Arabic listings), *A Current Bibliography on African Affairs*, and *African Affairs*. The *International Index Islamicus* and *International African Bibliography* are other important bibliographic aids. Though the American Historical Association's *Recently Published Articles* (ed. D. Gardinier) ended publication in 1990, it remains a significant source. The American Institute of Maghribi Studies (AIMS) *Newsletter* offers information on recent research and dissertations.

The *Annuaire de l'Afrique du Nord* (1962–) compiled by the Centre de Recherches et d'Etudes sur les Sociétés Méditerranéennes (CRESM) at Aix-en-Provence is the outstanding bibliographic tool for political, economic, social, and cultural research. It also includes Arabic bibliographies. The *Annuaire*'s own articles are also very useful. The Documentation Française's publication *Maghreb/Maghreb-Machrek* (1964–) includes articles and bibliographic assistance. *Grand Maghreb* was a short-lived (1980–1987) yet excellent source for chronologies, brief articles, book reviews, and bibliographies.

Three very useful biographical sources are Jean Déjeux, *Dictionnaire des auteurs maghrébines de langue française* (Paris: Karthala, 1984); Benjamin Stora, *Dictionnaire biographique de Militants nationalisties Algériens (E.N.A., P.P.A., M.T.L.D.) (1926–1954)* (Paris: L'Harmattan, 1985); and *Les Elites Algériennes*, 2 vols., 1st ed. (Paris: Ediafric-La Documentation africaine, 1985). Another valuable aid is Richard Bulliet, Reeva Simon, and Philip Mattar, eds. *The Encyclopedia of the Modern Middle East* (New York: Macmillan, 1994). See also editions of *Who's Who in the Arab World*.

English-language newspapers that give Algeria particular coverage include: the *Christian Science Monitor*, the *Financial Times*, the *New York Times*, the *Washington Post*, the *Wall Street Journal*, and the *Boston Globe*. *Le Monde* (Paris) provides frequent reports. The Agence France Presse (AFP) publishes the *Sahara* series, a collection of its reports. Algerian journalism has flourished since the 1988 upheaval, but publications are often unavailable at American universities except at specialized libraries. The more obtainable Saudi Arabian newspaper, *al-Sharq al-Awsat* (in Arabic), often contains reports on Algerian affairs (in particular, see issues in late 1992–early 1993 for in-depth analyses). The *Maghreb Report* is a new (1992) newsletter which features information on Algeria.

Magazines and journals that often feature reports or articles on Algeria include *The Economist*, *Jeune Afrique*, *Africa Report* (''Update'' section), and *Middle East Report*.

ADDITIONAL SOURCES IN ENGLISH AND FRENCH

Africa Contemporary Record.

Africa Research Bulletin. Series A: Political, Social, and Cultural. Series B: Economics, Financial, and Technical. (Provides information compiled primarily from newspapers.)

Alazard, A. et al. *Histoire et historiens de l'Algérie.* Vol. 4. *Collections du Centenaire de l'Algérie.* Paris: Librairie Félix Alcan, 1931.

Aldefer, H. F., comp. *Bibliography on Algeria.* Tangiers: Documentation Centre, African Training and Research Centre in Administration for Development (CAFRAD), 1971.

"The Algerian Literature of France." *North British Review,* 30 (February 1859): 1–21.

American University Field Staff. *Reports.*

Aspects of Agricultural Policy and Rural Development in Africa—North and North-East Africa: An Annotated Bibliography. Oxford: Commonwealth Bureau of Agricultural Economics, 1971.

Association France-Algérie. *Algérie informations.* (Includes documents and excerpts and articles from Algerian and French sources.)

Attal, Robert. "A Bibliography of Publications Concerning North African Jewry." *Isaiah Sonne Memorial Volume.*

Azzouz, Azzedine and others. *Selected Bibliography of Education Materials: Algeria-Libya, Morocco-Tunisia.* 10 vols. Tunis: Agence Tunisienne de Public Relations, 1967–1976. (Sponsored by the National Science Foundation and the Office of Education [DHEW], Washington, D.C.)

Bibliography on the Maghreb. Tangiers: Documentation Centre, African Training and Research Centre in Administration for Development, 1971.

Blackhurst, Hector (comp.). *Africa Bibliography.* In association with the International African Institute (London). Manchester, England: Manchester University Press, 1984–.

Brett, Michael. "The Colonial Period in the Maghrib and its Aftermath: The Present State of Historical Writing." *Journal of African History* 17, no. 2 (1976): 291–305.

Brill, E. J., ed. *First Encyclopedia of Islam, 1913–36* (Leiden: E. J. Brill, 1987).

Burke, Edmund. "Recent Books on Colonial Algerian History." *Middle Eastern Studies*, 7 (May 1971): 241–250.

Conover, Helen F., comp. *French North Africa (Algeria, Morocco, Tunis): A Bibliographical List.* Washington, D.C.: Division of Bibliography, Library of Congress, 1942.

———. *North and Northeast Africa: A Selected Annotated List of Writings, 1951–1957.* Washington, D.C.: Library of Congress, 1957.

Cooke, James. "The Army at Vincennes: Archives for the Study of North African History in the Colonial Period." *Muslim World* 61 (January 1971): 35–38.

Dictionary of African Biography, 2d ed. London: Melrose Press, 1971.

Foreign Broadcast Information Service. *Daily Reports.* (Near East and South Asia). Washington, D.C.

Gordon, David C. *Self-Determination and History in the Third World*. Princeton, N.J.: Princeton University Press, 1971.

Halpern, Manfred. "Recent Books on Moslem-French Relations in Algeria." *Middle East Journal* 3 (April 1949): 211–215.

————. "New Perspectives in the Study of North Africa." *Journal of Modern African Studies* 3, no. 1 (1965): 103–114.

Heggoy, Alf Andrew. "Books on the Algerian Revolution in English: Translations and Anglo-American Contributions." *African Historical Studies* 3, no. 1 (1970): 163–168.

————. *Historical Dictionary of Algeria*. 1st ed. Metuchen, N.J.: Scarecrow Press, 1981.

————. "On Oral Sources, Historians and the Fichier de Documentation." *African Studies Review* 14 (April 1971): 113–120.

————. "Some Useful French Depositories for the Study of the Algerian Revolution." *Muslim World* 58 (October 1968): 345–347.

————. "The Sources for Nineteenth Century Algerian History: A Critical Essay." *Muslim World* 54 (October 1964): 292–299.

————. *Through Foreign Eyes: Western Attitudes Toward North Africa*. Washington, D.C.: University Press of America, 1982.

Historical Abstracts. ABC-CLIO.

Kupferschmidt, Uri. "The French Foreign Office Records on North Africa and the Middle East in Nantes." *Middle East Studies Association Bulletin*, 23, no. 1 (1989): 9–15.

Middle East and North Africa (series). Europa Publications.

Rivlin, Benjamin. ''A Selective Survey of the Literature in the Social Science and Related Fields on Modern North Africa.'' *American Political Science Review*, 48 (September 1954): 826–848.

Rouina, Karim. *Bibliographie raisonnée sur l'émir Abdelkader*. Oran: Centre de Recherche et d'Information Documentaire en Sciences Sociales et Humaines, 1985.

Sahli, Mohamed Chérif. *Décoloniser l'histoire: Introduction à l'histoire du Maghreb*. Paris: Maspéro, 1965.

A Selected Functional and Country Bibliography for Near East and North Africa. Washington, D.C.: U.S. Department of State, Foreign Service Institute Center for Area and Country Studies, 1971.

United States Joint Publications Research Service.

Wansbrough, John. ''The Decolonization of North African History.'' *Journal of African History* 9 (Winter 1968): 643–650.

Prehistory to French Colonialism (Surveys)

For comparative historical perspectives of Algeria within African history, see J. D. Fage, ed., *The Cambridge History of Africa, II (from c. 500 to A.D. 1050* (Cambridge: Cambridge University Press, 1978), and John E. Flint, ed., *The Cambridge History of Africa, V (from c. 1790 to c. 1870)* (1976) (specific citations below), and UNESCO, *History of Africa*. Regional surveys include Jamil M. Abun-Nasr, *History of the Maghrib*, 2d ed. (Cambridge: Cambridge University Press, 1975); Abun-Nasr, *A History of the Maghrib in the Islamic Period* (Cambridge: Cambridge University Press, 1987); Abdallah Laroui, *The History of the Maghrib: An Interpretive Essay*, trans. Ralph Manheim (Princeton: Princeton University Press, 1977); and Charles-André Julien (q.v.) (ed. and revised by Roger Le Tourneau), trans. John

Petrie (ed. C.C. Stewart), *History of North Africa: Tunisia, Algeria, Morocco: From the Arab Conquest to 1830* (London: Routledge & Kegan Paul, 1970); and Ibn Khaldun, *The Muqaddimah: An Introduction to History,* trans. Franz Rosenthal (Princeton, N.J.: Princeton University Press, 1967). See also *Revue d'histoire maghrébine.*

ADDITIONAL SOURCES IN ENGLISH AND FRENCH

Abun-Nasr, Jamil M. *The Tijaniyya: A Sufi Order in the Modern World.* Oxford: Oxford University Press, 1965.

Albertini, Eugène. *L'Afrique romaine.* 2d ed. Algiers: Imprimerie officielle, 1955.

Augustine. *Confessions.* Translated by Henry Chadwick. Oxford: Oxford University Press, 1991.

Barnby, H. G. *The Prisoners of Algiers: An Account of the Forgotten American-Algerian War, 1785–1797.* London: Oxford University Press, 1966.

Benabou, Marcel. *La Résistance africaine à la romanisation.* Paris: François Maspero, 1976.

Bontemps, Claude. *Manuel des institutions Algériennes de la domination turque à l'indépendance. Tome premier—la domination turque et le régime militaire 1518–1870.* Vol. 1. Paris: Editions Cujas, 1976.

Bourouiba, Rachid. *Les Hammadides.* Algiers: PUB, 1982.

———. *Ibn Tumart.* Algiers: SNED, 1974.

Bousquet, Georges-Henri. *Les Berbères: Histoire et institutions.* Paris: PUF, 1961.

Boyer, Pierre. *La vie quotidienne à Alger à la veille de l'intervention française*. Paris: Hachette, 1963.

Braudel, Fernand. *The Mediterranean and the Mediterranean World in the Age of Philip II*. Translated by Siân Reynolds. 2 vols. London: Collins, 1972; New York: Harper & Row, 1972.

Brett, Michael. "The Arab Conquest and the Rise of Islam in North Africa." In *The Cambridge History of Africa, II*, 490–555.

Brown, Peter. *Augustine of Hippo: A Biography*. Berkeley: University of California Press, 1969.

Brunschvig, Robert. *La Berbérie orientale sous les Hafsides: Des origines à la fin du XVe siècle*. 2 vols. Paris: Librairie d'Amérique et d'Orient, 1940–1947.

Buck, D. J. "The Role of the State in the Eastern Maghreb, 500 B.C. to 500 A.D." *Maghreb Review* 9, nos. 1–2 (1984): 1–9.

Casanova, Paul, ed. *Histoire des Berbères et des dynasties musulmanes de l'Afrique Septentrionale*. 4 vols. Paris: Librairie Orientaliste, 1968–1969.

Charles-Picard, Gilbert. *La civilisation de l'Afrique romaine*. Paris: Librairie Plon, 1959.

Chouraqui, André. *Between East and West: A History of the Jews in North Africa*. Translated by Michael M. Bernet. New York: Atheneum, 1973.

Clissold, Stephen. *The Barbary Slaves*. London: Paul Elek, 1977.

Courtois, Christian. *Les Vandales et l'Afrique*. Aalen, Federal Republic of Germany: Scientia Verlag, 1964.

Dhina, Attallah. *Le Royaume abdelwaddide à l'époque d'Abdou*

Hammam Moussa 1ᵉʳ et d'Abou Tachfin 1ᵉʳ. Algiers: OPU, 1985.

Diehl, Charles. *L'Afrique byzantine: Histoire de la domination byzantine en Afrique, 533–709*. 2 vols. Philadelphia: Franklin, 1968 (reprint).

Dufourcq, Charles-Emmanuel. *L'Espagne catalane et le Maghrib aux XIIIᵉ et XIVᵉ siècles*. Paris: PUF, 1966.

Esposito, John. *Islam: The Straight Path*. 2d ed. Oxford: Oxford University Press, 1991.

Fisher, Sir Godfrey. *Barbary Legend: War, Trade and Piracy in North Africa, 1415–1830*. London: Oxford University Press, 1957.

Frend, W.H.C. *The Donatist Church: A Movement of Protest in Roman North Africa*. London: Oxford University Press, 1952.

Gaïd, Mouloud. *L'Algérie sous les Turcs*. Algiers: SNED, 1974.

Gallisot, René. "Precolonial Algeria." *Economy and Society* 4 (1975): 418–445.

Gautier, Emile-Félix. *Le passé de l'Afrique du Nord: Les siècles obscurs*. Paris: Payot, 1952.

Golvin, Lucien. *Le Maghrib central à l'époque des Zirides: Recherches d'archéologie et d'histoire*. Paris: Arts et métiers graphiques, 1957.

Gsell, Stéphane. *Histoire ancienne de l'Afrique du Nord*. 8 vols. Paris: Hachette, 1914–1928.

Hess, Andrew C. *The Forgotten Frontier: A History of the Sixteenth-Century Ibero-African Frontier* (Chicago: University of Chicago Press), 1978.

Hirschberg, H. Z. *A History of the Jews in North Africa*. Vol. 1: *From Antiquity to the Sixteenth Century*. Leiden: Brill, 1974.

Holsinger, Donald C. "Migration, Commerce, and Community: The Mizabis in Eighteenth and Nineteenth Century Algeria." *Journal of African History* 21, no. 1 (1980): 61–74.

Idris, Hady Roger. *La Berbérie orientale sous les Zirides: Xe-XIIe siècles*. 2 vols. Paris: Adrien-Maisonneuve, 1962.

Ikor, Roger. *La Kahina*. Paris: Encre Editions, 1979.

Irwin, Ray W. *The Diplomatic Relations of the United States with the Barbary Powers, 1776–1816*. Chapel Hill: University of North Carolina Press, 1931.

Johnson, Douglas. "The Maghrib." In *The Cambridge History of Africa, V*, 99–124.

Kaddache, Mahfoud. *L'Algérie médiévale*. Algiers: SNED, 1982.

Keenan, Jeremy. *The Tuareg: People of Ahaggar*. New York: St. Martin's Press, 1977.

Latham, J. D. "Towns and Cities of Barbary—the Andalusian Influence." *Islamic Quarterly* 16, nos. 3–4 (July-December 1972): 89–204.

Law, R.C.C. "North Africa in the Hellenistic and Roman Periods, 323 B.C. to A.D. 305." In *The Cambridge History of Africa, II*, 148–209.

———. "North Africa in the Period of Phoenician and Greek Colonization, c. 800 to 323 B.C." *The Cambridge History of Africa, II*, 87–147.

Le Tourneau, Roger. *The Almohad Movement in North Africa in the Twelfth and Thirteenth Centuries*. Princeton: Princeton University Press, 1969.

Lhote, Henri. *The Search for the Tassili Frescoes: The Story of the Prehistoric Rock-paintings of the Sahara*. Translated by Alan Houghton Brodrick. London: Hutchinson, 1959.

MacKendrick, Paul. *The North African Stones Speak*. Chapel Hill: The University of North Carolina Press, 1980.

Miller, Aurie Hollingsworth. "One Man's View: William Shaler and Algiers." In *Through Foreign Eyes*, ed. Alf Heggoy, 7–56.

Raven, Susan. *Rome in Africa*. 2d ed. London: Longman, 1984.

Seddon, David. "Tribe and State: Approaches to Maghreb History." *Maghreb Review* 2 (May-June 1977): 23–40.

Shaw, Brent D. "Rural Periodic Markets in Roman North Africa as Mechanisms of Social Integration and Control." *Research in Economic Anthropology* 2 (1979): 91–117.

Spencer, William. *Algiers in the Age of the Corsairs*. Norman: University of Oklahoma Press, 1976.

———. "Ottoman North Africa." In *Nationalism in a Non-National State: The Dissolution of the Ottoman Empire*, edited by William W. Haddad and William Ochsenwald, 103–127. Columbus: Ohio State University Press, 1977.

Thompson, Ann. *Barbary and Enlightenment: European Attitudes toward the Maghreb in the 18th Century*. Leiden: E. J. Brill, 1987.

Valensi, Lucette. *On the Eve of Colonialism: North Africa Before the French Conquest, 1790–1830*. Translated by Kenneth J. Perkins. New York: Africana Publishing Company, 1977.

Van der Meer, F. *Augustine the Bishop: Church and Society at the Dawn of the Middle Ages.* New York: Harper and Row, 1961.

Von Sivers, Peter. "Arms and Alms: The Combative Saintliness of the Awlad Sidi Shaykh in the Algerian Sahara, 16th to 19th Centuries." *Maghreb Review* 8, no. 4 (1983): 113–123.

Wellard, James. *The Great Sahara.* London: Hutchinson, 1964.

Wolf, John B. *The Barbary Coast: Algiers under the Turks, 1500–1830.* New York: W. W. Norton, 1979.

Zerouki, Brahim. *L'Imamat de Tahart: Premier état musulman du Maghreb (144/296 A.H.). Histoire politico-socio-réligieuse.* Paris: L'Harmattan, 1987.

FRENCH COLONIALISM AND THE WAR OF INDEPENDENCE

Three prominent works on French colonialism that also provide comprehensive bibliographies are: Charles-André Julien (q.v.), *Histoire de l'Algérie contemporaine: La Conquête et les débuts de la colonisation (1827–1871),* vol. 1 (Paris: PUF, 1964); Charles-Robert Ageron, *Histoire de l'Algérie contemporaine: De l'insurrection de 1871 au déclenchement de la Guerre de Libération (1954),* vol. 2 (Paris: PUF, 1979); and Jean-Claude Vatin, *L'Algérie politique: Histoire et société* (Paris: PUF, 1983). There are no works in English matching the scholarly magnitude of these works. Nevertheless, an important recent addition is John Ruedy, *Modern Algeria: The Origins and Development of a Nation* (Bloomington: Indiana University Press, 1992). This is a well-written synthesis that concentrates on colonial Algeria (with one chapter on the Regency and another on postcolonial Algeria).

Prominent specialized studies in the history of French colonialism include: Raphael Danzinger, *Abd al-Qadir and the Algerians: Resistance to the French and Internal Consolidation* (New York:

Holmes & Meier, 1977); John D. Ruedy, *Land Policy in Colonial Algeria: The Origins of the Rural Public Domain* (Berkeley: University of California Press, 1967); Vincent Confer, *France and Algeria: The Problem of Civil and Political Reform, 1870–1920* (Syracuse, N.Y.: Syracuse University Press, 1966); David Prochaska, *Making Algeria French: Colonialism in Bône, 1870–1920* (Oxford: Oxford University Press, 1990); Marnia Lazreg, *The Emergence of Classes in Algeria: A Study of Colonialism and Socio-Political Change* (Boulder, Colo.: Westview Press, 1976); and Tony Smith, *The French Stake in Algeria, 1945–1962* (Cornell, N.Y.: Cornell University Press, 1980). Jacques Goutor's, *Algeria and France, 1830–1963* (Muncie, Indiana: Ball State University Press, 1965) is a brief but useful survey for those beginning modern Algerian studies.

As for the War of Liberation, Alistair Horne, *A Savage War of Peace: Algeria, 1954–1962* (London: Penguin, 1977, 1987) is a popular history that captures the psychological drama of the war. The second edition includes additions and corrections. The book is particularly valuable for its interviews with participants. See also John Talbott, *The War Without a Name: France in Algeria, 1954–1962* (New York: Alfred A. Knopf, 1980); Martha Crenshaw Hutchinson, *Revolutionary Terrorism: The FLN in Algeria, 1954–1962* (Stanford University: Hoover Institute Press, 1978); Richard and Joan Brace, *Ordeal in Algeria* (New York: D. Van Nostrand, 1960); and Alf Andrew Heggoy, *Insurgency and Counterinsurgency in Algeria* (Bloomington: Indiana University Press, 1972).

Yves Courrière, *La Guerre de l'Algérie*, 4 vols. (Paris: Fayard, 1968–1971) is a monumental work that includes interviews with Belkacem Krim (q.v.). Other important publications among the massive number of works on the war include Henri Alleg and others, *La guerre d'Algérie*, 3 vols. (Paris: Temps Actuel, 1981); Bernard Droz and Evelyne Lever, *Histoire de la Guerre de l'Algérie, 1954–1962* (Paris: Seuil, 1982); Slimane Chikh, *L'Algérie en armes: Ou le temps des certitudes* (Paris: Economica, 1981); Mohammed Harbi, *Les archives de la Révolution Algérienne* (Paris: Editions Jeune Afrique, 1980); and *Le FLN, mirages et réalités: Des origines à la prise du pouvoir (1945–*

1962) (Paris: Editions Jeune Afrique, 1980). Germaine Tillion's concise contributions represent those of a very close observer of the Algerian War of Independence; see *Algeria: The Realities*, trans. Ronald Matthews (New York: Knopf, 1958); and *France and Algeria: Complementary Enemies*, trans. Richard Howard (New York: Knopf, 1961).

Finally, the works of Frantz Fanon (q.v.), including *A Dying Colonialism*, trans. Haakon Chevalier (New York: Grove Press, 1967); *Toward the African Revolution (Political Essays)*, trans. Haakon Chevalier (New York: Grove Press, 1969); and *The Wretched of the Earth*, trans. Constance Farrington (New York: Grove Press, 1968), examine the effect of the liberation struggle upon the consciousness of the colonized. Irene Gendzier, *Frantz Fanon: A Critical Study*, 2d ed. (New York: Grove Press, 1985) provides the best biography and analysis of this remarkable ideologue.

ADDITIONAL SOURCES IN ENGLISH

Abu-Lughod, Ibrahim, and Baha Abu-Laban, eds. *Settler Regimes in Africa and the Arab World: The Illusion of Endurance.* Wilmette, Illinois: Medina University Press, International, 1974.

Ageron, Charles-Robert. *Modern Algeria: A History from 1830 to the Present.* Translated by Michael Brett. Trenton, N.J.: Africa World Press, 1991.

Alleg, Henri. *The Question.* Translated by John Calder. London: Calder, 1958.

Alwan, Mohamed. *Algeria Before the United Nations.* New York: Robert Speller, 1959.

Ambassade de France. *Texts of Declarations Drawn up in Common Agreement at Evian, March 18, 1962 by the*

Delegations of the Government of the French Republic and the Algerian Liberation Front. New York: Service de Presse et d'Information, n.d. [1962].

Amrane, Djamila. "Algeria: Anticolonial War." In *Female Soldiers—Combatants or Non-combatants? Historical and Contemporary Perspectives,* edited by Nancy Loring Goldman, 123–135. Westport, Conn.: Greenwood Press, 1982.

Arab, Si Abderrahmane. "The National Liberation War in the French Language Novel of Algeria." *British Society for Middle Eastern Studies Bulletin* 17, no. 1 (1990): 33–46.

Bedjaoui, Mohammed. *Law and the Algerian Revolution.* Brussels: International Association of Democratic Lawyers, 1961.

Behr, Edward. *The Algerian Problem.* Harmondsworth, England: Penguin Books, 1961.

Berque, Jacques. *French North Africa: The Maghrib Between Two World Wars.* Translated by Jean Stewart. New York: Praeger, 1967.

Bocca, Geoffrey. *The Secret Army.* Englewood Cliffs, N.J.: Prentice-Hall, 1968.

Bookmiller, Robert. "The Algerian War of Words: Broadcasting and Revolution, 1954–62." *Maghreb Review* 14, nos. 3–4 (1989): 196–213.

Brace, Richard M. *Morocco, Algeria, Tunisia* (Englewood Cliffs, N.J.: Prentice-Hall, 1964).

Brace, Richard M. and Joan Brace. *Algerian Voices.* Princeton, N.J.: Van Nostrand, 1965.

Caute, David. *Frantz Fanon.* New York: Viking Press, 1970.

Christelow, Allan. "Algerian Islam in a Time of Transition: c. 1890–c. 1930." *Maghreb Review* 8, no. 4 (1983): 124–130.

————. *Muslim Law Courts and the French Colonial State in Algeria.* Princeton: Princeton University Press, 1985.

————. "Oral, Manuscript, and Printed Expressions of Historical Consciousness in Colonial Algeria." *Africana Journal*, 15 (1990): 258–275.

Clark, Michael K. *Algeria in Turmoil: A History of the Rebellion.* New York: Frederick A. Praeger, 1959.

Colonna, Fanny. "Cultural Resistance and Religious Legitimacy in Colonial Algeria." *Economy and Society* 3 (1974): 233–263.

Cooke, James J. "The Colonial Origins of *Colon* and Muslim Nationalism in Algeria—1880–1920." *Indian Political Science Review* 10 (January 1976): 19–36.

————. "Eugène Etienne and the Failure of Assimilation in Algeria." *Africa Quarterly* 9 (January-March 1972): 285–296.

————. "The Maghrib Through French Eyes: 1880–1929." In *Through Foreign Eyes*, ed. Alf A. Heggoy, 57–92.

————. "Tricolour and Crescent: Franco-Muslim Relations in Colonial Algeria, 1880–1940." *Islamic Studies* 29, no. 1 (1990): 57–75.

De Beauvoir, Simone and Gisèle Halimi. *Djamila Boupacha: The Story of the Torture of a Young Algerian Girl which Shocked Liberal French Opinion.* Translated by Peter Green. New York: Macmillan, 1962.

De Gaulle, Charles. *Memoirs of Hope: Renewal 1958–62; Endeavor 1962-*. Translated by Terence Kilmartin. London: Weidenfeld and Nicolson, 1971.

Dirlik, André. "The Algerian Response to Settlement." In *Settler Regimes*, eds. Abu-Lughod and Abu-Laban, 73–80.

Firestone, Ya'akov. "The Doctrine of Integration with France among the Europeans of Algeria, 1955–1960." *Comparative Political Studies* 4 (July 1971): 177–203.

Fitzgerald, E. Peter. "An Application of the Robinson Theory of Collaboration to Colonial Algeria after the Post-War Reforms: The *Instituteur indigène* and French Dominance in the 1920's." *Proceedings of the French Colonial Historical Society* (1976): 155–168.

————. "Civil Authority, Local Governments, and Native Administration in Colonial Algeria, 1834–1870." *French Colonial Studies* 2 (1978): 23–48.

————. "The District Commissioner of Colonial Algeria, 1875–1939." *Proceedings of the French Colonial Historical Society* (1978): 163–177.

Gendzier, Irene L. "Psychology and Colonialism: Some Observations." *Middle East Journal* 30 (Autumn 1976): 501–515.

Gillespie, Joan. *Algeria: Rebellion and Revolution*. New York: Praeger, 1960.

Gordon, David C. *North Africa's French Legacy, 1954–1962*. Cambridge, Mass.: Harvard University Press, 1962.

Harrison, Alexander. *Challenging de Gaulle: The OAS and the Counter Revolution in Algeria, 1954–1962*. New York: Praeger, 1989.

Hart, Ursula Kingsmill. *Two Ladies of Colonial Algeria*. Athens, Ohio: Ohio University Center for International Studies, 1987.

Heggoy, Alf Andrew. "Development or Control: French Policies in Colonial and Revolutionary Algeria." *Journal of African Studies* 5 (1978/79): 427–443.

————. *The French Conquest of Algiers, 1830: An Oral Tradition*. Athens, Ohio: Ohio University Center for International Studies, 1986.

————. "The Origins of Algerian Nationalism in the Colony and in France." *Muslim World* 58, no. 1 (January 1968): 128–140.

————, ed. *Through Foreign Eyes: Western Attitudes Toward North Africa*. Washington, D.C.: University Press of America, 1982.

Heggoy, Alf A. and Paul J. Zingg. "French Education in Revolutionary North Africa." *International Journal of Middle East Studies* 7 (1976): 571–578.

Hennissart, Paul. *Wolves in the City: The Death of French Algeria*. New York: Simon and Schuster, 1970.

Honisch, Ludmilla. "The Denunciation of Mysticism as a Bulwark against Reason: A Contribution to the Expansion of Algerian Reformism, 1925–1939." *Maghreb Review* 11, nos. 5–6 (1986): 102–106.

Howe, George F. *United States Army in World War II—the Mediterranean Theater of Operations, North Africa: Seizing the Initiative in the West*. Washington: Department of the Army, 1957.

Joesten, Joachim. *The Red Hand: The Sinister Account of the Terrorist Arm of the French Right-Wing "Ultras"—in Algeria and on the Continent.* New York: Abelard Schuman, 1962.

Kabak, Annette. *Isabelle: The Life of Isabelle Eberhardt.* New York: Knopf, 1989.

Knight, M. M. "The Algerian Revolt: Some Underlying Factors." *Middle East Journal* 10 (Autumn 1956): 355–367.

Kraft, Joseph. "Settler Politics in Algeria." *Foreign Affairs* 39 (July 1961): 591–600.

Lazreg, Marnia. *The Emergence of Social Classes in Algeria: A Study of Colonialism and Socio-Political Change.* Boulder, Colo.: Westview, 1976.

Leulliette, Pierre. *St. Michael and the Dragon: A Paratrooper in the Algerian War.* Translated by Tony White. London: Heinemann, 1964.

Lottman, Herbert R. *Albert Camus: A Biography.* Garden City, N.Y.: Doubleday, 1979.

Maran, Rita. *Torture: The Role of Ideology in the French-Algerian War.* New York: Praeger, 1989.

Naylor, Phillip C. "Abd el-Kader," *The International Military Encyclopedia* (Academic International Press, 1992): 62–66.

O'Ballance, Edgar. *The Algerian Insurrection, 1954–62.* London: Faber & Faber, 1967.

O'Brien, Conor Cruise. *Albert Camus of Europe and Africa.* New York: Viking Press, 1970.

Perinbam, Marie. "Fanon and the Revolutionary Peasantry: The

Algerian Case." *Journal of Modern African Studies* 11, no. 3 (1973): 427–445.

Perkins, Kenneth J. "The *Bureaux Arabes* and the *Colons*: Administrative Conflict in Algeria, 1844–1875." *Proceedings of the French Colonial Historical Society* (1976): 96–107.

———. *Qaids, Captains, and Colons.* New York: Africana, 1981.

———. "Pressure and Persuasion in the Policies of the French Military in Colonial North Africa." *Military Affairs* 40 (April 1976): 74–78.

Pickles, Dorothy. *Algeria and France: From Colonialism to Cooperation.* New York: Praeger, 1963.

Porch, Douglas. *Conquest of the Sahara.* New York: Knopf, 1984.

———. *The French Foreign Legion: A Complete History of the Legendary Fighting Force.* New York: Harper Collins, 1991.

Prochaska, David. "Approaches to the Economy of Colonial Annaba, 1870–1920." *Africa* 60, no. 4 (1990): 497–523.

———. "The Archives of *Algérie imaginaire.*" *History and Anthropology* 4, no. 2 (1990): 373–420.

Redouane, Jöelle. "British Trade with Algeria in the 19th Century: An Ally against France?" *Maghreb Review*, 13, nos. 3–4 (1988): 175–182.

Roy, Jules. *The War in Algeria.* Translated by Richard Howard. Westport, Conn.: Greenwood Press, 1975.

Saadallah, Belkacem. "The Algerian Ulemas, 1919–1931." *Revue d'histoire maghrébine*, no. 2 (1974): 138–150.

————. "The Rise of the Algerian Elite, 1900–1914." *Journal of Modern African Studies* 5 (May 1967): 69–77.

Sellin, Eric. "Alienation and Intellectual Invisibility of Algerian Nationals: The Writer's Vision." In *Settler Regimes in Africa*, eds. Ibrahim Abu-Lughod and Baha Abu-Laban, 125–135.

Shaler, William. *Sketches of Algiers: Political, Historical, and Civil*. Boston: Cummings, Hiliard and Company, 1826.

Sivan, Emanuel. "Colonialism and Popular Culture in Algeria." *Journal of Contemporary History* 14 (January 1979): 21–53.

————. "L'Etoile Nord-Africaine and the Genesis of Algerian Nationalism." *Maghreb Review* 3 (January-April 1978): 17–22.

Smith, Julia Clancy. "In the Eye of the Beholder: Sufi and Saint in North Africa and the Colonial Production of Knowledge, 1830–1900." *Africana Journal*, 15 (1990): 220–257.

Smith, Tony. "The French Colonial Consensus and Peoples' War, 1946–1958." *Journal of Contemporary History* 9 (October 1974): 217–247.

————. "The French Economic Stake in Colonial Algeria." *French Historical Studies* 9, no. 1 (Spring 1975): 184–189.

Stevens, Mary Anne, ed. *The Orientalists; Delacroix to Matisse: European Painters in North Africa and the Near East*. London: Royal Academy of Arts, 1984.

Sullivan, Antony Thrall. *Thomas-Robert Bugeaud, France and Algeria, 1784–1849: Politics, Power, and the Good Society*. Hamden, Conn.: Archon Books, 1983.

Sutton, Keith. "Population Resettlement—Traumatic Upheavals and the Algerian Experience." *Journal of Modern African Studies* 15 (June 1977): 279–300.

Talbott, John. "French Public Opinion and the Algerian War: A Research Note." *French Historical Studies* 9 (Fall 1975): 69–86.

———. "The Myth and Reality of the Paratrooper in the Algerian War." *Armed Forces and Society* 3, no. 1 (Fall 1976): 69–86.

———. "The Strange Death of Maurice Audin." *Virginia Quarterly Review* 52 (1976), 224–242.

———. "Terrorism and the Liberal Dilemma: The Case of the 'Battle of Algiers.' " *Contemporary French Civilization* 2 (Winter 1978): 177–190.

El Tayeb, Salah El Din El Zein. "The Europeanized Algerians and the Emancipation of Algeria." *Middle Eastern Studies* 22, no. 2 (1986): 206–235.

———. "The *Ulama* and Islamic Renaissance in Algeria." *American Journal of Islamic Social Sciences* 6, no. 2 (1989): 257–288.

Thomas, Ann. "Arguments for the Conquest of Algiers in the Late 18th and Early 19th Centuries." *Maghreb Review* 14, nos. 1–2 (1989): 108–118.

Van Dyke, Stuart. "Response to Rebellion: The Algerian French and the February 6, 1956 Crisis." *French Colonial Studies* 2 (1978): 97–112.

Von Sivers, Peter. "Insurrection and Accommodation: Indigenous Leadership in Eastern Algeria, 1840–1900." *Interna-*

tional Journal of Middle East Studies 6 (July 1975): 259–275.

———. "The Realm of Justice: Apocalyptic Revolts in Algeria (1849–1879)." *Humaniora Islamica* 1 (1973): 47–60.

Yacine, Kateb (Yacine Kateb). *Nedjma: A Novel*. Translated by Richard Howard. New York: Braziller, 1961.

ADDITIONAL SOURCES IN FRENCH

Abbas, Ferhat. *Autopsie d'une guerre*. Paris: Garnier, 1980.

———. *Guerre et révolution d'Algérie: La nuit coloniale*. Paris: Julliard, 1962.

Ageron, Charles-Robert. *«Algérie Algérienne» de Napoléon III à de Gaulle*. Paris: Sindbad, 1980.

———. *Les Algériens musulmans et la France (1871–1919)*. 2 vols. Paris: PUF, 1968.

Ainad-Tabet, Radouane. *Le mouvement du 8 mai 1945 en Algérie*. Algiers: OPU, 1985.

Ait Ahmed, Hocine. *La guerre et l'après guerre*. Paris: Minuit, 1964.

Azan, Paul. *Conquête et pacification de l'Algérie*. Paris: Librairie de France, 1931.

Ben Khedda, Benyoucef. *Les accords d'Evian*. Algiers/Paris: OPU-Publisud, 1986.

Boualam, Said (Bachaga). *Les Harkis au service de la France*. Paris: France-Empire, 1963.

————. *Mon pays . . . la France!* Paris: France-Empire, 1962.

Boudiaf, Mohamed. *La préparation du 1er novembre. Suivi d'une lettre ouverte aux Algériens.* Paris: Collection El Jarida, 1976.

Challe, Maurice. *Notre révolte.* Paris: Presses de la Cité, 1968.

Collot, Claude and Jean-Robert Henry, eds. *Le mouvement national Algérien: Textes, 1912–54.* Paris: L'Harmattan, 1978.

Duchemin, Jacques C. *Histoire du F.L.N..* Paris: Table Ronde, 1962.

Etienne, Bruno. *Les problèmes juridiques des minorités européennes au Maghreb.* Paris: Editions du Centre National de la Recherche Scientifique, 1968.

Favrod, Charles-Henri. *Le F.L.N. et l'Algérie.* Paris: Plon, 1962.

Gallissot, René. "Abdel Kader et la nationalité Algérienne: Interprétation de la chute de la Régence d'Alger et des premières résistances à la conquête française (1830–1839)." *Revue historique* 2 (1965): 339–368.

Gendarme, René. *L'économie de l'Algérie: Sous-développement et politique de croissance.* Paris: Armand Colin, 1959.

Hadj, Messali. *Les mémoires de Messali Hadj, 1898–1938.* Edited by Renaud de Rochebrun. Paris: Lattès, 1982.

Helie, Jerôme. *Les Accords d'Evian: Histoire secrète de la paix en Algérie.* Paris: Orban, 1992.

Jeanson, Francis. *La Révolution Algérienne: Problèmes et perspectives.* Milan: Feltrinelli, 1962.

Jouhaud, Edmond. *Ce que je n'ai pas dit.* Paris: Fayard, 1977.

Julien, Charles-André. *L'Afrique du Nord en marche: Nationalismes musulmans et souveraineté française.* Paris: René Julliard, 1972.

Kaddache, Mahfoud. *Histoire du nationalisme Algérien: Question nationale et politique Algérienne, 1919–1951.* 2 vols. Algiers: SNED, 1981.

Leconte, Daniel. *Les pieds-noirs: Histoire et portrait d'une communauté.* Paris: Seuil, 1980.

Le Tourneau, Roger. *Evolution politique de l'Afrique du Nord musulmane, 1920–1961.* Paris: Librairie Armand Colin, 1962.

Mahsas, Ahmed. *Le mouvement révolutionnaire en Algérie: De la 1ʳᵉ Guerre mondiale à 1954.* Paris: L'Harmattan, 1979.

Mameri, Khalfa. *Abane Ramdane.* Paris: L'Harmattan, 1988.

Mandouze, André, ed. *La Révolution Algérienne par les textes.* Paris: Maspéro, 1961.

Massu, Jacques. *La vraie bataille d'Alger.* Paris: Plon, 1971.

Mercier, Gustave, ed. *Le centenaire de l'Algérie: Exposé d'ensemble.* 2 vols. Algiers: Gouvernement général de l'Algérie, Commissariat général du Centenaire, Editions P. G. Soubiron, 1931.

Nouschi, André. *La naissance du nationalism Algérien.* Paris: Editions de Minuit, 1962.

Soustelle, Jacques. *Aimée et souffrante Algérie.* Paris: Plon, 1956.

Stora, Benjamin. *Messali Hadj (1898–1974): Pionnier du nationalisme Algérien*. Paris: L'Harmattan, 1986.

————. *Les sources du nationalisme Algérien: Parcours idéologiques; origines des acteurs*. Paris: L'Harmattan, 1989.

Turin, Yvonne. *Affrontements culturels dans l'Algérie coloniale: Ecoles, médecines, religion, 1830–1880*. Paris: François Maspéro, 1971.

Viollette, Maurice. *L'Algérie vivra-t-elle? Notes d'un ancien gouverneur général*. Paris: Librairie Félix Alcan, 1931.

SURVEYS OF POSTCOLONIAL ALGERIA

David C. Gordon's *The Passing of French Algeria* (London: Oxford University Press, 1966) is a well-integrated political, socioeconomic, and cultural survey that particularly describes the immediate difficulties in the transition from colonialism to independence. Arslan Humbaraci expresses his disillusionment (primarily ideological) concerning the course of newly independent Algeria in *Algeria: A Revolution that Failed* (London: Pall Mall, 1966). David and Marina Ottaway's *Algeria: The Politics of a Socialist Revolution* (Berkeley: University of California Press, 1970) surveys the Ben Bella-early Boumedienne periods. John P. Entelis complements these works with his timely study emphasizing the Benjedid period in *Algeria: The Revolution Institutionalized* (Boulder, Colo.: Westview Press, 1986).

Significant surveys in French include: Bernard Cubertafond, *La République Algérienne* (Paris: PUF, 1979); Jean Leca and Jean-Claude Vatin, *Algérie: Politique, institutions et régime* (Paris: Presses de la Fondation Nationale des Sciences Politiques, 1975); Bruno Etienne, *Algérie: Cultures et révolution* (Paris: Seuil, 1977); Paul Balta and Claudine Rulleau, *L'Algérie des Algériens* (Paris: Editions Ouvrières, 1981); Mohamed Dahmani, *Algérie: Légitimité historique et continuité politique* (Paris:

Editions Le Sycomore, 1979); and Yves Gauthier and Joël Kermarec, *Naissance et croissance de la République Algérienne démocratique et populaire* (Paris: Editions Marketing, 1978).

Richard B. Parker includes important sections on Algeria in his concise comparative survey *North Africa: Regional Tensions and Strategic Concerns* (New York: Praeger, 1984, 1987). See also Clement Henry Moore, *Politics in North Africa: Algeria, Morocco, and Tunisia* (Boston: Little, Brown, 1970); Richard F. Nyrop and others, *Area Handbook for Algeria*, DA Pam 550–44, 2d ed. (Washington, D.C.: U.S. Government Printing Office, 1972); Harold D. Nelson, ed., *Algeria: A Country Study*, DA Pam 550–44, (Washington: GPO for Foreign Area Studies, The American University, 3d ed., 1979; 4th ed., 1986).

ALGERIAN GOVERNMENT PUBLICATIONS

The Ministry of Information (and Culture) has published many works in English. Collectively, they present a positive, progressive national image. See *The Algerian Revolution: Facts and Prospects (10th Anniversary of Independence)* (Algiers, 1972) and especially the series entitled *The Faces of Algeria* (Algiers, 1970–1977), which examines different sectors including: public works, self-management, youth and sports, agricultural development, the Agrarian Revolution, trade policy, socialist organization of enterprises, education, hydrocarbons, and state-planning. These specific works relate directly to President Boumedienne's "state-building" policies.

The speeches of the presidents (in French) are also published under the general rubric of Ministry of Information («Orientation nationale» under Ben Bella; Information and Culture under Boumedienne).

SONATRACH'S "White Books" (Algiers, 1972) on the development of its hydrocarbon policy, and specifically, the French-Algerian relationship were printed in English. See: *The Algerian Oil Policy: Events, Studies, Declarations, 1965–1969*, vol. 1; *The Algerian Oil Policy: Events Studies Declarations,*

1970–1972, vol. 2; *The Algerian Oil Policy: President Houari Boumedienne's Speeches (1965–1972)*; *Background Information on the Relationship Between Algeria and the French Oil Companies*; *Hydrocarbons in Algeria: The 1971 Agreements.*

POLITICAL TOPICS

The Algerian elite has received particular attention. William B. Quandt, *Revolution and Political Leadership: Algeria 1954–1968* (Cambridge: MIT, 1969) represents one of the best works on Third World elite development. Henry F. Jackson contends that party development ended with Boumedienne's arrival to power in *The FLN in Algeria: Party Development in a Revolutionary Society* (Westport, Conn.: Greenwood Press, 1977). See also William H. Lewis, "The Decline of Algeria's FLN, "*Middle East Journal* 20 (Spring 1966): 161–172; John Entelis, "Elite Political Culture and Socialization in Algeria: Tensions and Discontinuities," *Middle East Journal* 35 (Spring 1981): 191–208; I. William Zartman, "L'Elite Algérienne sous la présidence de Chadli Benjedid," *Maghreb-Machrek*, no. 106 (1984): 37–53; and Robert A. Mortimer, "The Politics of Reassurance in Algeria," *Current History* 84 (May 1985): 201–204, 228–229.

The definition of Algeria's political culture was highlighted by the National Charter of 1976 (subsequently "enriched" in 1986). See John Nellis, *The Algerian National Charter of 1976: Content, Public Reaction, and Significance* (Washington, D.C.: Center for Contemporary Arab Studies, Georgetown University Press, 1980); and Nicole Grimaud, "La Charte Nationale Algérienne (27 juin 1976," *Notes et études documentaires*) (Documentation française), no. 4349–4350 (December 28, 1976); and Mostefa Lacheraf, *L'Algérie: Nation et société* (Algiers: SNED, 1978).

Any researcher in Algerian foreign policy will appreciate the contributions produced by Robert A. Mortimer. See, for example, "The Algerian Revolution in Search of the African Revolution," *Journal of Modern African Studies* 8 (October 1970): 363–387; "Algeria and the Politics of International Economic Reform,"

Orbis 21 (Fall 1977): 671–700; "Global Economy and African Foreign Policy: The Algerian Model," *African Studies Review* 27 (March 1984): 1–24; "Maghreb Matters," *Foreign Policy*, no. 76 (1989): 160–175; and "Algerian Foreign Policy in Transition," in John P. Entelis and Phillip C. Naylor, eds., *State and Society in Algeria*, 241–266. See also John P. Entelis, "Algeria in World Politics: Foreign Policy Orientation and the New International Economic Order," *American-Arab Affairs* 6 (Fall 1983): 70–78; and Assassi Lassassi, *Non-Alignment and Algerian Foreign Policy* (Aldershot, 1988).

Nicole Grimaud has often contributed her foreign policy analyses in *Maghreb/Maghreb-Machrek*. Her major work *La Politique extérieure de l'Algérie* (Paris, 1984) surveys the development of Algerian foreign policy. She contends that Algeria's most innovative initiatives concerned North-South relations (e.g., the "new economic order").

Among the works of specific foreign relationships, see Inga Brandell, *Les rapports franco-Algériens depuis 1962: Du pétrole et des hommes* (Paris: L'Harmattan, 1981); and Jean Offredo, *Algérie: Avec ou sans la France* (Paris: Cerf, 1973). Benjamin Stora examines historical memory (and amnesia) concerning the Algerian War of Independence and its influence on the postcolonial bilateral relationship in *La gangrène et l'oubli: La mémoire des années Algériennes* (Paris: La Découverte, 1991). The war in the Western Sahara has played a crucial role in regional policy. The Algerian dimension is included in Tony Hodges, *Western Sahara: The Roots of a Desert War* (Westport, Conn.: Lawrence Hill, 1983); John Damis, *Conflict in Northwest Africa: The Western Sahara Dispute* (Stanford: Hoover Institute Press, 1983); Maurice Barbier, *Le Conflit du Sahara occidental* (Paris: Harmattan, 1982); and Yahia H. Zoubir and Daniel Volman, eds., *International Dimensions of the Western Sahara Conflict* (Westport, Conn.: Praeger, 1993).

There are few specific works on Algerian leaders. Robert Merle compiled interview tapes of Ben Bella in *Ahmed Ben Bella*, trans. Camilla Sykes (New York: Walker and Company, 1967); and Ania Francos and Jean-Pierre Séréni, *Un Algérien nommé*

Boumediène (Paris: Stock, 1976), are both complimentary rather than critical.

For analyses concerning the causes and consequences of the October 1988 popular revolt, see John P. Entelis, "Algeria under Chadli: Liberalization without Democratization or, *Perestroika*, Yes; *Glasnost*, No!" *Middle East Insight* 6 (Fall 1988): 47–64; Robert A. Mortimer, "Algeria after the Explosion," *Current History* 89 (April 1990): 161–168; 180–182; Khalid Duran, "The Second Battle of Algiers," *Orbis* 33 (Summer 1989): 403–421; Nabeel Abraham, "Algeria's Facade of Democracy: An Interview with Mahfoud Bennoune," *Middle East Report* 20, no. 163 (March-April 1990): 9–13; and Rachid Tlemçani, "Chadli's Perestroika," 14–18; Arun Kapil, "Algeria's Elections Show Islamist Strength," *Middle East Report* 20, no. 166 (September-October 1990): 31–36; and Alfred Hermida, "Democracy Derailed," *Africa Report* 37, no. 2 (March-April 1992): 13–17. See also chapters listed below by John P. Entelis, Bradford Dillman, Lynette Rummel, and Boutheina Cheriet (under *Social and Cultural Topics*) in Entelis and Naylor, eds., *State and Society in Algeria*.

ECONOMIC TOPICS

There have been many significant contributions concerning economic affairs. Mahfoud Bennoune's *The Making of Contemporary Algeria, 1830–1987* (Cambridge: Cambridge University Press, 1988) is an economic survey of Algerian development. Unlike many others who now see the need for relegating the second sector, Bennoune claims that this direction is correct but must be complemented by greater democratization. See also M. E. Benissad, *Economie du développement de l'Algérie: Sous-développement et socialisme, 1962–1982* (Paris: Economica, 1982); and Benaouda Hamel, *Système productif Algérien et indépendance nationale* (Algiers: OPU, 1983).

As for the first sector, see Ian Clegg's *Workers' Self-Management in Algeria* (New York: Monthly Review Press,

1971) concerning the *autogestion* initiative and its subsequent bureaucratization. Slimane Bedrani's *L'Agriculture Algérienne depuis 1966: Etatisation ou privatisation?* (Algiers: OPU, 1981) is a critical survey of the sector's development as is Karen Pfeifer, *Agrarian Reform Under State Capitalism in Algeria* (Boulder, Colo.: Westview, 1985). See also Tony Smith, "Political and Economic Ambitions of Algerian Land Reform, 1962–1974," *Middle East Journal* 29 (Summer 1975): 259–278; Peter Knauss, "Algeria's 'Agrarian Revolution': Peasant Control or Control of Peasants?" *African Studies Review* 20 (December 1977): 65–78; and Nico Kielstra, "Algeria's Agrarian Revolution," *MERIP Reports*, no. 67 (1978): 3–11. Will D. Swearingen examines the alimentary crisis in "Agricultural Policies and the Growing Food Security Crisis," in John P. Entelis and Phillip C. Naylor, eds., *State and Society in Algeria*, 117–150.

The second sector was epitomized by the idea of "industrializing industries." The man asssociated with this model of development is Professor Gérard Destanne de Bernis. For example, see his "Le Plan quadriennal de développement de l'Algérie 1970–73," *Problèmes économiques* (Documentation française) no. 1.203 (1971): 19–25. The development of national companies is considered critical by Karen Farsoun in "State Capitalism in Algeria," *MERIP Reports*, no. 35 (1975), 3–30. See also Richard I. Lawless, "Algeria: The Contradictions of Rapid Industrialization," in *North Africa: Contemporary Politics and Economic Development*, ed. Richard Lawless and Allan Findlay, 153–190. Algeria's most significant postcolonial economic decolonization concerned hydrocarbons. See Nicole Grimaud, "Le conflit pétrolier franco-Algérien," *Revue française de science politique* 22 (December 1972): 1276–1307.

John C. Pawera's *Algeria's Infrastructure: An Economic Survey of Transportation, Communication, and Energy Resources* (New York: Praeger, 1964) is a useful work to start with when examining Algeria's postcolonial third-sector development.

John R. Nellis studies the difficulties in applying ideology to economic matters in "Socialist Management in Algeria," *Journal of Modern African Studies* 15 (December 1977): 529–554;

"Maladministration: Causes or Result of Underdevelopment? The Algerian Example," *Canadian Journal of African Studies* 13 (1980): 407–422; and "Algerian Socialism and Its Critics," *Canadian Journal of Political Science* 13 (September 1980): 481–587. See also Francis Ghiles, "Chadli's Pragmatic Economics," *Africa Report* 29 (November-December 1984): 10–13.

The *Middle East Economic Digest* and the Economist Intelligence Unit's *Quarterly Economic Report/Country Study* provide updated information.

SOCIAL AND CULTURAL TOPICS

Pierre Bourdieu's *The Algerians* (Boston: Beacon Press, 1962) remains an important work as well as the aforementioned analyses of Frantz Fanon. Peter R. Knauss examines the effect of "Liberation" upon gender relations in *The Persistence of Patriarchy: Class, Gender, and Ideology in Twentieth Century Algeria* (New York: Praeger, 1987). See also Boutheina Cheriet, "Islamism and Feminism: Algeria's 'Rites of Passage' to Democracy," in John P. Entelis and Phillip C. Naylor, eds., *State and Society in Algeria,* 171–216. See also the first number of a new publication entitled the *Journal of Maghrebi Studies* (Cambridge, Mass.), 1–2 (Spring 1993) (*Special Issue: Maghreni Women*), which includes a variety of articles on Algerian women.

The increasingly important role of Islam is considered by Jean-Claude Vatin, "Popular Puritanism versus State Reformism: Islam in Algeria," in James P. Piscatori, ed., *Islam in the Political Process* (Cambridge: Cambridge University Press, 1983), 98–121; Hugh Roberts, "Radical Islam and the Dilemma of Algerian Nationalism: The Embattled Arians of Algiers," *Third World Quarterly* 10, no. 2 (April 1988): 556–589; Robert Mortimer, "Islam and Multiparty Politics in Algeria," *Middle East Journal* 45, no. 4 (Autumn 1991): 575–593; and Ahmed Rouadjia, *Les frères et la mosquée: Enquête sur le mouvement islamiste en Algérie* (Paris: Editions Karthala, 1990).

Emigrant labor is a pressing issue. Among the many works on

this subject are Mahfoud Bennoune, "Maghribin Workers in France," *MERIP Reports*, no. 34 (1974): 1–12, 30; (Bennoune's dissertation especially describes the relationship between Algeria's government and the emigrant community ["Impact of Colonialism and Migration of an Algerian Peasant Community: A Study of Socio-economic Change," University of Michigan, 1976]); Tayeb Belloula, *Les Algériens en France* (Algiers: Editions Nationales Algériennes, 1965); and Malek Ath-Messaoud and Alain Gillette, *L'Immigration Algérienne en France* (Paris: Editions Entente, 1976); and Benjamin Stora, *Ils venaient d'Algérie: L'immigration Algérienne en France, 1912–1992* (Paris: Fayard, 1992). The "second generation" is examined by Abdelkader Chaker, *La jeunesse Algérienne en France: Eléments d'étude de l'émigration familiale* (Algiers: SNED, 1977); Martine Charlot and others, *Des jeunes Algériens en France: Leurs voix et les notres* (Paris: Editions CIEM, 1981); and Hervé-Frédéric Mecheri, *Les jeunes immigrés maghrébins de la deuxième génération: La Quête de l'identité* (Paris: L'Harmattan, 1984). The prospects of "reinsertion," or the return of emigrants to Algeria, is particularly studied by Mohamed Khandriche, *Développment et réinsertion: L'exemple de l'émigration Algérienne* (Paris: Editions Publisud, 1982); and Belkcem Hifi, *L'Immigration Algérienne en France: Origines et perspectives de non-retour* (Paris: L'Harmattan, 1985). See also the special issue "L'Immigration maghrébine en France: Les faits et les mythes," *Les Temps modernes*, 40 (March-April-May 1984). *Hommes et Migrations* is a journal that chronicles and studies emigration and immigration and is particularly useful concerning the Algerian community.

Arabization viewed as the instrument that would recover an authentic national identity has posed problems in postcolonial Algeria. Gilbert Grandguillaume's *Arabisation et politique linguistique au Maghreb* (Paris: Editions G.-P. Maisonneuve et Larose, 1983) surveys in depth the linguistic policies under the three Algerian presidents. Sid Ahmed Boghli's *Aspects of Algerian Cultural Policy* (Paris, UNESCO, 1978) is a short but valuable description of Algerian policy. Ahmed Taleb-Ibrahimi's

De la décolonisation à la révolution culturelle (1962–1972) (Algiers: SNED, 1973) chronicles the development of Arabization. This policy has particularly affected the Berbers. See Alf A. Heggoy, "Arabization and the Kabyle Language and Cultural Issues in Algeria," *Africana Journal*, 15 (1990): 292–304; Marnia Lazreg, "The Kabyle-Berber Cultural Movement in Algeria," in Peter Schwab and Adamantia Pollis, eds., (New York: Praeger, 1982), 223–238; and consult, too, Hugh Roberts, *Revolution and Resistance: Algerian Politics and the Kabyle Question* (London: I. M. Tauris, 1989), and his other contributions listed in this bibliography.

ADDITIONAL SOURCES IN ENGLISH

Aghrout, Ahmed, and Keith Sutton. "Regional Economic Union in the Maghreb." *Journal of Modern African Studies* 28, 1 (March 1990): 115–139.

Akre, Philip J. "Algeria and the Politics of Energy-Based Industrialization." *In State and Society in Algeria*, edited by John P. Entelis and Phillip C. Naylor, 73–96.

Amin, Samir. *The Maghreb in the Modern World: Algeria, Tunisia, Morocco*. Translated by Michael Perl. London: Penguin, 1970.

Anderson, Lisa. "Liberalism in Northern Africa." *Current History* 89, no. 546 (April 1990): 145–148; 174–175.

———. "Obligation and Accountability: Islamic Politics in North Africa." *Daedelus* 120, no. 3 (1991): 93–112.

Balta, Paul. "French Policy in North Africa." *Middle East Journal* 40 (Spring 1986): 238–251.

Barakat, Halim, ed. *Contemporary North Africa: Issues of Development and Integration.* Washington, D.C.: Center for Contemporary Arab Studies, 1985.

Beckett, Paul A. "Algeria v. Fanon: The Theory of Revolutionary Decolonization and the Algerian Experience." *Western Political Quarterly* 26 (March 1973): 5–27.

Bedrani, Slimane. "Self-sufficiency and Food Security: Political Principles and Practical Difficulties." In *La Dépendance Alimentaire/Food Security*, edited by B. Benhamouda and others, 34–56. Algiers: Institut National d'Etudes de Stratégie Global, 1988.

Bennoune, Mahfoud. "The Industrialization of Algeria: An Overview," in *Contemporary North Africa*, edited by Halim Barakat, 178–213.

———. "The Introduction of Nationalism into Rural Algeria, 1919–1954." *Maghreb Review* 2 (May-June 1977): 1–12.

———. "Maghribin Workers in France." *MERIP Reports*, no.34 (1975): 1–12; 30.

Blair, Thomas L. *'The Land to Those who Work It': Algeria's Experiment in Workers' Management.* Garden City, N.Y.: Doubleday, 1969.

Bookmiller, Robert J. "The Western Sahara: Future Prospects." *American-Arab Affairs*, no. 37 (1991): 64–76.

Bourdieu, Pierre. "The Algerian Subproletariat." In *Man, State, and Society*, ed. I. William Zartman, 83–92.

Brace, Richard M. *Morocco, Algeria, Tunisia.* Englewood Cliffs, N.J.: Prentice-Hall, 1964.

Brace, Richard, and Joan Brace. *Algerian Voices.* New York: D. Van Nostrand, 1965.

Brown, Leon Carl, ed. *State and Society in Independent North Africa.* Washington: Middle East Institute, 1966.

————. "The United States and the Maghrib." *Middle East Journal* 30 (Summer 1976): 273–290.

Burke, Edmond III. "Parties and Elites in North African Politics: Algeria and Morocco." *Africa Today* 18, no. 4 (October 1971): 50–59.

Causey, Margaret Cameron. "Public Enterprise in Algeria: Law as a Bridge between Ideology and Reality." *Public Administration and Development* 4, no. 2 (1984): 155–169.

Charrad, Mounira. "State and Gender in the Maghrib." *Middle East Report* 20, no. 163 (March-April 1990): 9–13.

Cheriet, Boutheina. "The Resilience of Algerian Populism." *Middle East Report* 22, no. 173 (1992): 9–14.

Christelow, Allan. "Ritual, Cultures, and Politics in Algeria." *Middle Eastern Studies*, 23, no. 3 (1987): 255–273.

Cohen, William B. "Legacy of Empire: The Algerian Connection." *Journal of Contemporary History* 15, no. 1 (1980): 97–123.

Damis, John. "Prospects for Unity/Disunity in North Africa. *Middle East Journal* 37, no. 2 (Apring 1983): 167–179.

————. "The U.S. Relations with North Africa." *Current History* 84 (May 1985): 193–196.

Daniel, Jean. "The Algerian Problem Begins." *Foreign Affairs* 40 (July 1962): 605–611.

————. "The Jewish Future in Algeria: A Dissenting View." *Commentary* 34 (September 1962): 198–203.

Davis, Hannah. "Taking Up Space in Tlemcen: The Islamist Occupation of Urban Algeria: An Interview with Rabia Bekkar." *Middle East Report,* 22, no. 179 (November/ December 1992): 11–15.

Descloitres, R., C. Descloitres, and J. C. Reverdy. "Urban Organization and Social Structure in Algeria." In *Man, State and Society,* ed. I. William Zartman, 424–438.

Dillman, Bradford. "Regime Strengthening: Results of Liberalization in Algeria since 1975." *Journal of Middle East Studies at Columbia University* 2, no. 1 (1988): 3–22.

————. "Transition to Democracy in Algeria." In *State and Society in Algeria,* edited by John P. Entelis and Phillip C. Naylor, 31–52.

Dominelli, Lena. *Love and Wages: The Impact of Imperialism, State Intervention and Women's Domestic Labour on Workers' Control in Algeria, 1962–1972.* Norwich, U.K.: Novata, 1986.

Elsenhans, Hartmut. "Algeria: The Contradiction of Rent-financed development." *Maghreb Review* 14, nos. 3–4 (1989): 226–248.

Entelis, John P. "Algeria: Technocratic Rule, Military Power." In *Political Elites in Arab North Africa,* edited by I. William Zartman and others, 92–143. New York: Longman.

————. *Comparative Politics of North Africa: Algeria, Morocco, and Tunisia.* Syracuse, N.Y.: Syracuse University Press, 1980.

————. "Democratic and Popular Republic of Algeria." In *The Government and Politics of the Middle East and North Africa*, ed. David E. Long and Bernard Reich, 415–436. Boulder, Colo.: Westview Press, 1980.

————. "Elite Political Culture and Socialization in Algeria: Tensions and Discontinuities." *Middle East Journal* 35, no. 2 (Spring 1981): 191–208.

————. "Introduction: State and Society in Transition." In *State and Society in Algeria*, edited by John P. Entelis and Phillip C. Naylor, 1–30.

————, and Phillip C. Naylor, eds. *State and Society in Algeria*. Boulder, Colo.: Westview Press, 1992.

Findlay, Allan, Anne Findlay, and Richard Lawless. "Algeria: Emigration from a Centrally Planned Economy." *Maghreb Review* 4 (May-June 1979): 82–85.

Friedman, Elizabeth. *Colonialism and After: An Algerian Jewish Community*. South Hadley, Mass.: Bergin and Garvey, 1988.

Gallagher, Charles F. "Language and Identity." In *State and Society*, ed. Leon Carl Brown, 73–96.

————. *The United States and North Africa: Morocco, Algeria, and Tunisia*. Cambridge: Harvard University Press, 1963.

Gelb, Alan, and Patrick Conway. "Algeria: Windfalls in a Socialist Economy." In *Oil Windfalls: Blessing or Curse?* ed. Alan H. Gelb, 147–169. Oxford: Oxford University Press, 1988.

Gellner, Ernest. "The Unknown Apollo of Biskra: The Social

Base of Algerian Puritanism.'' *Government and Opposition* 9, no. 3 (Summer 1974): 277–310.

Gordon, David C. *Women of Algeria: An Essay on Change.* Cambridge, Mass.: Harvard University Press, 1968.

Griffin, Keith B. ''Algerian Agriculture in Transition.'' In *Man, State and Society*, ed. I. William Zartman, 395–414.

Grimaud, Nicole. ''Algeria and Socialist France.'' *Middle East Journal* 40 (Spring 1986): 252–266.

Grohs, G. K. ''Franz Fanon and the African Revolution.'' *Journal of Modern African Studies* 6, no. 4 (December 1968): 543–556.

Hamouda, Naziha. ''Rural Women in the Aurès: A Poetry in Context.'' *Oral History* 13, no. 1 (1985): 43–53.

Harbi, Mohamed. ''The Party and the State.'' In *Man, State, and Society*, edited by I. William Zartman, 159–67.

Hargreaves, Alec G. *Voices from the North African Immigrant Community in France. Immigration and Identity in Beur Fiction.* New York. Berg, 1991.

Heggoy, Alf Andrew. ''Cultural Disrespect: European and Algerian Views on Women in Colonial and Independent Algeria.'' *Muslim World* 62, no. 4 (October 1972): 228–235.

———. ''The Evolution of Algerian Women.'' *African Studies Review* 17, no. 2 (September 1974): 449–456.

———. ''Colonial Origins of the Algerian-Moroccan Border Conflict of October 1963.'' *African Studies Review* 13, no. 1 (April 1970): 17–21.

————. "They Write in French Not in Arabic: Some Thoughts on North African Authors." *The Indiana Social Studies Quarterly* 30, no. 2 (1977): 98–102.

Helie, Damien. "Industrial Self-Management in Algeria." In *Man, State, and Society*, edited by I. William Zartman, 465–474.

Hermassi, Elbaki. *Leadership and National Development in North Africa: A Comparative Study*. Berkeley: University of California Press, 1972.

Himmelfarb, Milton. "Algeria's Jews and Other Matters." *Commentary* 33 (May 1962): 430–432.

Holsinger, Donald C. "Exiles in their Native Land: Algerian Novelists of French Expression." *Maghreb Review*, no. 3–4 (1986): 73–78.

Jansen, Willy. *Women Without Men: Gender and Marginality in an Algerian Town*. Kinderhook, N.Y.: E. J. Brill, 1986.

Joesten, Joachim. *The New Algeria*. Chicago: Follett, 1964.

El-Kenz, Ali. *Algerian Reflections On Arab Crises*. Translated by Robert W. Stookey. Austin, Tex.: Center for Middle Eastern Studies, 1991.

Knapp, Wilfrid. *North West Africa: A Political and Economic Survey*. 3d ed. Oxford University Press, 1977.

Knauss, Peter. "Algeria Under Boumedienne: The Mythical Revolution 1965 to 1978." In *The Performance of Soldiers as Governors: African Politics and the African Military*, ed. Isaac J. Mowoe, 27–100. Washington, D.C.: University Press of America, 1980.

————. "Algerian Women Since Independence." *In State and*

Society in Algeria, edited by John P. Entelis and Phillip C. Naylor, 151–170.

Korany, Bahgat. "Third Worldism and Pragmatic Radicalism: The Foreign Policy of Algeria." In *The Foreign Policies of Arab States*, ed. Bahgat Korany and Ali E. Hillal Dessouki, 79–118. Boulder, Colo.: Westview Press, 1984.

Lawless, Richard I., and Allan Findlay, ed. *North Africa: Contemporary Politics and Economic Development*. London: Croom Helm, 1984.

Layachi, Azzedine. *The United States and North Africa: A Cognitive Approach to Foreign Policy*. New York: Praeger, 1990.

Lazreg, Marnia. "Women, Work, and Social Change in Algeria." In *Women, Employment and the Family in the International Division of Labor*, ed. Sharon Stichner and Jane L. Parpart. London: Macmillan, 1990.

Leca, Jean. "Algerian Socialism: Nationalism, Industrialization, and State-Building." In *Socialism in the Third World*, eds. Helen Desfosses and Jacques Levesque, 121–160. New York: Praeger, 1973.

Lewis, William H. "Algeria Against Itself." *Africa Report* 12 (December 1967): 9–15.

———. "Algeria: The Cycle of Reciprocal Fear." *African Studies Bulletin* 12 (December 1969): 323–337.

———. "Algeria and the Maghreb at the Turning Point. *Mediterranean Quarterly* 1, no. 3 (Summer 1990): 62–74.

———. "Algeria: The Plight of the Victor." *Current History*, 44 (January 1963): 22–28.

————. "The Decline of Algeria's FLN." *Middle East Journal*, 20 (Spring 1966): 161–172.

Lippert, Anne. "Algerian Women's Access to Power: 1962–1985." In *Studies in Power and Class in Africa*, edited by Irving Leonard Markovitz, 209–232. New York: Oxford University Press, 1987.

Mandel, Arnold. "France's Algerian Jews." *Commentary* 35 (June 1963): 475–482.

Marshall, Susan E., and Randall G. Stokes. "Tradition and the Veil: Female Status in Tunisia and Algeria." *Journal of Modern African Studies* 19, no. 4 (December 1981), 625–646.

Michel, André. *The Modernization of North African Families in the Paris Area*. The Hague: Mouton & Company, 1974.

Miller, Mark J. "Reluctant Partnership: Foreign Workers in Franco-Algerian Relations, 1962–1979." *Journal of International Affairs* 33 (Fall/Winter 1979): 219–237.

Minces, Juliette. *The House of Obedience: Women in Arab Society*. London: Zed Press, 1982.

————. "Women in Algeria." In *Women in the Muslim World*, edited by Lois Beck and Nikki Keddie, 159–171. Cambridge: Harvard University Press, 1978.

Montagne, Robert. *The Berbers: Their Social and Political Organisation*. London: Frank Cass, 1973.

Moore, Kenny. "A Scream and a Prayer." *Sports Illustrated*, August 3, 1992: 46–56; 61.

Morray, J. P. *Socialism in Islam: A Study of Algeria*. Monmouth, Ore.: Institute for Theoretical History, 1980.

Mortimer, Mildred. *Journeys through the African Novel.* Portsmouth, N.H.: Heinemann, 1990.

————. "Language and Space in the Fiction of Assia Djeber and Leila Sebbar." *Research in African Literatures* (Austin, Tex.), 19, no. 3 (1988): 301–311.

Mortimer, Robert A. "Algeria's New Sultan." *Current History*, 80, no. 470 (December 1982): 418–421; 433–434.

————. "Boumedienne Redesigns His Regime." *Africa Report* 22 (July-August 1977): 14–18.

Naylor, Phillip C. "Algeria and France: The Post-Colonial Relationship." *Proceedings of the French Colonial Historical Society* (1979): 58–69.

————. "French-Algerian Relations, 1980–1990." In *State and Society in Algeria*, edited by John P. Entelis and Phillip C. Naylor, 217–240.

————. "Maghrib Unity: Illusive or Elusive?" *Africana Journal* 15 (1990): 305–315.

————. "A Post-Colonial Decolonization: French-Algerian Hydrocarbon Relations, 1962–71." *Proceedings of the French Colonial Society* (1982): 179–190.

Nellis, John R. "A Comparative Assessment of the Development Performances of Algeria and Tunisia." *The Middle East Journal* 37, no. 3 (Summer 1983): 370–393.

Ortzen, Len (Selector; translator; Introduction). *North African Writing.* London: Heinemann, 1970.

Pfeifer, Karen. "Algeria's Agrarian Transformation." *MERIP Reports*, no. 99 (1981): 6–14.

———. "Economic Liberalization in the 1980s: Algeria in Comparative Perspective." In *State and Society in Algeria*, ed. John P. Entelis and Phillip C. Naylor, 97–116.

Quandt, William B. "The Berbers in the Algerian Political Elite." In *Arabs and Berbers: From Tribe to Nation in North Africa*, ed. Ernest Gellner and Charles Micaud, 285–303. Lexington, Mass.: Lexington Books, 1972.

———. "Can We Do Business With Radical Nationalists? Algeria: Yes!" *Foreign Policy* 7 (Summer 1972): 108–131.

Robana, Abderrahman. "The Economic External Relations of the Maghreb Countries as seen through their Balance of Payments during the 1977–86 Decade." *Maghreb Review* 14, nos. 3–4 (1989): 249–270.

Roberts, Hugh. "Algeria: Thirty Years after the Revolution." *Africa Report* 29, no. 6 (November-December 1984): 4–9.

———. "The Algerian Constitution and the Restructuring of State Capitalism." *IDS Bulletin* 18, no. 4 (October 1987): 51–56.

———. "The Economics of Berberism: the Kabyle Question in Contemporary Algeria." *Government and Opposition* 18, no. 2 (1982): 218–231.

———. "In Troubled Waters." Africa Report 32, no. 5 (September-October 1987): 52.

———. "The Politics of Algerian Socialism." In *North Africa: Contemporary Politics*, eds. Richard Lawless and Allan Findlay, 5–49.

———. "Towards an Understanding of the Kabyle Question in Contemporary Algeria." *Maghreb Review* 5 (May-June 1980): 115–124.

————. "The Unforeseen Development of the Kabyle Question in Contemporary Algeria." *Government and Opposition* 17, 3 (1982): 312–324.

Roughton, Richard A. "Algeria and the June 1967 Arab-Israeli War." *Middle East Journal* 23, no. 4 (Autumn 1969): 434–444.

Rummel, Lynette. "Privatization and Democratization in Algeria." In *State and Society in Algeria*, edited by John P. Entelis and Phillip C. Naylor, 53–72.

Saivetz, Carol R. "Algerian Socialism under Ben Bella and Boumediene: The Soviet Assessment." *The Maghreb Review* 7, no. 3–4 (May-August 1982): 87–93.

Sherman, Alfred. "Algeria: An Intellectual Fashion Revisited." *World Today* 45, no. 1 (January 1989): 8–10.

Siabdelhadi, A. and R. H. Green. "Strategic Adjustment and Stabilization in a Hydrocarbon Exporter: The Case of Algeria. *IDS Bulletin*, 19, no. 1 (January 1988): 61–66.

Slymovics, Susan. "A Woman's Life on an Algiers Stage." *Middle East Report* 20, no. 166 (September-October 1990): 32–34.

Sutton, Keith. "Algeria: Centre-Down Development, State Capitalism, and Emergent Decentralization." In *Development from Above or Below?* eds. W. B. Stohr and D. R. Fraser Taylor, 351–375. London: John Wiley, 1981.

————. "The Progress of Algeria's Agrarian Reform and Its Settlement Implications." *Maghreb Review* 2 (January-April 1978): 10–16.

Swearingen, Will D. "Algeria's Food Security Crisis." *Middle East Report* 20, no. 166 (September-October 1990): 21–25.

Tlemcani, Rachid. *State and Revolution in Algeria*. Boulder, Colo.: Westview Press, 1986.

Vallin, Raymond. "Muslim Socialism in Algeria." In *Man, State, and Society*, ed. I. William Zartman, 50–64. New York: Praeger, 1973.

Vatin, Jean-Claude. "Religious Resistance and State Power in Algeria." In *Islam and Power in the Contemporary Muslim World*, eds. Alex Cudsi and Ali E. Hillal Dessouki. Baltimore: The Johns Hopkins Press, 1981.

Wolff, Ursala. "Report from Algeria's Mzab." *Africa Report* 21 (March 1976): 50–52.

Younger, Sam. "Ideology and Pragmatism in Algerian Foreign Policy." *World Today* 34 (March 1978): 107–114.

Zartman, I. William. "Algeria: A Post-revolutionary Elite." In *Political Elites and Political Development in the Middle East*, ed. Frank Tachau, 255–292. New York: Schenkman Publishing Co., 1975.

————. "The Algerian Army in Politics." In *Man, State, and Society in the Contemporary Maghrib*, ed. Zartman, 211–227.

————. *Government and Politics in Northern Africa*. New York: Praeger, 1963.

————, ed. *Man, State, and Society in the Contemporary Maghreb*. New York: Praeger, 1973.

————. "The Military in the Politics of Succession: Algeria." In *The Military in African Politics*, ed. John W. Harbeson, 21–45. New York: Praeger, 1987.

————, ed. *Political Elites in Arab North Africa.* New York: Longman, 1982.

Zingg, Paul J. "American Perceptions of North Africa." In Heggoy, ed., *Through Foreign Eyes*, 93–140.

Zoubir, Yahia. "Western Sahara Conflict Impedes Maghrib Unity." *Middle East Report* 20, no. 163 (March-April 1990): 28–29.

ADDITIONAL SOURCES IN FRENCH

Abbas, Ferhat. *L'indépendance confisquée.* Paris: Flammarion, 1984.

Abdessalem, Belaid. *Le gaz Algérien.* Algiers, Bouchène, 1989.

Achour, Christiane. *Anthologies de la littérature Algérienne de langue française.* Algiers: ENAP/Bordas, 1990.

Ageron, Charles-Robert. *Histoire de l'Algérie contemporaine (1830–1976).* Paris: PUF, 1977.

Aït Ahmed, Hocine. *L'affaire Mécili.* Paris: La Découverte, 1989.

Akkache, Ahmed. *Capitaux étrangers et libération économique: L'Expérience Algérienne.* Paris: François Maspéro, 1971.

Ammour, Kader, Christian Leucate, and Jean-Jacques Moulin. *La Voie Algérienne: Les contradictions d'un développement.* Paris: Maspero, 1974.

Arnaud, Jacqueline. *La Littérature maghrébine de langue française.* Vol. 1: *Origines et perspectives.* Vol. 2: *Le cas de Kateb Yacine.* Paris/Algiers: Publisud, 1986.

Balta, Paul. *Le grand Maghreb: des indépendances à l'an 2000.* Paris: Editions La Découverte, 1990.

Belvaude, Catherine. *L'Algérie.* Paris: Editions Karthala, 1991.

Benallègue, Nora. ''Algerian Women in the Struggle for Independence and Reconstruction.'' *International Social Science Journal* (Paris) 35, no. 4 (1983): 703–717.

Bennoune, Mahfoud, and Ali El-Kenz. *Le hasard et l'histoire: Entretiens avec Belaid Abdesselam.* 2 vols. Algiers: ENAG/ Editions, 1990.

Bonn, Charles. *Le Roman Algérien de langue française: Vers un espace de communication littéraire décolonisé?* Paris: L'Harmattan, 1985.

Boualam, Said (Bachaga). *Les Harkis sans la France.* Paris: France-Empire, 1964.

Boudiaf, Mohamed. *Où va Algérie?* Paris: Libraire de l'Etoile, 1964.

Bourdieu, Pierre, and Abdelmalek Sayed. *Le Déracinement: La Crise de l'agriculture traditionelle en Algérie.* Paris: Editions de Minuit, 1964.

Boutefnouchet, Mostefa. *La famille Algérienne: Evolution et caractéristiques récentes.* Algiers: SNED, 1980.

Bouzana, Belkacem. *Le Contentieux des hydrocarbures entre l'Algérie et les sociétés étrangères.* Algiers: OPU, 1985.

Brahimi, Brahim. *Le pouvoir, la presse, et les intellectuels en Algérie.* Paris: L'Harmattan, 1989.

Burgat, François. ''Islamisme au Maghreb.'' *Le Temps modernes* 45, no. 500 (March 1988): 75–118.

————. *L'Islamisme au Maghreb: La Voix du Sud*. Paris: Editions Karthala, 1988.

Burgat, François, and Michel Nancy. *Les Villages socialistes de la Révolution agraire Algérienne, 1972–1982*. Paris: Editions du CNRS, 1984.

Chaliand, Gérard. *L'Algérie est-elle socialiste?* Paris: Maspéro, 1964.

Chaliand, Gérard, and Juliette Minces. *L'Algérie indépendante: Bilan d'une révolution nationale*. Paris: Maspero, 1972.

Charlot, Martine, comp. *Des jeunes Algériens en France: Leurs voix et les nôtres*. Paris: Editions C.I.E.M.M., 1981.

Déjeux, Jean. *Femmes d'Algérie: Légendes, traditions, histoire, littérature*. Paris: Boite à Documents, 1987.

————. *La Littérature Algérienne contemporaine*. Paris: Presses Universitaires de France, 1975.

————. *Maghreb littératures de langue française*. Paris: Arcantère Editions, 1993.

Dersa [pseud.]. *L'Algérie en débat: Luttes et développement*. Paris: Maspero, 1981.

Fabre, T. "L'Algérie à la croisée des chemins." *Esprit*, no. 145 (December 1988): 8–18.

Mallarde, Eitenne. *L'Algérie depuis*. Paris: La Table Ronde, 1975.

Martens, Jean-Claude. *Le Modèle Algérien de développement: Bilan d'une décennie (1962–1972)*. Algiers: SNED, 1973.

Maschino, T. M., and Fadéla M'rabet. *L'Algérie des illusions: La Révolution confisquée*. Paris: Robert Laffont, 1972.

Mazouni, Abdallah. *Culture et enseignement en Algérie et au Maghreb*. Paris: François Maspéro, 1969.

Mazri, Hamid. *Les hydrocarbures dans l'économie Algérienne*. Algiers: SNED, 1975.

Minces, Juliette. *L'Algérie de Boumediène*. Paris: Presses de la Cité, 1979.

————. *L'Algérie de la révolution, 1963–64*. Paris: L'Harmattan, 1988.

M'rabet, Fadéla. *Les Algériennes*. Paris: Maspéro, 1967.

————. *La Femme Algérienne*. Paris: Maspéro, 1964.

Nouschi, André. *La naissance du nationalisme Algérien*. Paris: Editions du Minuit, 1962.

Perroux, François, comp. *L'Algérie de demain*. Paris: PUF, 1962.

Raffimot, Marc, and Pierre Jacquemot. *Le Capitalisme d'état Algérien*. Paris: Maspéro, 1977.

Ray, Marie-Christine, comp. *Le Cardinal Duval: «Evêque en Algérie»*. Paris: Centurion, 1984.

Redjala, Ramdane. *L'opposition en Algérie depuis 1962: Le PRS-CNDR et le FFS*. Vol. 1. Paris: L'Harmattan, 1988.

Roux, Michel. *Les Harkis ou les oubliés de l'histoire, 1954–1991*. Paris: La Découverte, 1991.

Rude-Antoine, Edwige. *Le Mariage maghrébin en France*. Paris: Editions Karthala, 1990.

Sanson, Henri. *Christianisme au miroir de l'Islam: Essai sur la rencontre des cultures en Algérie*. Paris: Editions du Cerf, 1984.

Zartman, I. William. "L'Elite Algérienne sous la présidence de Chadli Benjedid." *Maghreb-Machrek*, no. 106 (October-November-December 1984): 37–53.

CONCLUSION

In general, there is a need for more studies of Algerian history. Algeria's precolonial heritage deserves greater scholarly attention as well as postcolonial social and cultural issues (especially concerning the emerging younger generation). This country offers a multitude of rewarding scholarly pursuits and opportunities.

ABOUT THE AUTHORS

ALF ANDREW HEGGOY (1938–1987). Alf Heggoy was born in Algeria. He received his Ph.D. in History from Duke University. He helped organize the French Colonial Historical Society and served two nonconsecutive terms as its president. He also edited the Society's *Proceedings,* which are published regularly. He was a professor of history at the University of Georgia. Heggoy studied French imperial policy (e.g., *The African Policies of Gabriel Hanotaux* [1972]) before devoting his career to Algerian studies. He authored many articles and several that collectively expressed his wide range of interests concerning Algeria. Among his publications (besides the first edition of the *Historical Dictionary of Algeria*) are *Insurgency and Counterinsurgency in Algeria* (1972); *The French Conquest of Algiers, 1820: An Oral Tradition* (1986); *Through Foreign Eyes: Western Attitudes Toward North Africa* (editor) (1982); and several articles in scholarly journals.

PHILLIP CHIVIGES NAYLOR. Phillip Naylor received his Ph.D. in History from Marquette University. He was an Associate Professor and Chairman of his department at Merrimack College (North Andover, Mass.) before accepting the position of Director of the Western Civilization Program at Marquette University. Naylor has been particularly interested in the postcolonial relationship between France and Algeria and the war in the Western Sahara. He also acted as a free-lance reporter and photographer for the *Milwaukee Journal* while in Algeria researching his doctoral dissertation. His photography of Algeria and Sahrawi refugees has been exhibited. He is the coeditor (with John P. Entelis) of *State and Society in Algeria* (1992). He has also written the entries "Algeria" for the *Academic American Encyclopedia* (Grolier) and "Algeria" and "Algiers" for the *Encyclopedia Americana,* (Grolier), and several articles in scholarly journals.